STERLING
Test Prep

AP CHEMISTRY

Complete
Content Review

2nd edition

www.Sterling-Prep.com

2   1

ISBN-13: 978-1-9475560-4-1

Sterling Test Prep products are available at special quantity discounts for sales, promotions, academic counseling offices and other educational purposes.

For more information contact our Sales Department at:

Sterling Test Prep
6 Liberty Square #11
Boston, MA 02109

info@sterling-prep.com

© 2018 Sterling Test Prep

Published by Sterling Test Prep

Congratulations on choosing this book as part of your AP Chemistry preparation!

Scoring high on AP exams is important for admission to college. To achieve a high score on AP Chemistry, you need to develop skills to properly apply the science knowledge you have to solving each question. Understanding key concepts, having the ability to extract information from the provided data and distinguishing between similar answer choices is more valuable than simply memorizing terms.

This book provides a detailed and thorough review of topics tested on the AP Chemistry exam. The content covers foundational principles and theories necessary to answer related questions on the test. The information is presented clearly and organized in a systematic way to provide students with targeted AP Chemistry review tool. You can focus on one knowledge area at a time to learn and fully comprehend important concepts and theories, or to simply refresh your memory. By reading these review chapters thoroughly, you will learn important chemistry concepts and the relationships between them. This will prepare you for the exam and you will increase your score.

All the material in this book are prepared by chemistry instructors with years of experience in applied chemistry, as well as in academic settings. This team of experts analyzed the content of the test, released by the College Board, and designed essential review that will help you build and solidify the knowledge necessary for your success on the exam. The content was reviewed for quality and effectiveness by our science editors who possess extensive credentials, are educated in top colleges and universities and have years of teaching and editorial experience.

We wish you great success in your future academic achievements and look forward to being an important part of your successful preparation for the AP Chemistry!

Sterling Test Prep Team

180530gdx

Our Commitment to the Environment

Sterling Test Prep is committed to protecting our planet's resources by supporting environmental organizations with proven track records of conservation, environmental research and education and preservation of vital natural resources. A portion of our profits is donated to support these organizations so they can continue their important missions. These organizations include:

 Ocean Conservancy For over 40 years, Ocean Conservancy has been advocating for a healthy ocean by supporting sustainable solutions based on science and cleanup efforts. Among many environmental achievements, Ocean Conservancy laid the groundwork for an international moratorium on commercial whaling, played an instrumental role in protecting fur seals from overhunting and banning the international trade of sea turtles. The organization created national marine sanctuaries and served as the lead non-governmental organization in the designation of 10 of the 13 marine sanctuaries.

 For 25 years, Rainforest Trust has been saving critical lands for conservation through land purchases and protected area designations. Rainforest Trust has played a central role in the creation of 73 new protected areas in 17 countries, including Falkland Islands, Costa Rica and Peru. Nearly 8 million acres have been saved thanks to Rainforest Trust's support of in-country partners across Latin America, with over 500,000 acres of critical lands purchased outright for reserves.

 Since 1980, Pacific Whale Foundation has been saving whales from extinction and protecting our oceans through science and advocacy. As an international organization, with ongoing research projects in Hawaii, Australia and Ecuador, PWF is an active participant in global efforts to address threats to whales and other marine life. A pioneer in non-invasive whale research, PWF was an early leader in educating the public, from a scientific perspective, about whales and the need for ocean conservation.

Thank you for choosing our products to achieve your educational goals.

With your purchase you support environmental causes around the world.

Table of Contents

Table of Contents (*continued*)

Table of Contents (*continued*)

This book should be supplemented by our

"AP Chemistry Practice Questions" book

or online practice questions

at www.Sterling-Prep.com

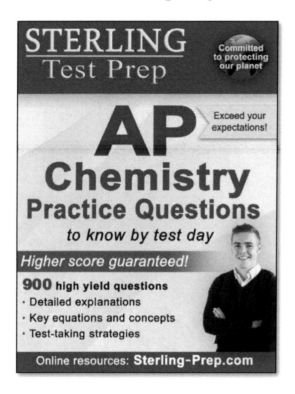

To access these and other AP questions online at a special pricing for book owners, see page 492

AP Chemistry: Exam Information and Strategies

AP Chemistry Exam

The AP Chemistry exam is 3 hours and 15 minutes long and includes a multiple-choice section (90 minutes) and a free-response section (105 minutes). The free-response section is divided into two parts, as shown in the table below. Student performance metrics on these three question types are compiled and weighted to determine an overall AP Exam score. Multiple-choice questions are answered filling in the appropriate oval on the answer sheet, while free-response questions are answered by writing in an answer booklet.

Section	Question Type	Number of Questions	Timing (minutes)	Percentage of Total Exam Score
I	Multiple-choice questions	60	90	50%
II	Long free-response questions	3	105	32%
	Short free-response questions	4		18%

Student will be provided both a periodic table of elements and a chart of formulas and constants to use on both sections of the test. Scientific and graphing calculators, however, may only be used by students on the free-response section, not on the multiple-choice section. A list of approved graphing calculators can be located on the College Board website on their "Calculator Policy" page. Calculators should not be used to store data/text or to communicate between other calculators. Proctors will monitor activity to ensure compliance during the exam.

Assessment of Student Learning

The AP Chemistry exam assesses students' ability to:

- solve problems both mathematically and symbolically;

- accurately describe and design experiments;

- execute keen data and error analysis;

- explain, reason or rationalize answers; and

- perform conceptual model interpretation and development.

Topics Covered on the AP Chemistry Exam

The AP Chemistry exam covers the following topics:

- Structure of Matter,

- Bonding and Intermolecular Forces,

- Chemical Reactions,

- Kinetics,

- Thermodynamics and

- Chemical Equilibrium.

Types of Questions

Multiple-Choice Questions

There are two types of multiple-choice questions featured on the AP Chemistry exam, both of which include four possible answer choices per question. The first type, *discrete items*, are stand-alone questions. The second type, *items in sets*, are questions in a sequential set that all share reference to the same provided prompt, which can include charts, diagrams, graphs, tables and text. Each question should be answered in no more than 1 minute and 30 seconds.

Free-Response Questions

There are two types of free-response questions featured on the AP chemistry exam, both of which can require written responses. The first type, *long free-response questions*, are questions that include five to eleven sub-questions (e.g., (a), (b), (i), (ii)) that each need to be answered in order to have a chance of receiving full credit. Typically, long free-response questions require approximately 20 minutes each to complete and are worth 10 points each. The second type, *short free-response questions*, are very similar to the longer varieties but only typically include two to four sub-questions. Additionally, short free-response questions require approximately 7 minutes each to complete and are worth 4 points each.

Test-Taking Strategies

The best way to do well on AP Chemistry is to be really good at chemistry. There is no way around that. Prepare for the test as much as you can, so you can answer with confidence as many questions as possible. With that being said, for multiple choice questions the only thing that matters is how many questions were answered correctly, not how much work you did to come up with those answers. A lucky guess will get you the same points as an answer you knew with confidence.

Below are some test-taking strategies you can apply to answering multiple choice questions on AP Chemistry exam to maximize your score. Many of these strategies you already know and they may seem like common sense. However, when a student is feeling the pressure of a timed test, these common sense strategies might be forgotten.

Mental Attitude

If you psych yourself out, chances are you will do poorly on the test. To do well on the test, particularly science, which calls for cool, systemic thinking, you must remain calm. If you start to panic, your mind won't be able to find correct solutions to the questions. Many steps can be taken before the test to increase your confidence level. Buying this book is a good start because you can begin to practice, learn the information you should know to master the topics and get used to answering chemistry questions. However, there are other things you should keep in mind:

Study in advance. The information will be more manageable, and you will feel more confident if you've studied at regular intervals during the weeks leading up to the test. Cramming the night before is not a successful tactic.

Be well rested. If you are up late the night before the test, chances are you will have a difficult time concentrating and focusing on the day of the test, as you will not feel fresh and alert.

Come up for air. The best way to take this test is not to keep your head down for all 90 minutes of multiple choice section. Even though you only have a relatively short time to answer each question and there is no time to waste, it is recommended to take a few seconds between the questions to take a deep breath and relax your muscles.

Time Management

Aside from good preparation, time management is the most important strategy that you should know how to use on any test. You have an average time of 90 seconds for each question. You will breeze through some in a minute or less and others you may be stuck on for 2-3 minutes.

Don't dwell on any one question for too long. You should aim to look at every question on the test. It would be unfortunate to not earn the points for a question you could have easily answered just because you did not get a chance to look at it. If you are still in the first half of the test and find yourself spending more than two minutes on one question and don't see yourself getting closer to solving it, it is better to move on. It will be more productive if you come back to this question with a fresh mind at the end of the test. You do not want to lose points because you were stuck on one or few questions and did not get a chance to work with other questions that are easy for you.

Nail the easy questions quickly. On the multiple choice section of AP Chemistry exam, you get as many points for answering easy questions as you do for answering difficult questions. This means that you get a lot more points for five quickly answered questions than for one hard-earned victory. Each student has their strong and weak points, and you might be a master on a certain type of questions that are normally considered difficult. Skip the questions you are struggling with and nail the easy ones.

Skip the unfamiliar. If you come across a question that is totally unfamiliar to you, skip it. Do not try to figure out what is going on or what they are trying to ask. At the end of the test, you can go back to these questions if you have time. If you are encountering a question that you have no clue about, most likely you won't be able to answer it through analysis. The better strategy is to leave such questions to the end and use the guessing strategy on them at the end of the test.

Understanding the Question

It is important that you know what the question is asking before you select your answer choice. This seems obvious, but it is surprising how many students don't read a question carefully because they rush through the test and select a wrong answer choice.

A successful student will not just read the question, but will take a moment to understand the question before even looking at the answer choices. This student will be able to separate the important information from distracters and will not get confused on the questions that are asking to identify a false statement (which is the correct answer). Once you've identified what you're dealing with and what is being asked, you should be able to spend less time on picking the right answer. If the question is asking for a general concept, try to answer the question before looking at the answer choices, then look at the choices. If you see a choice that matches the answer you thought of, most likely it is the correct choice.

Correct Way to Guess

Random guessing won't help you on the test, but educated guessing is the strategy you should use in certain situations if you can eliminate at least one (or even two) of the five possible choices.

For example, if you just randomly entered responses for the first 20 questions, there is a 25% chance of guessing correctly on any given question since each question has four answer choices. Therefore, the odds are you would guess right on 5 questions and wrong on 15 questions.

However, if for each of the 20 questions you can eliminate one answer choice because you know it to be wrong, you will have a 33% chance of being right. Therefore, your odds would move to 6 or even 7 questions right and 13-14 questions wrong. This may not seem like a dramatic increase, but it can make a difference for scoring 4 instead of 3, or 5 instead of 4.

Guessing is not cheating and should not be viewed that way. Rather it is a form of "partial credit" because while you might not be sure of the correct answer, you do have relevant knowledge to identify one or two choices that are wrong.

AP Chemistry Tips

Tip 1: Know the equations

Since many questions on the exam requires that you know how to use chemical equations, it is imperative that you memorize and understand when to use each one. It is not permitted to bring any papers with notes to the test. However, you will be provided with a sheet of main formulas and equations (provided in this book as well). Therefore you must memorize all the other equations you think you will need that are not provided on the exam.

As you work with this book, you will learn the application of all the important chemical formulas and equations and will use them in many different question types. If you are feeling nervous about having a lot of equations in your head and worry that it will affect your problem-solving skills, look over them right before you go into the examination space and write them down before you start the test. This way, you don't have to worry about remembering the equations throughout the exam. When you need to use them, you can refer back to where you wrote them down earlier.

Tip 2: Know how to manipulate the formulas

You must know how to apply the formulas in addition to just memorizing them. Questions will be worded in ways unfamiliar to you to test whether you can manipulate equations that you know to calculate the correct answer.

Tip 3: Estimating

This tip is only helpful for quantitative questions. For example, estimating can help you choose the correct answer if you have a general sense of the order of magnitude. This is especially applicable to questions where all answer choices have different orders of magnitude and you can save time that you would have to spend on actual calculations.

Tip 4: Write the reaction

Don't hesitate to write, draw or graph your thought process once you have read and understood the question. This can help you determine what kind of information you are dealing with. Write out the reactions that need to be balanced or anything else that may be helpful. Even if a question does not require a graphic answer, drawing a graph can allow a solution to become obvious.

Tip 5: Eliminating wrong answers

This tip utilizes the strategy of educated guessing. You can usually eliminate one or sometimes even two answer choices. In addition, there are certain types of questions for which you can use a particular elimination method.

By using logical estimations for quantitative questions, you can eliminate the answer choices that are unreasonably high or unreasonably low.

Roman numeral questions are the type of multiple-choice questions that list a few possible answers with five different combinations of these answers. Supposing that you know that one of the Roman numeral choices is wrong, you can eliminate all answer choices that include it. These questions are usually difficult for most test takers because they tend to present more than one potentially correct statement which is often included in more than one answer choice. However, they have a certain upside if you can eliminate at least one wrong statement.

Last helpful tip: fill in your answers carefully

This seems like a simple thing, but it is extremely important. Many test takers make mistakes when filling in answers whether it is a paper test or computer-based test. Make sure you pay attention and check off the answer choice you actually chose as correct.

Chapter 1

Atomic and Electronic Structure

- **Electronic Structure**
- **The Periodic Table: Variations of Chemical Properties with Group and Row**
- **The Periodic Table: Classification of Elements into Groups by Electronic Structure**

Electronic Structure

The *atom* is the smallest unit of an element that retains the characteristics of that element. An atom consists of several *subatomic particles*, including *protons*, *neutrons* and *electrons*. The *nucleus*, the densely-packed region at the center of an atom, consists of protons and neutrons. The diameter of the nucleus is approximately ~10,000 times smaller than the overall diameter of the atom. Most of an atom's volume comes from its *electron cloud*, which is the outer region of an atom that surrounds the nucleus.

The *proton* is the positively-charged particle located in the nucleus of the atom. Each proton has a charge of +1 and its mass is approximately equal to a neutron. The *neutron* is an uncharged particle that is also located in the nucleus of the atom. The *electron* is a small, negatively-charged particle located in the electron cloud. Each electron has a charge of -1, and its mass is about 2,000 times smaller than a proton or neutron. In a neutral atom, the number of electrons must equal the number of protons.

The *electrostatic attraction* between protons and electrons (due to their opposite charges) holds electrons around the nucleus. The *repulsion* between neighboring electrons allows them to spread out over the entire volume of the electron cloud. An *ion* is formed when an atom has either lost or gained electrons, causing it to incur either a net negative or a net positive charge. The loss of electrons produces positively-charged *cations*, and the gain of electrons produces negatively-charged *anions*. Cations and anions are often represented by a superscript positive or negative sign after a chemical symbol.

The *atomic number* (Z) equals the number of protons in an atom. If the atom has no charge, then Z also equals the number of electrons. On the periodic table, elements are arranged by their atomic numbers. The *mass number* (A) is the total number of protons and neutrons (i.e., *nucleons*) of an atom.

Isotopes are atoms of the same element with the same number of protons (i.e., identical atomic numbers) but a different number of neutrons; therefore, they have different mass numbers. However, isotopes still have virtually identical chemical properties because they have the same number of protons. Most elements naturally occur as a mixture of two or more stable isotopes.

For example, the element carbon ($Z=6$) includes the isotopes carbon-12, carbon-13 and carbon-14. The 12, 13 and 14 are the mass numbers (A) of the respective isotopes. Carbon-12 has six neutrons, carbon-13 has seven neutrons and carbon-14 has eight neutrons.

The *relative atomic mass* of an element (also known as *atomic weight*) is the weighted average of the masses of all its stable isotopes. *Mass spectrometry* is an experimental method used to determine the atomic masses of isotopes. In mass spectrometry, a sample is ionized by bombarding it with electrons, which causes it to break into charged fragments. The ions are separated by subjecting them to an electric or magnetic field. The amount of deflection that the ions experience is proportional to the ions' weight.

The unit of measurement used for atomic weight is the *atomic mass unit* (amu) or *dalton* (Da), which is approximately equivalent to the mass of one nucleon (a single proton and neutron). It is based on the atomic mass of the carbon-12 isotope, meaning 1 amu is equal to $\frac{1}{12}$ the mass of a ^{12}C atom, or 1.66×10^{-27} g. Carbon-12 is the only atomic species with an atomic mass that is exactly a whole number, but the atomic masses of other elements are always very close to whole numbers of atomic mass units. This can be represented in equation form as follows:

$$(mass_1) \cdot (abundance_1) + (mass_2) \cdot (abundance_2) + \ldots = avg. \ atomic \ mass$$

For example, hydrogen has two isotopes, and their masses and abundances are shown below:

Isotope	Mass	% Abundance
^{1}H	1.007825 amu	99.985
^{2}H	2.0140 amu	0.015

Based on this information, the relative atomic mass of hydrogen (i.e., atomic weight) can be calculated:

$$(0.99985 \times 1.007825 \ amu) + (0.0015 \times 2.0140 \ amu) = 1.007976 \ amu$$

Orbital structure of hydrogen atom, principal quantum number *n*, number of electrons per orbital

The *electron configuration* of an atom is the arrangement of electrons around the nucleus. Electron configurations describe electrons as each moving independently in an orbital.

Niels Bohr, a Danish physicist of the 20th century, was the first to apply quantum physics to restrict the energy of the atom to discrete values. A single-electron atom is an elementary form of matter that consists of only one electron around its nucleus. The *Bohr model*, which will be discussed in more detail later, focuses on the hydrogen atom and the single electron that orbits its nucleus. In quantum mechanics, the hydrogen electron exists in a spherical probability density cloud around its nucleus. The *principal quantum number* (*n*) defines which shell the electron occupies, which describes the *size* of the orbital. It can have only positive integer values. *Electron shells*, also called principle energy levels, are often labeled by their principal quantum numbers (*n* = 1, 2, 3. . .), but can also be labeled alphabetically (*n* = K, L, M. . .). Higher *n* shells indicate larger orbitals further from the nucleus and higher energy levels. The number of electrons per shell is given by $2n^2$. For example, the second shell can hold up to $2(2)^2 = 8$ electrons. Electrons usually occupy outer shells only after inner shells have been filled, although this is not necessary.

Conventional notation for electronic structure

The *Aufbau principle* states that electrons fill their orbitals in the order of lowest energy to highest energy. Orbitals are filled according to the diagonal lines.

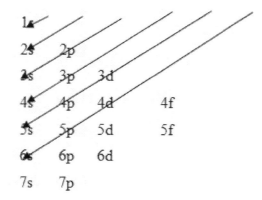

$1s^2\, 2s^2\, 2p^6\, 3s^2\, 3p^6\, 4s^2\, 3d^{10}\, 4p^6\, 5s^2\, 4d^{10}\, 5p^6\, 6s^2\, 4f^{14}\, 5d^{10}\, 6p^6\, 7s^2\, 5f^{14}\, 6d^{10}$

In multi-electron atoms, the energy level for an electron is affected by both the *n* and *l* quantum numbers. The *l* quantum number will be explained in further detail later, but know that it is represented by the letters *s, p, d* and *f* and it describes a particular subshell. Subshells are comprised of atomic orbitals, and each orbital can hold two electrons.

The 4*s* orbital is actually lower in energy than the 3*d* orbitals. Notice that electrons will populate the 4*s* orbital before the 3*d* orbital, despite the fact that 4*s* has a higher principal (*n*) value than 3*d*.

Another important guideline for writing electron configurations is *Hund's rule*, which states that every orbital in a sublevel has to be occupied by an electron before a second electron can occupy another orbital in that sublevel. This rule exists because maximizing the number of electrons with the same electron magnetic spin increases the stability of the atom. Double-occupied orbitals are much higher in energy and therefore less stable than orbitals with just a single electron.

The *octet rule* refers to the natural tendency of atoms to gain, lose or share electrons in order to achieve a full orbital of eight electrons in its *valence* (i.e., outermost) orbital. When atoms have an excess or deficiency in the number of electrons, they react with each other in order to form more stable compounds.

It is important to note that the octet rule only applies to the *s* and *p* orbital electrons, meaning that the octet rule is particularly useful when applied to the *representative elements* (i.e., elements not in the transition or inner-transition metal blocks). A complete octet would typically be represented as an electron configuration ending in s^2p^6.

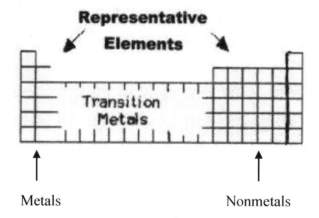

Using the Aufbau Principle and Hund's Rule for writing electron configurations, a typical electron configuration for an atom would appear as:

$$1s^2\ 2s^2\ 2p^6\ 3s^2\ 3p^6\ 4s^2\ 3d^{10}$$

- The first number indicates the principal energy level (n).

- The letter (s, p, d, f) indicates the subshell (which ranges from 0 to $n-1$).

- The superscript indicates the number of electrons occupying the subshell.

As the number of electrons in an atom increases across the periodic table, the length of written electron configurations can become very long and tedious. There is a shorthand approach of writing electron configurations that uses the configurations of noble gases. The noble gases are the elements located in the far right column of the periodic table (Group 18).

1. Identify the noble gas that comes before the element in the periodic table (the noble gas in the previous row).

   The noble gas before Na ($Z = 11$) is Ne ($Z = 10$). The noble gas before Cl ($Z = 17$) is also Ne ($Z = 10$) and not Ar ($Z = 18$).

2. Write the noble gas in square brackets:

   a. [Ne]

3. Write the rest of the electron configuration for the element after the noble gas:

   a. Ne: $1s^2\ 2s^2\ 2p^6$

   b. Na: $1s^2\ 2s^2\ 2p^6\ 3s^1$

4. Abbreviate the electron configuration for Na: [Ne] $3s^1$

When writing electron configurations for ions for a given element, simply add or subtract the number of electrons gained or lost from the atom when filling out the subshells. For example, consider sodium (Na), whose electron configuration is given below:

$$\text{Na:}\quad 1s^2\ 2s^2\ 2p^6\ 3s^1$$

However, when sodium reacts to form the Na^+ cation it loses one electron, and its electron configuration becomes:

$$Na^+: \quad 1s^2 \, 2s^2 \, 2p^6$$

Notice that the electron configuration for the sodium cation is identical to Ne because they both have 10 electrons.

When writing electron configurations, there are a few exceptions to the aforementioned guidelines because of the *stability rule*. The stability rule says that a sublevel is more stable when it is in half-filled configuration (one electron in every orbital) or full configuration (two electrons in every orbital). If an atom is only one short from achieving a half-filled or full configuration, it will take an electron from a neighboring *s* orbital to increase its stability. This is most commonly seen with the transition metals.

For example, chromium would appear to have the electron configuration [Ar] $4s^2 3d^4$. According to the stability rule, its electron configuration is actually more stable with a half-filled configuration [Ar] $4s^1 3d^5$. Notice that the $3d$ subshell took an electron from the neighboring $4s$ subshell. The $4s$ subshell now has a partially-filled orbital.

Another example is copper, whose default electron configuration is [Ar] $4s^2 3d^9$. Following the stability rule, its configuration changes into the more stable [Ar] $4s^1 3d^{10}$. Again, the $3d$ subshell takes an electron from the $4s$, which is now partially-filled.

Another way to express an atom's electron configuration is an *orbital diagram*, a visual representation that uses arrows to indicate electrons in orbitals, as shown on the left side below.

$\underset{1s}{\underline{1\downarrow}}\ \underset{2s}{\underline{1\downarrow}}\ \underset{2px}{\underline{1}}\ \underset{2py}{\underline{1}}\ \underset{2pz}{\underline{}}$	$1s^2\,2s^2\,2p^2$
Each fish hook arrow represents an electron. Each line represents an orbital, the subshell and energy level are written below. The spaces separate subshells *notice that there are three lines for *p*, since *p* has three orbitals (*x, y, z*)	Coefficient = energy level Letter = subshell Exponent = # of electrons in subshell This method does not give as much information as orbital diagrams.

Bohr atom

Before further exploring concepts on electronic structure, it is important to understand the scientific discoveries that contributed to the model of the atom that is currently used. By the beginning of the 19th century, chemists were able to show that simple compounds contained fixed and unvarying amounts of their constituent elements. In 1806, John Dalton provided a major step in explaining this with his particle theory, known as *Dalton's Atomic Theory*, which consisted of these important principles:

1. All matter is composed of very small particles, known as atoms.

2. Atoms of one element are the same shape, size, mass and other properties; atoms of one element differ in properties from atoms of other elements.

3. Atoms can neither be subdivided nor changed into one another.

4. Atoms cannot be created nor destroyed.

5. The atom is the smallest unit of matter that can partake in a chemical reaction.

In addition to these postulates, Dalton proposed the "rule of greatest simplicity," which suggested that atoms only combine in binary ratios (i.e., 1:1). This rule was problematic because Dalton assumed that the formula for water was HO instead of H_2O. Dalton eventually suggested that the rule of greatest simplicity was not correct, and in 1810 he suggested that a water molecule had three atoms. Now it is known that atoms combine in whole-number ratios (1:1, 1:2, 1:3, etc.) following the "law of multiple proportions."

There are some problems with Dalton's Atomic Theory. Dalton claimed that all atoms of one element must be the same mass, but the discovery of isotopes, which are atoms of the same element that vary in mass and density, proves otherwise. Additionally, it is now known that atoms can be subdivided into their constituent particles in nuclear processes; Dalton's postulate that atoms cannot be subdivided remains correct within the realm of chemical reactions.

In the early 1900s, German physicist Max Planck discovered that radiation is emitted in quantized amounts of energy, as opposed to a single continuous ray. Based on Planck's discovery, Niels Bohr conducted experiments on hydrogen atoms and was able to propose a revision to the accepted model for the atom of that time.

Bohr suggested that electrons orbit the nucleus in fixed orbits with defined energies and sizes, similar to how planets orbit the sun (except that the attraction within the atom is provided by electrostatic forces rather than gravity). When electrons move between orbits, they emit or absorb energy equivalent to the difference in energy levels between the orbits. Bohr identified each energy level using an integer *n*, which is now known as the principal quantum number (explained previously). Bohr also determined that additional electrons always occupy the lowest available energy level.

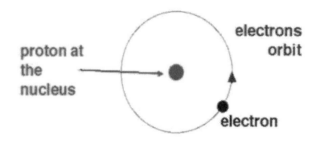

Bohr model of the Hydrogen atom

Quantum numbers *l*, *m*ₗ and *m*ₛ and number of electrons/orbital; Pauli Exclusion Principle

The second quantum number, called the *azimuthal* or *angular momentum quantum number* (*l*), is used to define the *shape* of an orbital. The principal energy levels, except for the first one where $n = 1$, have two or more possible subshells with differing energy levels. For any given *n*, the values for *l* may range from 0 to $(n-1)$. The number of subshells for any given energy level is equal to the value of *n* and is represented by the letters *s, p, d* and *f*.

Orbital	Angular Momentum Quantum Number
s	0
p	1
d	2
f	3

The third quantum number, called the *magnetic quantum number* (m_l), is used to describe the *orientation* of an orbital. This third magnetic quantum number defines the number of orbitals within a sublevel. The possible values for m_l range from $-l$ to $+l$, including 0.

- An *s* subshell has $l = 0$ which means that m_l can only have a single value (0), and thus it only has one orbital. The *s* sublevel can hold 2 electrons.

- A *p* subshell has $l = 1$ which means that m_l can have the values of -1, 0, +1. Thus, a *p* subshell has three orbitals and can hold up to 6 electrons.

- A *d* subshell has $l = 2$ which means that $m_l = -2, -1, 0, +1, +2$. Thus, a *d* subshell has five orbitals and can hold up to 10 electrons.

- An *f* subshell has $l = 3$ which means that $m_l = -3, -2, -1, 0, +1, +2, +3$. Thus a *d* subshell has seven orbitals and can hold up to 14 electrons.

Notice that each successive level holds 4 more electrons than its predecessor.

The fourth quantum number, called the *spin quantum number* (m_s), is used to describe the electron spin of any electron that occupies an orbital. This number is used to distinguish electrons within an orbital. There are two opposing values for electron-spin: $+\frac{1}{2}$ and $-\frac{1}{2}$. The first electron to occupy an orbital has a spin number of $+\frac{1}{2}$ while the second electron has a spin number of $-\frac{1}{2}$. In orbital diagrams, $+\frac{1}{2}$ electrons are represented by upward arrows and $-\frac{1}{2}$ electrons by downward arrows.

Energy Level	Number of sublevels	Sublevels	# of orbitals in that sublevel	Total number of electrons in sublevel
1	1	*s*	1	2
2	2	*s*	1	2
		p	3	6
3	3	*s*	1	2
		p	3	6
		d	5	10
4	4	*s*	1	2
		p	3	6
		d	5	10
		f	7	14

Quantum numbers represent locations of electrons within the atom.

The *Pauli Exclusion Principle* states that no two electrons in the same atom may have the same set of four quantum numbers (n, l, m_l and m_s). The maximum number of electrons in any orbital is two, and they must possess opposite spins ($+\frac{1}{2}$ or $-\frac{1}{2}$), because electrons of the same magnetic spin cannot both be simultaneously located in the same orbital.

Common names and geometric shapes for orbitals: *s, p, d, f*

There are four types of orbitals whose shapes have been predicted using wave mechanics (which are described further in the next section). They are: *s, p, d* and *f* from the initial letters of the words sharp, principal, diffuse and fundamental. Each energy level has between 1 and 4 sublevels and each sublevel is associated with a probability density of a particular shape. Each sublevel has a certain number of orbitals as given by the m_l value.

- *s orbitals* are spheres:

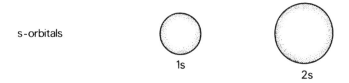

- *p orbitals have two lobes and are dumbbell-shaped – there are three different p orbitals (three orientations: p_x, p_y, p_z):*

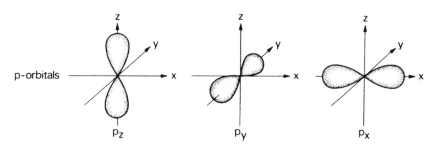

- *d orbitals have four lobes and are clover shaped– there are five different d orbitals (five orientations: d_{yz}, d_z^2, d_{xy}, d_{xz}, $d_{x^2-y^2}$):*

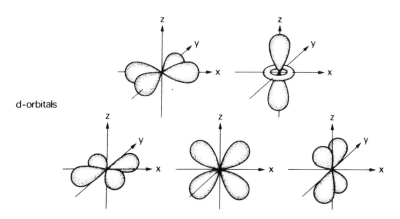

- *f orbitals are more complicated and the shape can be thought of as a mixture of the shapes of the other orbitals – there are seven f orbitals:*

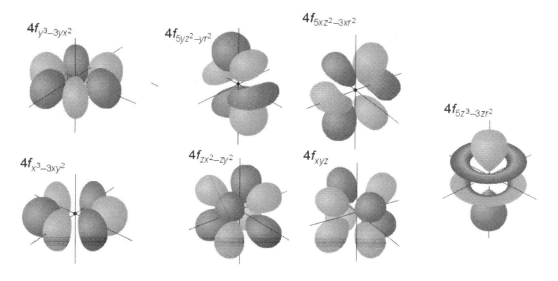

Heisenberg Uncertainty Principle

There were a series of important discoveries that led to quantum mechanics and enabled us to understand electron behavior. In 1924, Louis de Broglie published his work on *wave-particle duality*. He proposed that electrons could be classified as *particles* and *waves* simultaneously. Electrons are particles with mass and velocity, but they also possess *wave properties* such as wavelength and frequency. The following de Broglie equation demonstrates that all objects exhibit wave-behavior. Notice that the wave-behavior of real-life objects becomes negligible as the mass increases, as opposed to subatomic particles, which have extremely tiny masses:

$$\lambda = h \,/\, mv$$

λ = wavelength $\hspace{3cm}$ m = mass

h = Planck's constant $(6.626 \times 10^{-34}\,\text{J·s})$ $\hspace{1cm}$ v = velocity

Two years later, Erwin Schrödinger formulated a wave equation that models the movement of electrons based on their wave properties. In quantum mechanics, the solution to Schrödinger's wave equation yields a *wave function*, represented by the uppercase Greek letter psi (Ψ), which on its own does not indicate much about an atom. The square of the absolute value of psi, $|\Psi|^2$, gives the *probability density* of an electron's position. For example, the wave function $|\Psi(x)|^2$ yields the probability of finding an electron at position *x*. Orbitals are electron "clouds" because they represent the probability of an electron's location in the atom.

Since Schrödinger's equation showed that electrons behave similarly to waves, it implies that electrons do not travel in clearly defined paths, and that it is not possible to determine an electron's exact position and speed. German physicist Werner Heisenberg developed a theory based on the premise that there is a theoretical limit to how small the uncertainty in the measurements can be. This is known as *Heisenberg's Uncertainty Principle*, and states that both the position and momentum of an electron cannot be known simultaneously at any point in time. The uncertainty principle is given in the following equation:

$$\Delta x \times \Delta p \geq \frac{h}{4\pi}$$

where Δx is the *uncertainty in position*, and Δp is the *uncertainty in momentum*

Paramagnetism and diamagnetism

Electrons are constantly spinning in a fixed direction, which generates magnetic fields. According to the Pauli Exclusion Principle, if one electron is spinning in a clockwise direction, the other electron must be spinning in a counterclockwise direction, resulting in that orbital having no net spin. Since electrons occupying the same orbital must always have opposite values for their spin quantum numbers (m_s), they will always have different sets of quantum numbers.

Atoms can be classified based on their electron-induced magnetic behavior as ferromagnetic, diamagnetic or paramagnetic:

1. *Diamagnetic* materials generate an induced magnetic field in a direction opposite to an externally-applied magnetic field. These materials are therefore repelled by the applied magnetic field. All electrons in diamagnetic atoms are paired.

2. *Paramagnetic* materials, when in the presence of a magnetic field, generate internally-induced magnetic fields in the same direction as

the external field. A paramagnetic electron is an unpaired electron. An atom is paramagnetic if it has at least one paramagnetic electron in any orbital regardless of the number of its paired electrons. Paramagnetic atoms are slightly attracted to a magnetic field and cannot retain any magnetization in the absence of an external magnetic field.

3. *Ferromagnetic* materials generate permanent magnetic moments without needing an external magnetic field. Certain transition metals, such as iron and nickel, are known to have ferromagnetic properties. Electrons of ferromagnetic substances can spontaneously align themselves in the same direction, which reinforces each electron's magnetic properties.

Photoelectric effect

In 1905, Albert Einstein proposed a model known as the *photoelectric effect* that explained how incoming visible light interacts with electrons when it is reflected off surfaces of metals. Discrete packets of light energy, known as *photons*, are transferred to electrons on a metal surface as kinetic energy. When electrons possess sufficient energy to escape, *emission* of electrons from the metal may occur. This will occur only if the incident light possesses energy greater than or equal to the *work function* ϕ_W of the electron.

Energy (E) of light waves are calculated using the following formula:

$$E = h\nu$$

h = Planck's constant ν = frequency of light wave (Hz)

Einstein's model for the photoelectric effect also accurately predicts that the energy of a photon is proportional to its frequency and not its intensity.

Ground state, excited states

Every electron of an atom occupies a fixed orbital. When an electron occupies its default orbital, the electron is in its *ground state*. A ground state electron is at its lowest energy level and is the most stable. If an electron absorbs energy, it has greater potential energy and occupies a higher energy level. An electron in a higher energy level is known as an *excited state* electron. An electron can only stay in its excited state for a limited time before it drops back to its ground state and emits the excess energy as visible electromagnetic radiation.

Absorption and emission spectra

Electrons can only move between fixed orbitals, which means that the wavelength of light that is released or absorbed when they transition between energy levels is limited to a certain set of visible wavelengths known as the *line spectrum*. A line spectrum can only be produced by a gas under low pressure; solids, liquids and gases under low pressure produce *continuous spectra*, which contain all the colors of visible light.

Different elements have different numbers of electrons, which means that each element has a unique set of *atomic emission spectra,* represented by discrete lines along a frequency scale. Due to the uniqueness of this chemical property, it can be used to identify elements in a mixture.

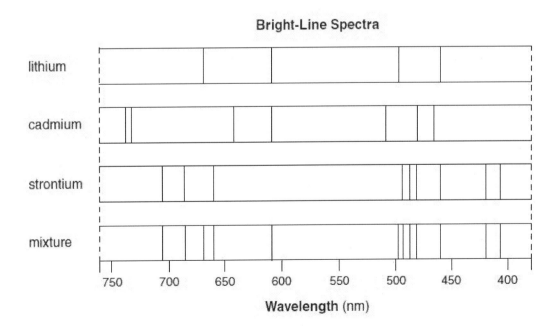

The same principle applies for *atomic absorption spectra*, which indicates the amount of energy absorbed when electrons jump to orbitals with higher energy levels. An element's absorption and emission spectrum correlate because the net difference between energy levels will be the same, regardless of the direction of the electron's movement.

The atomic emission spectrum of hydrogen has been widely observed. Its spectrum consists of five series of lines, and each series is named after its discoverer:

Lyman ($n = 1$), Balmer ($n = 2$), Paschen ($n = 3$), Brackett ($n = 4$), Pfund ($n = 5$) and Humphreys ($n = 6$). The most important emission series are the *Lyman, Balmer* and *Paschen* series, which correspond to *ultraviolet, visible* and *infrared* radiation, respectively.

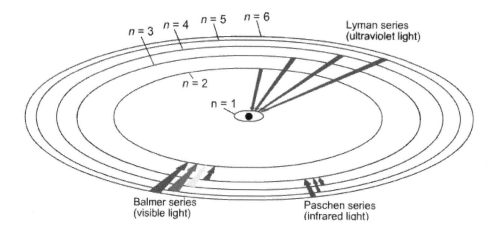

Swedish physicist Johannes Rydberg proposed an equation that could describe the relationship between the wavelengths of spectral lines of different elements. The *Rydberg formula* for hydrogen, which can be used to calculate energy emission of hydrogen electrons, is as follows:

$$E = \frac{hc}{\lambda}$$

$$= -R_h \left[\frac{1}{(n_i)^2} - \frac{1}{(n_f)^2} \right]$$

R_h = Rydberg's constant = 2.179×10^{-18}

n_i = principal number of initial orbital

n_f = principal number of final orbital

c = speed of light

λ = wavelength

h = Planck's constant

The Periodic Table: Variations of Chemical Properties with Group and Row

After the discovery of several new elements in the 18th and 19th centuries, scientists started noticing that elements could be categorized into groups with similar properties. The first significant development in this area occurred in 1869, when Russian chemist Dimitri Mendeleev and German chemist Lothar Meyer both published versions of the periodic table. In his table, Mendeleev arranged the elements by their atomic masses, which resulted in similarity of physical and chemical properties between elements in the same column. Mendeleev's table was revolutionary because it accurately predicted the position of elements that had not yet been discovered. Meyer arranged his table by increasing atomic volume.

Although Mendeleev's table exhibited patterns of similarities between elements in the same column, there were some exceptions. For example, argon exists in elemental form as a very unreactive gas, but it was categorized with the highly reactive sodium and lithium metals. In 1913, British physicist Henry Moseley improved Mendeleev's table by realizing that chemical properties of elements are related to their atomic number instead of atomic weight. This discovery became the foundation of the modern periodic table.

In today's periodic table, elements are arranged in rows and columns. The horizontal rows are called *periods*, which are identified by numbers (1-7). The vertical columns are called *groups* or *families*. There are several different standards for group nomenclature:

- In the older system, each group was assigned a Roman numeral (I-VIII) based on the number of their valence electrons. Additionally, the groups also got a letter (A or B) based on their location on the table. However, there were two different standards on the A/B designation. The American standard assigned A to the main group of elements on the sides and B to the transition group in the center, while the European standard assigned A to the left side and B to the right side of the table.

- To avoid confusion, a new naming standard was invented: from left to right, the groups are given consecutive integers (1-18).

hydrogen 1 **H** 1.0079																		helium 2 **He** 4.0026
lithium 3 **Li** 6.941	beryllium 4 **Be** 9.0122											boron 5 **B** 10.811	carbon 6 **C** 12.011	nitrogen 7 **N** 14.007	oxygen 8 **O** 15.999	fluorine 9 **F** 18.998	neon 10 **Ne** 20.180
sodium 11 **Na** 22.990	magnesium 12 **Mg** 24.305											aluminium 13 **Al** 26.982	silicon 14 **Si** 28.086	phosphorus 15 **P** 30.974	sulfur 16 **S** 32.065	chlorine 17 **Cl** 35.453	argon 18 **Ar** 39.948
potassium 19 **K** 39.098	calcium 20 **Ca** 40.078	scandium 21 **Sc** 44.956	titanium 22 **Ti** 47.867	vanadium 23 **V** 50.942	chromium 24 **Cr** 51.996	manganese 25 **Mn** 54.938	iron 26 **Fe** 55.845	cobalt 27 **Co** 58.933	nickel 28 **Ni** 58.693	copper 29 **Cu** 63.546	zinc 30 **Zn** 65.39	gallium 31 **Ga** 69.723	germanium 32 **Ge** 72.61	arsenic 33 **As** 74.922	selenium 34 **Se** 78.96	bromine 35 **Br** 79.904	krypton 36 **Kr** 83.80
rubidium 37 **Rb** 85.468	strontium 38 **Sr** 87.62	yttrium 39 **Y** 88.906	zirconium 40 **Zr** 91.224	niobium 41 **Nb** 92.906	molybdenum 42 **Mo** 95.94	technetium 43 **Tc** [98]	ruthenium 44 **Ru** 101.07	rhodium 45 **Rh** 102.91	palladium 46 **Pd** 106.42	silver 47 **Ag** 107.87	cadmium 48 **Cd** 112.41	indium 49 **In** 114.82	tin 50 **Sn** 118.71	antimony 51 **Sb** 121.76	tellurium 52 **Te** 127.60	iodine 53 **I** 126.90	xenon 54 **Xe** 131.29
caesium 55 **Cs** 132.91	barium 56 **Ba** 137.33	57-70 ★	lutetium 71 **Lu** 174.97	hafnium 72 **Hf** 178.49	tantalum 73 **Ta** 180.95	tungsten 74 **W** 183.84	rhenium 75 **Re** 186.21	osmium 76 **Os** 190.23	iridium 77 **Ir** 192.22	platinum 78 **Pt** 195.08	gold 79 **Au** 196.97	mercury 80 **Hg** 200.59	thallium 81 **Tl** 204.38	lead 82 **Pb** 207.2	bismuth 83 **Bi** 208.98	polonium 84 **Po** [209]	astatine 85 **At** [210]	radon 86 **Rn** [222]
francium 87 **Fr** [223]	radium 88 **Ra** [226]	89-102 ★★	lawrencium 103 **Lr** [262]	rutherfordium 104 **Rf** [261]	dubnium 105 **Db** [262]	seaborgium 106 **Sg** [266]	bohrium 107 **Bh** [264]	hassium 108 **Hs** [269]	meitnerium 109 **Mt** [268]	ununnilium 110 **Uun** [271]	unununium 111 **Uuu** [272]	ununbium 112 **Uub** [277]		ununquadium 114 **Uuq** [289]				

*Lanthanide series	lanthanum 57 **La** 138.91	cerium 58 **Ce** 140.12	praseodymium 59 **Pr** 140.91	neodymium 60 **Nd** 144.24	promethium 61 **Pm** [145]	samarium 62 **Sm** 150.36	europium 63 **Eu** 151.96	gadolinium 64 **Gd** 157.25	terbium 65 **Tb** 158.93	dysprosium 66 **Dy** 162.50	holmium 67 **Ho** 164.93	erbium 68 **Er** 167.26	thulium 69 **Tm** 168.93	ytterbium 70 **Yb** 173.04
**Actinide series	actinium 89 **Ac** [227]	thorium 90 **Th** 232.04	protactinium 91 **Pa** 231.04	uranium 92 **U** 238.03	neptunium 93 **Np** [237]	plutonium 94 **Pu** [244]	americium 95 **Am** [243]	curium 96 **Cm** [247]	berkelium 97 **Bk** [247]	californium 98 **Cf** [251]	einsteinium 99 **Es** [252]	fermium 100 **Fm** [257]	mendelevium 101 **Md** [258]	nobelium 102 **No** [259]

Since elements are ordered by increasing atomic number, there are recurring properties. A number of physical and chemical properties of elements can be predicted from their position in the periodic table. Among these periodic trends are number of valence electrons, ionization energy, electron affinity, atomic/ionic radii and electronegativity.

Valence electrons

Valence electrons are the outermost shell electrons and are responsible for participating in the formation of chemical bonds. On the periodic table, the given group numbers represent the number of valence electrons of each element. However, this rule only applies to the main group elements and does not apply to the transition metals.

Valence electrons experience the weakest electrostatic attractions from protons in the nucleus. There are two factors that contribute to this occurrence. The first one is distance. As seen in the formula for electrostatic force (known as *Coulomb's law*), increased distance leads to decreased attraction.

$$F = kq_1q_2 \,/\, r^2$$

where F is the electrostatic force, k is coulomb's constant (9×10^9 N·m^2/C^2), q_1 and q_2 are the respective charges of the two particles, and r is the distance between the particles.

The second factor is the presence of *screening electrons*, which are inner electrons that screen out the attractive force felt by the valence electrons.

Effective nuclear charge

Nuclear charge (*Z*) is the charge of all the protons in the nucleus, and it describes the extent to which electrons are pulled toward the nucleus.

Effective nuclear charge (Z_{eff}) is the net nuclear force experienced by valence electrons after accounting for electron shielding. This can be shown in the equation:

$$Z_{eff} = Z - S$$

where *Z* is the number of protons in the nucleus (i.e., the atomic number) and *S* is the average number of electrons between the nucleus and the electron in question (i.e., screening electrons)

The effective nuclear charge experienced by an electron is proportional to its stability: the more stable the electron, the greater the effective nuclear charge, and the more energy is required to remove the electron. Effective nuclear charge increases across a period, due to increasing nuclear charge but no accompanying increase in shielding effect. However, there is no general trend down a group, because both the nuclear charge and shielding effect increase (since more electron shells are added).

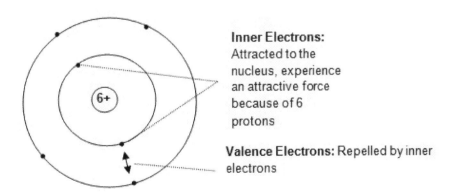

Inner Electrons: Attracted to the nucleus, experience an attractive force because of 6 protons

Valence Electrons: Repelled by inner electrons

Effective Nuclear Charge: Valence electrons only "feel" an attractive force = 4 protons.
2+ is cancelled out by the inner electrons due to shielding.

First and second ionization energy

The *ionization energy* (SI Units kJ/mol) is the energy required to remove an electron from a neutral atom of an element or an ion in the gaseous state. The ionization of an electron is always an endothermic process (i.e., it absorbs heat). While the electrons are leaving the atom, the number of protons in the nucleus are constant. Therefore, the remaining electrons would experience a stronger electrostatic force, as the force from the nucleus is divided among less electrons.

Ionization energies increase for each successive removal of an electron, due to the increase in electrostatic force; thus, the first electron is easiest to remove. The energy that is needed to remove this outermost electron is known as the *first ionization energy*. The energy that is needed to remove a second electron is called the *second ionization energy*.

Low ionization energy indicates that an electron is easily lost. This property is most commonly found in metals, with group I elements (alkali metal) having the lowest IE values. On the other hand, high IE indicates that an electron is not easily removed. This is mostly associated with nonmetals because of their natural tendency to gain electrons and form anions instead of losing electrons. The highest values are found for the inert gases (group VIII) because they have octets which make them extremely stable.

A larger, more positive nuclear charge results in a stronger bond and a higher ionization energy, while a larger atomic radius means that the outermost electrons will be further from the nucleus and thus have a weaker bond and a lower ionization energy. If an electron is in a lower sublevel, it will have a lower energy and be more difficult to dislodge; thus it will have a higher ionization energy. Half-filled shells are exceptions because these configurations are more stable than normal configurations (excluding filled shells). Half-filled shells occur when an atom's valence *p* or *d* orbital is half-filled (one electron in every orbital).

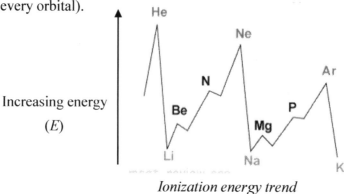

Ionization energy trend

From the ionization energy graph, ionization energy decreases down a group, because of increasing radii. The highest peaks on the graph are noble gases, while the lowest valleys are alkali metals. Local maxima occurs for filled subshells and half-filled *p* subshells.

Ionization energies generally increase from left to right across a given period, due to the increasing effective nuclear charge of the atom. Ionization energies generally decrease from top to bottom down a group, due to the increasing principal quantum number *n* and shielding effect of the inner shells.

Electron Affinity

Electron affinity is the energy released when an electron is added to a neutral atom. As the name implies, elements with high electron affinity are strongly attracted to electrons and are associated with exothermic reactions (i.e., reactions that release heat). Similar to ionization energy, electron affinity for nonmetals is indicative of their tendency to gain electrons and form negatively charged anions.

The first electron affinity is the energy released when one electron is added; it is always *exothermic*. The second electron affinity is always *endothermic* because adding an electron to an orbital where electrons are already present results in repulsion; thus, energy must be added to overcome the electrostatic repulsions and stabilize the additional electron.

The elements that need electrons most are the nonmetals, which have the highest electron affinities. The elements that do not need extra electrons are the metals, which have low electron affinities.

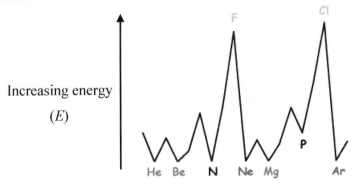

Electron affinity

On the electron affinity graph, the highest peaks are for the halogens and the lowest are for noble gases. Local minima occurs for filled subshells and half-filled *p* subshells.

Like ionization energy, electron affinity is a periodic trend that increases from left to right and decreases from top to bottom.

Electronegativity

In 1932, American chemist Linus Pauling derived a set of elemental values based on ionization energies and electron affinities, which indicate each element's tendency to gain electrons. This is known as *electronegativity*.

A more formal definition of electronegativity is the measure of the attraction of an atom for the electrons in the bond between itself and another atom. On the Pauling scale, electronegativity values range from a low of 0.7 for Fr to a high of 4.0 for F. Electronegativity generally increases from left to right and decreases from top to bottom, and as a result, nonmetals are typically more electronegative than metals.

The most electronegative elements are found at the top right corner and the least electronegative (i.e., most electropositive) elements are found at the bottom left corner. There are no electronegativity values given for the noble gases because they usually do not bond with other elements. In general, these trends can be explained in the same way as the previous concepts: as atomic number increases, the positive nuclear charge increases and the electrons within the same energy level are more strongly attracted to the nucleus.

Table of Pauling Electronegativity Values

IA	IIA	IIIB	IVB	VB	VIB	VIIB	VIII	VIII	VIII	IB	IIB	IIIA	IVA	VA	VIA	VIIA	VIIIA
1 **H** 2.1																	2 **He**
3 **Li** 1.0	4 **Be** 1.5											5 **B** 2.0	6 **C** 2.5	7 **N** 3.0	8 **O** 3.5	9 **F** 4.0	10 **Ne**
11 **Na** 0.9	12 **Mg** 1.2											13 **Al** 1.5	14 **Si** 1.8	15 **P** 2.1	16 **S** 2.5	17 **Cl** 3.0	18 **Ar**
19 **K** 0.8	20 **Ca** 1.0	21 **Sc** 1.3	22 **Ti** 1.5	23 **V** 1.6	24 **Cr** 1.6	25 **Mn** 1.5	26 **Fe** 1.8	27 **Co** 1.8	28 **Ni** 1.8	29 **Cu** 1.9	30 **Zn** 1.6	31 **Ga** 1.6	32 **Ge** 1.8	33 **As** 2.0	34 **Se** 2.4	35 **Br** 2.8	36 **Kr**
37 **Rb** 0.8	38 **Sr** 1.0	39 **Y** 1.2	40 **Zr** 1.4	41 **Nb** 1.6	42 **Mo** 1.8	43 **Tc** 1.9	44 **Ru** 2.2	45 **Rh** 2.2	46 **Pd** 2.2	47 **Ag** 1.9	48 **Cd** 1.8	49 **In** 1.8	50 **Sn** 1.8	51 **Sb** 1.9	52 **Te** 2.1	53 **I** 2.5	54 **Xe**
55 **Cs** 0.7	56 **Ba** 0.9	57 **La**	72 **Hf**	73 **Ta**	74 **W**	75 **Re**	76 **Os**	77 **Ir**	78 **Pt**	79 **Au**	80 **Hg**	81 **Tl** 1.8	82 **Pb** 1.9	83 **Bi** 1.9	84 **Po** 2.0	85 **At** 2.2	86 **Rn**
87 **Fr** 0.7	88 **Ra** 0.9	89 **Ac**	104 **Rf**	105 **Db**	106 **Sg**	107 **Bh**	108 **Hs**	109 **Mt**	110	111	112	114		116			

	58 **Ce**	59 **Pr**	60 **Nd**	61 **Pm**	62 **Sm**	63 **Eu**	64 **Gd**	65 **Tb**	66 **Dy**	67 **Ho**	68 **Er**	69 **Tm**	70 **Yb**	71 **Lu**
Lanthanides														
Actinides	90 **Th**	91 **Pa**	92 **U**	93 **Np**	94 **Pu**	95 **Am**	96 **Cm**	97 **Bk**	98 **Cf**	99 **Es**	100 **Fm**	101 **Md**	102 **No**	103 **Lr**

A *covalent bond* is the sharing of a pair of electrons between two nonmetal elements. If the electronegativity of the two atoms is the same, they will share the electrons equally. However, if there is an electronegativity difference, this results in a *polar covalent bond*. In this type of bond, the more electronegative element has a greater tendency to attract electrons to itself; thus, it gets a larger share of the electrons, giving it a partial negative charge. The less electronegative element in a polar covalent bond has a weaker tendency to attract electrons to itself; thus it gets a smaller share of the electrons, giving it partial positive charge.

An *ionic bond* occurs instead of a covalent one if the electronegativity difference is too great. Ionic bonds result from a transfer of electrons from the electropositive element to the electronegative element, and this generally occurs between a metal and a nonmetal element.

The difference in electronegativity between atoms participating in a bond is known as the *dipole moment* and is measured in units of *debye* (*D*). Based on the difference of electronegativity values, bonds can be classified as follows:

Type of Bond	Dipole Moment (*D*)
Covalent	$0 - 0.6$
Polar covalent	$0.6 - 1.6$
Ionic bonds	>1.6

Electron shells and the sizes of atoms

As previously discussed, electron shells are defined by the principal quantum number (*n* value). With increasing atomic number, elements have more electrons and therefore more electron shells to contain them. From top to bottom down a group, the shielding effect increases because the closer shells are between the nucleus and the outermost shell. Addition of an extra shell increases the atom size because of the physical presence of an extra orbit (i.e., higher shells have a larger distance from the nucleus than lower shells).

For elements going left to right across a row on the periodic table means filling up the same shell. As a shell is filled, the effective nuclear charge increases because the number of protons are increasing, while additional electrons fill the same orbit (so there is no increased shielding). With increasing effective nuclear charge, the electrostatic attraction between the nucleus and the electrons increases, so the atom becomes more compact.

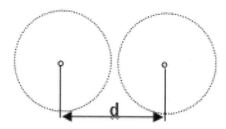

Atomic radius is ½ the distance between two nuclei. This is how the sizes of atoms are generally measured, since electron clouds are too ill-defined to measure precisely.

The trends in atomic radii in periods 2 and 3 are illustrated in the image below.

If a nucleus was the size of a ping-pong ball, the atom's diameter would be 25 miles. Therefore, an increase in the size of the nucleus does not substantially affect the overall size of an atom. From top to bottom down a group on the periodic table, the atoms become larger because electrons are added to new orbitals that are farther from the nucleus.

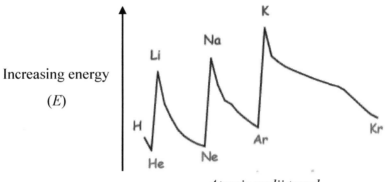

Atomic radii trend

The peaks on this graph represent atoms with a single electron in the valence shell, while the valleys are atoms with a filled valence shell.

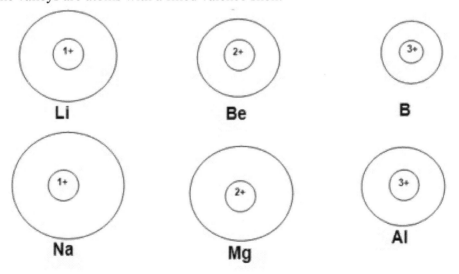

The size of an atom increases down a column due to increasing shells (*n* number) and decreases across a row due to increased nuclear attraction (greater number of protons).

The Periodic Table: Classification of Elements into Groups by Electronic Structure; Physical and Chemical Properties of Elements

The vertical columns (groups) of the periodic table have recurring trends. For this reason, some of the groups are given special names, sometimes referred to as trivial names or *unsystematic names* (e.g., alkali metals). Elements in the same group tend to show patterns in properties such as ionization energy, atomic radius and electronegativity.

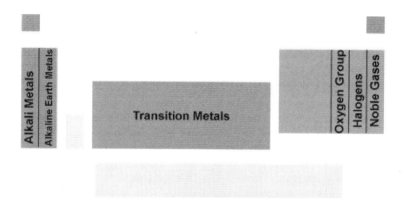

The periodic table can also be divided into blocks, which are named based on the subshell in which the valence (i.e., outermost) electron resides. In some of these blocks, the horizontal trends are very important. The four blocks are the *s*-block, the *p*-block, the *d*-block and the *f*-block.

This is seen in the figure below, although the *f*-block is generally displayed below the periodic table.

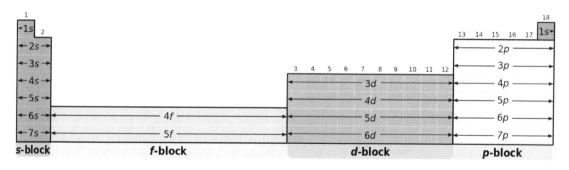

Representative elements

The representative (or main-group) elements (Groups 1A - 8A) comprise the *s* and *p*-blocks of the periodic table, and their properties are as follows:

- No free-flowing (loosely bound) outer *d* electrons, so number of valence electrons is given by group number

- Valence shell fills from left (1 electron) to right (8 electrons)

- Collectively make up the most important elements for life on Earth, comprising 80% of Earth's surface

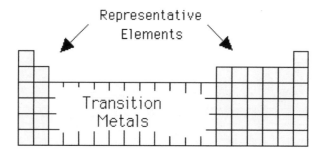

Alkali metals

The alkali metals (group 1 or 1A) include Li, Na, K, Rb, Cs and Fr, and the properties of the alkali metals are as follows:

- Single valence electron that is easily ionized - low ionization energy, very reactive

- Reacts to lose one electron and form cation in +1 oxidation state

- More reactive from top to bottom because of increasing atomic radii (Cs and Fr most reactive)

- Malleable, ductile, good conductor like all metals, but usually softer than other metals

- Reacts with oxygen to form oxides, which are strongly alkaline

- Reacts with water to form hydroxides and releases hydrogen

- Reacts with acids to form salts and releases hydrogen

- Most commonly found in nature in compounds with halogens

Alkaline earth metals

The alkaline earth metals (group 2 or 2A) include Be, Mg, Ca, Sr, Ba and Ra, and the properties of the alkaline earth metals are as follows:

- 2 valence electrons - relatively low in ionization energy, quite reactive

- Reacts to lose two electrons and form cation in +2 oxidation state

- More reactive from top to bottom because of increasing atomic radii

- Reacts with oxygen to form oxides, which are strongly alkaline

- Reacts with water to form hydroxides and releases hydrogen

- Reacts with acids to form salts and releases hydrogen

- Due to their reactivity, they are generally not found free in nature

Oxygen group

The oxygen group, also known as the chalcogens (group 16 or 6A) includes O, S, Se, Te and Po, and the properties of the chalcogens are as follows:

- Oxygen, sulfur and selenium are nonmetals, while tellurium and polonium are metalloids

- Lighter chalcogens (O, S) are typically nontoxic and critical to life, while heavier chalcogens are toxic

- Form ions with multiple oxidation numbers; sulfur's oxidation states are between –2 to +6

- Exist as polyatomic molecules in elemental state (e.g., O_2, S_8)

Halogens

The halogens (Group 17 or 7A) include F, Cl, Br, I and At, and the properties of halogens are as follows:

- 7 valence electrons (2 from *s* subshell and 5 from *p* subshell) - high electron affinity, very reactive (most reactive of all nonmetals)

- Most electronegative of all the elements

- Reacts to gain one electron and achieve full valence shell; forms anions with −1 oxidation state

- Less reactive from top to bottom because of decreasing atomic radii

- Reacts with alkali metals and alkaline earth metals to form salts (crystalline ionic solids)

- Form diatomic molecules in elemental state (e.g., Cl_2, Br_2, I_2)

Noble gases - physical and chemical characteristics

The noble gases (Group 18 or 8A) include He, Ne, Ar, Kr, Xe and Rn, and the properties of the noble gases are as follows:

- Full valence shell of 8 have high ionization energy coupled with low electron affinity

- Inert (i.e., very unreactive); only heavier elements of group react with few very electronegative elements, such as fluorine

- Exists in nature as monatomic gases (e.g., He, Ne, Ar)

Transition metals

The transition metals (groups 3-11 or 3B-1B) have unique chemical properties due to their loosely bound outermost *d* orbital electrons, and the properties of the transition metals are as follows:

- High conductivity and malleability due to loosely bound, free-flowing outer *d* electrons.

- When bonded with other ions to form metal complexes, the *d* orbitals become non-degenerate (different in energy). Electron transitions between non-degenerate *d* orbitals gives transition metal complexes vivid colors.

- Lose electrons from more than one shell to form cations of different oxidation states, indicated using Roman numerals (e.g., Iron (II) Fe2+ and Iron (III) Fe3+)

The periodic table has two detached rows of elements located under the table (the f-block). Those elements are collectively known as *inner transition elements* or the *lanthanide/actinide series*. They are located in the 6th and 7th periods starting at the *5d* block of the periodic table. They were once classified as rare-earth elements, due to the scarcity with which they naturally form. However, even the rarest of all the inner transition metals were found to be still more common than the platinum-group metals (which are transition metals). Most inner-transition metals, including plutonium and uranium, only exist in nature in radioactive form and decay rapidly.

Metals

The elements of the periodic table can be divided into metals, nonmetals and metalloids, according to their shared physical and chemical properties.

Metals are characterized by highly ordered, closely-packed atoms. They comprise almost three-fourths of all known Earth elements, such as aluminum, iron, calcium and magnesium. Many of the chemical and physical properties of metals are a result of their metallic bonds, where the valence electrons of *s* and *p* orbitals delocalize and form an aggregate of electrons that surrounds the nuclei of the interacting metal atoms.

The high degree of freedom with which their outermost electrons move between metal atoms gives rise to many of the following properties of metals:

- Metallic luster - can shine or reflect light

- Malleable - can be hammered or rolled into thin sheets

- Ductile - can be drawn into wire

- Hardness ranges from hard (iron and chromium) to soft (sodium, lead, copper)

- Conduct heat and electricity

- Crystalline solids at room temperature, with the exception of mercury (Hg) which is the only liquid metal

- High melting point

- Chemical reactivity varies greatly. Some are very unreactive (Au, Pt) while others are very reactive and will burst into flames upon contact with water (Na, K)

Nonmetals

The nonmetals are substances that do not exhibit any of the chemical or physical traits most associated with metal elements, owing to the fact that they bond with each other to form covalently-bonded compounds. They are located in the upper right hand corner of periodic table, and exhibit the following properties:

- Exist mostly as polyatomic elements, with the exception of the monoatomic noble gases

- At room temperature, nonmetal elements can be found in all phases: gas (H_2, O_2, N_2, F_2, Cl_2), solid (I_2, Se_8, S_8, P_4) and liquid (Br_2)

- Brittle - pulverize when struck

- Insulators (or very poor conductors) of electricity and heat, because electrons do not possess the high degree of movement as those in metal atoms

- Chemical reactivity ranges from inert (noble gases) to reactive (F_2, O_2, H_2). Nonmetals react with metals to form ionic compounds

- Some nonmetals have allotropes: different forms of the element in the same phase, such as carbon (diamond and graphite)

The following chart summarizes the differences between metals and nonmetals.

Chemical Properties	
Metals	**Nonmetals**
Likes to lose electrons to gain a positive (+) oxidation state (good reducing agent)	Likes to gain electrons to form a negative (–) oxidation state (good oxidizing agent)
Lower electronegativity – partially positive in a covalent bond with nonmetal	Higher electronegativity – partially negative in a covalent bond with metal
Forms basic oxides	Forms acidic oxides
Physical Properties	
Good conductor of heat and electricity	Poor conductor of heat and electricity
Malleable, ductile, luster and solid at room temperature (except Hg)	Solid, liquid, or gas at room temperature. Brittle if solid and without luster.

Metalloids (e.g., B, Si, As) are elements that exhibit both metal and nonmetal properties. They are found on the "stair-step" line of the periodic table that divides metals and nonmetals. Some metalloids are lustrous like metals, while others are brittle like nonmetals. Metalloids are also unique in that they do not normally conduct electricity at room temperatures, but conduct electricity when heated to higher temperatures.

electronegativity

Practice Questions

1. The attraction of the nucleus on the outermost electron in an atom tends to: 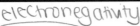 *electronegativity*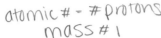

   A. decrease from right to left and bottom to top on the periodic table
   B. decrease from left to right and bottom to top on the periodic table
   C. decrease from left to right and top to bottom of the periodic table
   D. decrease from right to left and top to bottom on the periodic table

   atomic # = # protons
   mass #

2. Which species shown below has 24 electrons?

   A. $_{24}^{52}Cr$ B. $_{25}^{55}Mn$ C. $_{12}^{24}Mg$ D. $_{21}^{45}Sc$

3. Which characteristics describe the mass, charge and location of a proton, respectively?

   A. approximate mass 5×10^{-4} amu; charge +2; inside nucleus   *mass of a proton is 1 amu*
   B. approximate mass 1 amu; charge 0; inside nucleus
   C. approximate mass 1 amu; charge +1; inside nucleus
   D. approximate mass 5×10^{-4} amu; charge –1; outside nucleus

4. Which of the following subshell notations for electron occupancy is NOT possible?

   A. $4f^{11}$ *subshell*   B. $2p^1$ ← *electron*   C. $5s^3$ *princ. energy level*   D. $4p^5$

5. The *f* subshell can hold how many total electrons?

   A. 4   B. 8   C. 12   D. 14

6. Which of the following is the best description of the Bohr atom?

   A. Sphere with a heavy, dense nucleus containing electrons
   B. Sphere with a heavy, dense nucleus encircled by electrons in orbits
   C. Indivisible, indestructible particle
   D. Homogeneous sphere of protons, neutrons and electrons

7. Which of the following compounds does NOT exist?

   A. H^-, because H forms only positive ions
   B. PbO_2, because the charge on a Pb ion is only +2
   C. SF_6, because F does not have an empty *d* orbital to form an expanded octet
   D. OCl_6, because O does not have *d* orbitals to form an expanded octet

---

8. The elements in groups IA, VIIA and VIIIA are called, respectively:

   A. alkaline earth metals, transition metals and halogens
   B. alkali metals, halogens and noble gases
   C. alkali metals, alkali earth metals and halogens
   D. alkaline earth metals, halogens and alkali metals

9. Which of the following is a general characteristic of a metallic element?

   A. Reacts with nonmetals   C. Dull, brittle solid
   B. Reacts with metals   D. Low melting point

10. Which of the following elements would be shiny and flexible?

   A. bromine (Br)   C. helium (He)
   B. selenium (Se)   D. ruthenium (Ru)

11. The masses on the periodic table are expressed in what units?

   A. picograms   C. amu's
   B. nanograms   D. micrograms

12. Isotopes of an element have the same number of [ ] and different numbers of [ ].

   A. protons, electrons   C. neutrons, protons
   B. neutrons, electrons   D. protons, neutrons

13. Paramagnetism, the ability to be pulled into a magnetic field, is demonstrated by:

   A. any substance containing unpaired electrons
   B. nonmetal elements that have unpaired p orbital electrons
   C. transition elements that have unpaired d orbital electrons
   D. nonmetal elements that have paired p orbital electrons

14. Which element has the electron configuration $1s^2 2s^2 2p^6 3s^2 3p^6 4s^2 3d^{10} 4p^6 5s^2 4d^1$?

   A. Y   B. La   C. Si   D. Sc

15. Dmitri Mendeleev's chart of elements:

   A. predicted the behavior of unidentified elements
   B. developed the basis of our modern periodic table
   C. predicted the existence of elements undiscovered at his time
   D. all of the above

Solutions

1. D is correct. The attraction of the nucleus on the outermost electrons determines the ionization energy, which increases towards the right and increases up on the periodic table.

2. A is correct.

The number of protons is the atomic number (Z) of the element and is shown as a subscript.

Atoms of a particular element do not necessarily have the same mass (A), because they may have different numbers of neutrons (i.e., isotopes of the element).

For neutral elements, the number of electrons equals the number of protons (i.e., subscript).

Atoms of an element may also have different numbers of electrons, forming charged ions.

For neutral atoms, the number of electrons equals the number of protons.

3. C is correct.

Protons are the positively-charged particles located inside the nucleus of an atom. Like neutrons (also in the nucleus), protons have a mass of approximately 1 amu.

Protons have a +1 charge, while neutrons have a charge of 0 (i.e., neutral).

4. C is correct.

Each orbital can hold two electrons.

Maximum number of electrons in each shell:

The *s* subshell has 1 spherical orbital and can accommodate 2 electrons

The *p* subshell has 3 dumbbell-shaped orbitals and can accommodate 6 electrons

The *d* subshell has 5 lobe-shaped orbitals and can accommodate 10 electrons

The *f* subshell has 7 orbitals and can accommodate 14 electrons

Therefore, the *s* subshell can accommodate only 2 electrons.

5. D is correct.

The number of orbitals in a subshell is different than the maximum number of electrons in the subshell.

Each orbital can hold two electrons.

Maximum number of electrons in each shell:

> The *s* subshell has 1 spherical orbital and can accommodate 2 electrons
>
> The *p* subshell has 3 dumbbell-shaped orbitals and can accommodate 6 electrons
>
> The *d* subshell has 5 lobe-shaped orbitals and can accommodate 10 electrons
>
> The *f* subshell has 7 orbitals and can accommodate 14 electrons

The capacity of an *f* subshell is 7 orbitals × 2 electrons/orbital = 14 electrons.

6. B is correct. The Rutherford-Bohr model of the hydrogen atom, often referred to as simply the Bohr atom, depicts a sphere with a heavy, dense nucleus encircled by electrons in orbits, held together by the electrostatic forces between the positively-charged nucleus and the negatively-charged electrons.

7. D is correct.

O contains only *s* and *p* orbitals and isn't capable of forming 6 bonds due to the lack of *d* orbitals.

Hydrogen forms a negative ion in NaH (sodium hydride), LiAlH$_4$ (lithium aluminum hydride) or NaBH$_4$ (sodium borohydride). Each of these hydrides (i.e., H$^-$) is a strong base with a pK_a greater than 32.

Lead (Pb), although not a transition metal, does have two common valences: +2 and +4.

Fluorine in SF$_6$ does not have an expanded octet because each F is bonded only to S. The sulfur has an expanded octet but it is in the 3rd row of the periodic table and has empty *d* orbitals.

8. B is correct.

A group (or family) is a vertical column, and elements within groups share similar properties.

Group IA is the alkali metals which include lithium (Li), potassium (K), sodium (Na), rubidium (Rb), cesium (Cs) and francium (Fr).

Group VIIA is the halogens which include fluorine (F), chlorine (Cl), bromine (Br), iodine (I) and astatine (As). Halogens gain one electron to become a –1 anion and the resulting ion has a complete octet of valence electrons.

Group VIIIA is the noble gases that include helium (He), neon (Ne), argon (Ar), krypton (Kr) xenon (Xe), radon (Rn) and ununoctium (Uuo).

The alkaline earth metals (group IIA) include beryllium (Be), magnesium (Mg), calcium (Ca), strontium (Sr), barium (Ba) and radium (Ra).

9. A is correct.

The vast majority of elements on the periodic table (over 100 elements) are metals. There are about four times more metals than nonmetals.

Alkali metals (group IA) include lithium (Li), potassium (K), sodium (Na), rubidium (Rb), cesium (Cs) and francium (Fr).

The alkaline earth metals (group IIA) include beryllium (Be), magnesium (Mg), calcium (Ca), strontium (Sr), barium (Ba) and radium (Ra).

Metals form positive ions by losing electrons during chemical reactions; thus, metals are electropositive elements.

Metals are good conductors of both heat and electricity, because the molecules in metals are closely packed together.

Metals are not brittle or fragile (i.e., they do not break easily); to the contrary, they are malleable and can be pressed or hammered without breaking.

Metals are opaque and not transparent because all of the atoms in metal are surrounded by free moving electrons, therefore any light that strikes the metal will hit these electrons, which will absorb and re-emit it, and the light is not able to pass through.

Metals, except mercury, are solids under normal conditions. Potassium has the lowest melting point of the solid metals at 146 °F.

10. D is correct.

Transition metals occur in groups (vertical columns) 3–12 of the period table. They occur in periods (horizontal rows) 4–7. This group of elements includes silver, iron and copper.

11. C is correct.

The masses on the periodic table are the atomic masses of the elements. The atomic mass is a weighted average of the various isotopes of the element (the mass of each isotope multiplied by its relative abundance).

Atomic mass is sometimes called atomic weight, but the term atomic mass is more accurate. This mass is expressed in atomic mass units (amu), also called Daltons (D).

1 amu is equal to 1 g/mol.

An amu is one-twelfth the mass of a neutral carbon-12 atom.

12. D is correct. Elements are defined by the number of protons (i.e., atomic number).

The isotopes are neutral atoms: # electrons = # protons.

Isotopes are variants of a particular element which differ in the number of neutrons. All isotopes of the element have the same number of protons and occupy the same position on the periodic table.

The number of protons within the atom's nucleus is the atomic number (Z) and is equal to the number of electrons in the neutral (non-ionized) atom. Each atomic number identifies a specific element, but not the isotope; an atom of a given element may have a wide range in its number of neutrons.

The number of both protons and neutrons (i.e., nucleons) in the nucleus is the atom's mass number (A), and each isotope of an element has a different mass number.

13. A is correct. Paramagnetic elements are substances that move into a magnetic field and have one or more unpaired electrons.

Most transition metals and their compounds in oxidation states involving incomplete inner electron subshells are paramagnetic.

Diamagnetic elements are repelled by an applied magnetic field because they create an induced magnetic field in a direction opposite to an externally applied magnetic field.

14. A is correct.

Identify an element using the periodic table by using its atomic number. The atomic number is equal to the number of protons or electrons.

The total number of electrons can be determined by adding all the electrons in the provided electron configuration:

$$2 + 2 + 6 + 2 + 6 + 2 + 10 + 6 + 2 + 1 = 39.$$

Element #39 in the periodic table is yttrium (Y).

15. D is correct.

Russian chemist Dmitri Mendeleev (in 1869) created the prototype version of the periodic table of elements, in which he placed elements with the same number of valence electrons in the same group (i.e., vertical columns).

Mendeleev's table was the basis of the modern day periodic table, although our modern day table has an opposite system where elements with the same number of valence electrons are in the same group (or family) rather than periods (i.e., horizontal row).

Mendeleev predicted the existence of undiscovered elements, along with their behavior.

Chapter 2

Chemical Bonding

The Ionic Bond: Electrostatic Forces Between Ions

- **Electrostatic Energy $\propto q_1q_2 / r$**

- **Electrostatic Energy $\propto$ Lattice Energy**

- **Electrostatic Force $\propto q_1q_2 / r^2$**

The Covalent Bond: Electron Pair Sharing

- **Sigma (σ) and Pi (π) Bonds**

- **Lewis Electron Dot Formulas**

- **Partial Ionic Character**

THE IONIC BOND

Electrostatic Forces Between Ions

An ionic bond forms when electrons are transferred from one atom to another, resulting in oppositely-charged species that attract each other via electrostatic interaction. When atoms gain or lose electrons and become charged, they are known as ions. The table below summarizes the typical ions that are formed by elements in the periodic table:

Notice that nonmetals (on the right side of the periodic table) have a greater tendency to gain electrons and form negatively-charged anions. Metals (on the left side of the periodic table) exhibit weaker nuclear forces on valence electrons and tend to lose electrons and form positively-charged cations. Ionic bonds form between a metal cation and a nonmetal anion, so that both atoms obtain a full *valence shell*. If a metal has a low ionization energy and a nonmetal has a high electron affinity (concepts described in the previous chapter), ionic bonding is even more likely. A familiar ionic compound is sodium chloride (NaCl), or table salt.

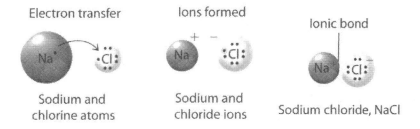

The cations and anions in an ionic compound can be thought of as the North and South poles of a magnet, which attract each other. Similarly, two cations (or anions) push away from each other. Therefore, the molecules are arranged into rigid crystalline structures.

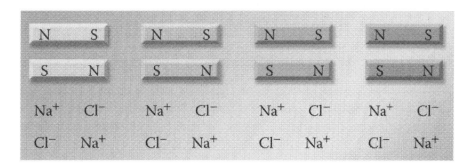

Due to the strong, polarized, intermolecular forces, ionic compounds generally possess high melting and boiling points, and are therefore solid at room temperature. *Ionic crystals* are three-dimensional arrangements of ions in an ionic compound, sometimes called a crystal lattice. The crystalline solid structure of sodium chloride is shown below. Sodium chloride has a high melting point (800 °C) and dissolves in water to give a conducting solution. Like all ionic compounds, sodium chloride is a strong electrolyte, so it dissociates completely in water. Solid ionic compounds are non-conductive; however, molten compounds (i.e., compounds that have been liquefied by heat) or compounds dissolved in water conduct electricity.

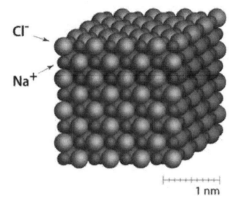

Cl⁻

Na⁺

1 nm

Crystalline Lattice Structure of Table Salt (NaCl)

Like in all types of bonding, the valence (outermost) electrons are the electrons involved in ionic bonding. Transfer of the lone 3*s* electron of a sodium atom to the half-filled 3*p* orbital of a chlorine atom generates a sodium cation and a chloride anion, forming the compound sodium chloride. Originally, the sodium and chlorine atoms each had a net charge of 0, but after the transfer of one electron took place, they had a charge of +1 and –1, respectively, due to the imbalance between protons and electrons in the atom.

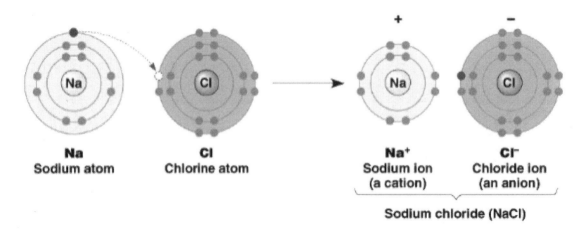

Sodium chloride (NaCl)

Electrostatic Energy $\propto q_1q_2 / r$

The strength of an ionic bond can be determined by the amount of *electrostatic potential energy* between the two opposing charges. The electrostatic potential energy can be determined by the following formula:

$$U_E = kq_1q_2 / r$$

where U_E is electrostatic potential energy, k is coulomb's constant (9×10^9 m/F), q_1 and q_2 are the two charges, and r is the distance between the charges.

Electrostatic energy is negative in ionic bonds because q_1 and q_2 have opposing charges. If q_1 and q_2 did not have opposing charges (i.e., both positive, or both negative), then they repel each other, and no ionic bond forms. However, the negative sign is often dropped and only the magnitude of the electrostatic energy is used. The greater the magnitude of electrostatic potential energy, the stronger the ionic bond. Strong ionic bonds are promoted by high charge magnitudes (q values) that are close together (small r value).

Ions that form strong ionic bonds have high charge density; that is, the charge-to-size ratio is high. A high charge density of a cation can distort the electron cloud of the anion to promote electron sharing.

Electrostatic Energy $\propto$ Lattice Energy

Lattice energy is the energy required to break an ionic bond. Conversely, it can also be the energy given off when oppositely-charged, gaseous ions come together to form an ionic crystalline solid. This energy released by the reaction is correlated to the ionic bond strength, which means that it is also proportional to electrostatic energy.

Electrostatic Force $\propto q_1q_2 / r^2$

The electrostatic force that holds charged particles together is defined in terms of the electrostatic energy. Coulomb's law defines the electrostatic force in terms of electrostatic charges and distance.

$$F = kq_1q_2 / r^2$$

where F is the electrostatic force, k is coulomb's constant (9×10^9 m/F), q_1 and q_2 are the two charges and r is the distance between the charges.

As seen in the equation, the electrostatic force is directly proportional to the product of opposite charges that attract (negative F) or same charges that repel (positive F). The electrostatic force is inversely proportional to the square of the distance between them. Therefore, larger charge magnitudes that are closer together exhibit a greater electrostatic force.

Coulomb's law is also analogous to the *universal law of gravitation* ($F = Gm_1m_2 / r^2$). G (gravitational constant) is analogous to k, and m (mass) is analogous to q. The big difference is that G is tiny compared to k, because gravitational force is weaker compared to the much stronger electrostatic force.

There is another way to write the formula for electrostatic force that is specific to ionic compounds. The equation below describes the force of attraction between the cation n^+ and the anion n^- at a distance d apart.

$$F = R(n^+ \times e) \cdot (n^- \times e) / d^2$$

where R is coulomb's constant (usually written as k), $n^+ \times e$ = charge of cation in coulombs = positive charge (n^+) × coulombs per electron (e) and $n^- \times e$ = charge of anion in coulombs = negative charge (n^-) × coulombs per electron (e)

THE COVALENT BOND

Electron Pair Sharing

A covalent bond is formed when electron pairs are shared between two atoms, rather than a complete transfer of electrons. These electron pairs are known as shared pairs or *bonding pairs*, and the formation of a covalent bond results in the overlap of their electron orbitals, as shown below.

Covalent bonds are typically formed between nonmetal elements.

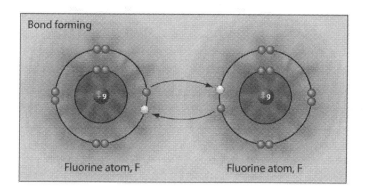
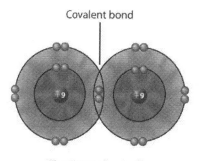

As described in the previous chapter, most atoms tend to share electrons to achieve a full valence shell of eight electrons (i.e., the octet rule).

Additional illustrations of covalent bonding that follows the octet rule are displayed below. These are simple Bohr notations, where the valence electrons are designated by dots.

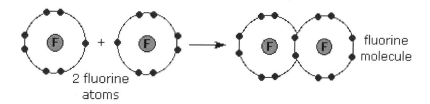

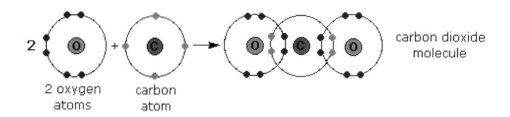

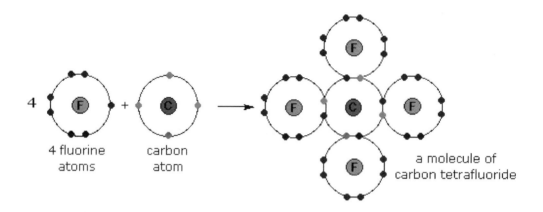

The hydrogen atom is an exception to the octet rule, because it is at its lowest energy when it has two electrons in its valence shell.

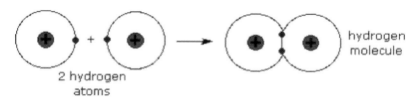

In the image below, the atoms form covalent bonds to obtain the ideal number of electrons. The electrons not involved in bonding are the *nonbonding lone pairs*.

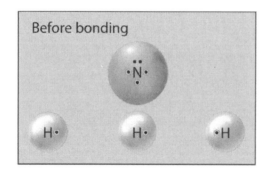

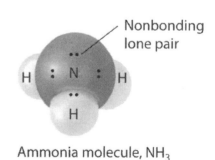

Ammonia molecule, NH_3

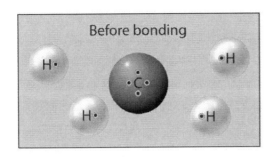

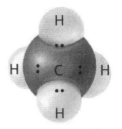

Methane molecule, CH_4

Covalent bonds can also involve more than a single pair of electrons, which results in double- and triple-bonded nonmetal atoms. In double bonds, two pairs of electrons (four electrons) are shared, and in triple bonds, three pairs of electrons (six electrons) are shared.

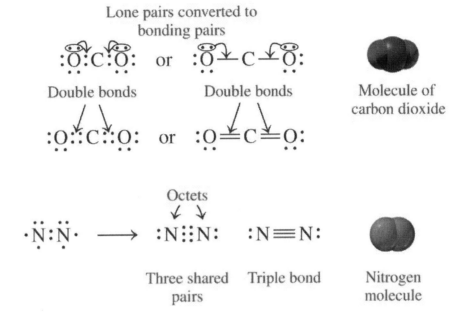

A covalent bond resulting from one atom donating an electron pair to another atom is a *coordinate covalent bond*. Both electrons in a coordinate covalent bond only come from one donor atom.

An example of a molecule with a coordinate covalent bond is ozone, O_3:

$$:\overset{..}{\underset{..}{O}}::\overset{..}{\underset{..}{O}}: \ + \ \overset{..}{\underset{..}{O}}: \longrightarrow \ :\overset{..}{\underset{..}{O}}::\overset{..}{\underset{}{O}}:\overset{..}{\underset{..}{O}}:$$

nonbonding electron pair   *coordinate covalent bond*

Sigma and *Pi* Bonds

The electron density of a chemical bond can be divided into different regions. *Sigma* (σ) *bonds* are formed when one orbital from each atom overlap and create a new orbital. Typically, a σ bond is a single bond and is the first bond involved in double and triple bonds. σ bonds lie along the imaginary line joining their two nuclei, called the *internuclear axis*. In σ bonds, the electron density is between the nuclei of the two atoms and is symmetrical about the internuclear axis. Atoms on both sides of a σ single bond are free to rotate with the bond as their axis.

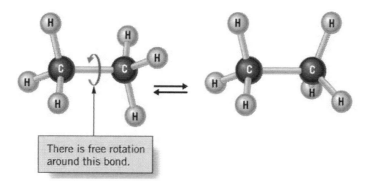

There is free rotation around this bond.

In the image below, the σ bonds of *s–s* and *p–p* orbitals are shown. Hybrid orbitals also exist, and are discussed in another section.

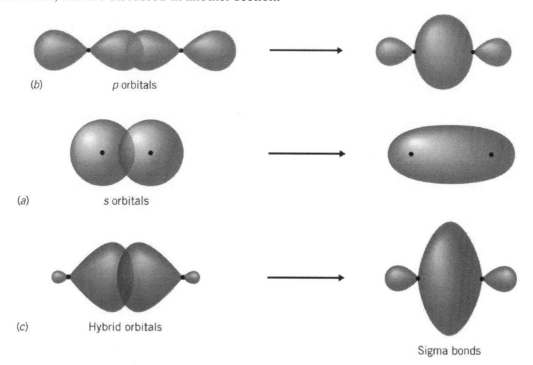

(b)   *p* orbitals

(a)   *s* orbitals

(c)   Hybrid orbitals

Sigma bonds

Pi (π) bonds are formed when unhybridized *p* orbitals on the top and bottom of the internuclear axis overlap, as illustrated in the image below. A single π bond consists of regions both above and below the intermolecular axis, and there is no electron density along the intermolecular axis.

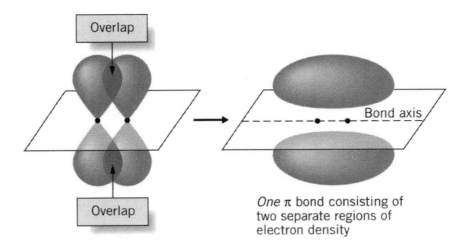

One π bond consisting of two separate regions of electron density

When electron density above and below σ bonds overlap, a multiple bond (i.e., double or triple) forms. Thus, π bonds can only form after a σ bond has connected two atoms together. A double bond is one σ bond and one π bond, while a triple bond is one σ bond and two π bonds. For example, nitrogen gas (N_2) is connected by a triple bond (N≡N). The first bond is a σ bond and the remaining two bonds are π bonds.

π bonds are distinct in that they introduce a special property of rigidity to molecules; they do not allow for the rotation of atoms. Molecules that involve π bonds are stronger and require more energy to break.

Hybrid orbitals

Hybrid orbitals are produced by the hybridization (mixing) of existing electron orbitals to create geometries that can facilitate better bonding.

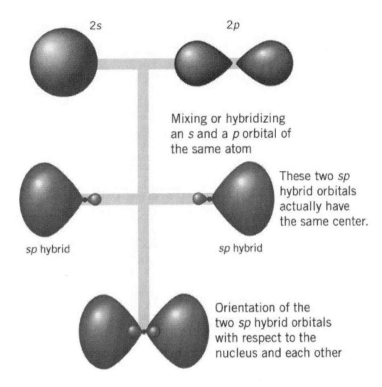

The possible hybridizations of the carbon atom are as follows.

- sp^3: a hybrid between one s with three p orbitals. Tetrahedral in geometry. Contains single bonds only.
- sp^2: a hybrid between one s with two p orbitals. Trigonal planar in geometry. Contains a double bond.
- sp: a hybrid between one s with one p orbital. Linear in geometry. Contains a triple bond.

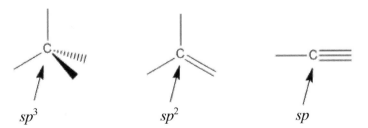

Hybridization of the carbon atom

Valence shell electron-pair repulsion (VSEPR) theory, predictions of shapes of molecules

Valence Shell Electron Pair Repulsion (VSEPR) theory states that electron pairs surrounding an atom repel each other, and the bonds and lone pairs around a central atom are separated by the largest possible bond angles. In VSEPR, *electron domains* refer to the electron pairs in the molecule.

Every molecule has bonding and non-bonding domains. When atoms bond to create molecules, the atoms arrange themselves as far apart as possible to minimize same-charge repulsion between electrons. VSEPR theory helps to predict the molecular geometry based on the number of electron pairs in the molecule.

The *electron pair domain geometry* (EDG) indicates the arrangement of bonding and non-bonding electron pairs around the central atom. The *molecular shape geometry* (MG) indicates the arrangement of atoms around the central atom after accounting for electron repulsion.

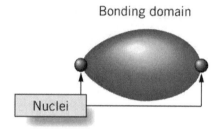

These are the configurations that maximize distance between the bonding electron pairs:

Molecules with two attached atoms: linear (a straight line, with one atom on each side of the central atom). Bond angle = 180°.

Molecules with three attached atoms: trigonal planar. Bond angle = 120°.

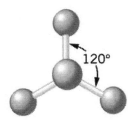

Molecules with four attached atoms: a tetrahedron. Bond angle = 109.5°.

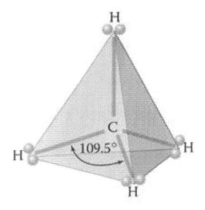

Molecules with five attached atoms: a trigonal bi-pyramid. Bond angles = 120° and 90°.

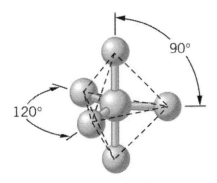

Molecules with six attached atoms: an octahedron. Bond angle = 90°.

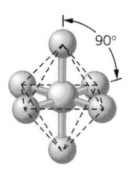

The molecular shapes above are true for molecules that contain only bonding domains (i.e., their central atoms do not have any non-bonding domains [lone pairs]). When the central atom has one or more non-bonding domains, the lone pair occupies the same space where a bond usually forms.

These non-bonding electron domains exert electrostatic repulsions that cause bonds to bend away. Lone pairs need to be closer to the atom than the bonding pairs, thus they take up more of the available space. An example is SF_4, which has one lone pair:

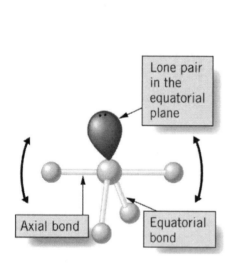

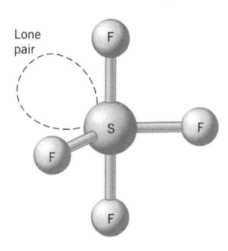

The structure of SF_4

General strategy to determine geometrical shape of a molecule:

1. Start by counting all the domains, both bonding and non-bonding, around the central atom. This determines the general shape of the molecule, which will be one of the shapes discussed above.

Number of electron domains	Arrangement of electron domains	Electron-domain geometry	Predicted bond angle
2		Linear	180°
3		Trigonal planar	120°
4		Tetrahedral	109.5°
5		Trigonal bipyramidal	120° 90°
6		Octahedral	90°

2. For every non-bonding domain, remove a surrounding atom.

   Example: a molecule with four total domains has a tetrahedral shape. If one of the domains is non-bonding, one of the surrounding atoms is removed, leaving a central atom with three surrounding atoms remaining. Now the molecule is in a shape of a trigonal pyramid. If there are two non-bonding domains, remove two surrounding atoms; now the molecule is in a bent shape.

3. For molecules with five domains, start by removing atoms above and below the pyramid before the 3 atoms surrounding it. Remember that the atoms always want the configuration with least repulsion. The angles between the top or bottom atoms and the three side atoms are 90°. The angles between the side atoms are 120°, thus the molecule gets rid of the more repulsive atoms first (i.e., the ones with the smaller bond angle). This is also true for molecules with six domains: the domains above and below are removed before the domains surrounding the central atom.

The following diagram summarizes the shapes of atoms based on the number of bonding and non-bonding electron pairs (also called unbonded electron pairs):

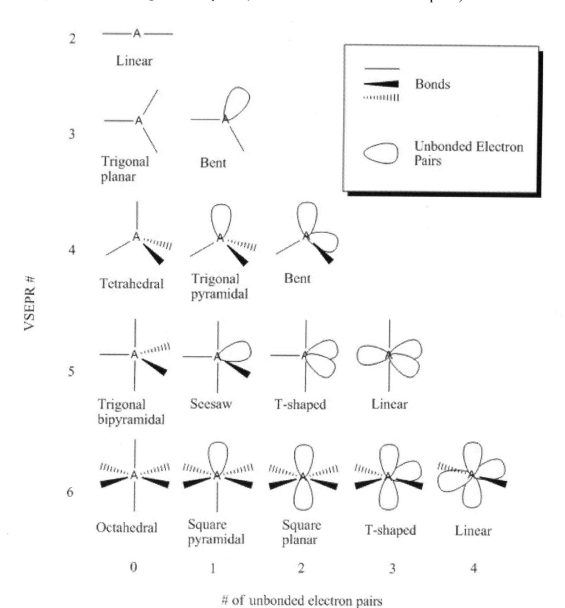

Non-bonding domains affect the angle of bonds in the molecule. Water (H_2O) has two bonding domains and two non-bonding domains, which means it experiences electron repulsion on its bonds and forms a bent shape (see previous chart). Its bent shape comes from a tetrahedral configuration with two of its vertices removed. All bonds in a tetrahedron are 109.5° wide, which means that bonds in a bent molecule should have 109.5° between them.

However, because of the repulsion between lone electron pairs and the bonding electrons, the actual bond angle is slightly decreased to approximately 105°.

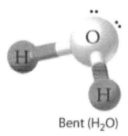

Bent (H_2O)

When determining geometric shapes using VSEPR, double bonds are counted as a single domain. For example, formaldehyde (CH_2O) has one double bond and two single bonds, which adds up to three bonding domains. Its molecular geometry is trigonal planar.

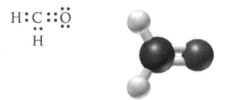

There are two major theories that explain how molecules bond with each other: valence bond theory and molecular orbital theory. They can both be used to help determine the structure of a molecule.

The *Valence Bond (VB) Theory* is largely based off valence electrons. This theory states that each atom has their own orbitals, and that orbitals overlap to form bonds. The extent of overlap of atomic orbitals is related to bond strength; the greater the overlap, the stronger the bond.

For example, the bonding of F_2 can be explained by VB theory. F_2 bonds form because atomic valence orbitals overlap (in this case, $2p$ orbitals), one from each fluorine.

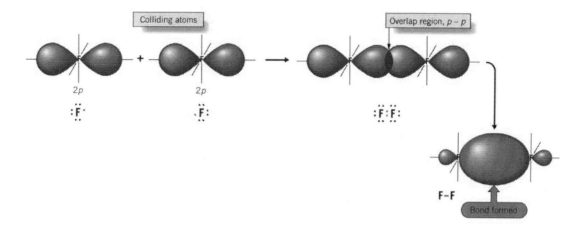

Orbital overlap is not limited to identical orbitals. Bonding in HF involves overlap between the $1s$ orbital of H and the $2p$ orbital of F.

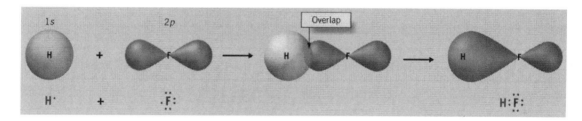

The bonding of H_2S can also be described according to VB theory. Sulfur has one filled orbital (contains two electrons) and two partially-filled orbitals (contains one electron). The partially filled p orbitals overlap with the s orbital from hydrogen. The predicted 90° bond angle is very close to the experimental value of 92°.

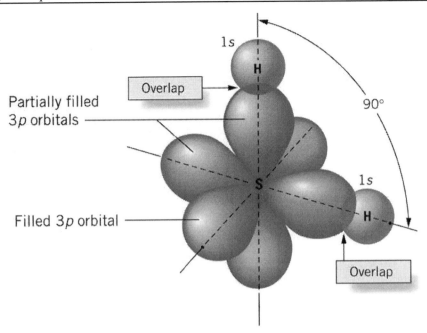

VB theory describes many bonds, however it cannot explain all existing molecular geometries properly. Methane (CH_4), for example, has a tetrahedral shape, seen in the image. Carbon's electron configuration ($1s^2 2s^2 2p^2$) indicates that all of its electrons are paired, except for two electrons that occupy p orbitals. VB theory predicts that carbon can only bond with two hydrogen molecules, resulting in a CH_2 molecule, and that the bond angle will be close to $90°$ (similar to H_2S from the previous example). However, observation of methane reveals that there are four equal bonds and the bond angles are all $109.5°$.

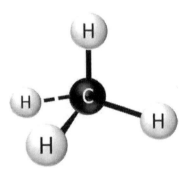

To resolve the difference between theoretical and experimental values, the concept of *hybridization* was introduced to improve upon the VB theory. Hybridization refers to the mixing of atomic orbitals to allow the formation of bonds that have realistic bond angles. *Atomic orbitals* are areas with the highest probabilities of finding electrons and hybridization is a rearrangement of orbital areas. Hybrid orbitals have new shapes, new directional properties and combined properties of the constituent orbitals.

Symbols for hybrid orbitals combine the symbols of the orbitals used to form them. The sum of exponents in hybrid orbital notation must add up to the number of atomic orbitals used.

- One *s* and one *p* orbitals form two *sp* hybrid orbitals

- One *s* and two *p* orbitals form three *sp²* hybrid orbitals

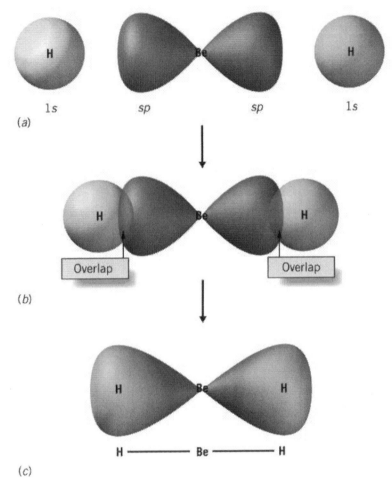

Bonding of BeH₂: Be $1s^2 2s^2$ H $1s^1$

Beryllium has two electrons in the *2s* orbital. In order to bond with two hydrogens, it needs to split the electrons into two orbitals. It uses the next available orbital (*2p*), and combines it with *2s* orbital, which results in two *sp* orbitals. Each of those *sp* orbitals overlap with hydrogen's *1s* orbital, creating a covalent bond. VSEPR predicts that this molecule would have a linear shape, which is confirmed by experiment.

Because of the octet rule, most atoms can only form up to four bonds. This means that four orbitals are needed (1 *s* and 3 *p* orbitals). For molecules that have more than four bonds/lone pairs around them, *d* orbitals are included in the hybridization to accommodate the extra bonds. This is known as *expanded octet hybridization*.

Bond angle experiments suggest that NH_3 and H_2O both use *sp*^{3} hybrid orbitals in bonding (with a total of four orbitals) even though each only has two bonds. This led to the conclusion that hybrid orbitals are not exclusively used for bonding; they also house the non-bonding electron pairs. Both bonding and non-bonding pairs contribute to the geometry of a molecule. Here is the orbital diagram of nitrogen in NH_3:

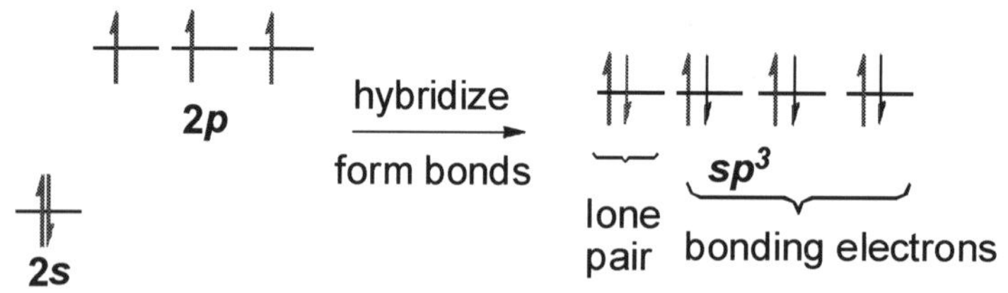

This diagram shows hybridization of oxygen in H_2O:

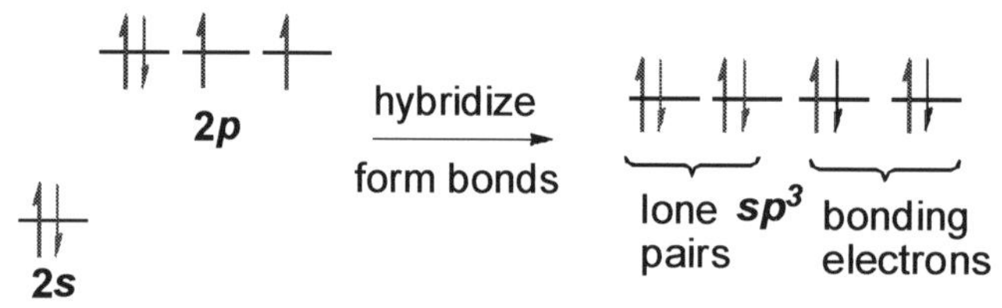

Molecular Orbital (*MO*) *Theory*, the second major theory, views molecules as a collection of positively-charged nuclei having a set of molecular orbitals that are filled with electrons (similar to filling atomic orbitals with electrons). It does not concern the way that atoms come together to form molecules. This is more difficult to visualize than the VB theory, but it can be advantageous because it allows for the accurate prediction of magnetic properties of molecules, along with other characteristics. The energies of molecular orbitals are determined by combining the electron waves of atomic orbitals.

For H_2, two $1s$ wave functions, one from each atom, combine to make two MO wave functions. This is constructive interference of waves. In this case, the energy of the bonding MO is lower than the energy of the atomic orbitals.

$$1s_A \ + \ 1s_B$$

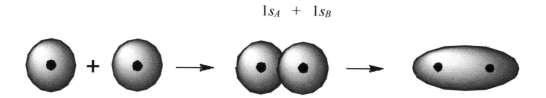

Just as there are σ orbitals, there are corresponding σ^* antibonding MOs. The other possible combination of two $1s$ orbitals involves destructive interference of the $1s$ waves. In this case, the energy of the antibonding MO is higher than the energy of parent atomic orbitals.

$$1s_A - 1s_B$$

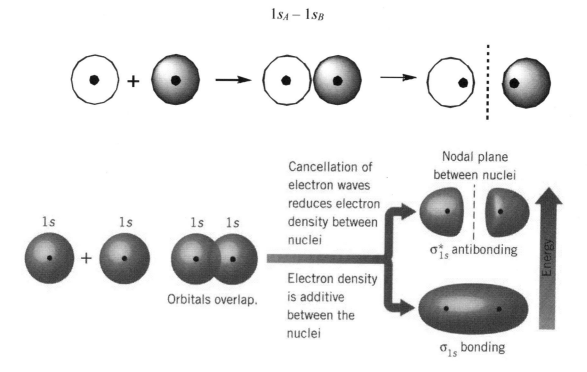

In the bonding MO, electron density builds up between nuclei; the electrons tend to stabilize the molecule. In the antibonding MO, cancellation of electron waves reduces electron density between nuclei. The electrons in antibonding MOs tend to destabilize the molecule.

MO energy diagrams can be created to represent the interactions between the atomic orbitals. An MO energy diagram displays the orbitals arranged vertically, from highest to lowest energy. The atomic orbitals for the atoms are listed on the left and right sides of the diagram, while the molecular orbitals are listed in a column down the center of the diagram. Below is the MO energy diagram for H_2.

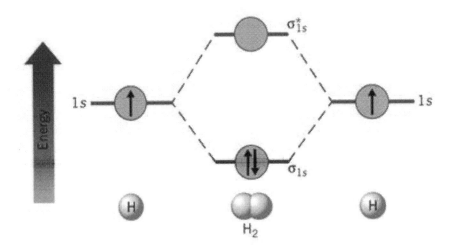

These are some rules for filling MO energy diagrams:

1. Electrons fill the lowest-energy orbitals that are available (Aufbau's principle).

2. No more than two electrons, with opposite spins, can occupy any orbital (Pauli exclusion principle).

3. Electrons with unpaired spins spread out as much as possible over orbitals of the same energy (Hund's rule).

Bond order indicates the number of electron pairs shared between two atoms (i.e., the number of bonds between two atoms). A bond order of one corresponds to a single bond. For example, the H_2 bond order and the C−H bond order are both one, while the N≡N bond order in diatomic nitrogen is three. The following formula can be used to calculate bond order.

$$\text{Bond order} = \frac{(\text{number of bonding } e^-) - (\text{number of antibonding } e^-)}{2 \text{ electrons/bond}}$$

Neither the valence bonding (VB) nor molecular orbital (MO) theory is entirely correct. Neither explains all aspects of bonding, and each has its strengths and weaknesses. VB theory is based on simple Lewis structures (explained later in this chapter) and related geometric figures. Yet, MO theory correctly predicts unpaired electrons in O_2, while Lewis structures do not. MO theory is difficult because even simple molecules have complex energy level diagrams, and molecules with three or more atoms require extensive calculations. VB theory, on the other hand, uses three dimensional structures based on electron domains, without extensive calculations. Simple hybrid orbitals are invoked where experimental evidence shows the need, and the integer bond orders are often correct.

Structural formulas for molecules involving H, C, N, O, F, S, P, Si, Cl

Lewis structures, which are explained in the next section, are frequently used to visually represent atoms and molecules. In general, Lewis structures for elements in the same column (group) of the periodic table are similar to one another. For example, sulfur can be substituted for oxygen in Lewis structures of oxygen. Here are the structural formulas for some important molecules.

- Hydrogen Lewis structures

    Hydrogen Proton: H^+

    Hydride ion: H^-

- Boron/Group 13 Lewis structures

Since group 13 elements only have three valence electrons, often they only have six total electrons in a molecule (exception to the octet rule).

Borane:

Borohydride ion:

- Carbon/Group 14 Lewis structures

Methane:

Carbocation:

Carbanion:

- Nitrogen/Group 15 Lewis structures

Some group 15 elements have more than eight electrons after bonding, which is an exception from the octet rule (e.g., PCl_5).

Amine / Ammonia:

Ammonium:

Imine:

- Oxygen/Group 16 Lewis structures

Some group 16 elements have more than eight electrons after bonding, which is an exception from the octet rule (e.g., SF_6).

Molecular oxygen:

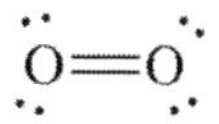

Water, alcohol, and ethers:

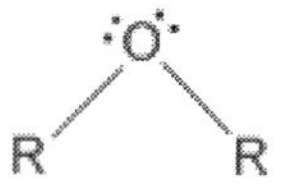

Ozone:

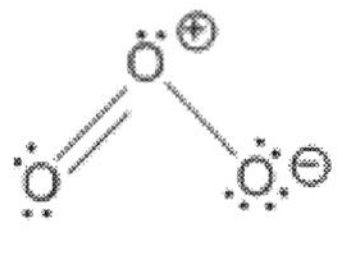

- Halogen/Group 17 Lewis structures

Hydrogen fluoride:

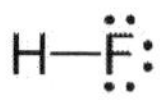

Chloromethane:

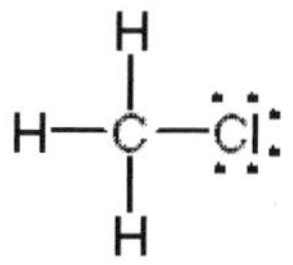

Bromide ion:

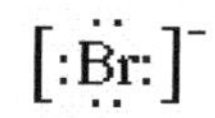

- R in the figures are either carbon or hydrogen.

Lewis Electron Dot Formulas

Lewis dot formulas, or *Lewis structures*, are notations used to describe bonds and electrons in a molecule. Each dot represents one electron and each line represents one bond (two electrons). A lone pair is represented by two dots.

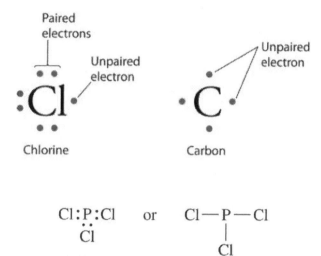

Lone pairs are usually omitted from the final structure:

Recall the octet rule: most atoms need a total of eight valence electrons to achieve stable electron configurations. All electrons in a bond are shared and can be used to satisfy the octet for both atoms on either side of the bond. This includes coordinate covalent bonds, where both electrons in a bond are contributed by only one atom, but the electron pair also counts towards the other atom's octet rule.

Exceptions for the octet rule include the boron column (they form three bonds and have a sextet), large elements (3rd row and below such as the dectet P in PO_4^{3-} and the duodectet S in SO_4^{2-}), and radicals (compounds with an odd number of total electrons that result in a single, unpaired electron). Those molecules have atoms with more or less than eight electrons.

Here are some general rules for Lewis structures:

- Due to the octet rule, most atoms can have up to eight electrons around them. When starting with atoms that have up to four valence electrons, separate them evenly around the molecule. If the atom has five or more valence electrons, divide them into four sections with a maximum of two electrons on each side. This is not a requirement, but drawing them in this fashion makes it easier to determine if an atom has achieved stability (eight total electrons).

- When sketching Lewis structures, use different symbols for electrons from different sources. Consider the Lewis structure of PCl_3 below; it is unclear which electrons around P came from itself or from Cl. Knowing that P has five valence electrons, one can quickly deduce that the remaining three must come from Cl.

  However, when the bonds get more complicated, such as SO_3, it can be confusing. Use clear designations to differentiate electrons from different sources. In the $BeCl_2$ example below, it is obvious that "x" represents electrons from Be and dots represent electrons from Cl.

- Place square brackets around complete Lewis structures and indicate the charge on the top of the right bracket.

Guide to drawing electron dot formulas:

1) Determine the arrangement of the atoms.

2) Determine the total number of valence electrons.

3) Attach each bonded atom to the central atom with a pair of electrons.

4) Place the remaining electrons using single or multiple bonds to complete the octet.

Using Valence Electrons to Draw Electron-Dot Formulas

Molecule or Polyatomic Ion	Total Valence Electrons	Form Single Bonds to Attach Atoms (electrons used)	Electrons Remaining	Completed Octets (or H:)
Cl_2	$2(7) = 14$	$Cl-Cl$ $(2\,e^-)$	$14 - 2 = 12$	$:\!\ddot{Cl}\!-\!\ddot{Cl}\!:$
HCl	$1 + 7 = 8$	$H-Cl$ $(2\,e^-)$	$8 - 2 = 6$	$H\!-\!\ddot{Cl}\!:$
H_2O	$2(1) + 6 = 8$	$H-O-H$ $(4\,e^-)$	$8 - 4 = 4$	$H\!-\!\ddot{O}\!-\!H$
PCl_3	$5 + 3(7) = 26$	$Cl-\overset{\displaystyle Cl}{\underset{\displaystyle \vert}{P}}-Cl$ $(6\,e^-)$	$26 - 6 = 20$	$:\!\ddot{Cl}\!-\!\overset{\displaystyle :\ddot{Cl}:}{\underset{\displaystyle \vert}{P}}\!-\!\ddot{Cl}\!:$
$ClO_3\text{-}$	$7 + 3(6) + 1 = 26$	$\left[O-\overset{\displaystyle O}{\underset{\displaystyle \vert}{Cl}}-O\right]^{-}$ $(6\,e^-)$	$26 - 6 = 20$	$\left[:\!\ddot{O}\!-\!\overset{\displaystyle :\ddot{O}:}{\underset{\displaystyle \vert}{Cl}}\!-\!\ddot{O}\!:\right]^{-}$
$NO_2\text{-}$	$5 + 2(6) + 1 = 18$	$\left[O-N-O\right]^{-}$ $(4\,e^-)$	$18 - 4 = 14$	$\left[:\!\ddot{O}\!-\!\ddot{N}\!=\!\ddot{O}\!:\right]^{-}$ $\updownarrow$ $\left[:\!\ddot{O}\!=\!\ddot{N}\!-\!\ddot{O}\!:\right]^{-}$

The following are more specific rules for the most common elements in Lewis structures:

- Carbon: four bonds total, zero lone pairs. (e.g., CH_4, CO_2)

- Oxygen:

    O: two bonds total, two lone pairs (e.g., H_2O, O_2)

    O^{1-}: one bond, three lone pairs, formal charge of -1

    O^{1+}: three bonds, one lone pair, formal charge of $+1$

- Nitrogen:

    N: three bonds total, one lone pair (e.g., amines or ammonia NH_3)

    N^+: four bonds, zero lone pairs, formal charge of $+1$ (e.g., ammonium NH_4^+)

- Halogens: one bond, three lone pairs (e.g., CCl_4)

- Hydrogen: one bond, zero lone pairs (exception to octet rule)

- Carbocation: C^+ has three bonds, no lone pairs

- Carbanion: C^- has three bonds, one lone pair

- Boron: three bonds, zero lone pairs (exception to octet rule) (e.g., BH_3)

Formal charge

Formal charge is the individual charge assigned to each atom in a Lewis structure on the basis of equal sharing of bonded electron pairs. Formal charges are used in drawing resonance structures (multiple Lewis structures that collectively describe a single molecule) of covalently-bonded molecules. This technique is used in describing, comparing and assessing resonance structures, similar to how oxidation numbers are used for balancing chemical equations in oxidation-reduction reactions.

Formal charge can be calculated using this formula:

$$\text{Formal Charge} = \text{Valence Electrons in Neutral Atom} - \left(\text{Unshared Valence Electrons} + \text{Half of the Shared Electrons} \right)$$

Every atom in a molecule has a formal charge. In a neutral molecule, the sum of atomic charges is zero. That does not mean the atoms are not charged, they simply cancel each other to create a neutral molecule. In charged molecules, the charge is not evenly distributed, and formal charges can help determine where the charge rests.

Here are some tips for determining formal charge:

Formal charge = [# of valence e^-] – [e^- in lone pairs + ½ the # of bonding e^-]

When using Lewis structures:

Formal charge = [# of valence e^-] – [dots around the atom + lines connected to atom]

The number of valence electrons is generally equal to the atom's group number on the periodic table (e.g., N has five valence electrons, O has six valence electrons and F has seven valence electrons).

The dots around the atom represent electrons that are held entirely by the atom.

The lines connected to the atom represent bonding electron pairs, in which the atom only gets one of the two electrons.

Formal charges (other than zero) must be labeled next to the atom with the formal charge.

Some examples of formal charges:

- Oxygen with only a single bond: –1

- Oxygen with no bonds but with an octet: –2

- Carbon with only three bonds: +1 if carbocation or –1 if carbanion

- Nitrogen with four bonds: +1

- Halogen with no bonds, but has an octet: –1

- Boron with 4 bonds: –1. (e.g., BH_4^-)

Carbon: Group 4A

$$=C=\qquad -C\equiv\qquad \diagdown C=\qquad -\overset{\textstyle |}{\underset{\textstyle |}{C}}-\qquad$$ 4 covalent bonds: Formal charge = 0

Nitrogen: Group 5A

$$=\overset{\oplus}{N}=\qquad -\overset{\oplus}{N}\equiv\qquad \diagdown\overset{\oplus}{N}=\qquad -\overset{\oplus}{\underset{\textstyle |}{N}}-\qquad$$ 4 covalent bonds: Formal charge = +1

$$-\overset{..}{N}=\qquad :N\equiv\qquad -\overset{..}{\underset{\textstyle |}{N}}-\qquad$$ 3 covalent bonds, 1 lone pair: Formal charge = 0

$$-\overset{..}{\underset{..}{N}}{}^{\ominus}\qquad {}^{\ominus}:N=\qquad$$ 2 covalent bonds, 2 lone pairs: Formal charge = −1

Oxygen: Group 6A

$$-\overset{\oplus}{\underset{..}{O}}=\qquad :\overset{\oplus}{O}\equiv\qquad -\overset{\overset{\oplus}{..}}{\underset{\textstyle |}{O}}-\qquad$$ 3 covalent bonds, 1 lone pair: Formal charge = +1

$$-\overset{..}{\underset{..}{O}}-\qquad \overset{..}{\underset{.}{O}}=\qquad$$ 2 covalent bonds, 2 lone pairs: Formal charge = 0

$$^{\ominus}:\overset{..}{\underset{..}{O}}-\qquad$$ 1 covalent bond, 3 lone pairs: Formal charge = −1

The number of valence shell electrons that an atom needs to gain or lose to achieve a valence octet is called "*valence*." In covalent compounds, the number of bonds which are characteristically formed by a given atom is equal to that atom's valence number.

Atom	H	C	N	O	F	Cl	Br	I
Valence	1	4	3	2	1	1	1	1

The valences in the chart above represent the most common form these elements assume in organic compounds. Many elements, such as chlorine, bromine and iodine, are known to exist in several valence states in different inorganic compounds. If the number of covalent bonds to an atom is greater than its normal valence, it carries a positive formal charge. If the number of covalent bonds to an atom is less than its normal valence, it carries a negative formal charge.

Here is a step-by-step approach to finding the formal charges of each atom in a molecule of nitric acid (HNO_3), using the structure displayed in the image below.

$$\begin{array}{c} O \\ \| \\ HO{-}N^+{\diagdown}O^- \end{array}$$

Formal charge of H

- Hydrogen shares two electrons with oxygen.
- Assign one electron to H and one to O.
- Hydrogen has one valence electron, and $1 - 1 = 0$.
- Therefore, the formal charge of H in nitric acid is zero.

Formal charge of the O that is bonded to N and H

- Oxygen has four electrons in covalent bonds (two with N, two with H).
- Assign two of these four electrons to O.
- Oxygen has two unshared pairs. Assign all four of these electrons to O.
- Therefore, the total number of electrons assigned to O is $2 + 4 = 6$.
- Oxygen has six valence electrons, and $6 - 6 = 0$.
- Therefore, the formal charge of the O bonded to H and N in nitric acid is zero.

Formal charge of the double-bonded O

- Oxygen has four electrons in covalent bonds with N.
- Assign two of these four electrons to O.
- Oxygen has two unshared pairs. Assign all four of these electrons to O.
- Therefore, the total number of electrons assigned to O is $2 + 4 = 6$.
- Oxygen has six valence electrons, and $6 - 6 = 0$.
- Therefore, the formal charge of the double-bonded O in nitric acid is 0.

Formal charge of the single-bonded O

- O has two electrons in a covalent bond.
- Assign one of those electrons to O.
- O has three unshared pairs. Assign all six of these electrons to O.
- Therefore, the total number of electrons assigned to O is $1 + 6 = 7$.

- Oxygen has six valence electrons, and $6 - 7 = -1$.
- Therefore, the normal charge of the single-bonded O in nitric acid is -1.

Formal charge of N

- N has eight electrons in covalent bonds.
- Assign four of those electrons to N.
- Nitrogen has five valence electrons, and $5 - 4 = 1$.
- Therefore, the formal charge of the N in nitric acid is $+1$.

If atoms in a molecule have a formal charge, it does not necessarily mean that the whole molecule has a charge.

For example, in the structure of ozone, the central oxygen atom has three bonds and is positively-charged. The right-hand oxygen has a single bond and is negatively-charged. The overall charge of the ozone molecule is therefore zero.

Similarly, nitromethane has a positively-charged nitrogen and a negatively-charged oxygen, the total molecular charge is again, zero. Finally, the azide anion has two negatively-charged nitrogens and one positively-charged nitrogen, and the total charge is minus one.

Resonance structures

When there is more than one possible structure for a molecule, it can exist in various forms as *resonance structures*. The averaging of electron distribution over two or more hypothetical contributing structures to produce a hybrid electronic structure is *resonance*.

Resonance structures can be used to describe molecules that may contain fractional bonds and charges. The forms all must have the same number of paired and unpaired electrons. No atoms change their positions within the common structural framework, as this would break an existing chemical bond. Only electrons (not atoms, as for isomers) are moved.

One can visualize the molecule quickly "shifting" between each of its possible resonance structures, and intermittently existing in several configurations at any given time. However, the molecule spends more time in the most stable resonance form. More accurately, the structure of the molecule is a "combination" (or a weighted average) of its resonance structures, borrowing from the most stable resonance structures. In a molecule with both a single-and a double-bond resonance structure, the bond length is between a single- and a double-bond length.

$$O=S-O \qquad O-S-O \qquad O-S=O$$
$$\quad\; | \qquad\qquad\quad || \qquad\qquad\quad |$$
$$\quad\; O \qquad\qquad\quad O \qquad\qquad\quad O$$

Resonance structure for SO_3 (single-bonded O have a (−) charge)

Resonance structure for CO_3^{2-}

The double-headed arrow seen in the image above acts as a symbol for resonance. The principles of resonance are very useful in rationalizing the chemical behavior of many compounds. The electron delocalization described by resonance significantly enhances the stability of the molecules.

To determine the most stable resonance structure of a molecule, the properties of a stable molecule must be known. In stable molecules, the octet group is satisfied in each atom (aside from hydrogen and the other exceptions, like the boron group). Neutral molecules are more likely to be stable, and it is best if the formal charges on atoms are spread accordingly (i.e., positive charge on positive atom and likewise for negative).

Resonance structure for formaldehyde

In the example above, the preferred charge distribution has the positive charge on the less electronegative atom (carbon) and the negative charge on the more electronegative atom (oxygen). Therefore, the middle formula represents a more reasonable and stable structure than the one on the right. This indicates that the molecule most likely spends the majority of time in this possible resonance structure over the others. If the double bond is broken heterolytically (both electrons going to one of the bonding atoms), formal charge pairs result, as shown in the other two structures. Since the middle, charge-separated contributor has an electron deficient carbon atom, this explains the tendency of electron donors (nucleophiles) to bond at this site.

The application of resonance to this example requires a weighted average of these structures. Consequently, if one structure has a much greater stability than the others, the hybrid closely resembles it both electronically and energetically. If two or more forms have identical low energy structures, the resonance hybrid is especially stable. Examples of identical low energy structures include sulfur dioxide and nitric acid.

There are three main aspects to consider when drawing resonance structures:

1. The number of covalent bonds in a structure - the greater the bonding, the more important and stable the contributing structure.

2. Formal charge separation - charge separation decreases the stability and importance of the contributing structure.

3. Electronegativity of charge bearing atoms and charge density - high charge density is destabilizing; positive charge is best accommodated on atoms of low electronegativity, and negative charge on highly electronegative atoms.

Lewis acids and bases

Molecules can be categorized based on the number of their free electron pairs: Lewis acids accept electron pairs, while Lewis bases donate electron pairs.

Acids have vacant orbitals and do not have lone pairs on the central atom (e.g., BF_3), while Lewis bases do have lone pair electrons (e.g., NH_3). Further discussions about acids and bases can be found in the chapter on acids and bases.

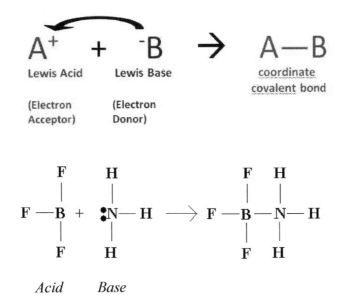

Partial Ionic Character

Covalent bonds can be categorized into polar covalent bonds and nonpolar covalent bonds. *Nonpolar covalent bonds*, occur between atoms of the same element (or very similar electronegativity).

Polar covalent bonds occur between atoms of different elements with differences in electrons. These bonds have *partial ionic character*, due to the way that the electrons are distributed. One end of the bond is more negative while the other end is more positive.

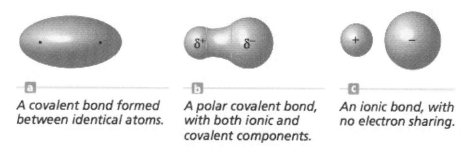

a	b	c
A covalent bond formed between identical atoms.	A polar covalent bond, with both ionic and covalent components.	An ionic bond, with no electron sharing.

The three possible types of bonds

Role of electronegativity in determining charge distribution

Electronegativity (*EN*) is the ability of an element to attract or hold onto electrons. Due to their differing nuclear charges, and as a result of shielding by inner electron shells, different atoms of the periodic table have different electronegativities. The polarity of a molecule is determined by calculating the difference of EN values of its atoms. Linus Pauling established a quantitative scale of electronegativity values, in which a larger number (e.g., F = 3.98) signifies a greater affinity for electrons.

H	Electronegativity Values					
2.20	for Some Elements					
Li	**Be**	**B**	**C**	**N**	**O**	**F**
0.98	1.57	2.04	2.55	3.04	3.44	3.98
Na	**Mg**	**Al**	**Si**	**P**	**S**	**Cl**
0.90	1.31	1.61	1.90	2.19	2.58	3.16
K	**Ca**	**Ga**	**Ge**	**As**	**Se**	**Br**
0.82	1.00	1.81	2.01	2.18	2.55	2.96

In the periodic table, EN values increase from left to right and from bottom to top.

Notice that higher electronegativity values are located towards the nonmetal side of the periodic table. Fluorine has the greatest electronegativity of all the elements, but the heavier alkali metals such as potassium, rubidium and cesium have lower electronegativity values. It should be noted that carbon (2.55) is roughly mid-range in regards to electronegativity, and is slightly more electronegative than hydrogen (2.20).

Of all the subatomic particles (protons, neutrons, electrons) of an atom, only the electron has the freedom to move within the atom. When two atoms bond, most of their electrons congregate between the two nuclei. However, the distribution depends on the electronegativity of the atoms. Shared electrons in a bond are attracted to the more electronegative atom, resulting in a shift of electron density toward the more electronegative atom.

Nonpolar covalent bonds are formed between identical atoms forming *homonuclear diatomic molecules*. For example, in diatomic hydrogen (H_2), both atoms are identical, hence they have identical EN values. The electrons therefore are evenly distributed between the two hydrogens.

Hydrogen fluoride (HF) has atoms of two different EN values – fluorine (3.98) is much more electronegative than hydrogen (2.20). Therefore, the electrons are more attracted to the fluorine nucleus, and are thus located closer to F than H.

H : F   H   F

If one atom in a molecule is more electronegative than the other, this causes a higher concentration of electrons to be located on one side of the bond, and the molecule is polar. *Polarity* of a molecule is proportional to the difference in electronegativity values between atoms.

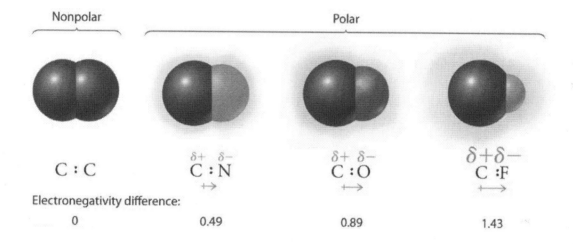

The lowercase Greek letter delta δ is used to denote partial charges on a polar molecule. A plus or minus sign indicates the partial positive or negative charges.

$$\delta^+ \; H - Cl \; \delta^-$$

Arrows are also used to indicate partial charges. In the diagram below the arrow is pointing in the direction of electron movement, originating in the positively charged atom and pointing toward the negatively-charged atom.

The partial positively- and negatively- charged ends are called dipoles. If the difference in electronegativity is great enough in a particular direction, the molecule acquires a net dipole moment.

Dipole moment

Dipole moment is the measure of polarity in a molecule. The dipole moment is calculated using the difference in electronegativity (EN) values of both atoms. The geometric shape of a molecule also affects its overall dipole moment. A molecule might have polar bonds, but if those bonds are arranged in such a way that cancels out the dipole moments, the molecule has zero net dipole moment and is nonpolar.

A molecule is only nonpolar if:

1) It is symmetrical.

2) It has identical atoms surrounding the central atom.

3) Any non-bonding electron pairs are evenly distributed and cancel each other (as seen in the illustration below).

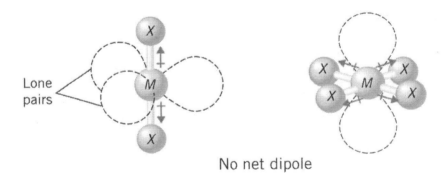

No net dipole

In the right-hand linear configuration of the figure below (bond angle 180°), the bond dipoles cancel each other, and the molecular dipole is zero. For other bond angles (90 to 120°), the molecular dipole varies in size. It is largest for the 90° configuration.

For example, boron trichloride (BCl_3) has three B−Cl bonds. B−Cl is a polar bond, but because the molecule is symmetrical and charges are evenly-distributed in a single plane, the charges cancel each other out. In addition, BCl_3 does not have any non-bonding electron pairs. As a result, BCl_3 has zero dipole moment.

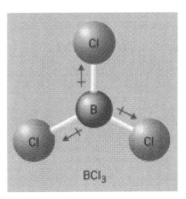

Similarly, the configurations of methane (CH_4) and carbon dioxide (CO_2) may be deduced from their zero molecular dipole moments. Since the bond dipoles have canceled, the configurations of these molecules must be tetrahedral and linear, respectively.

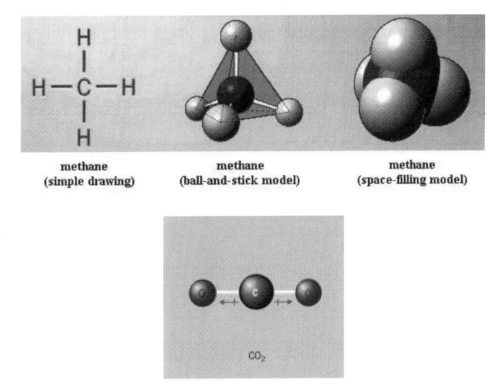

methane
(simple drawing)

methane
(ball-and-stick model)

methane
(space-filling model)

The methane molecule provides insight to other arguments that have been used to confirm its tetrahedral configuration. Substitution of one hydrogen by a chlorine atom gives a CH₃Cl compound.

Since the tetrahedral, square-planar and square-pyramidal configurations have structurally equivalent hydrogen atoms, they each give a single substitution product. However, in the trigonal-pyramidal configuration, one atom at the apex (chlorine) is structurally different from the other three hydrogens because of the pyramid base.

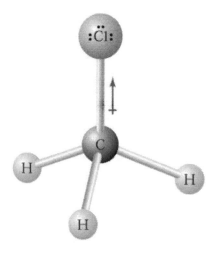

Methyl chloride (chloromethane)

Substitution in this example should give two different CH_3Cl compounds if all the hydrogens react. In the case of di-substitution, the tetrahedral configuration of methane leads to a single CH_2Cl_2 product, but the other configurations give two different CH_2Cl_2 compounds. These substitution possibilities are shown in the image below.

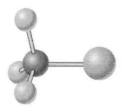

(a) Methyl Chloride
CH_3Cl, refrigerant, manufacture of synthetic rubber and silcones

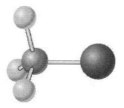

(b) Methyl Bromide
CH_3Br, in insecticides and weed killers

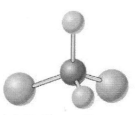

(c) Dichloromethane
(methylene chloride)
CH_2Cl_2, in paint and varnish strippers, industrial solvent

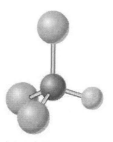

(d) Trichloromethane
(chloroform)
$CHCl_3$, industrial solvent

Most covalent compounds show some degree of local charge separation, resulting from differences in electronegativity between the atoms. If a molecule has polar bonds arranged so that the bonds are polar in a specific direction, then the molecule has a net dipole in that same direction. Some examples of polar molecules are PCl_3 and HCN. PCl_3 has three chlorine atoms positioned on one side of the molecule. Since chlorine is very electronegative, the electrons are attracted towards the chlorine side, creating a dipole moment.

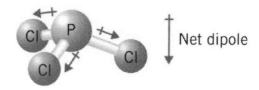

HCN is a symmetrical molecule in that it has one atom on each side of the middle carbon. However, nitrogen has stronger electronegative properties than hydrogen, which means electrons are concentrated on the nitrogen side of the molecule.

Some physical properties of matter are affected by molecular polarity, including melting and boiling points. Polar molecules tend to have stronger intermolecular forces, which results in higher boiling and melting points (displayed in the table below).

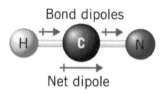

Boiling Points of Some Polar and Nonpolar Substances

Substance	Boiling Point (° C)
Polar	
Hydrogen fluoride, HF	20
Water, H_2O	100
Ammonia, NH_3	−33
Nonpolar	
Hydrogen, H_2	−253
Oxygen, O_2	−183
Nitrogen, N_2	−196
Boron trifluoride, BF_3	−100
Carbon dioxide, CO_2	−79

One important example of polarity is the water (H_2O) molecule. The center oxygen has two pairs of non-bonding electrons, two hydrogens (one on each side) and is symmetrical. VSEPR theory predicts that water will have a bent shape and the electron pairs will be grouped together, as seen in the images below.

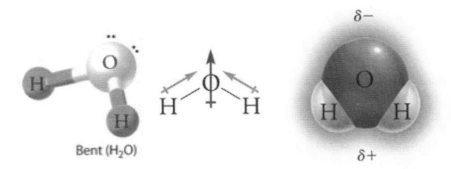

Bent (H₂O)

In the example of water, the electron pairs are not evenly distributed; they are shifted downwards and concentrated on one side of the oxygen atom. That side has a partial negative charge, while the opposing side has a partial positive charge. Therefore, the water molecule has a net dipole moment and is a polar molecule. Polar water molecules can also exert unique forces on each other known as hydrogen bonds.

hybridization

H
|
C = I
     |
     H

4 R + 6

Practice Questions

1. Unhybridized *p* orbitals participate in π bonds as double and triple bonds. How many distinct and degenerate *p* orbitals exist in the second electron shell, where n = 2?

   A. 3   **B.** 2   **C.** 1   **D.** 0

2. Which type of attractive forces occurs in all molecules regardless of the atoms they possess?

   A. Dipole–ion interactions
   B. London dispersion forces

   C. Dipole–dipole attractions
   D. Hydrogen bonding

3. Ignoring other factors, it is possible to make a rough approximation of the energy released when an ionic bond forms, simply by considering how much the electrostatic potential energy changes while forming the bond (i.e., bringing the two ions together from infinity). Using this approximation, what is the amount of energy released when 1 mole of NaCl is formed?

   For two ions with charges q_1 and q_2 that are separated by distance *r*, the electrostatic potential energy is given by $U_e = k \cdot q_1 q_2 / r$, where electrostatic constant $k = 9 \times 10^9$ J·m / C^2. (The charge on Na$^+$ = +e, charge on Cl$^-$ = –e, charge of electron $e = 1.602 \times 10^{-19}$ C, and separation distance $r = 282$ pm)

   A. –493 kJ/mol
   B. –288 kJ/mol

   C. +91.2 kJ/mol
   D. +421 kJ/mol

4. During strenuous exercise, why does perspiration on a person's skin forms droplets?

   A. Ability of H_2O to dissipate heat
   B. High specific heat of H_2O

   C. Adhesive properties of H_2O
   D. Cohesive properties of H_2O

5. Based on the Lewis structure, how many polar and nonpolar bonds are present in H_2CO?

   A. 1 polar bond and 2 nonpolar bonds
   B. 2 polar bonds and 1 nonpolar bond

   C. 3 polar bonds and 0 nonpolar bonds
   D. 0 polar bonds and 3 nonpolar bonds

6. Which of the following occur(s) naturally as nonpolar diatomic molecules?

   I. sulfur   II. chlorine   III. argon

   A. I only
   B. II only

   C. I and III only
   D. I and II only

7. In the nitrogen monoxide molecule, the dipole moment is 0.16 D and the bond length is 115 pm. What is the sign and magnitude of the charge on the oxygen atom? (Use the conversion factor of 1 D $= 3.34 \times 10^{-30}$ C·m and the charge of 1 electron $= 1.602 \times 10^{-19}$ C)

    A. $-0.098\ e$ **B.** $-0.71\ e$ **C.** $-1.3\ e$ **D.** $-0.029\ e$

8. From the electronegativity below, which covalent single bond is the most polar?

Element:	H	C	N	O
Electronegativity	2.1	2.5	3.0	3.5

    A. O–C   **B.** O–N   **C.** N–C   **D.** C–H

9. Under what conditions is graphite converted to diamond?

    A. low temperature, high pressure   **C.** high temperature, high pressure
    B. high temperature, low pressure   **D.** low temperature, low pressure

10. An ion with an atomic number of 34 and 36 electrons has what charge?

    A. +2   **B.** −36   **C.** +34   **D.** −2

11. Which of the following pairings of ions is NOT consistent with the formula?

    A. Co_2S_3 (Co^{3+} and S^{2-})   **C.** Na_3P (Na^+ and P^{3-})
    B. K_2O (K^+ and O^-)   **D.** BaF_2 (Ba^{2+} and F^-)

12. The ability of an atom in a molecule to attract electrons to itself is:

    A. ionization energy   **C.** electronegativity
    B. paramagnetism   **D.** electron affinity

13. All of the following are examples of polar molecules, EXCEPT:

    A. H_2O **B.** CCl_4 **C.** CH_2Cl_2 **D.** HF

14. When NaCl dissolves in water, what is the force of attraction between Na^+ and H_2O?

    A. ion–dipole   **C.** ion–ion
    B. hydrogen bonding   **D.** dipole–dipole

15. Which element likely forms a cation with a +2 charge?

    A. Na   **B.** S   **C.** Si   **D.** Mg

Solutions

1. A is correct. Three degenerate *p* orbitals exist for any atom with an electron configuration in the second shell or higher. The first shell only has access to *s* orbitals.

The *d* orbitals become available from $n = 3$ (third shell).

2. B is correct. London dispersion forces result from the momentary flux of valence electrons and are present in all compounds; they are the attractive forces that hold molecules together.

They are the weakest of all the intermolecular forces, and their strength increases with increasing size (i.e., surface area contact) and polarity of the molecules involved.

3. A is correct. Calculate potential energy for each molecule of NaCl:

$$U_e = k\, q_1 q_2 \,/\, r$$

$$U_e = [(9 \times 10^9 \text{ J·m·C}^{-2}) \cdot (1.602 \times 10^{-19} \text{ C}) \cdot (-1.602 \times 10^{-19} \text{ C})] \,/\, (282 \times 10^{-12} \text{ m})]$$

$$U_e = -8.19 \times 10^{-19} \text{ J per molecule of NaCl}$$

Calculate the energy released for one mole of NaCl:

$$[(-8.19 \times 10^{-19} \text{ J}) \times (6.02 \times 10^{23} \text{ mol}^{-1})] = -493,077 \text{ J} \approx -493 \text{ kJ/mol}$$

This approximation disregards a few important effects. For example, the orientation of the crystal lattice will affect the energy, and there are quantum mechanical effects that are not considered in this model.

4. D is correct. Water molecules stick to each other (i.e., cohesion) due to the collective action of hydrogen bonds between individual water molecules. These hydrogen bonds are constantly breaking and reforming, a large portion of the molecules are held together by these bonds.

Water also sticks to surfaces (i.e., adhesion) because of water's polarity. On an extremely smooth surface (e.g., glass) the water may form a thin film because the molecular forces between glass and water molecules (adhesive forces) are stronger than the cohesive forces between the water molecules.

5. C is correct. The molecule H_2CO (formaldehyde) is shown below and has one C=O bond and two C–H bonds. Because the bonds are between different atoms, there is a dipole moment and this results in three polar bonds.

6. B is correct.

The octet rule states that atoms of main-group elements tend to combine in a way that each atom has eight electrons in its valence shell.

7. D is correct.

Formula to calculate dipole moment:

$$\mu = qr$$

where μ is dipole moment (coulomb-meter or C·m), q is charge (coulomb or C), and r is radius (meter or m)

Convert the unit of dipole moment from Debye to C·m;

$$0.16 \times 3.34 \times 10^{-30} = 5.34 \times 10^{-31} \text{ C·m}$$

Convert the unit of radius to meter:

$$115 \text{ pm} \times 1 \times 10^{-12} \text{ m/pm} = 115 \times 10^{-12} \text{ m}$$

Rearrange the dipole moment equation to solve for q:

$$q = \mu / r$$

$$q = (5.34 \times 10^{-31} \text{ C·m}) / (115 \times 10^{-12} \text{ m})$$

$$q = 4.65 \times 10^{-21} \text{ C}$$

Express the charge in terms of electron charge (e).

$$(4.65 \times 10^{-21} \text{ C}) / (1.602 \times 10^{-19} \text{ C/e}) = 0.029 \text{ e}$$

In this NO molecule, oxygen is the more electronegative atom.

Therefore, the charge experienced by the oxygen atom is negative: –0.029e.

8. A is correct.

The greater the difference in electronegativity between two atoms in a compound, the more polar of a bond these atoms form, whereby the atom with the higher electronegativity is the partial (delta) negative end of the dipole.

9. C is correct.

The substantial difference between the two forms of carbon (i.e., graphite and diamonds) is mainly due to their crystal structure, which is hexagonal for graphite and cubic for diamond.

The conditions to convert graphite into diamond are high pressure and high temperature. That is why creating synthetic diamonds is time-consuming, energy-intensive and expensive, since carbon is forced to change its bonding structure

10. D is correct.

The valence shell is the outermost shell (i.e., highest principal quantum number, *n*) of an atom.

Valence electrons are those electrons of the outermost electron shell that can participate in a chemical bond.

11. B is correct.

If the charge of O is −1, the proper formula of its compound with K (+1) should be KO.

12. C is correct.

Electronegativity is a chemical property that describes an atom's tendency to attract electrons to itself.

The most common use of electronegativity pertains to polarity along the *sigma* (single) bond.

The most electronegative atom is F, while the least electronegative atom is Fr. The trend for increasing electronegativity within the periodic table is up and toward the right (i.e., fluorine).

13. B is correct.

The greater the difference in electronegativity between two atoms in a compound, the more polar of a bond these atoms form whereby the atom with the higher electronegativity is the partial (delta) negative end of the dipole.

Although each C−Cl bond is very polar, the dipole moments of each of the four bonds in CCl_4 (carbon tetrachloride) cancel because the molecule is a symmetric tetrahedron.

14. A is correct.

15. D is correct.

Group IA elements (e.g., Li, Na and K) have a tendency to lose 1 electron to achieve a complete octet to be cations with a +1 charge.

Group IIA elements (e.g., Mg and Ca) have a tendency to lose 2 electrons to achieve a complete octet to be cations with a +2 charge.

Group VIIA elements (halogens such as F, CL, Br and I) have a tendency to gain 1 electron to achieve a complete octet to be anions with a −1 charge.

Chapter 3

Properties of Matter

- **Gas Phase**
- **Intermolecular Forces**
- **Phase Equilibria**

Gas Phase

A *gas* is one of the fundamental states of matter, distinguished by the vast separation of the individual gas particles. Gases, unlike solids and liquids, have an indefinite shape and volume because they expand to fill their containers. As a result, gases are subject to changes in pressure, volume and temperature. Some common elements and compounds exist in the gaseous state under normal conditions of pressure and temperature, such as oxygen (O_2), nitrogen (N_2) and carbon dioxide (CO_2). A vapor is the gaseous form of a substance that normally exists as a liquid or solid at ordinary pressures and temperatures (e.g., water vapor).

To describe the gaseous state, four variables are needed:

1. Quantity of gas, *n* (in moles)

2. Temperature of the gas, *T* (in Kelvin)

3. Volume of gas, V (in liters)

4. Pressure of gas, *P* (in kPa)

Absolute temperature, Kelvin scale

Temperature is an objective measure of the kinetic energy of particles, and the volume of a gas (i.e., the space that it occupies) is proportional to its temperature. In the 19th century, experiments revealed that gases expand as temperature rises and compress when temperature drops, which led to the calculation of expansion coefficient per degree Celsius. This discovery posed an interesting question: what happens if the temperature is low enough to reach a point where the calculated volume of gas is zero? This *absolute zero* temperature was calculated to be –273.15° C. In actuality, gases do not reach zero volume because all gases liquefy or solidify before reaching this projected temperature. Additionally, a gas cannot have a volume of zero because the gas molecules themselves occupy a certain amount of space.

In 1848, British physicist Lord Kelvin (1824 – 1907) proposed a new temperature scale based on this absolute zero value. It starts with absolute zero as 0 K and the increments in this scale are identical to Celsius scale. To convert from Kelvin to Celsius, add 273.15; and for the opposite conversion, subtract 273.15. Temperature in Kelvin should be converted to Celsius before converting it into Fahrenheit. Also, by convention, Kelvin temperatures are not written with a degree symbol (273 K vs. 273 °C or 273 °F).

Some common temperatures expressed in K, °C and °F:

	K	°C	°F
Absolute zero	0	–273	–460
Freezing point of water / melting point of ice	273	0	32
Room temperature	298	25	77
Body temperature	310	37	99
Boiling point of water / condensation of steam	373	100	212

Pressure, simple mercury barometer

Pressure is the average force applied to or experienced by a given area. Gas molecules are always in motion, so if gas is put into a container, the gas molecules constantly move around and collide with the walls of the container. Since the force is applied over a certain area, this force is the gas pressure within a container.

Newton's Second Law, $F = ma$, can be used to determine the units of pressure. The SI units of mass (m) and acceleration (a) are the kilogram (kg) and the meter per second squared (m/s^2), respectively. The unit of force, derived from the equation $F = ma$, is kg·m/s^2. This derived unit is the newton (N). Pressure is force exerted over a specific area. The SI unit of length is meter (m), so the SI unit for area is m^2. Therefore, the unit for pressure is N/m^2, also known as the Pascal (Pa).

A *barometer* is a device that is used to measure Earth's atmospheric pressure. Dry air creates more pressure than wet air, so dry air is heavier than the same amount of wet air. Consequently, high barometer readings indicate dry air and fair weather. Low readings indicate an increased chance of rain or showers.

A mercury barometer is made by inverting a column that is completely filled with mercury and placing it in a mercury dish, without allowing any air to enter the tube. Some of the mercury flows out when the tube is inverted, leaving a space in the tube above the mercury. This space is nearly a vacuum, therefore there is no pressure pushing down on the column. The pressure exerted by the mercury column balances the pressure of the atmosphere. At sea level, the height of the mercury column is about 760 mm above the surface of the mercury in the dish.

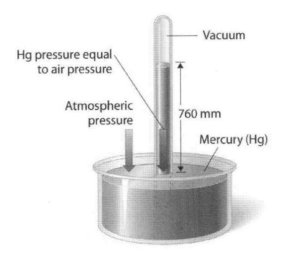

Any liquid may be used to measure atmospheric pressure; the height of the column depends on the density of the liquid. A comparison of mercury (density = 13.6 g/cm^3) and water (density = 1 g/cm^3) indicates that if a barometer were filled with water, the column would be almost 34 feet high.

Pressure exerted by a mercury barometer is recorded in units of millimeters of mercury (mmHg), a unit sometimes called the torr in honor of the Italian physicist Evangelista Torricelli (1608 – 1647), who invented the mercury barometer in 1643.

The standard atmosphere (atm) is another unit of pressure, and its conversion factors are listed below:

1 atm = 101,325 Pa

1 atm = 760 mm Hg = 760 torr = 76 cm Hg

1 atm = 14.7 lb/in^2 (psi, or pound per square inch)

The bar is a metric unit or pressure equal to 100,000 Pa. It is about equal to atmospheric pressure (101,325 Pa).

Pressure of gases is also measured by an instrument called a *manometer*, which is simply a bent piece of tubing. Its principle of operation is similar to that of a barometer. There are two major types. The first is the closed-tube manometer, which is used to measure pressures below atmospheric pressures, usually the pressure of gas in a container. Since the end is sealed, it contains a vacuum. The pressure is simply the difference in the heights of the mercury levels in the two arms.

The other type is the open-tube manometer, which is used to measure gas pressures that are near atmospheric pressures. The difference in the heights of the mercury levels in the two arms of the manometer relates the gas pressure to the atmospheric pressure.

In the below image, the closed tube manometer is on the right and the open tube manometer is on the left.

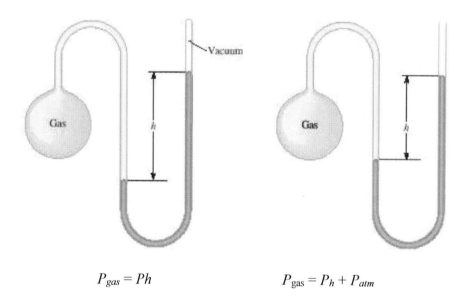

$$P_{gas} = Ph \qquad\qquad P_{gas} = P_h + P_{atm}$$

Two types of manometers used to measure gas pressures.

Left: Gas pressure is less than atmospheric pressure.

Right: gas pressure is greater than atmospheric pressure.

Molar volume at 0 °C and 1 atm = 22.4 L/mol

In 1811, Italian scientist Amedeo Avogadro suggested that "equal volumes of gases measured at the same conditions of temperature and pressure contain the same number of molecules."

In chemistry, *molar volume* is usually measured at the "standard temperature and pressure" or STP condition, which is 0 °C (273 K) and 101.3 kPa (760 mmHg). At these conditions, a mole of gas occupies 22.414 L of space.

In the 1980s, the International Union of Pure and Applied Chemistry (IUPAC), the organization that governs chemistry standards, changed their definition of STP. It was only a minor change on the pressure: it went from 101,325 Pa (1 atm) to 100,000 Pa (1 bar). In this new standard, the volume of 1 mol of gas in STP condition is 22.7 L. However, in general chemistry problems, the volume of one mole of gas is 22.4, unless indicated otherwise.

Kinetic Molecular Theory of Gases

The *kinetic molecular theory* (*KMT*) uses atomic theory to describe the behavior of gases. This theory was developed throughout a period of over 100 years, eventually culminating in a paper written by German physicist Rudolf Clausius (1822 – 1888) published in 1857. KMT is used to explain the macroscopic properties of a gas, such as pressure and temperature, in terms of its microscopic components, such as molecules or atoms.

The kinetic theory of gases originated in the ancient idea that matter consists of tiny invisible atoms in rapid motion. Between the 17th century and the 19th century, the idea was revived and developed to explain the properties of gases, among other phenomena. In order to apply the kinetic theory to the observed behavior of gases, five important assumptions need to be made.

1. Gas molecules move in random molecular motion. They continue in a straight line until they collide with something.

2. The gas molecule is considered to be a "point mass," which is a particle so small that its mass is nearly zero. Therefore, an ideal gas particle has negligible volume.

3. No molecular forces are participating.

4. Collisions between gas molecules are "perfectly elastic." Therefore, the total kinetic energy (*KE*) of the gas molecules remains constant before and after the collision, since intermolecular attractive and repulsive forces are nonexistent.

5. The average kinetic energy (*KE*) for all gas particles is proportional only to its absolute temperature, regardless of the chemical identity or atomic mass. At 0 K (absolute zero), the molecules are not moving and have no volume.

The final assumption can be written in equation form as follows:

$$KE = \frac{1}{2}\, mv^2 = (3/2)\, k_B T$$

where *KE* is kinetic energy, *m* is mass, *v* is velocity, *T* is temperature (in Kelvin) and k_B is *Boltzmann's constant* ($k_B = 1.38 \times 10^{-23}$ J/K), which relates the macroscopic and microscopic behavior of gases to their individual gas particles.

This equation is significant in that it states that the average kinetic energy of a gas particle is proportional to the absolute temperature of the gas. As the temperature of the gas particles increases, their total speed and overall energy also increase. Since gas atoms are infinitesimally small in size, it is close to impossible to accurately measure the speed of any one given particle. As a result, the speed of gas particles is defined in terms of the root-mean-square speed (u_{rms}). The root-mean-square speed is given by the following equation:

$$u_{rms} = \sqrt{\frac{3RT}{MM}}$$

where *R* is the ideal gas constant, *T* is the absolute temperature (in Kelvin) and *MM* is the molar mass of the gas sample.

This equation can also be written in terms of the Boltzmann constant, k_B:

$$u_{rms} = \sqrt{\frac{3kT}{m}}$$

where *k* is the Boltzmann constant, *T* is the absolute temperature (in Kelvin) and *m* is the mass of one molecule of gas.

At a given temperature, a plot of the distribution of speeds of each gas particle shows a slightly asymmetric curve. This speed-distribution curve is known as the *Maxwell-Boltzmann distribution curve*. The Boltzmann distribution plot below shows that the peak of the curve corresponds to the most probable speed.

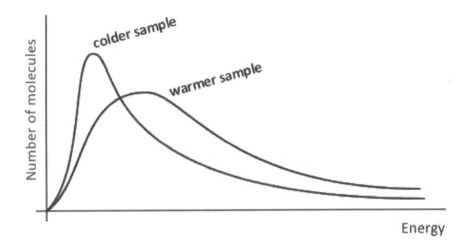

Maxwell-Boltzmann Distribution Curves of Molecular Speeds at Two Different Temperatures

If the temperature (in Kelvin) remains constant, the total kinetic energy remains unchanged. However, the energy can be distributed in many ways, and the gas particles can be traveling at many different speeds at any given point in time. This distribution changes continually as the gas atoms collide with each other and with the container walls. The curve flattens and shifts to the right at higher temperatures, indicating that a greater number of gas molecules are moving at higher speeds, and therefore possess greater kinetic energy.

Diffusion, the process whereby a substance (solute or particle) spreads from a region of high concentration to one of lower concentration, can be explained by kinetic theory.

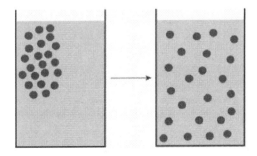

Diffusion of solutes in solvent

According to the kinetic theory, heavier gases diffuse more slowly than lighter gases because of the difference in the speed at which they travel. Scottish chemist Thomas Graham developed *Graham's law*, which states that at constant temperature and pressure conditions, the rates at which two gases diffuse are inversely proportional to the square root of their molar masses. This can be written in equation form as follows:

$$\frac{r_1}{r_2} = \sqrt{\frac{MM_2}{MM_1}}$$

where r_1 and r_2 are the diffusion rates of gas 1 and gas 2, respectively, and MM_1 and MM_2 are the molar masses of the gases, respectively.

Effusion is the flow of gas particles under pressure from one compartment to another through a small opening, as shown in the figure below:

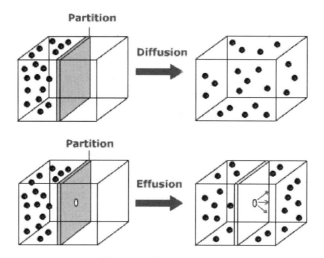

Effusion of gas particles

Graham's law also applies to the effusion of gas particles, and the equation for effusion is the same as the equation for diffusion.

Ideal gas - Definition

The kinetic theory described in the previous section is based on the idea of a theoretical ideal gas. An *ideal gas* is one that follows all five assumptions of KMT (gas molecules move in random motion, they are point masses with no volume, there are no intermolecular forces, all collisions are elastic and kinetic energy of molecules is proportional to temperature).

In comparison to an ideal gas, real gas behavior is very complex. However, by conceptualizing ideal gas behavior, real gas behavior becomes easier to understand.

In the 17th and 18th centuries, scientists began to realize that there are several relationships between properties of gases. Today, these are called the gas laws. Boyle's Law, Charles' Law, and Avogadro's Law all deal with the properties of pressure, volume and temperature. These laws, which were all developed empirically, are special cases of the ideal gas equation, which is discussed later in this section.

Boyle's Law

Robert Boyle studied the compressibility of gases in 1661 and observed that *the volume of a fixed amount of gas at a given temperature is inversely proportional to the pressure exerted on the gas.* This is *Boyle's Law*.

$$P_1 V_1 = P_2 V_2$$

where the subscripts 1 and 2 refer to the same sample of gas under two different sets of pressure and volume conditions.

A plot of volume vs. pressure for a gas illustrates that Boyle's Law is indeed a special case of the ideal gas law, where n (moles of gas) and T (temperature) are held constant, as shown in the following figure:

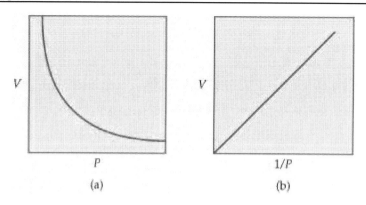

Boyle's Law: as pressure increases, volume decreases

Example: Suppose there is gas in a 15.0 L container at 5.00 atm, and the volume is decreased to 0.500 L. What is the new pressure in the container?

Solution: Substitute known quantities into the equation for Boyle's Law. It is important to note, however, that the volume units need to be consistent. In this case, the volume units are both expressed in liters.

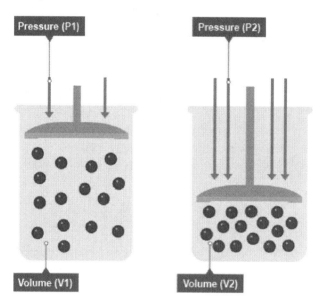

$$(5.00 \text{ atm}) \cdot (15.0 \text{ L}) = P_2(0.500 \text{ L})$$

Next, solve for the new pressure, P_2, by dividing both sides of the equation by V_2, 0.500 L.

$$P_2 = [(5.00 \text{ atm}) \cdot (15.0 \text{ L})] / 0.500 \text{ L} = 150 \text{ atm}$$

Charles' Law

French scientist Jacques Charles (1746 – 1823) discovered the relationship between temperature and volume of a gas through a series of experiments. *Charles' law* states that at constant pressure, the volume of a given sample of gas is directly proportional to its absolute temperature (in Kelvin). This can be written in equation form as follows:

$$\frac{V_1}{T_1} = \frac{V_2}{T_2}$$

where the subscripts 1 and 2 refer to the same sample of gas but under two different sets of temperature and volume conditions.

A plot of temperature vs. volume for a gas illustrates that Charles' law is another special case of the ideal gas law, where n and P are held constant, as shown in the figure below:

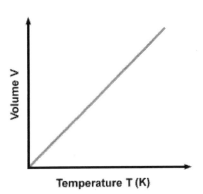

Charles' law: temperature increases, volume increases

Example: Suppose there is 25.0 L of gas at 0 °C, and the temperature is raised to 100 °C. What is the new volume of the gas?

Solution: First, the temperature units need to be converted into units of Kelvin.

$$T_1 = 0 \text{ °C} + 273 = 273 \text{ K}$$

$$T_2 = 100 \text{ °C} + 273 = 373 \text{ K}$$

Next, substitute known quantities into the equation for Charles' law.

$$25.0 \text{ L} / 273 \text{ K} = V_2 / 373 \text{ K}$$

Then solve for the new volume, V₂, by multiplying both sides of the equation by T₂, 373 K.

$$V_2 = (25.0 \text{ L}) \cdot (373 \text{ K}) / 273 \text{ K} = 34.2 \text{ L}$$

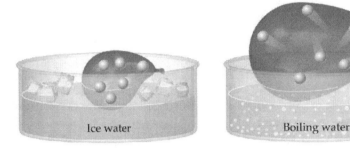

Gay-Lussac's Law

Gay-Lussac's law, developed by French chemist Louis Joseph Gay-Lussac in 1802, states that at a constant volume, the pressure of a given sample of gas is directly proportional to its absolute temperature (in Kelvin). In equation form:

$$\frac{P_1}{T_1} = \frac{P_2}{T_2}$$

where the subscripts 1 and 2 refer to the same sample of gas but under two different sets of temperature and pressure conditions.

A plot of temperature vs. pressure for a gas illustrates that Gay-Lussac's law is another special case of the ideal gas law, where n andare held constant, as shown in the figure below:

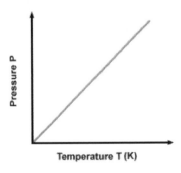

Gay-Lussac's law: as temperature increases, pressure increases

Example: Suppose a gas is at 30.0 atm pressure and 100 °C, and the temperature is changed to 400 °C. What is the new pressure of the gas?

Solution: Again, the first step is to convert the temperature into units of Kelvin.

$$T_1 = 100 \text{ °C} + 273 = 373 \text{ K}$$

$$T_2 = 400 \text{ °C} + 273 = 673 \text{ K}$$

Next, substitute given quantities into the equation for Gay-Lussac's Law.

$$30.0 \text{ atm} / 373 \text{ K} = P_2 / 673 \text{ K}$$

Then solve the above expression for the new pressure, P₂, by multiplying both sides of the equation by T₂ (673 K).

$$P_2 = [(30.0 \text{ atm}) \cdot (673 \text{ K})] / 373 \text{ K} = 54.1 \text{ atm}$$

Avogadro's Law

The volume of a gas in a container is affected not only by pressure and temperature but also by the amount of gas as well. The relationship between the quantity of a gas and its volume was investigated by Joseph Louis Gay- Lussac (1778 − 1823) and by Amadeo Avogadro.

Avogadro's law states that all gases at a given temperature and pressure occupy a volume that is directly proportional to the number of moles of gas present. This can be written in equation form as follows:

$$\frac{n_1}{V_1} = \frac{n_2}{V_2}$$

where n_1 and n_2 are the number of moles of gas 1 and gas 2, respectively, and V_1 and V_2 are the volumes of the gases, respectively.

A plot of volume vs. moles of gas illustrates that Avogadro's law is a special case of the ideal-gas law where *T* and *P* are held constant, as shown below:

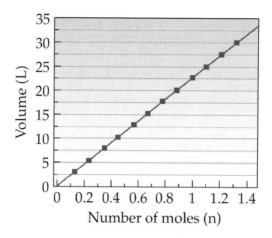

Avogadro's law: as moles of gas increase, volume increases

Example: Suppose that 8.00 moles of a gas occupies a volume of 4.00 L at a constant pressure and temperature. What volume of gas would 16.0 moles of this gas occupy at the same temperature and pressure?

Solution: Substitute given quantities into the equation for Avogadro's law:

$$4.00 \text{ L} / 8.00 \text{ mol} = V_2 / 16.0 \text{ mol}$$

Solve the above equation for the volume, V_2, by multiplying both sides of the equation by n_2, 16.0 mol:

$$V_2 = [(4.00 \text{ L}) \cdot (16.0 \text{ mol})] / 8.00 \text{ mol}$$

Combined Gas Law

The *combined gas law* is essentially an amalgam of the previously discussed gas laws. It is important to note that the combined gas law is not the ideal gas law. It is expressed in equation form to relate changes in temperature, volume and pressure of a gas as follows:

$$\frac{P_1 V_1}{T_1} = \frac{P_2 V_2}{T_2}$$

where, again, the subscripts 1 and 2 refer to the same sample of gas but under two different sets of temperature, pressure and volume conditions.

Example: Suppose a gas is at 15.0 atm pressure, with a volume of 25.0 L and a temperature of 300 K. What would the volume of the gas be at a standard temperature and pressure?

Solution: Substitute given quantities into the equation for the combined gas law. Standard pressure is 1.00 atm and standard temperature is 273 K.

$$[(15.0 \text{ atm}) \cdot (25.0 \text{ L})] / 373 \text{ K} = [(1.00 \text{ atm}) \cdot V_2] / 273 \text{ K}$$

Next, solve for the volume, V_2. Multiply both sides of the equation by T_2 (273 K) and divide both sides of the equation by P_2 (1.00 atm):

$$V_2 = [(15.0 \text{ atm}) \cdot (25.0 \text{ L}) \cdot (273 \text{ K})] / [(300 \text{ K}) \cdot (1.00 \text{ atm})]$$

$$V_2 = 341 \text{ L}$$

Ideal Gas Law

The *ideal gas law* was first stated in 1834 by French physicist Émile Clapeyron. It is a combination of laws discussed above, and it is the equation regarding the state of a hypothetical ideal gas. The general form of the ideal gas law is:

$$PV = nRT$$

where P is the pressure, V is the volume, T is the temperature, n is the number of moles and R is the gas constant ($R = 0.082$ L·atm/K·mol; although depends on the units).

Example: Suppose 2.5 moles of a gas is at standard temperature and pressure. What is the volume occupied by the gas?

Solution: Substitute given quantities into the equation for the ideal gas law. Standard pressure is 1.00 atm and standard temperature is 273 K.

$$PV = nRT$$

$$(1.00 \text{ atm})V = (2.5 \text{ mol}) \cdot (0.082 \text{ L} \cdot \text{atm/K} \cdot \text{mol}) \cdot (273 \text{ K})$$

Next, solve for the volume, V. Divide both sides of the equation by P, 1.00 atm.

$$V = [(2.5 \text{ mol}) \cdot (0.082 \text{ L} \cdot \text{atm/K} \cdot \text{mol}) \cdot (273 \text{ K})] / (1.00 \text{ atm})$$

$$V = 56 \text{ L}$$

From the ideal gas law, $PV = nRT$, useful expressions can be derived that relate the molar mass and density of gases to pressures and temperatures. This is often done by substituting a different known expression for one of the variables in the ideal gas law. For instance, the moles of a gas, n, can also be expressed as the mass of the gas in grams over the molar mass of that gas:

$$n = m / MM$$

where MM = molar mass, m = mass of the gas in grams and n = moles of gas

Substitute this into the ideal gas law, and one obtains the equation:

$$PV = mRT / MM$$

Multiplying both sides by the molar mass, MM, obtains:

$$(MM)PV = mRT$$

This equation is useful for determining the molar mass of a gas from experimental data, where the mass, pressure, volume and temperature of the gas is measured.

Now, divide both sides of the above expression by the volume, V:

$$(MM)P = gRT / V$$

Since it is known that g/V is density, φ, substitute density for g/V in the equation:

$$(MM)P = \varphi RT$$

This equation is useful for relating the pressure, density and temperature of a gas, similar to the other empirical gas laws.

Example: The density of a gas is measured at 1.855 g/L at 0.95 atm and 297 K. What is its molar mass?

Solution: Substitute given quantities into the equation above.

$$(MM)\cdot(0.95 \text{ atm}) = (1.855 \text{ g/L})\cdot(0.082 \text{ L}\cdot\text{atm/K}\cdot\text{mol})\cdot(297 \text{ K})$$

Solve for the molar mass, MM. Divide both sides of the equation by P, 0.95 atm.

$$MM = [(1.855 \text{ g/L})\cdot(0.082 \text{ L}\cdot\text{atm/K}\cdot\text{mol})\cdot(297 \text{ K})] / (0.95 \text{ atm})$$

$$MM = 47.55 \text{ g/mol}$$

Deviation of real-gas behavior from ideal gas law: a) qualitative; b) quantitative (van der Waals equation)

The kinetic molecular theory and the ideal gas law are just approximations of gas behavior. They are based on the theoretical ideal gas, while real gases have deviations from this behavior. When molecules are far apart (under conditions of low pressure and high temperature), a real gas behaves more like an ideal gas. When molecules are brought close together (under conditions of high pressure and low temperature), they experience intermolecular attraction and may therefore deviate significantly from ideal gas behavior.

The largest deviations from the ideal occur at high pressure and low temperature. At these conditions, the gas molecules are "squished" together, and thus experience more intermolecular interactions. Also, the molecular volume becomes significant when the total volume is "squished" down so much. The intermolecular attractions cause collisions to be sticky and inelastic. At extremely high pressures and low temperatures, gases condense into liquids.

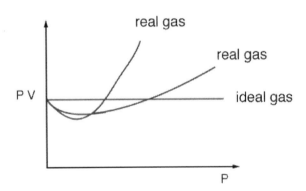

Recall that an ideal gas is considered to be a point mass (a particle so small that the volume of that particle is negligible). A real gas particle has real volume. This is because real gases liquefy as they cool and cannot compress to zero volume because their molecules are not dimensionless points. For an ideal gas, the collisions between gas particles was said to be "elastic" –no attractive or repulsive forces exist– and thus, no energy is exchanged during collisions. For a real gas, collisions are inelastic. There are a number of real gas laws.

Dutch theoretical physicist Johannes Diderik van der Waals (1873 – 1923) developed an equation of state that describes the behavior of real gases and their condensation to the liquid phase. In 1873, he derived the *van der Waals equation*, displayed below:

$$[P + (n^2a) / V^2] (V - nb) = nRT$$

Notice how "corrections" are being made to the pressure term and the volume term. Since collisions of real gases are inelastic, the term "n^2a / V^2" corrects for the interactions of these particles. Since real gas particles have real volume, the "nb" term is correcting for the excluded volume. The values of a and b are constant and are determined experimentally for each gas. The constants a and b would be given in a problem that needs to be solved using this equation and only pressure or temperature can be solved for easily. Solving for the volume is nontrivial and involves solving a cubic polynomial equation.

Here, the van der Waals equation is rearranged to solve for pressure. Begin by dividing both sides of the equation by the volume term, $V - nb$:

$$P + (n^2a) / (V^2) = (nRT) / (V - nb)$$

Next, subtract the intermolecular interaction term, n^2a / V^2, from both sides of the equation:

$$P = [(nRT) / (V - nb)] - [(n^2a) / (V^2)]$$

$$\underset{\text{Repulsion}}{\nearrow} \qquad \underset{\text{Attraction}}{\nwarrow}$$

Example: Using the real gas law, find the pressure of 2.00 moles of carbon dioxide gas at 298 K in a 5.00 L container. The van der Waals constants for carbon dioxide are: $a = 3.592$ L$^2 \cdot$atm/mol^2 and $b = 0.04267$ L/mol.

Solution: Substitute all variables into the appropriate terms of the equation, and solve for P to find the pressure:

$$P = \frac{(2.00 \, \text{mol})(0.0821 \, \text{L} \cdot \text{atm})(298 \, \text{K})}{5.00 \, \text{L} - (2.00 \, \text{mol})\text{mol} \cdot \text{K}(0.04267 \, \text{L})} - \frac{(2.00 \, \text{mol})^2(3.592 \, \text{L}^2 \cdot \text{atm})}{(5.00 \, \text{L})^2 \text{mol}^2} = 9.38 \, \text{atm}$$

Compare this to the pressure calculated using the ideal gas law:

$$PV = nRT$$

$$P = nRT / V$$

$$P = \frac{(2.00\,\text{mol})(0.0821\,\text{L}\cdot\text{atm})(298\,\text{K})}{(5.00\,\text{L})\text{mol}\cdot\text{K}} = 9.77\,\text{atm}$$

Although the results from the two equations are similar, they are not identical, illustrating the difference in behavior of a real gas from an ideal gas.

Partial pressure, mole fraction

There is so much space between the molecules in a gas that the molecules of another gas can readily share the space; therefore, gases often combine to form homogeneous mixtures. The *partial pressure* of a gas is the pressure that the gas would exert if it were the only gas in the container. Therefore each gas behaves independently of the other, and makes its own contribution to the total pressure.

Mole fraction indicates the ratio between moles of a certain component and the total number of moles. A symbol that is often used for mole fraction is X_a, which indicates the mole fraction of a component in the mixture.

Dalton's law relating partial pressure to composition

When two or more nonreactive gases are present in the same container, they behave independently of one another. *Dalton's law of partial pressures* states that the total pressure of a given mixture of gases is equal to the sum of the partial pressures of the individual gas components. This can be written in equation form as follows:

$$P_T = P_A + P_B + P_C \,...$$

where P_T is the total pressure in the container, and P_A, P_B and P_C equal the partial pressures of gases A, B and C, respectively.

The partial pressure of a given sample of gas is also related to its mole fraction in the following way:

$$P_A = X_A P_T$$

$$\text{where } X_A = \frac{[\text{moles of gas A}]}{[\text{total moles of gas}]}$$

Example: Suppose there is 1.0 L oxygen at 1.0 atm pressure in one container, 1.0 L nitrogen at 0.5 atm pressure in a second container and 1.0 L hydrogen at 3.0 atm pressure in a third container. What would the total pressure be if the gases were combined in a single 1.0 L container?

Solution: If the samples are combined in a single 1.0 L container, the total pressure is the sum of the pressures of each individual gas component:

1.0 atm + 0.5 atm + 3 atm = 4.5 atm

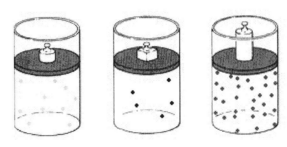

$P_{O_2} = 1.0$ atm $P_{N_2} = 0.5$ atm $P_{H_2} = 3.0$ atm

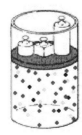

$$P_{\text{Total}} = P_{O_2} + P_{N_2} + P_{H_2} = 4.5 \text{ atm}$$

Dalton's law of partial pressures: the total pressure of a mixture of gases equals the sum of the individual gas pressures.

One important application of the law of partial pressures is for determining *vapor pressure* (the pressure exerted by a vapor in thermodynamic equilibrium with its liquid or solid phase). It is frequently used to determine the amount of a water-insoluble gaseous reaction product, or a slightly soluble gas such as hydrogen or oxygen. A common way to determine the amount of gas present is by collecting it over water and measuring the height of displaced water; this is accomplished by placing a tube into an inverted bottle, the opening of which is immersed in a larger container of water. As the gas bubbles into the test tube, it displaces the water until the test tube is full. The collected gas is not the only gas in the test tube since liquid water is always in equilibrium with its vapor, so the collected gas in the test tube is a mixture of two gases: the gas being collected and the water vapor.

The partial pressure of water is known as the vapor pressure of water and is dependent on temperature. Thus, the volume of gas collected consists of a mixture of the gas collected and water vapor; total pressure is the sum of the two contributing partial pressures.

From a list of water vapor pressure values at various temperatures (shown below), the value of the pressure of dry gas collected can be calculated. It is found by the vapor pressure of water being subtracted from the total vapor pressure of the gas mixture (equalizing the atmospheric pressure to give the partial pressure of the gaseous product collected). With volume and temperature known, the amount of gaseous product can be determined.

Vapor Pressure of Water at Various Temperatures

Temperature (°C)	Vapor Pressure (kPa)	Temperature (°C)	Vapor Pressure (kPa)
0	0.61	26	3.36
5	0.87	27	3.57
10	1.23	28	3.78
15	1.71	29	4.00
16	1.82	30	4.24
17	1.94	35	5.62
18	2.06	40	7.38
19	2.20	45	9.58
20	2.34	50	12.33
21	2.49	60	19.92
22	2.64	70	31.16
23	2.81	80	47.34
24	2.98	90	70.10
25	3.17	100	101.3

Example: A small piece of zinc reacts with dilute hydrochloric acid to form hydrogen gas, which is collected over water at 16.0 °C. The total pressure is adjusted to barometric pressure, 100.24 kPa, and the volume of hydrogen gas is measured as 1,495 cm³. Calculate the partial pressure of the hydrogen gas and the mass of the hydrogen gas.

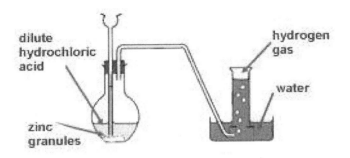

Solution:

The partial pressure of hydrogen gas = 100.24 kPa – 1.82 kPa = 98.42 kPa

To calculate the mass of the hydrogen gas, use the ideal gas equation and solve for moles. Hydrogen gas exists as H_2, so first multiply the mass of one hydrogen atom (1.008 g/mol) by two to obtain the molecular mass.

Since the temperature and volume have been given in the equation, and the partial pressure of hydrogen has been calculated in the first part of the problem, the ideal gas equation can now be used.

$PV = nRT$

$n = PV / RT$

$n = 98.42 \text{ kPa} \times 1.495 \text{ L} / 8.314 \text{ L kPa K}^{-1} \text{ mol}^{-1} \times 289 \text{ K}$

$n = 0.061 \text{ mol}$

mass = moles × molecular mass

mass = 0.061 mol × 2.016 g/mol

mass = 0.123 g

Intermolecular Forces

Intermolecular forces are forces of attraction or repulsion that occur between molecules. In the previous chapter, covalent and ionic bonding were discussed. However, there are a number of other interactions that are not quite as strong as covalent or ionic bonds, but still play a significant role in determining the properties of substances.

Dipole interactions

Molecules with dipole moments (described in the previous chapter) are attracted to each other. The more polar the molcule is, the stronger the dipole attraction. There are four different types of dipole attractions:

- *Ion-dipole attraction*: between an ion and a polar molecule. Since a polar molecule has a slight charge on either side and an ion is a charged atom, these particles may be attracted to each other.

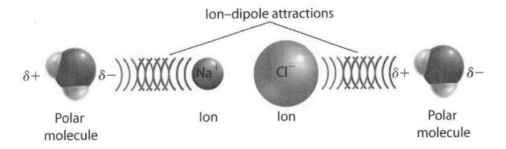

- *Dipole-dipole attraction*: between two polar molecules. The postive side of one polar molecule attracts the negative side of another polar molecule.

- *Dipole-induced dipole attraction*: between a polar molecule and a nonpolar molcule. Polar molecules can induce nonpolar molecules, shifting electrons and turning the nonpolar molecules temporarily into polar molecules.

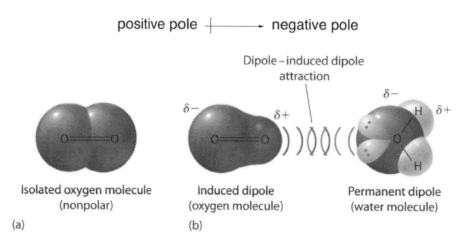

positive pole +———→ negative pole

Dipole–induced dipole attraction

Isolated oxygen molecule (nonpolar)

(a)

Induced dipole (oxygen molecule)

(b)

Permanent dipole (water molecule)

Induced dipole-induced dipole attraction/London dispersion force: between two nonpolar molecules. These molecules are both temporarily polar due to instantaneous induction by a polar molecule. Longer molecules tend to experience greater London dispersion forces. For example, octane (C_8H_{18}) has a stronger dispersion force than methane (CH_4).

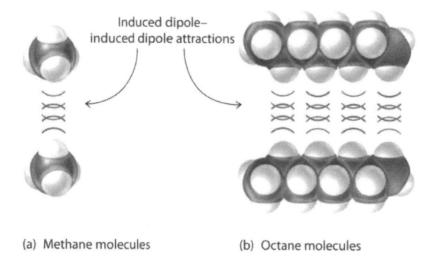

Induced dipole–induced dipole attractions

(a) Methane molecules

(b) Octane molecules

Molecular Attractions Involving Dipoles

Attraction	Relative Strength
Ion–dipole	Strongest
Dipole–dipole	
Dipole–induced dipole	
Induced dipole–induced dipole	Weakest

Hydrogen bonding

Hydrogen bonding is a special type of bonding that is categorized as a dipole-dipole attraction. When hydrogens are bonded directly to the electronegative atoms N, O and F (known as hydrogen bond donors), the bonding electrons spend most of the time closer to the more electronegative atom. In addition to that, hydrogen has only one valence electron. Due to these factors, the hydrogen nucleus is very exposed. The highly positive hydrogen nucleus attracts the electronegative atom from a neighboring molecule, creating a very strong intermolecular force comparable to covalent polar bonds. The neighboring molecule must possess a lone electron pair to form a hydrogen bond, and this molecule is known as the hydrogen bond acceptor.

The more polar a bond is, the stronger the hydrogen bond. The H−F bond is the most polar, followed by the H−O bond, and lastly the H−N bond.

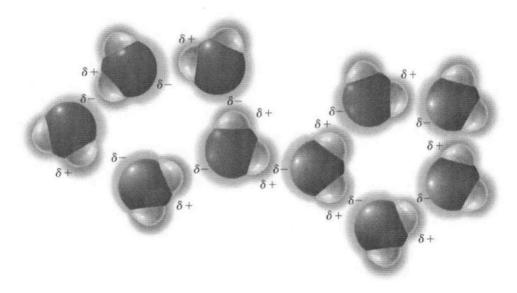

A significant consequence of hydrogen bonding is differences in physical properties. For example, hydrogen bonding significantly increases the boiling point of compounds. Methanol (CH$_3$OH) and methane (CH$_4$) have similar molecular structures. However, methanol is liquid at room temperature while methane is gaseous. This is mainly due to hydrogen bonding between methanol molecules, which is much stronger than the dispersion forces between nonpolar methane molecules.

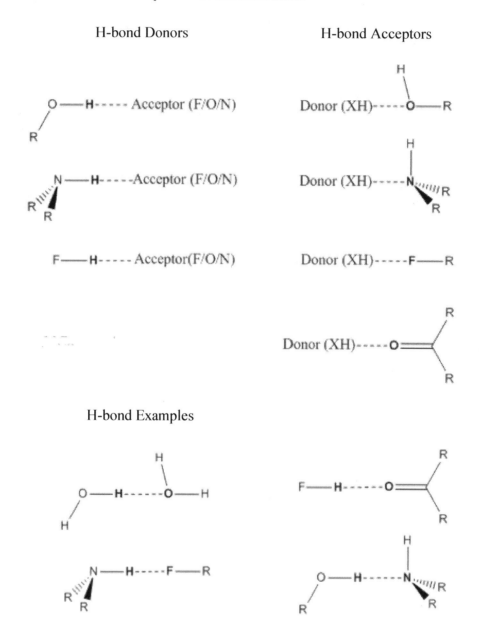

Van der Waals' Forces (London dispersion forces)

Atoms and molecules have a weak attraction for each other, known as *van der Waals forces*. This results from the weak residual attraction of one molecule's nuclei to another molecule's electrons. The van der Waals equation, described previously in the section on real gas behavior, takes these forces into account. These forces have a large effect on the boiling point of a substance, because the boiling point reflects the kinetic energy needed to release a molecule from the cooperative attractions of the liquid state.

Nonpolar molecules have fluctuating dipoles that tend to align with one another from one instant to the next. Van der Waals' forces can result from these temporarily fluctuating molecules ("induced dipole/induced dipole attraction"), and this category of van der Waal's forces is known as the *London dispersion force*. Dispersion forces exist for all molecules, but are only significant for nonpolar molecules (for polar molecules, dipole forces are predominant).

In general, larger molecules have higher boiling points compared to smaller molecules of the same type, due to the increase in dispersion forces.

Phase Equilibria

Phase changes

Most substances can exist in solid, liquid or gas form. A *solid* (e.g., ice) has a definite shape and volume. The molecules in a solid vibrate about a fixed position, and a solid cannot be compressed. A *liquid* (e.g., water) has a definite volume but takes the shape of its container. The molecules can move about, but are close together and bound by intermolecular forces. A gas (e.g., water vapor) has neither a definite volume nor a definite shape; it takes both the volume and shape of its container. The molecules fly apart from each other and are not held together by intermolecular forces. A gas is easily compressible.

Freezing point, melting point, boiling point, condensation point

Freezing point is the temperature at which liquids turn into solids. The *melting point* is the temperature at which a solid melts to become a liquid. Theoretically, the melting point and freezing point of a particular substance should be the same. In reality, a difference in those quantities may be observed.

Vaporization is the phase transition from liquid to gas. There are two types of vaporization: boiling and evaporation. When liquid is heated, it reaches a temperature where the vapor pressure is large enough for bubbles to form inside the body of the liquid; this temperature is called the *boiling point*. As a liquid is boiling, the temperature remains constant until all of the liquid has been converted into gas. Since the boiling point is based on pressure, it can differ depending on the environment. For example, at high-altitude, low-pressure locations, the boiling point of a substance is lower.

Evaporation, on the other hand, occurs at temperatures below the boiling point. It occurs from the surface of the liquid into a gaseous phase that is not saturated with the substance (as opposed to boiling, which occurs from the bulk of the liquid, not just the surface). Evaporation tends to occur more quickly in liquids with higher vapor pressure. *Condensation*, the opposite of evaporation, is the change from the gas phase to liquid phase. It commonly occurs when a vapor is cooled or compressed to its saturation limit, and the temperature at which condensation occurs is known as the condensation point. One example of condensation is the formation of water droplets in clouds.

Sublimation, the phase transition from a solid to a gas, is essentially evaporation that occurs directly from the solid phase below the melting point. The opposite of sublimation is *deposition*, which is the phase transition where a gas forms directly into a solid.

Molality

Molality, also known as molal concentration, is a measure of the concentration of solutes in a solvent, in terms of the mass of the solvent. The SI unit for molality is mol/kg. Molality is often given the symbol *m*. (This is different than the uppercase *M* given to molarity).

Molality = mols of solute / mass (in kg) of solvent

Example: Suppose a person had 3.00 moles of sucrose and proceeded to mix it into 1.00 L water until it was entirely dissolved. What is the molality of the solution?

Solution: First, determine the mass of 1.00 L water. Water has a density of 1.00 g/mL, or 1.00 kg/L. Therefore, the mass of the liter of water is 1.00 kg. Using this solvent mass, solve for molality.

Molality = 3.00 mol / 1.00 kg = 3.00 mol/kg

The molality of the solution is 3.00 m.

More commonly, instead of giving the number of moles, the mass of the solute is given in grams, as in the problem below.

Example: Suppose someone had 116.88 grams of NaCl and dissolved it into 4.00 kg of water. What is the molality of the solution?

Solution: Convert grams of NaCl into moles. The molar mass of NaCl is 58.44.

Moles = mass / molar mass

Moles = 116.88 / 58.44

Moles = 2.00 mol

Solve for molality:

Molality = 2.00 mol / 4.00 kg = 0.500 mol/kg

The molality of the solution is 0.500 mol/kg.

It is important to remember that when calculating molality, the mass of the solvent is only of the pure solvent, excluding the mass of the solute. This is different from molarity, where the volume used is solution volume, which includes both solute and solvent. In short, molality is (mol solute/kg solvent) while molarity is (mol solute/L solution).

Colligative properties

Colligative properties are physical properties that depend on the ratio of solute particles to the solvent, but not on the type of chemical species present. Colligative properties include relative lowering of vapor pressure, elevation of boiling point, depression of freezing point and osmotic pressure.

All colligative properties take the van 't Hoff factor (i) into consideration. It is the ratio of the concentration of particles produced when a substance is dissolved, to the concentration of a substance as calculated from its mass. Basically, it means that the concentration should be converted to reflect the total number of particles in solution. For example, glucose has i of 1 because it does not dissociate in solution. This is true of most non-electrolytes. NaCl has i of 2, because in solution, it breaks into 2 particles: Na^+ and Cl^-.

Vapor pressure lowering (Raoult's law)

In 1888, French chemist Francois-Marie Raoult proved that the vapor pressure of a solution is equal to the mole fraction of the solvent times the vapor pressure of the pure solvent. This is *Raoult's law*:

$$P = \chi_{solvent} \cdot P^{\circ}_{solvent}$$

where P is the vapor pressure, $\chi_{solvent}$ = mol fraction of the solvent (# mols of solvent / # total mols of both solute and solvent), and $P^{\circ}_{solvent}$ is the vapor pressure of the pure solvent alone.

When calculating χ_{solute}, make sure the van't Hoff factor is taken into account (i.e., 1 mol of NaCl in solution is actually 2 mol of particles).

Example: Suppose 2.00 moles of sucrose are added to a pitcher containing 2.00 liters of water. The vapor pressure of water alone is 23.8 mmHg. What is the new vapor pressure of the solution?

Solution: Convert the 2.00 L of water into moles, knowing that 1.00 L water is 1.00 kg, 2.00 L water = 2000 g.

Then, convert the mass of the water into moles, using the molar mass of water (18.02 g).

$$2000 \text{ g} / 18.02 \text{ g} = 110.9 \text{ moles } H_2O$$

Solve for the mole fraction, $\chi_{solvent}$.

$$\chi_{solvent} = \text{mols of solvent / total mols of both solute and solvent}$$

$$\chi_{solvent} = 110.9 \text{ moles } H_2O \text{ / total moles}$$

$$\chi_{solvent} = 110.9 \text{ moles } / 110.9 + 2 \text{ moles}$$

$$\chi_{solvent} = 0.98$$

Finally, use Raoult's law.

$$P = \chi_{solvent} \cdot P^{\circ}_{solvent}$$

$$P = (0.98) \cdot (23.8 \text{ mmHg})$$

$$P = 23.3 \text{ mmHg}$$

The addition of a solute caused the vapor pressure to be lowered.

Boiling point elevation ($\Delta Tb = Kbm$)

Adding a solute to a solvent stabilizes the solvent in the liquid phase, thus lowering the tendency of the solvent molecules to move to the gas or solid phases. Therefore, the boiling point increases. The *boiling point elevation* is proportional to the lowering of vapor pressure in a dilute solution and is calculated as follows:

$$\Delta T_b = k_b \cdot m \cdot i$$

where ΔT_b is the increase in boiling point. k_b is the molal boiling point constant (a value that will be given), m is the molality (mol solute/kg solvent) and i is the van 't Hoff factor.

Example: What is the boiling point elevation when 6.4 g of ammonia (NH_3) is dissolved in 0.3 kg of water? The k_b for water is 0.52 °C/m.

Solution: Determine the moles of ammonia, using the molar mass of ammonia (17.031 g/mol).

$$6.4 \text{ g} / 17.031 \text{ g/mol} = 0.38 \text{ mol}$$

$$\text{Molality} = \text{mols of solute} / \text{mass (in kg) of solvent}$$

$$\text{Molality} = 0.38 \text{ mol} / 0.3 \text{ kg}$$

$$= 1.27 \text{ m}$$

Then, use the formula for boiling point elevation.

$$\Delta T_b = k_b \cdot m \cdot i$$

$$\Delta T_b = (0.52 \text{ °C/m}) \cdot (1.27 \text{ m}) \cdot (1)$$

$$= 0.66 \text{ °C}$$

Therefore, the boiling point has increased by 0.66 °C due to the addition of 6.4 g of ammonia.

Freezing point depression (ΔTf = Kfm)

Solute particles in mixtures increase the strength of intermolecular bonds. This is why it makes it harder to boil (due to boiling point elevation, described in the previous section) and also makes it harder to freeze (by lowering the freezing point).

The lowering of the freezing point, known as the *freezing point depression*, is given by the following equation (the negative sign indicates that the change is a decrease).

$$\Delta T_f = -k_f\,m \cdot i$$

where ΔT_f is the decrease in freezing point, k_f is the molal freezing point constant (a value that will be given), m is the molality (mol solute/kg solvent) and i is the van 't Hoff factor.

Example: A 48.0 g sample of a non-electrolyte was dissolved in 500.0 g of water. The solution's freezing point was –3.5 °C. The k_f of water is 1.86 °C/m. What is the molar mass of the compound?

Solution: The freezing point of pure water is 0 °C; therefore the freezing point depression ΔT_f is 3.5 °C. Use the formula for freezing point depression:

$$\Delta T_f = k_f \cdot m \cdot i$$

$$3.5\ °C = (1.86\ °C/m) \cdot (x\,/\,0.5\ kg) \cdot (1)$$

$$3.5\ °C = (3.72\ °C/m) \cdot (x)$$

$$x = 0.94\ mol$$

Then, divide the mass of the sample by the moles in the sample to obtain the molar mass.

$$48.0\ g\,/\,0.94\ mol = 51.1\ g/mol$$

The molar mass of the unknown compound is 51.1 g/mol.

Osmotic pressure

Osmotic pressure is the minimum pressure that needs to be applied to a solution to prevent the inward flow of water across a semipermeable membrane. This membrane allows the passage of solvent particles, but not solute particles. The formula for osmotic pressure is:

$$\pi = MRT \cdot i$$

where π is the osmotic pressure, M is the molarity in mol/L, R is the ideal gas constant and T is the temperature in K.

Osmotic pressure determines whether and in what direction osmosis will occur. *Osmosis* is the movement of solvent across a semi-permeable membrane from an area of low solute concentration (and therefore a high solvent concentration) to an area of high solute concentration (and conversely a low solvent concentration). Solvent moves from an area with low Π value to an area with high π value.

Example: What is the osmotic pressure of a solution prepared by adding 10.5 g of sucrose ($C_{12}H_{22}O_{11}$) to enough water to make 300 mL of solution at 25 °C?

Solution: Using the periodic table, the molar mass of sucrose is calculated as 342 g/mol. Then, find the concentration of sucrose by dividing the mass of the sample by the molar mass.

$$10.5 \text{ g} / 342 \text{ g/mol} = 0.03 \text{ mol}$$

Then, find the molarity, M:

$$\text{Molarity} = \text{mol solute/L solution}$$

$$= 0.03 \text{ mol} / 0.3 \text{ L}$$

$$= 0.1 \text{ mol/L}$$

Convert temperature into Kelvin (i.e., absolute temperature).

$$T = {}^{\circ}C + 273$$

$$T = 25 + 273$$

$$T = 298 \text{ K}$$

Use the formula for osmotic pressure. Since sucrose does not dissociate, $i = 1$.

$$\pi = MRT \cdot i$$

$$\Pi = (0.1 \text{ mol/L}) \cdot (0.08206 \text{ L} \cdot \text{atm/mol} \cdot \text{K}) \cdot (298 \text{ K}) \cdot (1)$$

$$\pi = 2.4 \text{ atm}$$

The osmotic pressure for the sucrose solution is 2.4 atm.

Colloids

Previously, a *solution* was described as a homogeneous mixture that consists of only one phase, meaning that it stays mixed. A *colloid* is a substance with microscopic insoluble particles that are dispersed throughout the solution. A colloid has a dispersed phase (the actual suspended particles) and a continuous phase (the medium of suspension, essentially what holds the particles). A colloid stays mixed (i.e., the particles will not settle), unless it is centrifuged. The common colloid example is homogenized milk, which consists of butterfat globules dispersed within a water-based solution. Also, when water and oil are vigorously shaken together, an emulsion is formed, which is a colloid.

Henry's law

In 1803, English chemist William Henry showed that at a constant temperature, the solubility of a gas in a liquid is directly proportional to the partial pressure of the gas above the liquid (when the gas is in equilibrium with the liquid). This came to be known as *Henry's law*, and it is described by the following formula:

$$P_{\text{solute}} = k_{\text{H}} \cdot c$$

where P_{solute} is the partial pressure of the solute at the solution's surface, k_{H} is Henry's law constant (which is different for each solute-solvent pair) and c is the concentration of dissolved gas.

Example: How many grams of carbon dioxide (CO_2) gas are dissolved in a 0.5 L bottle of carbonated water if the manufacturer uses a pressure of 2.5 atm in the bottling process? K_{H} of CO_2 in water = 29.76 atm/(mol/L).

Solution: Use Henry's law to determine the concentration of CO_2.

$$P_{solute} = k_H \cdot c$$

$$2.7 \text{ atm} = [29.76 \text{ atm/(mol/L)}] \cdot c$$

$$c = 0.09 \text{ mol/L}$$

Determine how many moles of CO_2 are in 0.5 L carbonated water by dividing the mol/L by 2. 0.09 / 2 = 0.045 mol

Convert moles to grams by using the molar mass of CO_2, which is 44 g/mol (can be determined from periodic table).

$$0.045 \text{ mol} \times (44 \text{ g/mol}) = 1.98 \text{ g}$$

There are 1.98 grams of CO_2 in a 0.5 L bottle of carbonated water.

Practice Questions

1. Consider the phase diagram for H_2O. The termination of the gas-liquid transition at which distinct or liquid phases do NOT exist is the:

    A. critical point   **C.** triple point

    B. end point   **D.** condensation point

2. When liquids and gases are compared, liquids have [ ] compressibility compared to gases and a [ ] density.

    A. lower… lower   **C.** higher… lower

    B. higher … higher   **D.** lower … higher

3. How does a real gas deviate from an ideal gas?

    I. Molecules occupy a significant amount of space

    II. Intermolecular forces may exist

    III. Pressure is created from molecular collisions with the walls of the container

    A. I only   **C.** I and II only

    B. II only   **D.** II and III only

4. Under which conditions does a real gas behave most nearly like an ideal gas?

    A. High temperature and high pressure

    B. High temperature and low pressure

    C. Low temperature and low pressure

    D. Low temperature and high pressure

5. Which of the following compounds has the highest boiling point?

    A. CH_3OH **C.** $CH_3OCH_2CH_2CH_2CH_3$

    B. $CH_3CH_2CH_2CH_2CH_2OH$ **D.** $CH_3CH_2CH_2C(OH)HOH$

6. Consider the phase diagram for H_2O. The termination of the gas-liquid transition at which distinct or liquid phases do NOT exist is the:

    A. critical point   **C.** triple point

    B. end point   **D.** condensation point

7. The boiling point of a liquid is the temperature:

    A. where sublimation occurs

    B. where the vapor pressure of the liquid equals the atmospheric pressure over the liquid

    C. equal to or greater than 100 °C

    D. where the rate of sublimation equals evaporation

8. Which of the following statements about gases is correct?

    A. Formation of homogeneous mixtures, regardless of the nature of non-reacting gas components

    B. Relatively long distances between molecules

    C. High compressibility

    D. All of the above

9. What is the proportionality relationship between the pressure of a gas and its volume?

    A. directly

    B. inversely

    C. pressure is raised to the 2nd power

    D. pressure raised to the $\sqrt{2}$ power

10. How does the volume of a fixed sample of gas change if the pressure is doubled?

    A. Decreases by a factor of 2

    B. Increases by a factor of 4

    C. Doubles

    D. Remains the same

11. What is the ratio of the diffusion rate of O_2 molecules to the diffusion rate of H_2 molecules, if six moles of O_2 gas and six moles of H_2 gas are placed in a large vessel, and the gases and vessel are at the same temperature?

    A. 4:1

    B. 1:4

    C. 12:1

    D. 1:1

12. Under ideal conditions, which of the following gases is least likely to behave as an ideal gas?

    A. CF_4

    B. CH_3OH

    C. N_2

    D. O_3

Solutions

1. A is correct.

At a pressure and temperature corresponding to the triple point (point D on the graph) of a substance, all three states (gas, liquid and solid) exist in equilibrium.

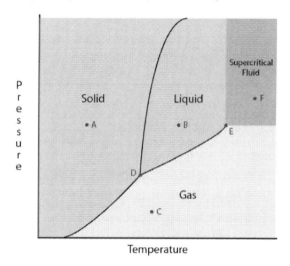

Phase diagram of pressure vs. temperature

The critical point (point E on the graph) is the end point of the phase equilibrium curve where the liquid and its vapor become indistinguishable.

2. D is correct.

Density = mass / volume

Gas molecules have a large amount of space between them, therefore they can be pushed together and thus gases are very compressible. Because there is such a large amount of space between each molecule in a gas, the extent to which the gas molecules can be pushed together is much greater than the extent to which liquid molecules can be pushed together. Therefore, gases have a greater compressibility than liquids.

Gas molecules are further apart than in liquid molecules, which is why gases have a smaller density.

3. C is correct.

The molecules of an ideal gas do not occupy a significant amount of space and exert no intermolecular forces, while the molecules of a real gas do occupy space and do exert (weak attractive) intermolecular forces.

However, both an ideal gas and a real gas have pressure, which is created from molecular collisions with the walls of the container.

4. B is correct.

The molecules of an ideal gas exert no attractive forces. Therefore, a real gas behaves most nearly like an ideal gas when it is at high temperature and low pressure, because under these conditions the molecules are far apart from each other and exert little or no attractive forces on each other.

5. D is correct. Hydroxyl (~OH) groups greatly increase the boiling point because they form hydrogen bonds with ~OH groups of neighboring molecules.

Hydrocarbons are nonpolar molecules, which means that the dominant intermolecular force is London dispersion. This force gets stronger as the number of atoms in each molecule increases. Stronger force increases the boiling point.

Branching of the hydrocarbon also affects the boiling point. Straight molecules have slightly higher boiling points than branched molecules with the same number of atoms. The reason is that straight molecules can align parallel against each other and all atoms in the molecules are involved in the London dispersion forces.

Another factor is the presence of other heteroatoms (i.e., atoms other than carbon and hydrogen). For example, the electronegative oxygen atom between carbon groups or in an ether (C–O–C) slightly increases the boiling point.

6. A is correct.

At a pressure and temperature corresponding to the triple point (point D on the graph) of a substance, all three states (gas, liquid and solid) exist in equilibrium.

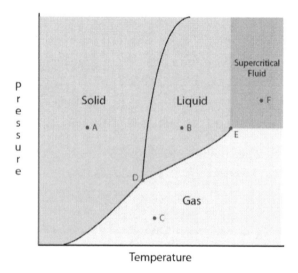

Phase diagram of pressure vs. temperature

The critical point (point E on the graph) is the end point of the phase equilibrium curve where the liquid and its vapor become indistinguishable.

7. B is correct. Boiling occurs when the vapor pressure of a liquid equals atmospheric pressure.

Vapor pressure is the pressure exerted by a vapor in equilibrium with its condensed phases (i.e., solid or liquid) in a closed system, at a given temperature.

Atmospheric pressure is the pressure exerted by the weight of air in the atmosphere.

Vapor pressure is inversely correlated with the strength of intermolecular force.

With stronger intermolecular forces, the molecules are more likely to stick together in the liquid form and fewer of them participate in the liquid-vapor equilibrium; therefore, the molecule would boil at a higher temperature.

8. D is correct. Gases form homogeneous mixtures, regardless of the identities or relative proportions of the component gases. There is a relatively large distance between gas molecules (as opposed to solids or liquids where the molecules are much closer together).

When a pressure is applied to gas, its volume readily decreases, and thus gases are highly compressible.

There are no attractive forces between gas molecules, which is why molecules of a gas can move about freely.

9. B is correct.

Boyle's law (i.e., pressure-volume law) states that pressure and volume are inversely proportional:

$$(P_1 V_1) = (P_2 V_2)$$

or

$$P \times V = \text{constant}$$

If the volume of a gas increases, its pressure decreases proportionally.

10. A is correct.

Boyle's law (i.e., pressure-volume law) states that pressure and volume are inversely proportional:

$$(P_1 V_1) = (P_2 V_2)$$

or

$$P \times V = \text{constant}$$

If the pressure of a gas increases, its volume decreases proportionally.

Doubling the pressure reduces the volume by half.

11. B is correct.

Graham's law of effusion states that the rate of effusion (i.e., escaping through a small hole) of a gas is inversely proportional to the square root of the molar mass of its particles.

Rate 1 / Rate 2 = $\sqrt{}$(molar mass gas 1 / molar mass gas 2)

The diffusion rate is the inverse root of the molecular weights of the gases.

Therefore, the rate of effusion is:

O_2 / H_2 = $\sqrt{}$(2 / 32)

rate of diffusion = 1 : 4

12. B is correct.

Methanol (CH_3OH) is an alcohol that participates in hydrogen bonding.

Therefore, this gas experiences the strongest intermolecular forces.

Chapter 4

Stoichiometry

- **Molecular Weight**

- **Empirical Formula vs. Molecular Formula**

- **Metric Units Commonly Used in the Context of Chemistry**

- **Description of Composition by Percent Mass**

- **Mole Concept, Avogadro's Number N**

- **Definition of Density (φ)**

- **Oxidation Number**

- **Description of Reactions by Chemical Equations**

Molecular Weight

A *molecular compound* is an electrically neutral particle that consists of two or more nonmetals that are covalently bonded together. As described in the chapter on chemical bonding, a covalent bond arises from sharing electrons between two atoms. Groups of atoms that make up a molecule behave as single particles or discrete units. For example, a single water molecule consists of two hydrogen atoms bonded to one oxygen atom. Each type of molecule has a specific molecular weight (MW).

Molecular weight is the weight of 1 mole of molecules, where 1 mole equals 6.02×10^{23} particles. This number is also known as Avogadro's number (N_A). In general, molecular weight is expressed in grams per mole. Sometimes it is also expressed in *atomic mass units* (amu, or simply u), where 1 u equals 1 g/mol. For example, ^{12}C weighs 12 amu = 12 g/mol. 1 amu is also 1 Dalton (Da).

The molecular weight of a substance is obtained by adding the atomic masses of its constituent atoms. The *atomic mass* of an element can be found on the periodic table; it is the number directly below the symbol for the element, as indicated by the red arrow in the image to the right.

For example, determine the MW of H_2O. First, look at the periodic table and see that the mass of a hydrogen atom is 1.008 amu. The mass of an oxygen atom is 15.999 amu. Water contains two hydrogens and one oxygen (given its chemical formula), so use the following equation to determine the MW of water (H_2O):

$$2 \,(H) + 1 \,(O) = 2 \,(1.008) + (15.999) = 18.015 \text{ g/mol.}$$

Another example can be seen in the graphic below. A single carbon atom is approximately 12 amu. However, oxygen exists as a diatomic molecule, O_2.

Therefore, the mass of an oxygen atom, approximately 16 amu, should be multiplied by two to obtain the MW of O_2, which is around 32 amu.

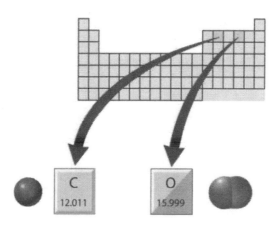

The mass of one carbon atom is approximately 12 amu. The mass of one oxygen molecule is approximately 32 amu. A carbon atom is 12/32, or 3/8, as massive as an oxygen molecule.

Empirical Versus Molecular Formula

There are two different ways of expressing the chemical formula of a molecular compound. The *molecular formula* describes the atomic composition of a molecule in its naturally occurring form. It specifies the number of each type of atom present. The *empirical formula* describes the *simplest integer ratio* of atoms of a molecule. For example, the molecular formula of hydrogen peroxide is H_2O_2. The empirical formula of hydrogen peroxide is simply HO.

The chart below shows the structure, molecular formula and empirical formula of glucose:

Molecular Structure	Molecular Formula	Empirical Formula
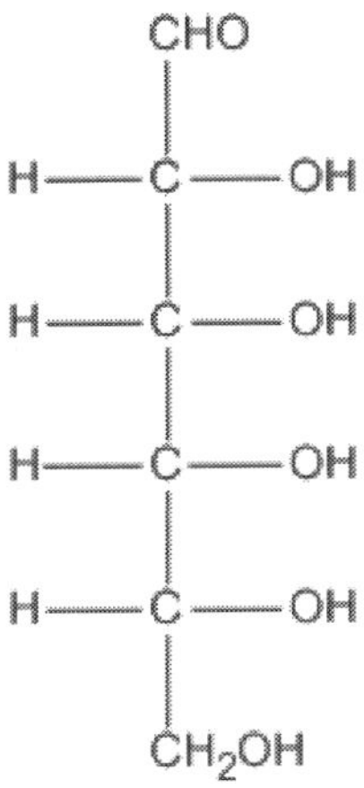	$C_6H_{12}O_6$	CH_2O

Binary molecular compounds are covalently-bonded compounds composed of two elements, generally nonmetals. Writing the molecular formula of a binary molecular compound is quite simple; these rules can be followed:

1. The first element in the formula is given first, using the full name of the element.

2. The second element is named as if it were an anion.

3. The number of each element in the compound is indicated by a prefix, as in the chart below.

Numerical Prefixes for Naming Compounds

Prefix	Meaning
mono-	1
di-	2
tri-	3
tetra-	4
penta-	5
hexa-	6
hepta-	7
octa-	8

For example, the formula for carbon dioxide is CO_2 since the name indicates one carbon (no prefix because the "mono-" prefix is eliminated when the first element exists as a single atom) and two oxygens (prefix "di-" means 2). Disulfur tetrafluoride has the formula S_2F_4 since the "di-" prefix indicates two sulfur atoms, and the "tetra-" prefix indicates four fluorine atoms.

Ionic compounds are named differently. An *ionic compound* consists of a metal and nonmetal atom that have transferred electrons and are bonded together due to electrostatic forces between oppositely-charged particles. When writing a chemical formula from the name of an ionic compound, one must consider the ions contained in the compound. These include the cations, as well as the monatomic and polyatomic anions. The inability to recognize these ions is the main cause of difficulty in writing chemical formulae of inorganic compounds; memorization of the ions is essential. In the name of an ionic compound or the chemical formula, the cation is first and the anion is second. For example, sodium chloride is NaCl, which is formed from a sodium cation (Na^+) and a chlorine anion (Cl^-).

Recall that some cations only form one ion (Group IA, IIA and IIIA elements, except Thallium). Cations that can form more than one ion have a stock number, shown as a Roman numeral in parentheses. For the monatomic anions, the charge is equivalent to the group number minus 8. For example, oxygen has the monatomic anion O^{2-}. The group number is 6, so the charge is $6 - 8 = -2$.

The polyatomic anions shown in the table below should be learned.

Common Polyatomic Ions

$C_2H_3O_2^-$	acetate	OH^-	hydroxide
NH_4+	ammonium	ClO^-	hypochlorite
CO_3^{2-}	carbonate	NO_3^-	nitrate
ClO_3^-	chlorate	NO_2^-	nitrite
ClO_2^-	chlorite	$C_2O_4^{2-}$	oxalate
CrO_4^{2-}	chromate	ClO_4^-	perchlorate
CN^-	cyanide	MnO_4^-	permanganate
$Cr_2O_7^{2-}$	dichromate	PO_4^{3-}	phosphate
HCO_3^-	bicarbonate	SO_4^{2-}	sulfate
HSO_4^-	bisulfate	SO_3^{2-}	sulfite
HSO_3^-	bisulfite		

Metric Units Commonly Used in the Context of Chemistry

The metric system is a decimal system of measurement referred to as the *International System of Units* (commonly abbreviated as SI). The SI has seven base units: length (meters), mass (kilograms), time (seconds), electric current (amperes), temperature (Kelvin), amount of substance (moles) and luminous intensity (candelas). Other SI units of measurements, such as volume (liters), density (kg/m^3) and pressure (atmospheres) are derived from those base units. All the units are based on 10 or multiples of 10. As a result, conversions between units are uniform and easy to apply.

The SI system uses prefixes to indicate the magnitude of a measured quantity; the prefix itself gives the conversion factor. Learn some of the common prefixes shown below, as they are used regularly.

Prefix	Symbol	Power	Prefix	Symbol	Power
mega-	M	10^6	centi-	c	10^{-2}
kilo-	k	10^3	milli-	m	10^{-3}
hecto-	h	10^2	micro-	μ	10^{-6}
deca-	D	10^1	nano-	n	10^{-9}
deci-	d	10^{-1}	pico-	p	10^{-12}

SI units do not allow for double prefixes (e.g., 1,000 g is not 1 hectodecagram); instead only one prefix is used for any given quantity of base units (e.g., 1,000 g = 1 kilogram).

Conversions between metric units involve adding or subtracting zeros from the number. Suppose the mass of a 250 mg aspirin tablet needs to be converted to grams. Start by using the units to set up the problem. If a unit is to be converted (in this case, mg), it is placed in the numerator. That unit must then be in the denominator of the conversion factor in order for it to cancel:

$$(250 \text{ mg}/1) \cdot (1 \times 10^{-3} \text{ g}/1 \text{ mg}) = 0.250 \text{g}$$

Notice how the units cancel to give grams. The conversion factor is shown as a numerator of 1×10^{-3} because on most calculators it must be entered in this fashion, not as just 10^{-3}. Also, mg is assigned the value of 1, and the prefix "milli-" is applied to the gram unit. In other words, 1 mg literally means 1×10^{-3} g.

Conversions between English/imperial and metric units work in a similar fashion. The difference is the conversion factors; they are not powers of ten and they are different for each unit, which makes conversions more complex. This is why the imperial system is not ideal for scientific calculations. It is a good idea to memorize a few basic metric-imperial conversions:

Length: 2.54 cm = 1 inch

Mass: 454 g = 1 pound

Volume: 0.946 L = 1 quart

Temperature: $^\circ$C = ($^\circ$F − 32) / 1.8

Notice that all of the above conversions are given to three significant figures. *Significant figures* are used to indicate the number of digits known exactly for a measured or calculated quantity within a degree of uncertainty. For example, if a thermometer indicates a boiling point of 36.2 $^\circ$C, and has an uncertainty of ± 0.2 $^\circ$C, all three figures in 36.2 are significant (including the 0.2, which is uncertain). The notation 36.2 ± 0.2 $^\circ$C indicates the known quantity, along with the digits of uncertainty.

How does one convert the mass of a 23 lb object to kilograms? This is done in two steps: the pound units are converted to grams, and then grams are converted to kilograms. Use the units to help set up the problem:

$$\frac{23\,\text{lb}}{1} \times \frac{454\,\text{g}}{1\,\text{lb}} \times \frac{1\,\text{kg}}{1 \times 10^3\,\text{g}} = 10\,\text{kg}$$

A conversion problem may include multiple units. For example, convert the pressure 14 lb/in^2 to g/cm^2. When setting up a problem that involves multiple conversions, work with one unit at a time. Start by converting the pound units to gram units:

$$\frac{14\,\text{lb}}{\text{in}^2} \times \frac{454\,\text{g}}{1\,\text{lb}}$$

Next, convert in^2 to cm^2. Set up the conversion without the exponent first, using the conversion factor 1 in = 2.54 cm. Since in^2 and cm^2 are needed, raise everything to the second power:

$$\frac{14\,\text{lb}}{\text{in}^2} \times 0\frac{454\,\text{g}}{1\,\text{lb}} \times \frac{1^2\,\text{in}^2}{2.54^2\,\text{cm}^2} = 9.9 \times 10^2\,\text{g/cm}^2$$

Remember, when the units are squared, the numbers associated with them have to be squared too. In the case of 1 in^2, it does not make a difference because $1^2 = 1$. In most cases, however, the squaring of numbers when units are squared is essential.

Always check the units, because they indicate if the problem has been set up correctly.

Description of composition by percent mass

Percent mass (% mass) is a unit of concentration that compares the mass of one part of a substance to the mass of the whole. This unit is often used for solutions, especially concentrated acid or base solution, where the concentration is often expressed as percent by mass on the bottle. Percent mass is:

% mass = (mass of species of interest / total mass) × 100%

Example: Find the % mass of sodium (Na) in sodium bicarbonate (NaHCO$_3$).

Solution: Use the periodic table to find the atomic mass. Na is 22.99 g/mol, H is 1.01 g/mol, C is 12.01 g/mol and O is 16.00 g/mol. Use this information to find the molecular weight of NaHCO$_3$:

1(22.99) + 1(1.01) + 1(12.01) + 3(16.00) = 84.01 g/mol.

Then, find the percent mass of Na by using the formula given above:

% mass = (22.99 g/mol / 84.01 g/mol) × 100%

% mass = 27.4%

Sometimes concentration is also expressed as % volume, which is calculated in the same manner as % mass.

Mole Concept, Avogadro's Number *N*

In *stoichiometry*, the section of chemistry that involves using quantitative relationships between products and reactants, the quantity of molecules is expressed in the mole unit. *Avogadro's number* (N_A) is the number of particles in 1 mole of a substance, and is equal to 6.02×10^{23}.

In a reaction equation, the mass of a substance and the moles of a substance can be determined for each reactant and product, as seen in the image below.

$\underline{2\ H_2}$ + $\underline{1\ O_2}$ → $\underline{2\ H_2O}$

2 moles = 4 *g*   1 mole = 32 *g*   2 moles = 36 *g*

= 12.04×10^{23} molecules   = 6.02×10^{23} molecules   = 12.04×10^{23} molecules

Most stoichiometry problems follow a set strategy that involve the mole:

Quantity A → Moles A → Moles B → Quantity B

Many stoichiometry problems can be solved using this strategy. Each step will be examined and then combined to solve more complicated problems.

Converting Quantity A to Moles A:

Example: How many moles of $CaCO_3$ are in a 25.0 g sample?

Solution: Calculate the molar mass of $CaCO_3$, using the atomic mass information from the periodic table. The molar mass should be calculated to at least the same number of significant figures as the quantity needed convert:

1 Ca = 40.08 g/mol × 1 = 40.08 g/mol

1 C = 12.01 g/mol × 1 = 12.01 g/mol

3 O = 16.00 g/mol × 3 = 48.00 g/mol

40.08 g/mol + 12.01 g/mol + 48.00 g/mol = 100.09 g/mol $CaCO_3$

Use the molar mass to convert the 25.0 g mass of $CaCO_3$ to moles $CaCO_3$.

25.0 g $CaCO_3$ × (1 mol $CaCO_3$ / 100.09 g $CaCO_3$) = 0.250 mol $CaCO_3$

Converting moles into grams:

Example: Given 0.750 mol $CaCO_3$, the number of grams of $CaCO_3$ is calculated as:

0.750 mol $CaCO_3$ × (100.09 g $CaCO_3$ / 1 mol $CaCO_3$) = 75.1 g $CaCO_3$

Moles A to Moles B Conversions:

Example: How many moles of sodium ion (Na^+) does 0.100 mol of sodium carbonate (Na_2CO_3) have?

Solution: One mole of sodium Na_2CO_3 contains two moles of sodium, one mole of carbon and three moles of oxygen. In a solution, Na_2CO_3 completely dissociates into ions, which is why the sodium atoms are referred to as ions. In this case, compare the moles of sodium carbonate and moles of sodium ions:

0.100 mol Na_2CO_3 × (2 mol Na^+ / 1 mol Na_2CO_3) = 0.200 mol Na^+

Relating Moles of Reactants and Products:

In other problems, a reaction may be involved, and a comparison of two different compounds is necessary. Given a balanced chemical reaction, the stoichiometric coefficients represent the mole ratio between all species. The following is a typical reaction:

$$2 \, KClO_3 \quad \rightarrow \quad 2 \, KCl + 3 \, O_2$$

In this reaction, two moles of potassium chlorate ($KClO_3$) decompose into two moles of potassium chloride (KCl) and three moles of oxygen (O_2). How many O_2 molecules are produced from this reaction?

Solution: If there are 0.400 mol of $KClO_3$ and the moles of O_2 are needed, use the stoichiometric coefficients to set up a mole ratio in which moles of $KClO_3$ cancel and moles of O_2 remain:

0.400 mol $KClO_3$ × (3 mol O_2 / 2 mol $KClO_3$) = 0.600 mol O_2

From moles, the number of particles can be calculated by using Avogadro's number:

0.600 mol O_2 × (6.02×10^{23} molecules O_2 / 1 mol O_2) = 3.61 × 10^{23} O_2 molecules

Notice that the mole units of O_2 successfully cancel in the final answer.

Definition of Density

Density (φ) is the ratio of mass over volume of a given substance. The SI unit of density is kg/m^3.

Specific gravity is a unit-less ratio between the density of some material and the density of a *reference substance* (most times, the reference is water).

Some important density units to remember:

- Density of water = 1 g/mL = 1 g/cm^3

- Specific gravity of water = 1 g/cm^3 / 1 g/cm^3 = 1

- Density of lead = 11 g/cm^3

- Specific gravity of lead = 11 g/cm^3 / 1 g/cm^3 = 11

The densest element on the periodic table is osmium, with density of 22.587 g/cm^3.

The least dense element on the periodic table is hydrogen, with density of 8.99×10^{-5} g/cm^3. It is about 250,000 times less dense than osmium.

Molarity (*M*) of a substance is the moles of solute per liter of solution.

$$\text{Molarity} = \frac{\text{moles of solute}}{\text{L solution}}$$

Molarity is the most common concentration unit used when dealing with solutions.

The molality (*m*) of a substance is the moles of solute per kilogram of solvent, and is described in the chapter on Phase Equilibria.

$$\text{Molality} = \frac{\text{moles of solute}}{\text{kg solvent}}$$

A different unit of measurement is more often used to express the concentration of very dilute solutions. This unit of measurement is known as parts per million (ppm). The definition of parts per million is:

$$ppm = \frac{grams\ of\ solute}{grams\ of\ solution} \times 10^6$$

Since the amount of solute relative to the amount of solvent is typically very small, the density of the overall solution is, to a first approximation, the same as the density of the solvent. For this reason, parts per million may also be expressed in the following way:

$$ppm = \frac{mg\ solute}{kg\ solution}$$

If the solvent is water, which has a density of 1.00 kg/L, then ppm can also be expressed as:

$$ppm = \frac{mg\ solute}{L\ solution}$$

Another unit of measurement used to express the concentration of even more dilute solutions is parts per billion (ppb). The expression for parts per billion is:

$$ppb = \frac{grams\ of\ solute}{grams\ of\ solution} \times 10^9$$

Owing to the dilute nature of the solution, the density of the solution is almost equal to the density of the solvent. Thus, parts per billion may also be expressed as:

$$ppb = \frac{\mu g\ solute}{kg\ solution}$$

$$ppb = \frac{\mu g\ solute}{L\ solution}$$

The *mole fraction* (χ) is the ratio between moles of a specific molecule over the total moles of all components in the mixture.

The *mole percent* (%χ) is the mole ratio multiplied by 100.

$$\chi_{solute} = \frac{mol\ solute}{total\ moles\ of\ all\ components}$$

$$\chi_{solute}\ \% = \frac{mol\ solute}{total\ moles\ of\ all\ components} \times 100$$

When converting between different units, start by choosing an arbitrary amount of solution in the denominator of the concentration to be converted. For example, if converting percent mass to molarity, assume 100 grams of solution. If converting molarity to percent mass, assume one liter of solution.

Example: For a concentrated solution of HCl known to be 37.0% HCl by mass and its density is 1.19 g/ml, what is the molarity, molality and mole fraction of HCl?

Solution: Begin with the valid assumption that the HCl solution is 100 g. Since the % mass of HCl is 37%, that means 37.0 g of the solution is HCl (grams of solute) and the remaining 63.0 g is water (grams of solvent).

To find molarity, determine the moles of HCl (solute) per liter of solution. First, convert the mass of HCl to moles:

$$mol\ HCl = 37.0\ g\ HCl \times \frac{1\ mol\ HCl}{36.5\ g\ HCl} = 1.01\ mol\ HCl$$

Then, using the density of the solution, convert the known mass of solution (100 g) to liters of solution.

$$L\ solution = 100\ g\ solution \times \frac{1\ mL\ solution}{1.19\ g\ solution} \times \frac{1\ L\ solution}{1000\ mL\ solution}$$

$$= 0.0840\ L\ solution$$

Using the moles of solute (HCl) and volume of solution in liters, calculate the molarity (*M*) of the solution as moles of solute per liter of solution:

$$M = \frac{1.01 \text{ mol HCl}}{0.0849 \text{ L solution}} = 12.0 \text{ mol HCl/L solution}$$

$$= 12.0 \, M \text{ HCl}$$

From the information above, find the molality of the HCl solution. The moles of solute are already known (1.01 mol HCl). Determine the mass of solvent (H_2O) in kilograms:

$$63.0 \text{ g } H_2O \times (1 \text{ kg } H_2O \, / \, 1000 \text{ g } H_2O) = 0.0630 \text{ kg } H_2O$$

Using the moles and the mass of solvent, calculate the molality (m or b):

$$m = 1.01 \text{ mol HCl} \, / \, 0.0630 \text{ kg } H_2O = 16.0 \text{ mol HCl/kg } H_2O = 16.0 \text{ m } H_2O$$

Finally, determine the mole fraction of HCl.

From previous calculations, there are 1.01 moles of HCl. Calculate moles of H_2O:

$$\text{mol } H_2O = 63.0 \text{ g } H_2O \times (1 \text{ mol } H_2O \, / \, 18.0 \text{ g } H_2O) = 3.50 \text{ mol } H_2O$$

Now that moles of all molecules present are known, calculate the mole fraction of HCl:

$$\chi_{solute} = \frac{\text{mol solute}}{\text{total moles of all components}}$$

$$\chi_{HCl} = 1.01 \text{ mol HCl} \, / \, (1.01 \text{ mol HCl} + 3.50 \text{ mol } H_2O) = 0.244$$

Oxidation Number

The *oxidation number* (or *oxidation state*) is the charge an atom has, or appears to have, when the electrons of the compound are counted in accordance with a set of rules. Oxidation numbers are typically used in ionic compounds for oxidation-reduction reactions, which involve the transfer of electrons. For compounds that are not ionic, oxidation numbers can be used as a form of bookkeeping to determine if the chemical formula of the compound has been written correctly.

Basic Guidelines in Assigning Oxidation States:

1. The oxidation state of an element is always zero.

2. For main group metals (Groups IA-IIIA), the charge of the ion is the same as the valence electrons or group number.

    a. Important Note: Transition metals, however, do not obey this rule: their oxidation states are sometimes not given by their group number. They may also have multiple oxidation states.

3. The oxygen ion in a compound is typically –2 with the exception of the peroxide ion (O_2^{2-}), which is –1.

4. For polyatomic ions or compounds, the sum of oxidation states is equal to the overall charge of the polyatomic ion or neutral molecule.

Example: Determine the oxidation states of the elements in potassium permanganate ($KMnO_4$).

Solution: Apply rule two. Since potassium is a Group IA alkali metal, its oxidation state must be +1. Assign x to Mn for now, since manganese may exist in several oxidation states. There are four oxygen atoms in the permanganate ion, with oxidation states of –2 per O atom. The overall charge of the neutral compound equals zero:

$$K \quad Mn \quad O_4$$

$$+1 \quad x \quad 4(-2)$$

The algebraic expression is:

$$1 + x - 8 = 0$$

Solving for x gives the oxidation state of manganese:

$$x - 7 = 0$$

$$x = +7$$

$$K \quad Mn \quad O_4$$

$$+1 \quad +7 \quad 4(-2)$$

Example: Now suppose the species under consideration is a polyatomic ion. What is the oxidation state of chromium in dichromate ion $Cr_2O_7^{2-}$?

Solution: As before, start by assigning –2 as the oxidation state for oxygen. Since the oxidation state for chromium is not known, and two chromium atoms are present, assign the algebraic value of $2x$ for chromium:

$$Cr_2 \quad O_7^{2-}$$

$$2x \quad 7(-2)$$

Set up the algebraic equation to solve for x. Since the overall charge of the ion is – 2, the expression is set equal to –2, rather than 0:

$$2x + 7(-2) = -2$$

Solve for x:

$$2x - 14 = -2$$

$$2x = 12$$

$$x = +6$$

Each chromium in the ion has an oxidation state of +6.

Example: What are the oxidation states of the elements in the polyatomic compound $Fe_2(CO_3)_3$?

Solution: Here, two elements (iron and carbon) have more than one possible oxidation state. When considering molecules formed from cations (positive ions) and anions (negative ions), start by splitting the molecule into its constituent ions. Then, determine the charge on each ion.

Iron (Fe) has more than one oxidation state, but a carbonate ion always has an oxidation state of -2 (CO_3^{2-}). With this information, Fe's oxidation state can be determined:

$$Fe_2 \quad (CO_3)^3$$

$$2x \quad 3(-2)$$

$$2x - 6 = 0$$

$$2x = 6$$

$$x = 3$$

Each iron ion in the compound has an oxidation state of $+3$.

Next, consider the carbonate ion independent of the iron (III) ion:

$$CO_3^{2-}$$

$$x \quad 3(-2)$$

$$x - 6 = -2$$

$$x = +4$$

The oxidation state of carbon is $+4$ and each oxygen is -2.

An *oxidation-reduction reaction* is any process whereby a transfer of electrons occurs between two chemicals. For an oxidation-reduction (or redox) reaction to proceed, one substance in a reaction is oxidized, while another substance in the reaction is reduced; reduction or oxidation processes cannot occur separately.

Oxidation involves a loss of electrons. Oxidation is typically associated with metals and may involve the addition of oxygen or removal of hydrogen. *Reduction* involves a gain of electrons. Reduction is normally observed in nonmetals, and may involve the addition of hydrogen or a removal of oxygen.

In biological systems, cells oxidize and reduce metals. A protein called cytochrome c plays an important role in ATP production. This protein contains a Fe^{2+} cation that undergoes oxidation to form Fe^{3+}, followed by a reduction back into Fe^{2+}.

In organic reactions, look for the movement of oxygen and hydrogen. *Combustion* (i.e., burning) is a reaction with oxygen, and it is an example of a redox reaction.

Common oxidizing and reducing agents

An *oxidizing agent* (or *oxidant*) is a substance that oxidizes another substance by removing electrons. The oxidizing agent gains the removed electrons, thus reducing itself. Therefore, the oxidation number of the oxidizing agent becomes less positive.

A *reducing agent* is a substance that reduces another substance by giving away its own electrons to the substance being reduced. Thus, the reducing agent loses these electrons and is oxidized. Therefore, the oxidation number of the reducing agent becomes more positive (or less negative).

Using a number line like shown below may be helpful in identifying the substances being reduced or oxidized, and whether they are oxidizing agents or reducing agents, respectively.

Oxidation number decreased, substance reduced

$\longrightarrow$

-|---|---|---|---|---|---|---|---|---|---|---

–5 –4 –3 –2 –1 0 +1 +2 +3 +4 +5

$\longleftarrow$

Oxidation number increased, substance oxidized

The image below summarizes the relationship between reducing agents and oxidizing agents. Essentially, atoms that lose electrons during a chemical reaction undergo oxidation. Atoms that gain electrons during a chemical reaction undergo reduction.

The oxidized species is the reducing agent, and the reduced species is the oxidizing agent.

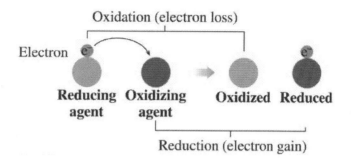

A useful mnemonic for remembering what is happening to the electrons in a redox reaction is "OIL RIG," which stands for "**O**xidation **I**s **L**oss, **R**eduction **I**s **G**ain. Remember that this mnemonic device refers to the loss and gain of electrons.

Example 1: Identify the substance being oxidized, the substance being reduced, the oxidizing agent and the reducing agent in the following reaction:

$$Cu\ (s) + 4\ HNO_3\ (aq) \rightarrow Cu(NO_3)_2\ (aq) + 2\ NO_2\ (g) + 2\ H_2O\ (l)$$

Solution: Determine the oxidation state for each element in the reactants and products.

Elemental copper, Cu (s), has an oxidation state of zero (0).

For nitric acid, HNO_3, set N equal to x:

$$H \quad N \quad O_3$$

$$+1 \quad x \quad 3(-2)$$

$$1 + x - 6 = 0$$

$$x = +5$$

$$H = +1, N = +5, O = -2$$

For copper (II) nitrate, $Cu(NO_3)_2$:

$$Cu(NO_3)_2$$

Nitrates are always -1, while Cu might be $+1$ or $+2$.

$$Cu(NO_3)_2$$

$$Cu \quad (NO_3)_2$$

$$x + 2(-1) = 0$$

$$x = 2$$

In this example, Cu's oxidation state is $+2$. Oxygen is -2.

For nitrate ion, NO_3^-, set N equal to x:

$$N \quad O_3^-$$

$$x \quad 3(-2)$$

$$x - 6 = -1$$

$$x = +5$$

$$\text{so, } Cu = +2, N = +5, O = -2$$

For nitrogen dioxide, NO_2, set N equal to x:

$$N \quad O_2$$

$$x \quad 2(-2)$$

$$x - 4 = 0$$

$$x = +4$$

so, N = +4, O = –2

For water, H_2O:

$$H_2 \quad O$$

$$2(+1) \quad -2$$

so, H = +1, O = –2

Element	Oxidation State: Reactants	Oxidation State: Products
Cu	0	+2
H	+1	+1
N	+5	+5 (in NO_3^-), +4 (in NO_2)
O	–2	–2

The next step is to identify the molecules that changed oxidation states.

Copper's oxidation number increased from 0 to +2, which means that copper has been oxidized (lost electrons), and therefore it is the reducing agent. Copper reduced nitric acid by giving away its own electrons to the nitrogen in nitric acid.

Similarly, the nitrogen in nitric acid changed from +5 to +4 in nitrogen dioxide, which means that nitric acid has been reduced by copper. Since the nitric acid has been reduced, it is the oxidizing agent.

Oxidation cannot occur without also having a reduction.

Table of common oxidizing and reducing agents:

Common oxidizing agents	Common reducing agents
Oxygen O_2, Ozone O_3, Permanganates MnO_4^-, Chromates CrO_{42}^-, Dichromates $Cr_2O_7^{2-}$, peroxides H_2O_2, Lewis acids, compounds with many oxygens	Hydrogen H_2, metals (such as K), Zn/HCl, Sn/HCl, LAH (Lithium Aluminum Hydride), $NaBH_4$ (Sodium Borohydride), Lewis bases, compounds with many hydrogens

Disproportionation reactions

In *disproportionation reactions*, an atom undergoes both oxidation and reduction to form two different atoms with different oxidation states. Consider the following reaction:

$$2Cu^+ \rightarrow Cu + Cu^{2+}$$

Here, the Cu^+ acts as both oxidizing and reducing agent and simultaneously reduces and oxidizes itself. The oxidized Cu^+ becomes Cu^{2+}. The reduced Cu^+ becomes Cu.

Redox titration

Titration, or *volumetric analysis*, is a common experimental procedure carried out in the lab to determine the unknown concentration of a given substance. A reagent of known concentration is slowly added to a sample of unknown concentration, until the neutralization reaction (i.e., reaction between an acid and a base) is complete. The *analyte* is the substance of unknown concentration being analyzed, and the *titrant* is the analytical reagent of known concentration being added to the sample. For more information, refer to the chapter on acid-base neutralization.

To determine the endpoint of a redox titration (i.e., when all the sample molecules have been used), an *indicator* is added to the reaction. A redox indicator undergoes a definite color change at the equivalence point of the neutralization reaction.

An example of a redox reaction is the titration of ascorbic acid (a form of vitamin C) using iodine. Ascorbic acid oxidizes iodine to form iodide ions. Starch is added as an indicator because excess iodine reacts with starch and turn the solution's color from clear to dark blue. Using the initial volume of ascorbic acid (analyte), and the measured volume of iodine (titrant) added, the concentration of ascorbic acid can be calculated.

Description of Reactions by Chemical Equations

Predicting the products which will form in a given reaction is no easy task. Since many chemical compounds exist, memorizing every possible reaction is not necessary. Fortunately, most chemical reactions can be classified into several groups. Being able to identify the type of reaction is a major step towards predicting the products of a given chemical reaction. The most important classes of reactions encountered in general chemistry are shown in the figure below:

Reaction Type	General Reaction Scheme
Synthesis	$A + B \rightarrow AB$
Decomposition	$AB \rightarrow A + B$
Replacement	$AB + C \rightarrow AC + B$ (single)
	$AB + CD \rightarrow AD + CB$ (double)

1. *Combination* (Synthesis) *Reactions*: Two (or more) substances react to form a single product. The general form of reaction is $A + B \rightarrow AB$, in which two substances combine to form one compound.

2. *Decomposition Reactions*: One material reacts to form two or more products. This is the reverse of a combination reaction. The general form of this type of reaction is $AB \rightarrow A + B$, in which one compound decomposes to form two (or more) of its constituent elements.

3. *Replacement Reactions* (also called substitution or displacement reactions): One atom or group replaces another species in a compound.

   o In a *Single Replacement Reaction*, an element replaces the corresponding element in a compound. The general form of this type of reaction is $AB + C \rightarrow AC + B$, in which element C is replacing element B.

○ In a *Double Replacement* (or *Metathesis Reaction*), two compounds react and switch partners; cations and anions in one compound exchange places with their counterparts in the other compound. The general form of this type of reaction is AB + CD → AD + CB.

○ <u>Important Note</u>: In both of these types of replacement reactions, the number of substances on the reactant side of the equation is the *same* as on the product side.

These are some examples of more specific types of reactions.

• Oxidation-Reduction Reaction (also called *redox*): A transfer of electrons occurs between the two reactants. A loss of electrons (increase in oxidation number) is oxidation, while a gain of electrons (or decrease in oxidation number) is reduction.

○ Many combination and decomposition reactions involve oxidation and reduction, as well as all single displacement reactions.

• *Combustion* involves a carbon-containing molecule (e.g., a hydrocarbon) reacting with oxygen to produce carbon dioxide (CO_2) and water (H_2O).

○ Combustion reactions tend to be highly exothermic and are considered irreversible, and therefore spontaneous (refer to the chapter on thermodynamics).

○ Combustion reactions are a type of decomposition reaction and are also oxidation-reduction reactions. Combustion reactions use O_2 and produce energy, which dissipates as heat or performs useful work.

○ The general formula for the combustion of a hydrocarbon:

$$C_xH_y + O_2 \rightarrow CO_2 + H_2O$$

• *Condensation* involves water being produced as part of a double replacement reaction. Condensation reactions occur among functional groups that contain –H and –OH: those two groups break away from their respective compounds and form H_2O.

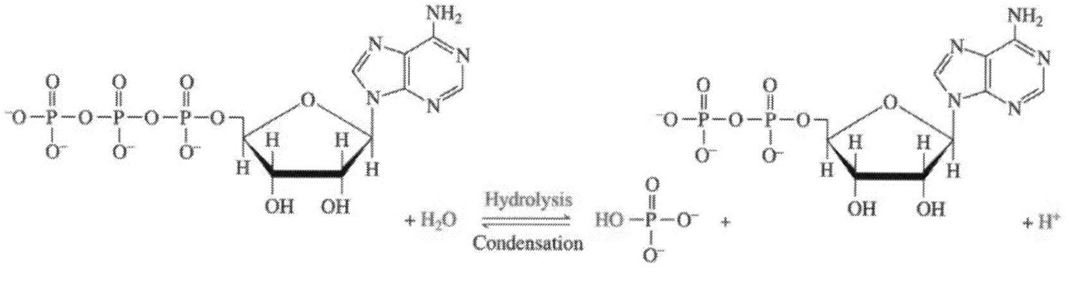

Adenosine triphosphate (ATP)   Adenosine diphosphate (ADP) + Energy

- *Hydrolysis* (hydro- means "water," lysis means "break") is the reverse process of condensation, where water is consumed as a reactant and the other reactant molecule is split into two smaller molecules in the products. An example of hydrolysis (and the reverse condensation reaction) is shown in the figure above. The more general form is shown in the figure below.

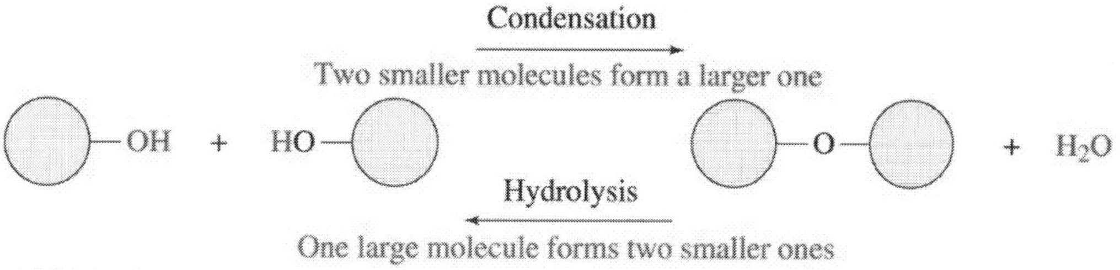

- *Carboxylation* reactions involve the addition of a carboxyl ($-C=O$) or carboxylic acid (–COOH) group. As carbon dioxide moves through the cell, it is added to and removed from biomolecules by the two enzymes carboxylase and decarboxylase, respectively.

- An example of carboxylation is shown in the figure below.

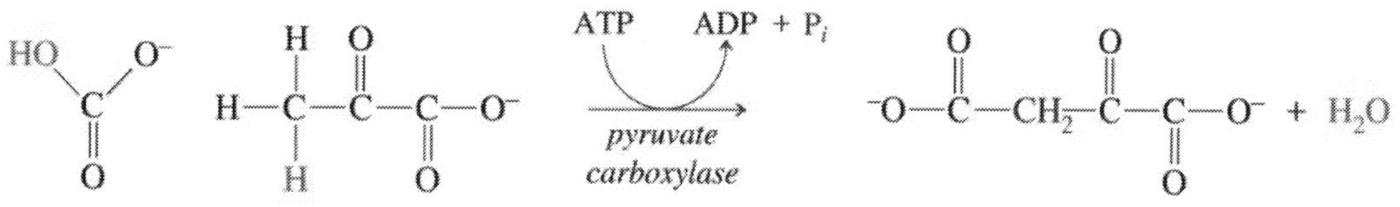

Bicarbonate   Pyruvate   Oxaloacetate

Conventions for writing chemical equations

Chemical equations have several important parts:

$$H_2SO_4\ (aq) + 2\ NaOH\ (aq) \rightarrow 2\ Na^+\ (aq) + SO_4^{2-}\ (aq) + 2\ H_2O$$

phase   coefficient   direction   charge

- The *phase* of a substance is indicated with a letter subscript, such as solid (*s*), liquid (*l*), gas (*g*) or aqueous solution (*aq*).

- The *coefficient* indicates the quantity or moles of reactant or product, relative to other components in the reaction.

- The *direction* is represented as single-headed arrow, which denotes the forward direction of the reaction as written.

  o *Reversible reactions* are at a state of *chemical equilibrium* and are represented with a double-headed arrow. This indicates that the rates of the forward and reverse reactions are equal and constant and no net products are formed.

  o A double-sided arrow with one side *larger* than the other denotes a *nonequilibrum condition*, which spontaneously favors the direction of the larger arrow.

- The *charge* is indicated with a numerical superscript and +/– sign. It is common practice to not indicate the charge on a neutral compound or substance.

Balancing equations including redox equations

The *law of mass conservation* (refer to the chapter on thermodynamics) states that atoms are neither created nor destroyed in a chemical reaction—they are simply rearranged.

Therefore, in a chemical reaction, the coefficients of the reactants and products have to be balanced, which means that there are equivalent amounts of all atoms on both sides of the reaction.

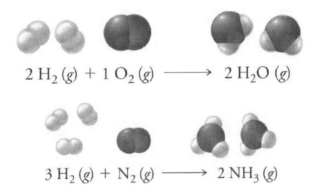

$$2\ H_2\ (g) + 1\ O_2\ (g) \longrightarrow 2\ H_2O\ (g)$$

$$3\ H_2\ (g) + N_2\ (g) \longrightarrow 2\ NH_3\ (g)$$

To balance a given chemical equation, coefficients are assigned to each species until all atoms are balanced on both sides.

Example: Balance the combustion of propanol: $C_3H_8O + O_2 \rightarrow CO_2 + H_2O$

Solution: Pick the atom (or ion) that is only present in one species on each side of the equation. Start with carbon. Add the coefficient 3 to CO_2 on the right side since there are three carbons on the left side, indicated by C_3.

$$C_3H_8O + O_2 \rightarrow \mathbf{3}\ CO_2 + H_2O$$

Next, hydrogen is the other species present in one molecule on each side, so the hydrogens can be balanced. Add the coefficient 4 to H_2O on the right side because $4 \times 2 = 8$, equals the number of hydrogens on the left side, indicated by H_8.

$$C_3H_8O + O_2 \rightarrow 3\ CO_2 + \mathbf{4}\ H_2O$$

Starting with hydrogen before balancing carbon yields the same result.

Balance all the elements that are present in one species on each side first, because it prevents needing to go back to change coefficients of species that are already balanced.

Oxygen is present in every term of the equation, so if O was balanced first, it would be more difficult. However, because of the adjustments made to balance the other atoms, at this point there is only one oxygen-containing species that has not yet been balanced.

Count oxygen atoms: there is one from C_3H_8O, six from 3 CO_2 (because $3 \times 2 = 6$) and four from 4 H_2O.

Set up this equation: $1 + 2x = (3 \times 2) + 4$, where x is the coefficient of the last term, O_2. Solve for x, which equals $^9/_2$.

$$C_3H_8O + x\,\mathbf{O_2} \rightarrow 3\ CO_2 + 4\ H_2O$$

$$C_3H_8O + {^9/_2}\,\mathbf{O_2} \rightarrow 3\ CO_2 + 4\ H_2O$$

Remove any fractions, so multiply every term by 2.

$$2\ C_3H_8O + 9\ O_2 \rightarrow 6\ CO_2 + 8\ H_2O$$

With all non-integer coefficients removed, the equation is now balanced.

When solving oxidation-reduction equations, a different approach is required. Balancing redox reactions is a much more complicated; it involves splitting the redox reaction into half-reactions. There are two methods of balancing half-reactions:

- *The Ion-Electron Method*: balance the elements first, then balance charge by adding electrons.

- *The Oxidation-State Method*: treat the species of interest as a single element (i.e., undergo a change in oxidation number) and then balance it.

Learn the following procedure when approaching problems that require the balancing of oxidation-reduction reactions:

1. Separate the equation into two *half-reactions*. A half-reaction contains only the species of interest (i.e., those containing the atom that undergoes a change in oxidation state).

   a. Each half-reaction corresponds to the oxidation half-reaction or reduction half-reaction. Anything that is not covalently attached to the atom is not part of the species of interest. A species that does not undergo a change in oxidation state is a *spectator ion*, (i.e., an ion that is present in solution but is not involved in the reaction).

2. Balance each of the separate half-reactions with respect to both the *charge* and *number of atoms*.

    a. There are two methods for balancing oxygen elements:

        i. Under acidic conditions: add H_2O to the side that needs the oxygen atom, then add H^+ to the other side.

        ii. Under basic conditions: add 2 OH^- to the side that needs the oxygen atom, then add H_2O to the other side.

3. After the half-reactions are balanced, recombine the half-reactions:

    a. Multiply each half-reaction by a factor, such that when they are added together, the electrons cancel.

    b. It is similar to solving a simultaneous equation where the electron term must be eliminated.

4. Lastly, perform these additional steps:

    a. Combine identical species on the same side of the equation.

    b. Cancel identical species on opposite sides of the equation.

    c. Add back in the spectator ions.

    d. For the oxidation-state method, now balance the oxygen and hydrogen elements.

    e. Check that both sides of the equation have an equal number of atoms and neutral net charge.

Example: Balance the redox reaction below using the ion-electron method:

$$K_2Cr_2O_7 \, (aq) + HCl \, (aq) \rightarrow KCl \, (aq) + CrCl_3 \, (aq) + H_2O \, (l) + Cl_2 \, (g)$$

Solution: Step 1 – Separate into half-reactions:

- Reduction: $Cr_2O_7^{2-} \rightarrow Cr^{3+}$

- Oxidation: $Cl^- \rightarrow Cl_2$

The species of interest for the oxidation reaction is Cl^- (not HCl), because the H^+ is not covalently attached to Cl^- and the ions separate in an aqueous solution.

Similarly, $Cr_2O_7^{2-}$ is used, not $K_2Cr_2O_7$, because K^+ and H^+ are spectator ions.

Step 2 – Balance each of the half-reactions:

For the ion-electron method, balance the elements first, then balance charge.

Balance elements for the reduction half-reaction (ion-electron method):

1. $Cr_2O_7^{2-} \rightarrow Cr^{3+}$

2. $Cr_2O_7^{2-} \rightarrow 2Cr^{3+}$

3. $Cr_2O_7^{2-} + 14 \, H^+ \rightarrow 2 \, Cr^{3+} + 7 \, H_2O$

Balance charge for the reduction half-reaction (ion-electron method):

1. $Cr_2O_7^{2-} + 14 \, H^+ + 6 \, e^- \rightarrow 2 \, Cr^{3+} + 7 \, H_2O$

Balance charge for the oxidation half-reaction (ion-electron method):

1. $Cl^- \rightarrow Cl_2$

2. $2 \, Cl^- \rightarrow Cl_2$

3. $2 \, Cl^- \rightarrow Cl_2 + 2 \, e^-$

Step 3 – Recombine the half-reactions:

- $Cr_2O_7^{2-} + 14\ H^+ + 6\ e^- \rightarrow 2\ Cr^{3+} + 7\ H_2O$

- $2\ Cl^- \rightarrow Cl_2 + 2\ e^-$

Multiply each species in the second equation by 3:

- $6\ Cl^- \rightarrow 3\ Cl_2 + 6\ e^-$

Add the two equations:

- $Cr_2O_7^{2-} + 14\ H^+ + 6\ e^- + 6\ Cl^- \rightarrow 2\ Cr_3+ + 7\ H_2O + 3\ Cl_2 + 6\ e^-$

Step 4 – Complete the process:

Except for the electrons, there are no identical species to combine or cancel at this time.

- $Cr_2O_7^{2-} + 14\ H^+ + 6\ Cl^- \rightarrow 2\ Cr^{3+} + 7\ H_2O + 3\ Cl_2$

Step 5 – For the ion-electron method, the equation is now balanced. However, the spectator ions need to be added into the equation. When adding the spectator ions, always add equal numbers of ions to both sides of the reaction.

- To the left side: The dichromate ion was paired with K^+, so add 2 K^+ for the dichromate.

- To the right side: Match the left side by adding 2 K^+ ions.

$$K_2Cr_2O_7 + 14\ H^+ + 6\ Cl^- \rightarrow 2\ Cr^{3+} + 7\ H_2O + 3\ Cl_2 + \textbf{2 K}^+$$

Step 6 – There are 14 H^+ on the left side and 14 on the right, so they are balanced. Referring back to the original equation, the H and Cl elements on the left originated from the HCl. Add 8 Cl elements to the product side.

- $K_2Cr_2O_7 + 14\ HCl \rightarrow 2\ Cr^{3+} + 7\ H_2O + 3\ Cl_2 + 2\ K^+ + \textbf{8 Cl}^-$

Step 7 – The right side shows that two of the Cl^- need to be combined with the 2 K^+, and the remaining 6 Cl^- goes with the Cr.

Thus, the final balanced redox equation is:

$$K_2Cr_2O_7 \ (aq) + 14 \ HCl \ (aq) \rightarrow \mathbf{2 \ CrCl_3} \ (aq) + 7 \ H_2O \ (l) + 3 \ Cl_2 \ (g) + \mathbf{2 \ KCl} \ (aq)$$

Example: Balance the same reaction using the oxidation-state method:

$$K_2Cr_2O_7 \ (aq) + HCl \ (aq) \rightarrow KCl \ (aq) + CrCl_3 \ (aq) + H_2O \ (l) + Cl_2 \ (g)$$

Step 1 - Separate into half-reactions (same as the ion-electron method):

$$\text{Reduction: } Cr_2O_7^{2-} \rightarrow Cr^{3+}$$

$$\text{Oxidation: } Cl^- \rightarrow Cl_2$$

Step 2 - Balance each half reaction.

Balance the elements of interest first when using the oxidation-state method.

Balance the elements for the reduction half reaction (oxidation-state method):

1. $Cr_2O_7^{2-} \rightarrow Cr^{3+}$

2. $Cr_2O_7^{2-} \rightarrow 2 \ Cr^{3+}$

3. Each oxygen is 2^- so the 2 Cr on the left must be 6^+

4. $2 \ Cr^{6+} \rightarrow 2 \ Cr^{3+}$

Balance charge for the elements in the reduction half-reaction (oxidation-state method):

1. $2 \ Cr^{6+} + 6 \ e^- \rightarrow 2 \ Cr^{3+}$

Balance charge for the oxidation half-reaction (oxidation-state method):

1. $Cl^- \rightarrow Cl_2$

2. $2 \ Cl^- \rightarrow Cl_2$

3. $2 \ Cl^- \rightarrow 2 \ Cl^0$

4. $2 \ Cl^- \rightarrow 2 \ Cl^0 + 2 \ e^-$

Step 3 - Recombine the half-reactions:

$$2 \, Cr^{6+} + 6 \, e^- \rightarrow 2 \, Cr^{3+}$$

$$2 \, Cl^- \rightarrow 2 \, Cl^0 + 2 \, e^-$$

To cancel the electrons, multiply each term in the second equation by 3:

$$2 \, Cr^{6+} + 6 \, e^- \rightarrow 2 \, Cr^{3+}$$

$$6 \, Cl^- \rightarrow 6 \, Cl^0 + 6 \, e^-$$

Add the two equations:

$$2 \, Cr^{6+} + 6 \, e^- + 6 \, Cl^- \rightarrow 2 \, Cr^{3+} + 6 \, Cl^0 + 6 \, e^-$$

Step 4 - Except for the electrons, there are no like terms to combine or cancel.

$$2 \, Cr^{6+} + 6 \, Cl^- \rightarrow 2 \, Cr^{3+} + 6 \, Cl^0$$

Convert the elements into species by referring to the original equation.

$$K_2Cr_2O_7 + 6 \, HCl \rightarrow 2 \, CrCl_3 + 3 \, Cl_2$$

Unlike the ion-electron method, where the equation is balanced and spectator ions are added into the equation, the oxidation-state method requires the equation to be balanced again. This is because after the elements are combined to recreate the molecules, the equation is no longer balanced.

Step 5 - Oxygen: there are seven O atoms on the left, so add 7 H_2O molecules to the right. (Remember that this method applies to acidic reactions – refer to the explanation for basic reactions).

$$K_2Cr_2O_7 + 6 \, HCl \rightarrow 2 \, CrCl_3 + 3 \, Cl_2 + \mathbf{7 \, H_2O}$$

Step 6 - Hydrogen: there are 6 H atoms on the left, but 14 H atoms on the right. Eight H atoms should be added to the left for a total of 14 H atoms. All 14 H atoms on the left should be as HCl (refer to the original equation).

$$K_2Cr_2O_7 + \mathbf{14 \, HCl} \rightarrow 2 \, CrCl_3 + 3 \, Cl_2 + 7 \, H_2O$$

<u>Important Note</u>: HCl here is both the species of interest and also the spectator species. Some of the HCl contributes to the $Cl^- \rightarrow Cl_2$ oxidation, but the other HCl do not undergo redox. It merely provides the H^+ ions for the water and the Cl^- ions for the KCl and $CrCl_3$.

Step 7 - Chlorine: there are 14 Cl atoms on the left, and 12 Cl atoms on the right. Add 2 Cl atoms to the right. Referring to the original equation, all the right-sided Cl atoms come in the form of KCl (do not modify the Cl_2 since it has already been balanced by the oxidation state method. When balancing equations at this stage, only manipulate the water and spectator species.

$$K_2Cr_2O_7 + 14\,HCl \rightarrow 2\,CrCl_3 + 3\,Cl_2 + 7\,H_2O + \textbf{2 KCl}$$

Upon examination, every element is balanced. The balanced redox equation is:

$$K_2Cr_2O_7\,(aq) + 14\,HCl\,(aq) \rightarrow 2\,CrCl_3\,(aq) + 3\,Cl_2\,(g) + 7\,H_2O\,(l) + 2\,KCl\,(aq)$$

<u>Summary of Steps for Balancing Redox Half-Reactions</u>:

1. Split the equation into two half-reactions.

2. Balance any atom other than O or H.

3. Balance oxygens using H_2O. Add water as needed to balance oxygens on the side deficient in O.

4. Balance hydrogens using H^+ if in acidic solution. Add H^+ ions as needed to the side deficient in H.

5. If in basic solution, add OH^- ions equal to the number of H^+ ions to both sides of the chemical equation.

6. The mass should now be balanced. To balance the charge, determine the charge on each side of the reaction, and add electrons as needed to the more positive side, so the charge is the same on each side.

7. Repeat steps 1 through 4 for both half-reactions.

8. If the number of electrons lost does not equal the number of electrons gained, multiply each half-reaction by the necessary factor.

9. Sum both half-reactions to obtain the balanced, net ionic reaction. In many cases, inspect for H^+ ions and H_2O molecules to cancel.

10. Check the final equation for mass and charge balance.

<u>Important Note</u>: If expressing H^+ as H_3O^+, then change the number of H^+ into the same number of H_3O^+ and add that same number of H_2O to the opposite side of the equation.

Limiting reactants

The *limiting reactant* is the component of a chemical reaction in the lowest stoichiometric quantity, which limits the amount of product that can be formed in a reaction. Therefore, the limiting reactant is the reagent that is depleted first and stops the reaction.

Example: Consider a 50.6 g sample of magnesium hydroxide $Mg(OH)_2$ that reacts with 45.0 g of hydrogen chloride HCl, according to the reaction given below:

$$Mg(OH)_2 + 2\ HCl \rightarrow MgCl_2 + 2\ H_2O$$

Solution: Identify the limiting reactant of this reaction. Notice how quantities of both reactants are known. There are numerous ways of approaching a limiting reagent problem.

Method 1 for determining limiting reactants

To identify the limiting reagent, convert each of the grams of reactants given to moles using their molar mass:

$$50.6\ g\ Mg(OH)_2 \times (1\ mol\ Mg(OH)_2 / 58.3\ g\ Mg(OH)_2) = 0.868\ mol\ Mg(OH)_2$$

$$45.0\ g\ HCl \times (1\ mol\ HCl / 36.5\ g\ HCl) = 1.23\ mol\ HCl$$

Select one of these reactants and calculate how many moles of the other reactant is needed to completely use up the reactant picked. For example, begin with magnesium hydroxide:

$$0.868\ mol\ Mg(OH)_2 \times (2\ mol\ HCl\ needed / 1\ mol\ Mg(OH)_2) = 1.74\ mol\ HCl\ needed$$

Compare the moles of HCl needed to the actual moles of HCl available. In this example, 1.74 mole of HCl is needed and 1.23 mole of HCl is available. So, even though it appears that there are more moles of HCl than $Mg(OH)_2$, HCl is the limiting reagent. The HCl is completely consumed before the magnesium hydroxide, thereby limiting the amount of product formed.

Method 2 for determining limiting reactants

This method compares the *theoretical ratio* of the reactants to the *actual ratio* of reactants available. First, determine the moles of each reactant using their molar mass:

$50.6 \ g \ Mg(OH)_2 \times (1 \ mol \ Mg(OH)_2 \ / \ 58.3 \ g \ Mg(OH)_2) = 0.868 \ mol \ Mg(OH)_2$ available

$45.0 \ g \ HCl \times (1 \ mol \ HCl \ / \ 36.5 \ g \ HCl) = 1.23 \ mol \ HCl$ available

Consider the balanced reaction:

$$Mg(OH)_2 + 2 \ HCl \rightarrow MgCl_2 + 2 \ H_2O$$

From the balanced equation, the theoretical mole ratio is:

$$2 \text{ moles of HCl needed } / \ 1 \text{ mol } Mg(OH)_2$$

The actual mole ratio, based on the actual amounts of reactants present:

$$\frac{1.23 \, \text{mol HCl}}{0.868 \, \text{mol Mg(OH)}_2} = \frac{1.42 \, \text{mol HCl present}}{1 \, \text{mol Mg(OH)}_2}$$

Comparing these two ratios, one can easily see that there is not enough HCl, so HCl must be the limiting reagent:

$(2 \text{ mol HCl needed } / \ 1 \text{ mol } Mg(OH)_2)$ compared to $(1.42 \text{ mol HCl present } / \ 1 \text{ mol } Mg(OH)_2)$

Method 3

Calculate the theoretical yield of product produced by each reactant and choose the lesser amount:

$50.6 \ g \ Mg(OH)_2 \times (1 \ mol \ Mg(OH)_2 \ / \ 58.3 \ g \ Mg(OH)_2) \times (1 \ mol \ MgCl_2 \ / \ 1 \ mol \ Mg(OH)_2)$
$\times (95.3 \ g \ MgCl_2 \ / \ 1 \ mol \ MgCl_2) = 82.7 \ g \ MgCl_2$

45.0 g HCl × (1 mol HCl / 36.5 g HCl) × (1 mol $MgCl_2$ / 2 mol HCl) × (95.3 g $MgCl_2$ / 1 mol $MgCl_2$) = 58.6 g $MgCl_2$

Since HCl produced less product, HCl is the limiting reagent and 58.6 g $MgCl_2$ is the theoretical yield.

Theoretical yields

The *theoretical yield* is the calculated amount of product expected from a reaction. In reality, reactions almost always yield less product than the predicted yield for various reasons (e.g., equipment inefficiency or human error). The ratio between experimental (actual) and theoretical yields is called *percent yield.*

percent yield = (experimental yield / theoretical yield) × 100%

Example: If the reaction of 30.0 grams of calcium carbonate ($CaCO_3$) produces 15.0 grams of calcium oxide, (CaO), what is the percent yield for the following reaction?

$$CaCO_3 \rightarrow CaO + CO_2$$

Solution: It is known that the experimental yield was 15.0 g, so now the theoretical yield needs to be determined. For every mole of $CaCO_3$ reacted, there is one mole of CaO produced.

Using the periodic table, the molar mass of $CaCO_3$ is 100.0896 and the molar mass of CaO is 56.0774. Use these conversion factors to perform the stoichiometric calculations and determine the theoretical yield.

30.0 g $CaCo_3$ × (1 mol $CaCO_3$ / 100.0869 g) × (1 mol CaO / 1 mol $CaCO_3$) × (56.0774 g CaO / 1 mol CaO) = 16.8 g CaO

Theoretical yield = 16.8 g CaO

Then, use the formula given above to calculate the percent yield.

% Yield = (Actual Yield / Theoretical Yield) × 100%

% Yield = (15.0 g CaO / 16.8 g CaO) × 100% = 89.3%

% Yield = 89.3%

Practice Questions

1. Which substance listed below is the strongest reducing agent, given the following spontaneous redox reaction?

$$Mg\ (s) + Sn^{2+}\ (aq) \rightarrow Mg^{2+}\ (aq) + Sn\ (s)$$

A. Sn   **B.** Mg^{2+} **C.** Sn^{2+} **D.** Mg

2. Which of the following is a guideline for balancing redox equations by the oxidation number method?

    A. Verify that the total number of atoms and the total ionic charge are the same for reactants and products

    B. In front of the substance reduced, place a coefficient that corresponds to the number of electrons lost by the substance oxidized

    C. In front of the substance oxidized, place a coefficient that corresponds to the number of electrons gained by the substance reduced

    D. All of the above

3. Which of the following represents the oxidation of Co^{2+}?

    A. $Co \rightarrow Co^{2+} + 2\ e^-$ **C.** $Co^{2+} + 2\ e^- \rightarrow Co$

    B. $Co^{3+} + e^- \rightarrow Co^{2+}$ **D.** $Co^{2+} \rightarrow Co^{3+} + e^-$

4. What is the molecular formula of a compound that has an empirical formula of CHCl with a molar mass of 194 g/mol?

    A. $C_4H_4Cl_4$ **C.** $C_3H_5Cl_3$

    B. $C_2H_4Cl_3$ **D.** CHCl

5. What is the term for the amount of substance that contains 6.02×10^{23} particles?

    A. molar mass   **C.** Avogadro's number

    B. mole   **D.** formula mass

6. How many grams are in 0.7 mole of $CaCO_3$?

    A. 25 g   **B.** 40 g   **C.** 70 g   **D.** 48 g

7. What is the coefficient for CO_2 in the balanced reaction?

$$\_\_C_5H_{12} + \_\_O_2 \rightarrow \_\_CO_2 + \_\_H_2O$$

    A. 5   **B.** 7   **C.** 8   **D.** 10

8. What are the products for this double-replacement reaction?

$BaCl_2$ (*aq*) + K_2SO_4 (*aq*) →

A. $BaSO_3$ and $KClO_4$

B. $BaSO_4$ and 2 KCl

C. BaS and $KClO_4$

D. $BaSO_3$ and KCl

9. Which coefficients balance the following equation: __P_4 (*s*) + __H_2 (*g*) → __PH_3 (*g*)?

A. 2, 10, 8

B. 1, 4, 4

C. 1, 6, 4

D. 4, 2, 3

10. After balancing the following redox reaction in acidic solution, what is the coefficient of H^+?

Mg (*s*) + NO_3^- (*aq*) → Mg^{2+} (*aq*) + NO_2 (*aq*)

A. 1   **B.** 2   **C.** 4   **D.** 6

11. How many atoms are in a sample of phosphorus trifluoride (PF_3) that contains 1.40 moles?

A. 3.37×10^{24}

B. 5.38

C. 3.46

D. 2.218×10^{24}

12. Which of the following is the percent mass composition of acetic acid (CH_3COOH)?

A. 48% carbon, 8% hydrogen and 44% oxygen

B. 52% carbon, 12% hydrogen and 36% oxygen

C. 32% carbon, 6% hydrogen and 62% oxygen

D. 40% carbon, 7% hydrogen and 53% oxygen

13. If one mole of Ag is produced in the following reaction, how many grams of O_2 gas are produced?

$2 Ag_2O → 4 Ag + O_2$

A. 6g   **B.** 8g   **C.** 2g   **D.** 12g

14. Which metal in the free state has an oxidation number of zero?

A. Mg

B. Na

C. Al

D. All of the above

15. What is the oxidation number of Cr in $K_2Cr_2O_7$?

A. +6   **B.** +5   **C.** +4   **D.** +2

Solutions

1. D is correct.

Use the mnemonic OIL RIG: <u>O</u>xidation <u>I</u>s <u>L</u>oss, <u>R</u>eduction <u>I</u>s <u>G</u>ain (of electrons).

Oxidation is the loss of electrons, while reduction is the gain of electrons.

An oxidizing agent undergoes reduction, while a reducing agent undergoes oxidation.

Because the reaction is spontaneous, the reducing agent as a reactant is the strongest reducing agent in the reaction.

Mg is the reducing agent being oxidized because it went from 0 as a reactant to +2 as a product.

2. D is correct.

All statements are correct for balancing redox equations by the oxidation number method.

3. D is correct.

Use the mnemonic OIL RIG: <u>O</u>xidation <u>I</u>s <u>L</u>oss, <u>R</u>eduction <u>I</u>s <u>G</u>ain (of electrons).

Oxidation is the loss of electrons, while reduction is the gain of electrons.

An oxidizing agent undergoes reduction, while a reducing agent undergoes oxidation.

Co^{2+} is the starting reactant because it has to lose electrons and produce an ion with a higher oxidation number.

4. A is correct.

Formula mass is a synonym for molecular mass/molecular weight (MW).

Start by calculating the mass of the formula unit (CHCl):

$$CHCl = (12.01 \text{ g/mol} + 1.01 \text{ g/mol} + 35.45 \text{ g/mol}) = 48.47 \text{ g/mol}$$

Divide the molar mass by the formula unit mass:

$$194 \text{ g/mol} / 48.47 \text{ g/mol} = 4.0025$$

Round it to the closest whole number: 4

Multiply the formula unit by 4:

$$(CHCl)_4 = C_4H_4Cl_4$$

5. B is correct.

A mole is a unit of measurement used to express amounts of a chemical substance.

The number of molecules in a mole is 6.02×10^{23}, which is Avogadro's number.

However, Avogadro's number relates to the number of molecules, not the amount of substance.

Molar mass refers to the mass per mole of a substance.

Formula mass is a term that is sometimes used to mean molecular mass or molecular weight, and it refers to the mass of a certain molecule.

6. C is correct.

MW of $CaCO_3$:

$(Ca = 40.08$ g/mol$) + (C = 12$ g/mol$) + (O = 3 \times 16$ g/mol$) = 100$ g/mol

Mass of 0.7 moles of $CaCO_3$:

0.7 mole $CaCO_3 \times 100$ g/mole $= 70$ g $CaCO_3$

7. A is correct.

The number of oxygens on both sides of the reaction equation must be equal.

On the right side, there are 5 CO_2 molecules; since each CO_2 molecule contains 2 oxygens, multiply $5 \times 2 = 10$.

Also on the right side are 6 H_2O molecules; $6 \times 1 = 6$.

Add 10 and 6 to get the total number of oxygens on the right side: $10 + 6 = 16$.

Since there are 16 oxygens on the right side, there should be 16 oxygens on the left side.

Each O_2 molecule contains 2 oxygens; $16 / 2 = 8$.

Therefore, the coefficient 8 is needed to balance the equation.

Balanced equation (combustion):

$C_5H_{12} + 8\ O_2 \rightarrow 5\ CO_2 + 6\ H_2O$

8. B is correct.

Balanced reaction:

$BaCl_2$ (*aq*) $+ K_2SO_4$ (*aq*) $\rightarrow BaSO_4$ and 2 KCl

Double replacement reaction indicates an exchange of cations and anions between the reactants.

Separate the reactants into ions and then exchange the cation and anion pairings.

9. C is correct.

Balanced equation (synthesis):

$$P_4 \, (s) + 6 \, H_2 \, (g) \rightarrow 4 \, PH_3 \, (g)$$

10. C is correct.

Balancing Redox Equations

From the balanced equation, the coefficient for the proton can be determined. Balancing a redox equation not only requires balancing the atoms that are in the equation, but the charges must be balanced as well.

The equations must be separated into two different half-reactions. One of the half-reactions addresses the oxidizing component, and the other addresses the reducing component.

Magnesium is being oxidized, therefore the unbalanced oxidation half-reaction will be:

$$Mg \, (s) \rightarrow Mg^{2+} \, (aq)$$

Furthermore, the nitrogen is being reduced, therefore the unbalanced reduction half-reaction will be:

$$NO_3^- \, (aq) \rightarrow NO_2 \, (aq)$$

At this stage, each half reaction needs to be balanced for each atom, and the net electric charge on each side of the equations must be balanced as well.

Order of operations for balancing half-reactions:

1) Balance atoms except for oxygen and hydrogen.

2) Balance the oxygen atoms by adding water.

3) Balance the hydrogen atoms by adding protons.

   a) If in basic solution, add equal amounts of hydroxide to each side to cancel the protons.

4) Balance the electric charge by adding electrons.

5) If necessary, multiply the coefficients of one half-reaction equation by a factor that cancels the electron count when both equations are combined.

6) Cancel any ions or molecules that appear on both sides of the overall equation.

After determining the balanced overall redox reaction, the stoichiometry indicates the moles of protons that are involved.

For magnesium:

$$Mg \, (s) \rightarrow Mg^{2+} \, (aq)$$

The magnesium is already balanced with a coefficient of 1. There are no hydrogen or oxygen atoms present in the equation. The magnesium cation has a +2 charge, so to balance the charge, 2 moles of electrons should be added to the right side.

The balanced half-reaction for oxidation:

$$Mg\,(s) \rightarrow Mg^{2+}\,(aq) + 2\,e^-$$

For nitrogen:

$$NO_3^-\,(aq) \rightarrow NO_2\,(aq)$$

The equation is already balanced for nitrogen because one nitrogen atom appears on both sides of the reaction. The nitrate reactant has three oxygen atoms, while the nitrite product has two oxygen atoms.

To balance the oxygen, one mole of water should be added to the right side:

$$NO_3^-\,(aq) \rightarrow NO_2\,(aq) + H_2O$$

Adding water to the right side of the equation introduces hydrogen atoms to that side. Therefore, the hydrogen atom count needs to be balanced. Water possesses two hydrogen atoms, therefore, two protons need to be added to the left side of the reaction:

$$NO_3^-\,(aq) + 2\,H^+ \rightarrow NO_2\,(aq) + H_2O$$

The reaction is occurring in acidic conditions. If the reaction was basic, then OH^- would need to be added to both sides to cancel the protons.

The net charge needs to be balanced. The left side has a net charge of +1 (+2 from the protons and –1 from the electron), while the right side is neutral. Therefore, one electron should be added to the left side:

$$NO_3^-\,(aq) + 2\,H^+ + e^- \rightarrow NO_2\,(aq) + H_2O$$

When half reactions are recombined, the electrons in the overall reaction must cancel.

The reduction half-reaction will contribute one electron to the left side of the overall equation, while the oxidation half-reaction will contribute two electrons to the product side.

Therefore, the coefficients of the reduction half-reaction should be doubled:

$$2 \times [NO_3^-\,(aq) + 2\,H^+ + e^- \rightarrow NO_2\,(aq) + H_2O]$$

$$= 2\,NO_3^-\,(aq) + \mathbf{4\,H^+} + 2\,e^- \rightarrow 2\,NO_2\,(aq) + 2\,H_2O$$

The answer is 4 at this step.

Combining both half reactions gives:

$$Mg\,(s) + 2\,NO_3^-\,(aq) + 4\,H^+ + 2\,e^- \rightarrow Mg^{2+}\,(aq) + 2\,e^- + 2\,NO_2\,(aq) + 2\,H_2O$$

Cancel the electrons that appear on both sides of the reaction in the following balanced net equation:

$$Mg\,(s) + 2\,NO_3^-\,(aq) + 4\,H^+ \rightarrow Mg^{2+}\,(aq) + 2\,NO_2\,(aq) + 2\,H_2O$$

This equation is now fully balanced for mass, oxygen, hydrogen and electric charge.

11. A is correct.

Number of molecules = moles × Avogadro's constant

Number of molecules = 1.40 mol × 6.02 × 10^{23} molecules/mol

Number of molecules = 8.428 × 10^{23} molecules

4 atoms in each PF_3 molecule:

$$4 \times 8.428 \times 10^{23} = 3.37 \times 10^{24} \text{ atoms}$$

12. D is correct. CH_3COOH:

mass of O atoms = 2 × 16 g/mol = 32 g/mol

mass of H atoms = 4 × 1 g/mol = 4 g/mol

Therefore, the mass % of O is 8 times (32 / 4) greater than the mass % of H.

Calculate the molecular mass (MW) of acetic acid:

MW of CH_3COOH:

= (2 × atomic mass of C) + (4 × atomic mass of H) + (2 × atomic mass of O)

MW of CH_3COOH = (2 × 12.01 g/mole) + (4 × 1.01 g/mole) + (2 × 16.00 g/mole)

MW of CH_3COOH = 60.05 g/mole

To obtain percent mass composition of each element, calculate the total mass of each element, divide it by the molecular mass, and multiply with 100%.

% mass composition of carbon = [(2 × 12.01 g/mole) / 60.05 g/mole] × 100%

% mass composition of carbon = 40.00%

% mass composition of hydrogen = [(4 × 1.01 g/mole) / 60.05 g/mole] × 100%

% mass composition of hydrogen = 6.71%

% mass composition of oxygen = [(2 × 16.00 g/mole) / 60.05 g/mole] ×100%

% mass composition of oxygen = 53%

13. B is correct.

From the balanced equation:

4 moles of Ag are produced for each mole of O_2.

Therefore, if 1 mole of Ag is produced, ¼ mole of O_2 is produced.

The mass of ¼ mole of O_2 is:

(¼ mol)·(2 × 16 g/mol) = 8 g

14. D is correct.

All metals (and elements) have an oxidation number of zero in their elemental state.

15. A is correct.

Assign oxidation number to each species:

K_2	Cr_2	O_7
$2(+1)$	$2x$	$7(-2)$

The sum of charges in a neutral molecule is zero:

$$2 + (2x) + (7 \times -2) = 0$$

$$2 + (2x) + (-14) = 0$$

$$2x = -2 + 14$$

$$2x = +12$$

$$+6 = \text{oxidation number of Cr}$$

Chapter 5

Solution Chemistry

- **Introduction to Solutions**
- **Ions in Solution**
- **Solubility**

Introduction to Solutions

A *solution* is a homogeneous mixture of two or more substances, in which individual components in the mixture are indistinguishable from one another. A solution is always composed of one or more solutes and a *solvent* – the solvent being the substance that is present in the largest quantity.

Aqueous solutions are solutions that have water as the solvent.

The formation of a solution involves disruption of the crystalline lattice structure of solute and the mixing of solute particles with solvent molecules. Solute particles diffuse into solution and become uniformly dispersed. For this to happen, there must be sufficiently strong interactions between solute particles and solvent molecules (i.e., strong enough to overcome the intermolecular attractive forces between solute particles in the liquid state or in crystalline solids). Solution processes may be divided into three main stages:

1. pure solvent $\rightarrow$ separated solvent molecules (endothermic); $\Delta H_1 > 0$

2. pure solute $\rightarrow$ separated solute particles (endothermic); $\Delta H_2 > 0$

3. separated solvent and solute molecules $\rightarrow$ solution (exothermic); $\Delta H_3 < 0$

Net: Solute(s) + Solvent $\rightarrow$ Solution; $\Delta H_{soln} = \Delta H_1 + \Delta H_2 + \Delta H_3$

Depending on the magnitudes of ΔH_1, ΔH_2 and ΔH_3, solution processes can be exothermic (if $|\Delta H_3| > |\Delta H_1 + \Delta H_2|$) or endothermic (if $|\Delta H_3| < |\Delta H_1 + \Delta H_2|$).

For solutions, remember the phrase "like dissolves like." Polar solutes dissolve in polar solvents, and nonpolar solutes dissolve in nonpolar solvents.

Ions in Solution

Many ionic compounds dissolve in water but not in organic (nonpolar) solvents. Water molecules are very polar and interact strongly with the ionic species (cations and anions) through ion-dipole interactions. Such interactions result in negative enthalpies, called the *solvation* or *hydration energy*. The overall solution process may be exothermic or endothermic, depending on which enthalpy is larger.

When ionic compounds dissolve in water, they dissociate (ionize) to produce free ions. For example, when NaCl dissolves, it produces free Na^+ and Cl^- ions, which become hydrated with water molecules. Sodium chloride and many other ionic compounds dissolve in water because of the strong ion-dipole interactions between solute and solvent particles.

The energy needed to overcome the lattice energy and disrupt ions in the crystalline solids is provided by the hydration energy produced from these ion-dipole interactions. For NaCl, the lattice energy is only slightly greater than the sum of hydration energy for Na^+ and Cl^- ions, and the solution process for NaCl is only slightly endothermic.

Strong electrolytes (solutions of ionic compounds) completely dissociate, and the ions are good conductors of electric current.

Weak electrolytes (solutions of polar covalent compounds) only partially dissociate in solution. *Nonelectrolytes* do not dissociate at all, and dissolve as molecules rather than ions (e.g., sugar as a nonelectrolyte).

Anion, cation: common names, formulas, and charges for familiar ions, such as ammonium (NH_4^+); phosphate (PO_4^{3-}); sulfate (SO_4^{2-})

The following table lists common ions. It begins with anions (negatively charged), follows by cations (positively charged). The charge is written as a superscript. A single negative sign indicates a charge of −1, and a single positive sign indicates a charge of +1.

Common name	Formula
Anions	
Hydroxide	OH^-
Chloride	Cl^-
Hypochlorite	ClO^-
Chlorite	ClO_2^-
Chlorate	ClO_3^-
Perchlorate	ClO_4^-
Halide, hypohalide, etc.	X^-, XO^-, etc.
Carbonate	CO_3^{2-}
Hydrogen Carbonate (Bicarbonate)	HCO_3^-
Sulfate	SO_4^{2-}
Hydrogen Sulfate (Bisulfate)	HSO_4^-
Sulfite	SO_3^{2-}
Thiosulfate	$S_2O_3^{2-}$
Nitrate	NO_3^-
Nitrite	NO_2^-
Phosphate	PO_4^{3-}
Hydrogen Phosphate	HPO_4^{2-}
Dihydrogen Phosphate	$H_2PO_4^-$
Phosphite	PO_3^{3-}
Cyanide	CN^-

Common name	Formula
Thiocyanate	SCN^-
Peroxide	O_2^{2-}
Oxalate	$C_2O_4^{2-}$
Acetate	$C_2H_3O_2^-$
Chromate	CrO_4^{2-}
Dichromate	$Cr_2O_7^{2-}$
Permanganate	MnO_4^-
Cations	
Hydronium	H_3O^+
Ammonium	NH_4^+
Metal	M^{n+}

Qualitative analysis is the separation and identification of ions in a mixture. The technique employs the different solubilities of ionic compounds in aqueous solution, as well as the ability of certain cations to form *complex ions* with ligands. The complex ions of many transition metals are often colored, which can be used in their identification.

The general approach in the qualitative analysis of cations is to separate them into various *ion groups*.

Ion group 1: Insoluble chlorides. Treating the mixture with 6 M HCl precipitates Ag^+, Hg_2^{2+} and Pb^{2+} ions as chlorides, leaving other cations in solution. The formation of a *white precipitate* indicates the presence of at least one of these cations in the mixture.

Ion group 2: Acid-insoluble sulfides. The supernatant from the above treatment with HCl is adjusted to pH ≈ 0.5 and then treated with aqueous H_2S. The high $[H_3O^+]$ in solution keeps $[HS^-]$ very low, which precipitates only the following group of cations: Cu^{2+}, Cd^{2+}, Hg^{2+}, Sn^{2+} and Bi^{3+}. Centrifuging and decanting gives the next solution.

Ion group 3: Base-insoluble sulfides. The supernatant from acidic sulfide treatment is treated with a NH_3/NH_4^+ buffer to make the solution slightly basic (pH ≈ 8). The excess OH^- in solution increases $[HS^-]$, which causes the precipitation of the more soluble sulfides and some hydroxides. The cations that precipitate under this condition are: Zn^{2+}, Mn^{2+}, Ni^{2+}, Fe^{2+} and Co^{2+} as sulfides, and Al^{3+}, Cr^{3+}, and Fe^{3+} as hydroxides. The precipitate is centrifuged and the supernatant decanted to give the next solution.

Ion group 4: Insoluble phosphates. The slightly basic supernatant separated from the group 3 ions is treated with $(NH_4)_2HPO_4$, which precipitates $Mg_3(PO_4)_2$, $Ca_3(PO_4)_2$ and $Ba_3(PO_4)_2$.

Ion group 5: Alkali metal and ammonium ions. The final solution contains any of the following ions: Na^+, K^+ and NH_4^+.

Hydration, the hydronium ion

Hydration, also known as *solvation*, is where water forms a shell around ions in solution. The oxygen atom on water is partially negative, so it surrounds cations. The hydrogen atoms on water is partially positive, so they surround anions.

H^+ does not exist as a proton in water, it exists as the hydronium ion (H_3O^+). This is because the high charge density of a proton attracts it to any part of a nearby molecule that has a negative charge. Since water has two lone pairs of electrons on the oxygen atom, the proton can interact with one of the lone pairs, forming the hydronium ion.

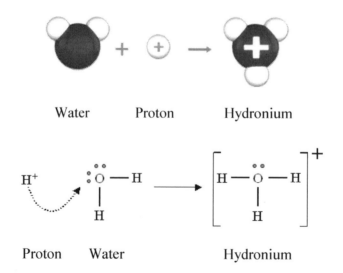

Water   Proton   Hydronium

Proton   Water   Hydronium

Solubility

The *solubility* of a substance is the amount of solute (in grams) that is dissolved in a given quantity of solvent to give a saturated solution at a particular temperature. A *saturated* solution contains the maximum quantity of dissolved solute that is normally possible at a given temperature, and where a state of dynamic equilibrium exists between dissolution and crystallization.

Solubility is temperature dependent. For example, the solubility of KNO_3 is about 30 g per 100 g water at 20 °C and 63 g per 100 g water at 40 °C. When a solution that is almost saturated at a higher temperature is cooled to a lower temperature where the solubility is lower, the excess solute normally precipitates out to give a saturated solution at the lower temperature. However, if the solution is cooled down too rapidly, precipitates do not form, and the resulting solution contains more dissolved solute than it would in a normal saturated solution (*supersaturated* solution). The supersaturated solution is unstable, and crystallization occurs readily by seeding (introducing particles that provide nuclei for precipitation).

A *concentrated solution* contains a relatively large amount of dissolved solute, while a *dilute solution* is one that contains very little dissolved solute in a relatively large amount of solvent. A solution containing 40 g or more of dissolved solute in 100 mL of water is considered concentrated, whereas one with less than 10 g of solute per 100 mL of water is called a dilute solution. A concentrated solution does not necessarily imply a saturated solution. Likewise, a saturated solution does not necessarily imply a concentrated solution.

The solubility of most liquids and solids in water increases with temperature, but the solubility of gases decreases with temperature. However, the pressure of a gas strongly affects its solubility, as described by *Henry's law*. Henry's law states that as pressure increases, solubility increases (i.e., they are directly proportional). Other factors that affect solubility include the surface area of the solute (e.g., granulated sugar dissolves faster than a sugar cube) and heating or agitating a solution (e.g., stirring leads to faster dissolving).

221

The terms *miscible* and *immiscible* are often used to describe liquids that dissolve or do not dissolve in another liquid, respectively. Thus, ethanol and water are completely miscible because they dissolve in each other freely when mixed, while oil and water are immiscible since they remain separate.

Units of concentration

The concentration of a solution is expressed in terms of the amount of solute dissolved in the solution and may be expressed in the different ways listed below.

1. Mass Percent, % (w/w) = $\dfrac{\text{mass of solute}}{\text{mass of solution}} \times 100\%$

2. Volume Percent % (v/v) = $\dfrac{\text{volume of solute}}{\text{volume of solution}} \times 100\%$

3. Molarity (M) = $\dfrac{\text{number of moles of solute}}{\text{liters of solution}}$

4. Molality (m) = $\dfrac{\text{number of moles of solute}}{\text{kg of solvent}}$

5. Normality (N) = $\dfrac{\text{number of equivalents of solute}}{\text{liters of solution}}$

   where

   Number of equivalents of solute = $\dfrac{\text{grams of solute}}{\text{equivalent weight of solute}}$

6. Mole fraction, (X_i) = $\dfrac{\text{moles of a component}}{\text{total moles of components in solution}}$

Normality is based on a unit of chemical mass known as the equivalent weight.

The *equivalent weight* is the amount of solute needed to be the equivalent of one mole of hydrogen ions, and the equivalent weight is thus dependent on the valence of the solute.

For solutes with a valence of 1 (e.g., HCl), the molecular weight and equivalent weight are the same. For solutes with a valence of more than 1 (e.g., H_3PO_4, valence of 3), the equivalent weight is equal to the molecular weight divided by the valence.

Therefore, molarity is related to normality, as in the examples below:

1 M HCl = 1 N HCl

1 M H_2SO_4 = 2 N H_2SO_4

1 M H_3PO_4 = 3 N H_3PO_4

Since ionic compounds dissociate into ions, the total number of particles in a solution of an ionic compound is always greater than that in a solution of a nonionic (molecular) compound.

The total concentration of ions in solution is the sum of the concentrations of cations and anions, which is dependent on the formula of the compound.

For example, a solution of 1.0 M aluminum nitrate, $Al(NO_3)_3$, contains 1.0 M of Al^{3+} and 3.0 M NO_3^- ions. The total concentration of ions in solution is 4.0 M.

Before dissolving After dissolving

$$Al(NO_3)_3 \, (aq) \rightarrow Al^{3+} \, (aq) \, + \, 3 \, NO_3^- \, (aq)$$

$$(1.0 \, M) \rightarrow (1.0 \, M) \, + \, (3 \times 1.0 \, M)$$

A solution of 1.0 M $MgCl_2$ contains 1.0 M of Mg^{2+} and 2.0 M of Cl^- ions, and the total ion concentration is 3.0 M.

Solubility product constant, the equilibrium expression (K_{sp})

Solubility product constants (K_{sp}) describe saturated solutions of ionic compounds of relativity low solubility. For example, when a slightly soluble salt such as silver chloride (AgCl) is dissolved in water, a saturated solution is quickly obtained. This is because only a very small amount of the solid dissolves, while the rest remains undissolved.

The following equilibrium between solid AgCl and the free ions occurs in solution:

$$AgCl\ (s) \rightleftarrows Ag^+\ (aq)\ +\ Cl^-\ (aq)$$

$$K_{sp} = [Ag^+] \cdot [Cl^-]$$

A more general expression of the solubility product constant K_{sp} for solubility equilibrium is: $M_aX_b\ (s) \rightleftarrows aM^{b+}\ (aq)\ +\ bX^{a-}\ (aq)$,

$$K_{sp} = [M^{b+}]^a \cdot [X^{a-}]^b$$

In some problems, the K_{sp} may be given and the solubility may need to be calculated, or vice versa. How to proceed depends on the type of equilibria.

Some examples are given below.

A. For ionic equilibria of the type: $MX\ (s) \rightleftarrows M^{n+}\ (aq) + X^{n-}\ (aq)$

$$K_{sp} = [M^{n+}] \cdot [X^{n-}]$$

If the solubility of compounds is S mol/L, $K_{sp} = S^2; \rightarrow S = \sqrt{(K_{sp})}$

For example, the solubility equilibrium for $BaSO_4$ is

$$BaSO_4\ (s) \rightleftarrows Ba^{2+}\ (aq) + SO_4^{2-}\ (aq)$$

$$K_{sp} = [Ba^{2+}][SO_4^{2-}] = 1.5 \times 10^{-9}$$

If the solubility of $BaSO_4$ is S mol/L, a saturated solution of $BaSO_4$ has

$$[Ba^{2+}] = [SO_4^{2-}] = S\ mol/L$$

$$K_{sp} = S^2 \text{ and } S = \sqrt{(K_{sp})} = \sqrt{(1.5 \times 10^{-9})} = 3.9 \times 10^{-5}\ mol/L$$

B. For ionic equilibria of the type: $MX_2(s) \rightleftarrows M^{2+}(aq) + 2X^-(aq)$

$K_{sp} = [M^{2+}][X^-]^2$

and for the type: $M_2X(s) \rightleftarrows 2M^+(aq) + X^{2-}(aq)$

$K_{sp} = [M^+]^2[X^{2-}]$

For both types, if the solubility is S mol/L

$K_{sp} = 4S^3; \rightarrow S = (K_{sp}/4)^{1/3}$

For example,

$CaF_2(s) \rightleftarrows Ca^{2+}(aq) + 2F^-(aq)$

$K_{sp} = [Ca^{2+}][F^-]^2 = 4.0 \times 10^{-11}$

The solubility of calcium fluoride is $S = (K_{sp}/4)^{1/3} = (4.0 \times 10^{-11}/4)^{1/3} = 2.2 \times 10^{-4}$ mol/L

C. For solubility equilibria of the type:

$MX_3(s) \rightleftarrows M^{3+}(aq) + 3X^-(aq)$

$K_{sp} = [M^{3+}][X^-]^3$

Or one of the type: $M_3X(s) \rightleftarrows 3M^+(aq) + X^{3-}(aq)$

$K_{sp} = [M^+]^3[X^{3-}]$

If the solubility of the compound (MX_3 or M_3X) is S mol/L,

$K_{sp} = 27S^4; \rightarrow S = \sqrt[4]{(K_{sp}/27)}$

For example,

$Ag_3PO_4(s) \rightleftarrows 3Ag^+(aq) + PO_4^{3-}(aq)$

$K_{sp} = [Ag^+]^3[PO_4^{3-}] = 1.8 \times 10^{-18}$

The solubility of silver phosphate is:

$$S = \sqrt[4]{(K_{sp}/27)} = \sqrt[4]{(1.8 \times 10^{-18})/27} = 1.6 \times 10^{-5} \text{ mol/L}$$

D. For solubility equilibria:

$$M_2X_3\,(s) \rightleftarrows 2M^{3+}\,(aq) + 3X^{2-}\,(aq)$$

$$K_{sp} = [M^{3+}]^2[X^{2-}]^3$$

Or, one of the type:

$$M_3X_2\,(s) \rightleftarrows 3M^{2+}\,(aq) + 2X^{3-}\,(aq)$$

$$K_{sp} = [M^{2+}]^3[X^{3-}]^2$$

If the solubility of the compound M_3X_2 is S mol/L,

then $[M^{2+}] = 3S$, and $[X^{3-}] = 2S$

$$K_{sp} = (3S)^3(2S)^2 = 108S^5$$

$$\rightarrow S = \sqrt[5]{K_{sp}/108}$$

For example, $Ca_3(PO_4)_2\,(s) \rightleftarrows 3\,Ca^{2+}\,(aq) + 2\,PO_4^{3-}\,(aq)$,

$$K_{sp} = [Ca^{2+}]^3[PO_4^{3-}]^2 = 1.3 \times 10^{-32}$$

The solubility of $Ca_3(PO_4)_2$ is $S = \sqrt[5]{(1.3 \times 10^{-32})/108} = 1.6 \times 10^{-7}$ mol/L

An example of calculating K_{sp} from solubility:

Suppose the solubility of $PbSO_4$ in water is 4.3×10^{-3} g/100 mL solution at 25 °C.

What is the K_{sp} of $PbSO_4$ at 25 °C?

Solubility of $PbSO_4$ in mol/L = $\dfrac{4.3 \times 10^{-3} \text{ g}}{100 \text{ mL}} \times \dfrac{1000 \text{ mL/L}}{303.26 \text{ g/mol}} = 1.40 \times 10^{-4}$ mol/L

A saturated solution of $PbSO_4$, contains $[Pb^{2+}] = [SO_4^{2-}] = 1.4 \times 10^{-4}$ mol/L

For the equilibrium: $PbSO_4(s) \rightleftarrows Pb^{2+}(aq) + SO_4^{2-}(aq)$;

$$K_{sp} = [Pb^{2+}] \cdot [SO_4^{2-}]$$

$$S^2 = (1.4 \times 10^{-4} \text{ mol/L})^2 = 2.0 \times 10^{-8}$$

This next example displays how to determine solubility from K_{sp}:

If the K_{sp} of $Mg(OH)_2$ is 6.3×10^{-10} at 25 °C, what is its solubility at 25 °C (a) in mol/L, and (b) in g/100 mL solution at 25 °C?

(a) Solubility equilibrium for $Mg(OH)_2$ is:

$$Mg(OH)_2(s) \rightleftarrows Mg^{2+}(aq) + 2 OH^-(aq)$$

$$K_{sp} = [Mg^{2+}][OH^-]^2$$

$$4S^3 = 6.3 \times 10^{-10}$$

Solubility of $Mg(OH)_2$: $S = \sqrt[3]{K_{sp}/4} = \sqrt[3]{(6.3 \times 10^{-10})/4} = 5.4 \times 10^{-4}$ mol/L

(b) Solubility in g/100 mL solution:

$(5.4 \times 10^{-4} \text{ mol/L}) \cdot (58.32 \text{ g/mol}) \cdot (0.1 \text{ L/100 mL}) = 3.1 \times 10^{-3}$ g/100 mL solution.

Common-ion effect, its use in laboratory separations

The *common-ion effect* is simply Le Châtelier's principle applied to K_{sp} reactions; it states that the presence of common ion decreases the solubility of a slightly soluble ionic compound. A common ion is any ion in the solution that is common to the ionic compound.

For example, in the following equilibrium:

$$PbCl_2\,(s) \rightleftharpoons Pb^{2+}\,(aq) \;+\; 2\,Cl^-\,(aq)$$

If some NaCl is added to a saturated solution of $PbCl_2$, the $[Cl^-]$ increases, and according to Le Châteliler's principle, the equilibrium shifts in the direction that tends to reduce $[Cl^-]$. In this example, the equilibrium shifts left, to form more $PbCl_2$ solid, hence decreasing the amount of $PbCl_2$ that dissolves into solution. More $PbCl_2$ can dissolve in pure water than in water containing Cl^- ions.

In laboratory separations, the common-ion effect can be used to selectively precipitate out one component in a mixture. For example, to separate AgCl from a mixture of AgCl and Ag_2SO_4, add NaCl. This selectively displaces AgCl by the common-ion effect (Cl^- being the common ion).

Complex ion formation

A *complex ion* consists of a central metal ion that is covalently bonded to two or more *ligands*, which can be anions such as OH^-, Cl^-, F^- and CN^-, or neutral molecules such as H_2O, CO and NH_3.

For example, in the complex ion $[Cu(NH_3)4]^{2+}$, Cu^{2+} is the central metal ion, with four NH_3 molecules covalently bonded to it. All complex ions are Lewis adducts (i.e., the addition of a Lewis acid and a Lewis base). The metal ions act as Lewis acids (electron-pair acceptors) and the ligands are Lewis bases (electron-pair donors).

$$\text{Metal}^+ + \text{Lewis base} \rightarrow \text{Complex ion}$$

$$M^+ + L \rightarrow M - L_n^{\;+}$$

The Lewis base can be charged or uncharged.

The K_{eq} for this reaction is K_f, or the *formation constant*.

In aqueous solutions, metal ions form complex ions with water molecules as ligands. When another ligand is introduced into the solution, ligand exchanges occur and equilibrium is established.

For example, when NH_3 is added to aqueous solution containing Cu^{2+} ion, the following equilibrium occurs:

$$Cu(H_2O)_6^{2+} (aq) + 4 NH_3 (aq) \rightleftarrows [Cu(NH_3)_4]^{2+} (aq) + 6 H_2O$$

$$K_f = \frac{[Cu(NH_3)_4^{2+}]}{[Cu(H_2O)_6^{2+}][NH_3]^4}$$

At molecular level, the ligand exchange process occurs in stepwise manner; each water molecule is replaced with an NH_3 molecule, one at a time, to give a series of intermediate species, each with its own formation constant. For convenience, the water molecules can be omitted from the equation.

1. $Cu^{2+} (aq) + NH_3 (aq) \rightleftarrows Cu(NH_3)^{2+} (aq)$;

$$K_{f1} = \frac{[Cu(NH_3)^{2+}]}{[Cu^{2+}][NH_3]}$$

2. $Cu(NH_3)^{2+} (aq) + NH_3 (aq) \rightleftarrows Cu(NH_3)_2^{2+} (aq)$;

$$K_{f2} = \frac{[Cu(NH_3)_2^{2+}]}{[Cu(NH_3)^{2+}][NH_3]}$$

3. $Cu(NH_3)_3^{2+} (aq) + NH_3 (aq) \rightleftarrows Cu(NH_3)_4^{2+} (aq)$;

$$K_{f4} = \frac{[Cu(NH_3)_4^{2+}]}{[Cu(NH_3)_3^{2+}][NH_3]}$$

The overall formation constant is the product of all intermediate formation constants:

$$K_f = K_{f1} \times K_{f2} \times K_{f3} \times K_{f4}$$

$$K_f = \frac{[Cu(NH_3)_4^{2+}]}{[Cu^{2+}][NH_3]^4}$$

Complex ions and solubility

The *complex-ion effect* is the opposite of the common-ion effect. A ligand increases the solubility of slightly soluble ionic compounds if complex ions form with the metal ions.

For example, silver chloride, AgCl, is more soluble in ammonia solution because silver ions form complex ions with NH_3:

$$AgCl\ (s) \rightleftarrows Ag^+\ (aq)\ +\ Cl^-\ (aq) \qquad\qquad K_{sp} = 1.6 \times 10^{-10}$$

$$Ag^+\ (aq)\ +\ 2\ NH_3\ (aq) \rightleftarrows\ Ag(NH_3)_2^+\ (aq) \qquad\qquad K_f = 1.7 \times 10^7$$

$$AgCl\ (s)\ +\ 2\ NH_3\ (aq)\ \rightleftarrows\ Ag(NH_3)_2^+\ (aq)\ +\ Cl^-\ (aq)$$

$$K_{net} =\ K_{sp} \times K_f$$

$$K_{net} =\ (1.6 \times 10^{-10}) \cdot (1.7 \times 10^7)\ =\ 2.7 \times 10^{-3}$$

When a complex ion forms, the Cl^- ion is reduced, so more of AgCl dissolves.

Alternatively:

$$AgCl\ (s) \leftrightarrow Ag^+\ (aq) + Cl^-\ (aq)$$

$$NH_3 + Ag^+ \leftrightarrow Ag\text{-}(NH_3)_n \text{ complex ion.}$$

The complex ion formation reduces Ag^+, causing more AgCl to dissolve.

Solubility and pH

pH affects the solubility of slightly soluble compounds containing anions that are conjugate bases of weak acids, such as F^-, NO_2^-, OH^-, SO_3^{2-} and PO_4^{3-}, but not those containing anions, which are conjugate bases of strong acids, such as SO_4^{2-}, Cl^- and Br^-.

For example, in a saturated solution of calcium fluoride, CaF_2, the following equilibrium exists:

$$CaF_2\ (s)\ \rightleftarrows\ Ca^{2+}\ (aq)\ +\ 2F^-\ (aq)$$

When a strong acid is added to the saturated solution, the following reaction occurs:

$$H^+ (aq) \ + \ F^- (aq) \ \rightarrow \ HF (aq)$$

This reaction has the net effect of reducing the concentration of F^- ions, which causes the equilibrium to shift to the right, and more of CaF_2 to dissolve.

Acids are more soluble in bases.

$$HA \rightarrow H^+ + A^-$$

Placing the above reactions in a base reduces the H^+, thus, more HA dissolves, according to Le Châtelier's principle.

Bases are more soluble in acids.

$$B + H^+ \rightarrow BH^+$$

Putting the above reactions in an acid adds more H^+, and thus, more B dissolves, according to Le Châtelier's principle.

Practice Questions

1. Which of the following statements describing solutions is NOT true?

    A. Solutions are colorless

    B. The particles in a solution are atomic or molecular

    C. Making a solution involves a physical change in size

    D. Solutions are homogeneous

2. Which of the following describes a saturated solution?

    A. When the ratio of solute to solvent is small

    B. When it contains less solute than it can hold at 25 °C

    C. When it contains as much solute as it can hold at a given temperature

    D. When it contains 1 g of solute in 100 mL of water

3. An ionic compound that strongly attracts atmospheric water is said to be:

    A. immiscible   **C.** diluted

    B. miscible   **D.** hygroscopic

4. What happens when the molecule-to-molecule attractions in the solute are less than those in the solvent?

    A. The material has only limited solubility in the solvent

    B. The solution will become saturated

    C. The solute can have infinite solubility in the solvent

    D. The solute does not dissolve in the solvent

5. What does negative heat of solution indicate about solute-solvent bonds as compared to solute-solute bonds and solvent-solvent bonds?

    A. Solute-solute and solute-solvent bond strengths are greater than solvent-solvent bond strength

    B. Solute-solute and solvent-solvent bonds are weaker than solute-solvent bonds

    C. Solute-solute and solvent-solvent bonds are stronger than solute-solvent bonds

    D. Solute-solute and solvent-solvent bond strengths are equal to solute-solvent bond strength

6. Which statement supports the fact that calcium fluoride is much less soluble in water than sodium fluoride?

> I. calcium fluoride is not used in toothpaste
> II. calcium fluoride is not used to fluoridate city water supplies
> III. sodium fluoride is not used to fluoridate city water supplies

A. I only

B. II only

C. I and II only

D. I and III only

7. The principle *like dissolve like* is NOT applicable for predicting solubility when the solute is a/an:

A. nonpolar liquid

B. polar gas

C. nonpolar gas

D. ionic compound

8. Which of the following is the most soluble in benzene (C_6H_6)?

A. glucose ($C_6H_{12}O_6$)

B. sodium benzoate

C. octane (C_8H_{18})

D. hydrobromic acid

9. Apply the *like dissolves like* rule to predict which of the liquids is immiscible in water.

A. ethanol, CH_3CH_2OH

B. acetone, C_3H_6O

C. acetic acid, CH_3COOH

D. none of the above

10. What is the equilibrium constant expression (K_{sp}) for slightly soluble silver sulfate in an aqueous solution: $Ag_2SO_4(s) \leftrightarrow 2\,Ag^+(aq) + SO_4^{2-}(aq)$?

A. $K_{sp} = [Ag^+]^2\,[SO_4^{2-}]$

B. $K_{sp} = [Ag^+]^2 \cdot [SO_4^{2-}] / [Ag_2SO_4]$

C. $K_{sp} = [Ag^+] \cdot [SO_4^{2-}]$

D. $K_{sp} = [Ag^+] \cdot [SO_4^{2-}]^2 / [Ag_2SO_4]$

11. In the reaction KHS (aq) + HCl (aq) → KCl (aq) + H_2S (g), which ions are the spectator ions?

A. H^+ and HS^-

B. K^+ and HS^-

C. K^+ and Cl^-

D. K^+ and H^+

12. What is the mass of a 10.0% blood plasma sample that contains 2.50 g of dissolved solute?

A. 21.5 g

B. 25.0 g

C. 0.215 g

D. 0.430 g

13. What is the molarity of KCl in sea water, if KCl is 12.5% (m/m) and the density of seawater is 1.06 g/mL?

A. 1.78 M

B. 17.8 M

C. 2.78 M

D. 0.845 M

14. If 25.0 mL of urine has a mass of 25.5 g and contains 1.8 g of solute, what is the mass/mass percent concentration of solute in the urine sample?

A. 12.48%

B. 17.42%

C. 7.06%

D. 3.82%

15. With increasing temperature, many solvents expand to occupy greater volumes. What happens to the concentration of a solution made with such a solvent as temperature increases?

A. Concentration decreases because the solution has a greater ability to dissolve more solute at a higher temperature

B. Concentration increases because the solution has a greater ability to dissolve more solute at a higher temperature

C. Concentration of a solution decreases as the volume increases because concentration depends on how much mass is dissolved in a given volume

D. Concentration of a solution increases as the solute fits into the new spaces between the molecules

Solutions

1. A is correct.

Some solutions are colored (e.g., Kool Aid powder dissolved in water).

The color of chemicals is a physical property of chemicals from (most common) the excitation of electrons due to an absorption of energy by the chemical. The observer sees not the absorbed color, but the wavelength that is reflected.

Most simple inorganic (e.g., sodium chloride) and organic compounds (e.g., ethanol) are colorless.

Transition metal compounds are often colored because of transitions of electrons between *d*-orbitals of different energy.

Organic compounds tend to be colored when there is extensive conjugation (i.e., alternating double and single bonds), causing the energy gap between the HOMO (i.e., highest occupied molecular orbital) and LUMO (i.e., lowest occupied molecular orbital) to decrease, bringing the absorption band from the UV to the visible region. Color is also due to the energy absorbed by the compound, when an electron transitions from the HOMO to the LUMO.

2. C is correct.

A saturated solution contains the maximum amount dissolved material in the solvent under normal conditions. Increased heat allows for a solution to become supersaturated. The term also refers to the vapor of a compound that has a higher partial pressure than the vapor pressure of that compound.

A saturated solution forms a precipitate more solute is added to the solution.

3. D is correct.

A hygroscopic substance (e.g., honey, glycerin) is one that readily attracts water from its surroundings, through either adsorption or absorption. *Adsorption* is the process in which atoms, ions or molecules from a substance (e.g., gas, liquid or dissolved solid) adhere to a surface of the *adsorbent*.

4. C is correct.

If the attraction between solute molecules is less than the attraction between solvent molecules, a solute has (a virtually) infinite solubility because solvent-solute attraction is stronger than solute-solute attraction.

5. B is correct.

Bond formation releases energy: if the heat of the solution is negative, then energy is released.

Heat of solution is the net of enthalpy changes for making and breaking bonds. During solution formation, solvent-solvent bonds and solute-solute bonds break while solute-solvent bonds form.

The breaking of bonds absorbs energy while the formation of bonds releases energy.

6. C is correct.

Fluorides (e.g., BaF_2, MgF_2 PbF_2) are frequently insoluble.

7. D is correct.

Like dissolves like means that polar substances tend to dissolve in polar solvents, and nonpolar substances in nonpolar solvents.

Molecules that can form hydrogen bonds with water are soluble.

Ionic compounds form anions and cations that bond with the polar water molecule and therefore are soluble in water.

8. C is correct.

Like dissolves like means that polar substances tend to dissolve in polar solvents, and nonpolar substances in nonpolar solvents.

Benzene is a nonpolar molecule and octane is also nonpolar. Therefore, nonpolar octane is soluble in nonpolar benzene.

9. D is correct.

The "like dissolves like" rule applies when a solvent is miscible (soluble) with a solute that has similar properties.

A polar solute is miscible with a polar solvent.

All the molecules are polar and therefore are miscible in water.

10. A is correct.

Calculation of solubility constant (K_{sp}) is similar to equilibrium constant.

For K_{sp}, only aqueous species are included in the calculation.

The concentration of each species is raised to the power of their coefficients and multiplied with each other.

Therefore, $K_{sp} = [Ag^+]^2 \cdot [SO_4^{2-}]$

11. C is correct.

Spectator ions appear on both sides of the net ionic equation.

Ionic equation of the reaction:

$K^+ (aq) + HS^- (aq) + H^+ (aq) + Cl^- (aq) \rightarrow BaSO_4 (s) + 2 K^+ (aq) + 2 NO_3^- (aq)$

12. B is correct.

Mass % = mass of solute / mass of solution

Rearrange that equation to solve for mass of solution:

mass of solution = mass of solute / mass %

mass of solution = 2.50 g / 10.0%

mass of solution = 2.50 g / 0.1

mass of solution = 25.0 g

13. A is correct.

Assume 1 L of seawater.

Molarity is the number of moles in 1 L of solution, so starting with 1 L makes the calculation easier.

Mass of sea water = volume × density

Mass of sea water = (1 L × 1,000 L/mL) × 1.06 g/mL

Mass of sea water = 1,060 g

Use the mass of the sea water to determine the mass of KCl:

Mass of KCl = mass % of KCl × mass of sea water

Mass of KCl = 12.5% × 1,060 g

Mass of KCl = 132.5 g

Calculate the number of moles:

Moles of KCl = mass of KCl / molar mass of KCl

Moles of KCl = 132.5 g / (39.1 g/mol + 35.45 g/mol)

Moles of KCl = 1.78 moles

Divide moles by volume to calculate molarity:

Molarity of KCl = moles of KCl / volume of KCl

Molarity of KCl = 1.78 moles / 1 L

Molarity of KCl = 1.78 M

14. C is correct.

Mass % of solute = (mass of solute / total urine mass) × 100%

Mass % of solute = (1.8 g / 25.5 g) × 100%

Mass % of solute = 7.06%

15. C is correct.

As the volume of a solution increases, the concentration of a solution decreases

because concentration depends on how much mass is dissolved in a given volume.

Chapter 6

Kinetics and Reaction Rates

- **Reaction Rates**

- **Dependence of Reaction Rate on Concentrations of Reactants**

- **Rate-Determining Step**

- **Dependence of Reaction Rate on Temperature**

- **Kinetic Control vs. Thermodynamic Control of a Reaction**

- **Catalysts, Enzyme Catalysis**

- **Equilibrium in Reversible Chemical Reactions**

- **Relationship of the Equilibrium Constant and ΔG^o**

- **Relationship of the Equilibrium Constant and ΔH^o, ΔS^o**

Reaction Rates

Reaction rate is the rate of change in the concentration of reactants or products (i.e., how fast a reactant is consumed and how fast a product is formed). This is shown in the formula below:

$$\text{rate of reaction} = \frac{\text{change in concentration of reactant or product}}{\text{change in time}}$$

$$\text{rate of reaction} = \frac{\Delta \text{ concentration}}{\Delta \text{ time}}$$

Since rate is given by concentration divided by time, the unit is molarity per second (M/s).

The rate of reaction can be written for both the forward and reverse directions of a given chemical reaction. A subscript "fwd" or "rev" is often used to specify the direction in which the reaction rate is being given.

Forward Rate of Reaction:

$$\text{rate}_{fwd} = \frac{-\Delta \text{reactant}}{\Delta \text{time}} = \text{how fast a reactant disappears}$$

$$\text{rate}_{fwd} = \frac{\Delta \text{product}}{\Delta \text{time}} = \text{how fast a product forms}$$

Reverse Rate of Reaction:

$$\text{rate}_{rev} = \frac{-\Delta \text{Product}}{\Delta \text{Time}} = \text{how fast a product disappears}$$

$$\text{rate}_{rev} = \frac{\Delta \text{reactant}}{\Delta \text{time}} = \text{how fast a reactant reforms}$$

A reaction between two molecules occurs if the molecules have sufficient *kinetic energy* and both molecules are oriented properly to start a reaction, shown in the image below.

This is explained by the *collision theory*, which focuses on gas-phase chemical reactions.

There are three collision-related factors that affect the rate of a chemical reaction:

1. *Collision frequency:* An increase in the frequency at which molecules collide, increases the rate of reaction. The more collisions, the greater the probability that a collision produces product.

2. *Collision energy:* The molecules must collide with enough energy to form new bonds for a reaction to occur.

3. *Collision orientation:* The reactants must have the correct orientation (i.e., properly aligned) for products to be formed.

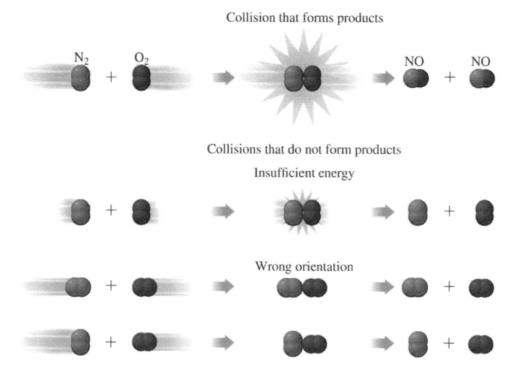

Dependence of Reaction Rate on Concentrations of Reactants

If the initial concentration of the reactants is increased, there are more reactant molecules; thus the molecules are closer together and collide more frequently. A higher collision frequency results in a higher rate of reaction. As the reaction proceeds, the concentration of reactant molecules decreases and the forward rate of reaction decreases. Thus, the concentration of product molecules increases, and the reverse rate of reaction increases.

Rate law, rate constant

The *rate law expression* describes how the rate of a reaction changes with the concentration of reactants and products. Consider the general expression for a homogeneous reaction:

$$a\mathbf{A} + b\mathbf{B} \longrightarrow c\mathbf{C} + d\mathbf{D}$$

Its rate law expression is:

$$rate = -\frac{\Delta[A]}{\Delta t} = k[A]^x[B]^y$$

where $[A]$ and $[B]$ are initial concentrations of the reactants, x and y are partial rate orders determined experimentally and k is the rate constant.

The rate constant k quantifies the rate of a chemical reaction; it takes into account other factors influencing reaction rate, including temperature and solvent used. Therefore, the constant is specific to the experimental conditions.

There is no correlation between stoichiometric coefficients (*a*, *b*) and rate exponents (*x*, *y*). In general, exponents tend to be small integers, but may be simple fractions (e.g., ½, ¾) or zero.

Reaction order

The *partial rate order* is the exponent associated with each concentration term.

- For a reaction that is *zero order* in a reactant, the rate of reaction is constant and does not depend on the concentration of that reactant. In this case, the reactant's exponent is zero, thus the term is equal to one (since anything to the zeroth power is one). Since it is equal to one, it disappears from the rate law expression, as the reaction rate does not depend on a zero order reactant.

- For a reaction that is *first order* in a reactant, the rate of reaction is directly proportional to the concentration of that reactant. The exponent is one.

- For a reaction that is *second order* in a reactant, the rate of reaction is directly proportional to the square of the concentration of that reactant. The exponent is two.

The *overall order of the reaction* is the sum of the partial orders. Most differential rate laws for chemical reactions are zero, first, or second order overall:

- *Zero order overall*: For a zero order overall reaction, the differential rate law is in the general form $r = k$. The units of the rate constant k are mole $\times$ L^{-1} $\times$ sec^{-1} (or M/s).

- *First order overall*: For a first order overall reaction, the differential rate law is in the general form $r = k[A]$. The units of the rate constant k are sec^{-1}.

- *Second order overall*: For a second order overall reaction, the differential rate law is in the general form $r = k[A]^2$. The units of the rate constant k are L $\times$ mole^{-1} $\times$ sec^{-1} (or M$^{-1} \cdot$ s^{-1}).

The example illustrates how to sum the partial orders to obtain the overall order for an equation.

From the reaction:

$$2\,NO\,(g) + O_2\,(g) \rightleftharpoons 2\,NO_2\,(g)$$

the rate law was experimentally determined to be $r = k[NO]^2[O_2]$.

In the rate law, the partial order for NO is two. The partial order for O_2 is one. The overall order is three; therefore, this reaction is third order overall.

Note that in this reaction, the orders happen to match the coefficients from the reaction, but that rate orders and coefficients are not necessarily correlated. Coefficients only equal rate orders for elementary-step reactions. In most problems, it is not known if the reaction is elementary or multi-step unless it is specifically given.

In defining the overall order of a given reaction, it is important to discuss its *molecularity*. The molecularity of a reaction mechanism is determined by the number of molecules (typically the coefficients) or ions that participate in the rate-determining step.

If a single reactant makes up the transition state, the reaction is called *unimolecular*. A mechanism that consists of two reacting species is *bimolecular*. The least likely scenario is when three independent molecules collide and react, which is called *termolecular*. However, note that bimolecular reactions are already very unlikely, and the factors necessary for a successful reaction are so specific that termolecular reactions are unlikely.

Reaction Type	Overall Reaction Order	Rate Law(s)
Unimolecular	1	$r = k[A]$
Bimolecular	2	$r = k[A]^2$, $r = k[A]\cdot[B]$
Termolecular	3	$r = k[A]^3$, $r = k[A]^2[B]$, $r = k[A]\cdot[B]\cdot[C]$
Zero order	0	$r = k$

The *differential rate law* and the *integrated rate law* are the two forms in which a rate law can be expressed. The differential rate law is the form that is expressed above. Integrated rate laws are written to express change in concentration of component vs. time, whereas differential rate laws are used to express the rate of reaction vs. concentration.

The integrated rate laws are listed below:

- Integrated rate law for 0 order: $[A]_t = -kt + [A]_0$

- Integrated rate law for 1st order: $\ln[A]_t = -kt + \ln[A]_0$

- Integrated rate law for 2nd order: $1 / [A] = 1 / [A]_0 + kt$

The *method of initial rates* described below is one way to determine the rate law of a reaction by finding the order of each reactant from experimental data.

Example: Results of an experiment show the reaction rates relative to initial concentrations of reactants:

	Rate (M/s)	Initial Concentrations (M)	
		[NO]	[O_2]
Trial 1	1.2×10^{-8}	0.10	0.10
Trial 2	2.4×10^{-8}	0.10	0.20
Trial 3	1.08×10^{-7}	0.30	0.10

Based on the data above, determine:

a) reaction orders of the reactants, and

b) value and units of k

To determine the rate law, start by comparing two trials in which the concentration of one reactant is changed, while the concentration of the other reactant is held constant. This is necessary in determining the partial order for the reactant with changing concentration. By keeping the concentration of the other reactant constant, the change in rate is due only to the change in concentration of one reactant.

Consider the results for Trial 1 and Trial 2. A comparison of these two trials, shows that the concentration of NO is constant, while the concentration of O_2 is doubled. To determine the partial order of O_2, note that doubling the concentration of O_2 also doubles the rate of the reaction. This may be expressed as:

$$2^x = 2 \quad \longrightarrow \text{ rate has doubled}$$

partial order for O_2

concentration doubled

For equality, x must equal one. Therefore, the partial order for O_2 is first order.

The same procedure is used to determine the partial order of NO. Select two trials in which the concentration of O_2 is constant while the concentration of NO is varied. These criteria are met with Trial 1 and Trial 3. The concentration of O_2 is held constant, while the concentration of NO has tripled. Under these conditions, the rate of the reaction increased nine-fold. This may be expressed as:

$$3^x = 9$$

partial order for NO → rate has increased nine-fold → concentration tripled

For equality, x must be two. Therefore, the partial order for NO is second order.

The orders can be substituted into the rate law:

$$\text{rate} = k[NO]^2[O_2]$$

Partial first orders are typically omitted from the rate law of most reactions, which is why $[O_2]$ does not have an exponent. The exponent is assumed to be one.

With partial rate orders, it is also possible to solve for the rate constant, k.

For example, choose any experimental trial, and substitute the values of rate and concentrations of NO and O_2.

Using data from Trial 1:

$$k = \frac{\text{rate}}{[NO]^2[O_2]} = \frac{1.2 \times 10^{-8}\,\text{Ms}^{-1}}{(0.10\,\text{M})^2(0.10\,\text{M})} = 1.2 \times 10^{-5}\,\text{M}^{-2}\text{s}^{-1}$$

Thus the rate law becomes:

$$\text{rate} = 1.2 \times 10^{-5}\,\text{M}^{-2}\cdot\text{s}^{-1}[NO]^2[O_2].$$

The reaction is third order overall, and the units are $\text{M}^{-2} \times \text{s}^{-1}$.

Notice that the units of k cancel to yield M/s for the rate of reaction.

Rate-Determining Step

Most chemical reactions occur in several steps known as a *reaction mechanism*. The mechanism is a sequence of events that takes place as reactant molecules are converted into products.

Each individual step in a multiple-step mechanism is an *elementary step*, which has its own rate constant and its own rate law.

The step with the slowest rate is the largest contributor to the overall rate of the reaction; this slowest step is called the *rate-determining step*. In most cases, the overall rate of reaction is almost equal to the rate-determining step's rate, because the other steps are very fast (almost instantaneous) and they do not affect the overall rate significantly.

Example: For this reaction, these steps were experimentally observed:

Overall:

$$(CH_3)_3CCl \ (aq) + OH^- \ (aq) \rightarrow (CH_3)_3COH \ (aq) + Cl^- \ (aq)$$

Step 1:

$$(CH_3)_3CCl \ (aq) \rightarrow (CH_3)_3C^+ \ (aq) + Cl^- \ (aq) \quad \text{(slow)} \qquad r_1 = k[(CH_3)_3CCl]$$

Step 2:

$$(CH_3)_3C^+ \ (aq) + OH^- \ (aq) \rightarrow (CH_3)_3COH \ (aq) \quad \text{(fast)} \qquad r_2 = k[(CH_3)_3C^+] \cdot [OH^-]$$

The first step, which is the formation of the carbonium ion $(CH_3)_3C^+$, is very slow compared to the second step, where the carbocation immediately reacts with the OH^- ion. Thus, the first step is the rate-determining step and the overall rate law is determined by the rate law of this step where $r_1 = k[(CH_3)_3CCl]$.

There are also cases when the rate-determining step, or slowest step, is not the first step in the reaction mechanism. In these cases, an intermediate may appear in the rate-determining step. The intermediate must be substituted for so that it is not in the rate law. This requires a slightly more detailed approach to determining the rate law of the reaction mechanism.

Dependence of Reaction Rate on Temperature

An increase in temperature increases the average kinetic energy of the colliding molecules; thus, the molecules move faster. These faster molecules are more likely to possess the energy necessary to overcome the activation energy, and successfully collide and react. Faster molecules also collide with each other at an increased frequency. Therefore, using the collision theory, an increase in temperature increases the reaction rate.

However, some reactions might slow down or even stop as temperature increases. This is quite common among reactions in biological systems, because enzymes involved in the reaction could be damaged by higher temperatures, reducing the enzymes' capability to participate in reactions.

Activation energy

For a reaction to start, the reactants need to have enough energy to break existing bonds and create new ones. This minimum energy threshold is the *activation energy* (E_a).

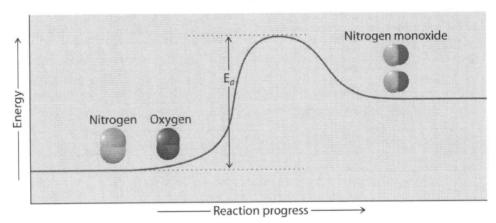

On the diagram above, the *energy barrier* (hill) between the reactants and the products. The reacting molecules need to increase their energy and proceed over the energy barrier before the reaction can produce products.

The activation energy E_a is the difference between energies of the reactant and the top of the reaction profile.

Activated complex or transition state

The transition state is located at the peak of the energy profile. In this state, bonds that are going to form are just beginning to form, and bonds that are going to break are just beginning to break. A molecule in transition can go either way; it can revert back to reactants, or it can form new molecules (i.e., products).

Unlike reaction *intermediates* (products that are produced in one elementary step and then consumed in the next step), molecules in the transition state cannot be isolated.

Transition states are formed once the reactants have enough energy to overcome the activation energy. Image (a) below shows steps of a complete reaction, whereas image (b) shows what happens if the activation energy is not overcome: no transition state and no products are formed.

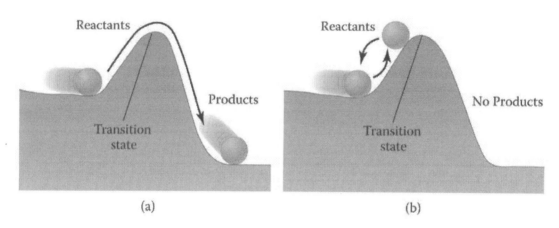

(a)

(b)

Exergonic reaction

Endergonic reaction

Transition states are denoted by adding square brackets [ ] around the molecule, while the dashed lines symbolize temporary bonds where bonds are being simultaneously formed and broken, as shown in the image below.

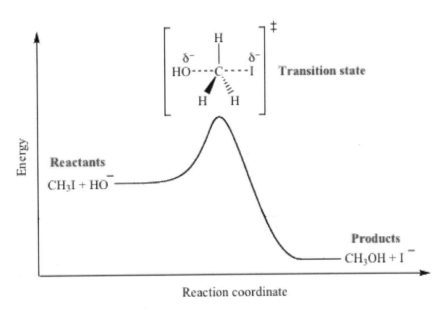

Interpretation of energy profiles showing energies of reactants and products, activation energy (E_{ac}), enthalpy (ΔH) for the reaction

In a reaction, the products and reactants often have different energy levels. The energy differential is released or absorbed from the system as heat. This heat is the heat of reaction (or enthalpy) of reaction (ΔH).

Based on their enthalpies, reactions can be classified as endothermic and exothermic.

In endothermic reactions, the products are at a higher energy level than reactants. To balance the energy levels, heat is absorbed by the system from its surroundings ($+\Delta H$). Energy is absorbed to break bonds. This is an energetically unfavorable reaction, and the temperature of the surroundings decreases.

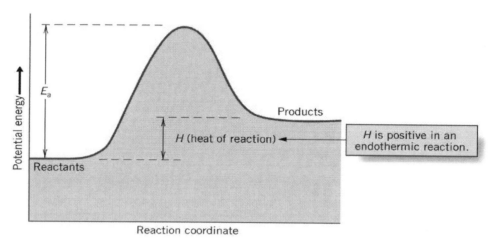

In exothermic reactions, the products are at a lower energy level than the reactants. Excess heat is released by the system towards its surroundings ($-\Delta H$). Energy is released when bonds are formed. This is an energetically favorable reaction, and the temperature of the surroundings increases.

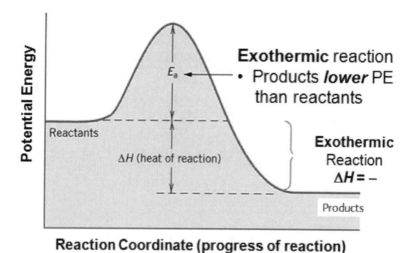

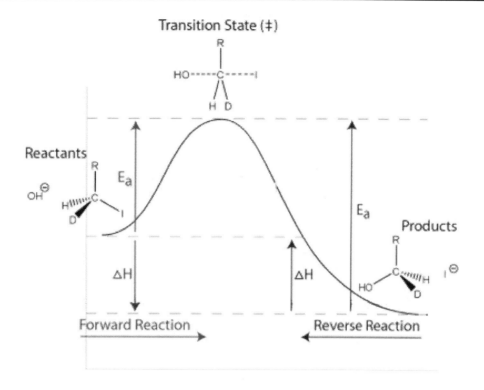

In any energy profile, the diagram summarizes the energies involved in a reaction, and gives the ΔH and E_A.

Arrhenius equation

As described previously, chemical reactions generally occur more rapidly at higher temperatures. This is represented by the Arrhenius equation, which was developed by Svante Arrhenius in 1889. The equation is as follows:

Arrhenius equation describes the relationship between the rate constant (k), temperature (T) and activation energy (E_a):

$$k = Ae^{-E_a/RT}$$

where k is the rate constant, R is the ideal gas constant ($R = 8.314$ J mol^{-1} K^{-1}), E_a is the activation energy, T is the temperature and A is the *Arrhenius frequency factor* (the pre-exponential factor or the collision factor), because it represents the frequency of collisions between molecules.

When using this equation, ensure that the units for the different quantities are correct. T should be in Kelvin, E_a should be in J/mol and A has the same units as rate constant k.

Taking the natural logarithm of both sides of this equation yields the Arrhenius equation in point-slope form:

$$\ln k = -(E_a / RT) + \ln A$$

If experimental data is graphed, where $\ln k$ is on the y-axis and $1 / T$ is on the x-axis, a straight line is obtained. On a plot of $\ln k$ vs. $1 / T$, the slope of the line is E_a / R and the y-intercept corresponds to $\ln A$.

By determining the slope of the line mathematically, the E_a can be determined. Similarly, by extrapolation, the line to the y-intercept, the $\ln A$ collision factor can be determined.

Since the slope embodies the activation energy (E_a), a simplified form of the Arrhenius equation can be used to determine the E_a. The information required is rate constants of the reaction at two different temperatures. Recall that the slope of a line is determined by the change in y over the change in x ("rise" over "run"). The following equation can be generated:

$$\ln\left(\frac{k_2}{k_1}\right) = -\frac{E_a}{R}\left[\frac{1}{T_2} - \frac{1}{T_1}\right]$$

The equation can be used to calculate the rate constant k of a reaction at two different temperatures (in Kelvin). The y-intercept ($\ln A$) can be ignored because it is a constant and not part of the slope calculation.

Example: A rate of reaction for a chemical process is investigated at two different temperatures. The rate of a reaction at 25 °C is 1.55×10^{-4} s^{-1}. At 50 °C, the rate of reaction is 3.88×10^{-4} s^{-1}.

Based on this data, what is the energy of activation for the chemical process expressed in J/mol?

Start by looking at the units of the quantities given in the problem. The units for both rates, s^{-1}, cancel each other. Since the energy of activation is to be expressed in J/mol, the logical choice of the gas constant, R, is 8.314 J/mol·K. This choice of R dictates the units for temperature. Since the R constant has temperature units expressed in Kelvin, K, the given temperatures must be converted to Kelvin:

$$T_1 = 25\ °C + 273 = 298\ K$$

$$T_2 = 50\ °C + 273 = 323\ K$$

Substitute the rate constants and temperatures into the Arrhenius equation:

$$\ln\left[\frac{3.88 \times 10^{-4}\ s^{-1}}{1.55 \times 10^{-4}\ s^{-1}}\right] = -\frac{E_a}{8.314\ J/mol \cdot K}\left[\frac{1}{323\ K} - \frac{1}{298\ K}\right]$$

Solve for E_a:

$$-17.503 = -\frac{E_a}{8.314\ J/mol \cdot K} \times (-2.60 \times 10^{-4})$$

$$-17.503 = (-3.13 \times 10^{-5}\ mol/J)\ E_a$$

$$E_a = -17.503 / -3.13 \times 10^{-5}\ mol/J = 5.59 \times 10^5\ J/mol$$

A slightly modified version of Arrhenius' equation replaces E_a with ΔH; this modified equation is the van't Hoff equation:

$$\ln\left(\frac{K_{T_2}}{K_{T_1}}\right) = \frac{\Delta H°}{R}\left(\frac{1}{T_1} - \frac{1}{T_2}\right)$$

Note that this equation is not the same as the Arrhenius equation, although the format looks similar. The van't Hoff equation is used to calculate the equilibrium constant K of a reaction at two different temperatures (in Kelvin).

Kinetic Control Versus Thermodynamic Control of a Reaction

There are a number of reactions in chemistry that can have two possible products, and the reaction conditions affect the selectivity of the reaction. One product is the *kinetic product*, which requires a lower activation energy and is formed preferentially at lower temperature. The other product is the *thermodynamic product*, which has a lower (i.e., negative and more favorable) ΔG, and is formed preferentially at higher temperature.

Thermodynamics explains how ΔG and other variables affect whether a reaction occurs spontaneously.

However, kinetics describes how fast a reaction occurs (based on the activation energy), and kinetics has no impact on the spontaneity or thermodynamics of a reaction.

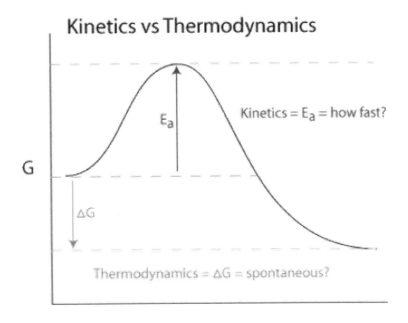

The energy profile diagram displays a reaction under kinetic control vs. thermodynamic control. Note that the starting materials are the same for both, but the ΔG, the transition states and the intermediates are different. The end product of the reaction is also different, depending on whether it is under thermodynamic or kinetic control.

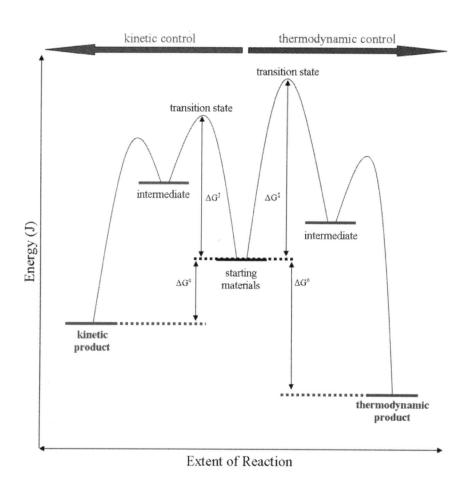

For example, when strong acids are added to certain conjugated dienes, such as butadiene, there are two possible products: the 1,2-product and the 1,4-product, in the image below.

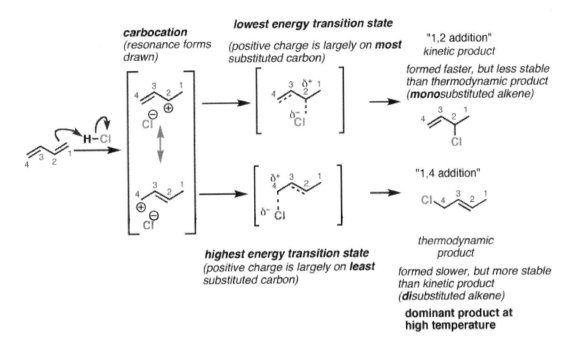

In the top transition state on the picture, the positive charge is localized on the most substituted carbon, and therefore this transition state is lower in energy. This indicates that the top reaction has a lower activation energy; thus, the 1,2 kinetic product is preferentially formed at lower temperatures.

Although the bottom transition state is higher in energy, the final 1,4-product is more stable than the kinetic 1,2-product because it is a disubstituted alkene, as opposed to a monosubstituted alkene.

Therefore, the bottom product is more thermodynamically stable and is dominant at higher temperatures.

The energy profile diagram for this particular reaction is given below.

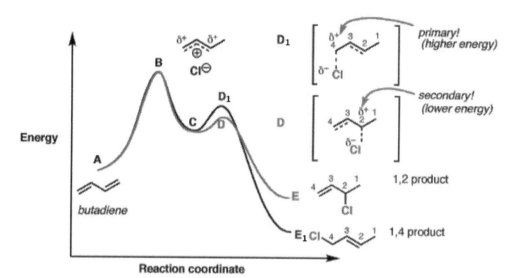

Energy coordinate for 1,2- versus 1,4- additions to butadiene

The height of transition states D and D_1 (and therefore their reaction rate from carbocation C) is related to the stability of the positive charge in D and D_1.

The lower the energy, the faster reaction. Therefore, E is formed faster from the primary carbocation intermediate C, since the energy of transition state D is less than D_1.

The energy of E and E_1 is related to the greater stability of the 1,4-alkene in this case (disubstituted versus monosubstituted). E_1 has a more substituted (internal) double bond than E, so it is more stable.

Catalysts, Enzyme Catalysis

Catalysts are substances added to a chemical reaction to increase the reaction rate. They lower the activation energy that needs to be reached for the reaction to proceed.

A catalyst participates in a chemical reaction, but remains chemically unchanged and can be used again. When a reaction mechanism is separated into its elementary steps, a catalyst appears at the start of the reaction and at the end of the reaction; therefore, a catalyst is neither a product nor a reactant.

Acids, bases and metal ions often act as catalysts.

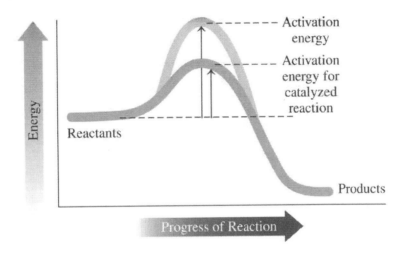

There are homogeneous catalysts and heterogeneous catalysts. *Homogeneous catalysts* are in the same phase as the reactants (e.g., both the reactant and the catalyst are in the gas phase).

A *heterogeneous catalyst* is in a different phase than the reactants. These catalysts often immobilize reactants near each other, increasing the likelihood of collision and therefore the rate of reaction. An example of a heterogeneous catalyst is a dissolved acid that catalyzes the hydrolysis of esters in an aqueous solution. The majority of heterogeneous catalysts are solids, and the reactants are generally gases or liquids. An example is iron, which catalyzes the synthesis of ammonia from gaseous N_2 and H_2.

Modern cars are equipped with *catalytic converters* in their exhaust systems. These are heterogeneous catalysts that provide a solid surface for the molecules to bind to and react. Catalytic converters help to reduce pollutants such as carbon monoxide (CO), nitrogen oxide (NO) and hydrocarbons, including octane (C_8H_{18}). The catalyst usually consists of solid particles, including platinum (Pt) and palladium (Pd).

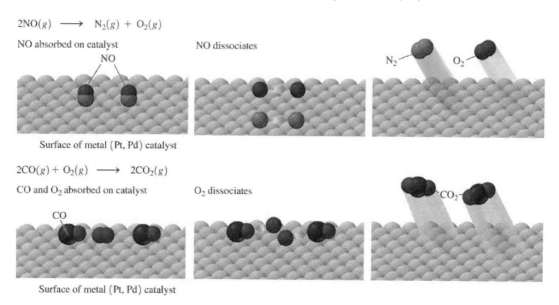

$$2NO(g) \longrightarrow N_2(g) + O_2(g)$$

NO absorbed on catalyst   NO dissociates

Surface of metal (Pt, Pd) catalyst

$$2CO(g) + O_2(g) \longrightarrow 2CO_2(g)$$

CO and O_2 absorbed on catalyst O_2 dissociates

Surface of metal (Pt, Pd) catalyst

Enzymes are biological catalysts (usually proteins) that increase the reaction rates of biochemical reactions. Biological enzymes are much more efficient than normal chemical catalysts; enzymes can enhance the rate of a chemical reaction by a factor of more than ten million (1×10^7). Enzymes are also highly specific; they form enzyme-substrate complexes with the reactants. A *substrate* is the molecule on which an enzyme acts.

For example, when hydrogen peroxide is put on a cut, oxygen gas is produced by the decomposition of hydrogen peroxide by an enzyme, catalase, found in the blood.

$$2\,H_2O_2\,(l) \xrightarrow{\text{catalase}} 2\,H_2O\,(l) + O_2\,(g)$$

Catalysts are written above or below the arrow in the reaction equation.

Previously, it was discussed how changing variables (i.e., reactant concentration and temperature) can increase the rate of reaction. The addition of a catalyst has a similar effect on reaction rate, but simply uses a different method.

Factor	Reason
Increasing reactant concentration	More collisions
Increasing temperature	More collisions exceeding energy of activation
Adding a catalyst	Lowers energy of activation

Equilibrium in Reversible Chemical Reactions

Some chemical reactions are reversible; they can form products in either direction, resulting in an equilibrium mixture of reactants and products. If a chemical bond can be formed, it can also be broken with enough input of energy. Reversible chemical reactions are indicated by either a double-headed arrow or two arrows facing opposite directions:

$$A + B \leftrightarrow AB$$

$$A + B \leftrightarrows AB$$

The forward reaction occurs when A and B form AB. When a sufficient amount of AB builds up, the reverse reaction occurs and A and B are reformed. At the point when both the forward and the reverse reactions are occurring at the same rate, the reaction is said to be in a state of chemical *equilibrium.*

Equilibrium does not mean that there are equal amounts of reactants and products but is the point where the amount of reactants and products remain constant: the forward and reverse reactions proceed at equal rates.

For example, take the following reaction:

$$2\,SO_2\,(g) + O_2\,(g) \; \rightleftarrows \; 2\,SO_3\,(g)$$

Starting with the reactants, SO_2 and O_2, the reaction proceeds in the forward direction and the product SO_3 is formed until equilibrium is reached. Starting with only the product SO_3, the reaction proceeds in the reverse direction, and forms SO_2 and O_2 until equilibrium is reached. As shown in the image below, the equilibrium concentrations of SO_2, O_2, and SO_3 are the same for both the forward and reverse reactions.

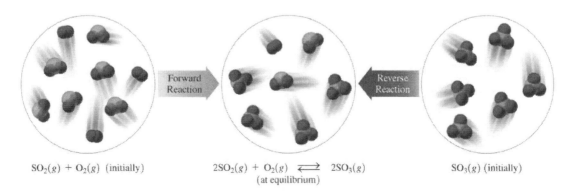

$SO_2(g) + O_2(g)$ (initially) $2SO_2(g) + O_2(g) \rightleftarrows 2SO_3(g)$ $SO_3(g)$ (initially)
(at equilibrium)

Consider another example of a reversible reaction: evaporation and condensation of water. If water is placed over a gas-filled chamber, separated by a moving piston (see diagram below), work on/by the system can be observed by measuring the compression or expansion of the gas. As water evaporates, the water weighs less and it allows the gas to expand. Similarly, when water vapor condenses, it increases the weight of water and compresses the gas. However, once the system reaches equilibrium, the liquid-to-vapor ratio is constant and the gas will not compress or expand, which leads to the conclusion that there is no work being done by or against the system at equilibrium. Water molecules are still constantly transforming between liquid and gas phases, but the rate of evaporation matches the rate of condensation, so there is not any noticeable shift in composition.

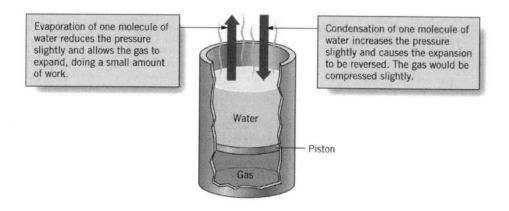

Law of mass action

The *law of mass action* states that the rate of a reaction depends on the concentration of the substances participating in the reaction.

$$a\text{A} + b\text{B} \rightleftharpoons c\text{C} + d\text{D}$$

$$\text{rate}_{\text{rxn}} = \left(-\frac{1}{a}\right)\frac{\Delta \text{A}}{\Delta t} = \left(-\frac{1}{b}\right)\frac{\Delta \text{B}}{\Delta t} = \left(+\frac{1}{c}\right)\frac{\Delta \text{C}}{\Delta t} = \left(+\frac{1}{d}\right)\frac{\Delta \text{D}}{\Delta t}$$

Using the law of mass action, the equilibrium constant is derived by setting the forward reaction rate equal to the reverse reaction rate, which is what happens at equilibrium.

For the reaction:

$$a\text{A} + b\text{B} \rightleftharpoons c\text{C} + d\text{D}$$

The following relationships are true:

- $r_{\text{forward}} = r_{\text{reverse}}$

- $k_{\text{forward}} \cdot [\text{A}]^a \cdot [\text{B}]^b = k_{\text{reverse}} \cdot [\text{C}]^c \cdot [\text{D}]^d$

- $K_c = k_{\text{forward}} / k_{\text{reverse}} = [\text{C}]^c \cdot [\text{D}]^d / [\text{A}]^a \cdot [\text{B}]^b$

The law of mass action is based on the equilibrium constant K_c, which is the ratio of the concentration of the products to the concentration of the reactants.

When writing the mass action expression of an equilibrium, only include the components in the equilibrium that are in the same phase. Notice that pure solids and liquids do not appear in the mass action expression.

This is seen in the following example:

$$CaCO_3\,(s) \rightleftharpoons CaO\,(s) + CO_2\,(g)$$

$$K_c = [CO_2]$$

$$2\,HCl\,(aq) + CaCO_3\,(s) \rightleftharpoons CaCl_2\,(aq) + CO_2\,(g) + 2\,H_2O\,(l)$$

The net ionic equation for the above reaction is:

$$2\,H^+\,(aq) + CaCO_3\,(s) \rightleftharpoons Ca^{2+}\,(aq) + CO_2\,(g) + 2\,H_2O\,(l)$$

(Cl^- ions were present on both sides of the equation; therefore, they are spectator ions and can be removed from the net equation.)

$$K_{c1} = [Ca^{2+}]\,/\,[H^+]^2 \qquad or \qquad K_{c2} = [CO_2]$$

There are two forms of the mass action equilibrium constant: K_{c1} is expressed in terms of the concentrations of the aqueous species, while K_{c2} is expressed in terms of the concentration of the gaseous species. These two constants have different values; the commonly used K values are based on the easiest phase to experimentally measure. Do not mix phases, and do not include the solid in either expression. When dealing with mass action problems, always check the phases of molecules in the reaction.

Equilibrium Constant

Equilibrium constant (K_c) represents the ratio of molar concentrations of products and reactants at equilibrium. It can also be abbreviated as K_{eq}, which is a more general term for an equilibrium constant that can refer to either equilibrium with respect to concentration, or equilibrium with respect to partial pressures.

For the reaction $\quad aA + bB \rightleftharpoons cC + dD \quad$ the equilibrium constant is:

$$K_c = \frac{[C]^c[D]^d}{[A]^a[B]^b} = \frac{[products]}{[reactants]}$$

The equilibrium constant is a temperature-specific constant. It always has the same value, regardless of the molar concentrations, as long as the temperature does not change.

The units of K_c depend on the specific reaction, and K_c is without units.

Here is a guide to calculating the K_c value:

1. State the given and needed qualities.
2. Write the K_c expression for the equilibrium.
3. Substitute equilibrium (molar) concentrations and calculate K_c.

Example: What is the value of K_c at 443 °C if the equilibrium concentrations are:

$$H_2\,(g) + I_2\,(g) \;\rightleftharpoons\; 2\,HI\,(g)$$

$[H_2] = 1.2$ mol/L $\qquad$ $[I_2] = 1.2$ mol/L $\qquad$ $[HI] = 0.35$ mol/L

Step 1: State the given and needed quantities.

Given		Need
Reactants	*Products*	
$[H_2] = 1.2$ mol/L	$[HI] = 0.35$ mol/L	
$[I_2] = 1.2$ mol/L		K_c

Step 2: Write the K_c expression for the equilibrium.

$$K_c = \frac{[HI]^2}{[H_2] \cdot [I_2]}$$

Step 3: Substitute equilibrium (molar) concentrations and calculate K_c.

$$K_c = \frac{[0.35]^2}{[1.2] \cdot [1.2]} = 8.5 \times 10^{-2}$$

Small K_c	$K_c \approx 1$	Large K_c
Mostly reactants		Mostly products
Products << Reactants Little reaction takes place	Reactants ≈ Products Moderate reaction	Products >> Reactants Reaction essentially complete

The value of K_c depends on whether equilibrium is reached with more products or reactants. However, the size of the equilibrium constant does not affect how fast equilibrium is reached.

Reactions with a large K_c have large amounts of products created from the forward reaction at equilibrium, and these products predominate at equilibrium.

Reactions with a small K_c have large amounts of reactants that predominate at equilibrium. This is demonstrated by the examples below.

The equilibrium constant for the reaction of SO_2 and O_2 has a large K_c.

$$2\,SO_2\,(g) + O_2\,(g) \;\rightleftharpoons\; 2\,SO_3\,(g)$$

At equilibrium, the reaction contains mostly products and few reactants.

$$K_c = \frac{[SO_3]^2}{[SO_2]^2[O_2]} = \frac{\text{Mostly products}}{\text{Few reactants}} = 3.4 \times 10^2$$

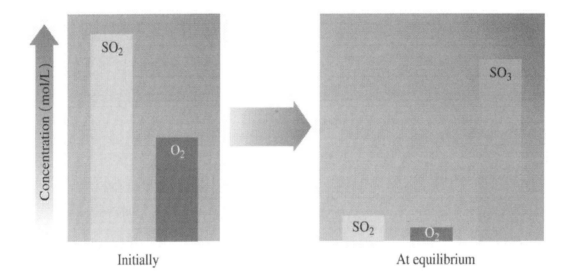

$$2\,SO_2\,(g) + O_2\,(g) \rightleftharpoons 2SO_3\,(g)$$

Meanwhile, reactions with a small K_c have an equilibrium mixture with a low concentration of products and a high concentration of reactants.

The equilibrium constant for the reaction of N_2 and O_2 has a small K_c.

$$N_2\,(g) + O_2\,(g) \rightleftharpoons 2\,NO\,(g)$$

At equilibrium, the reaction mixture contains few products and mostly reactants.

$$K_c = \frac{[NO]^2}{[N_2][O_2]} = \frac{\text{few products}}{\text{mostly reactants}} = 2 \times 10^{-9}$$

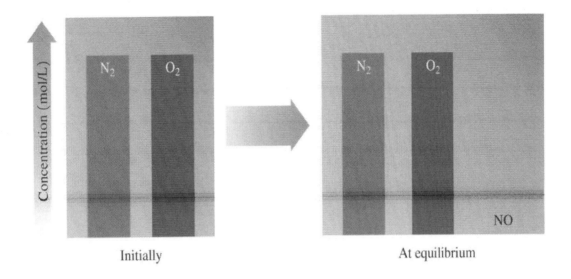

Initially   At equilibrium

$$N_2 \, (g) + O_2 \, (g) \leftrightarrows 2NO \, (g)$$

A *homogeneous equilibrium* is a reaction in which all of the products and reactants are in the same physical state, such as the reaction in the following example:

$$2\, SO_2 \, (g) + O_2 \, (g) \rightleftarrows 2\, SO_3 \, (g)$$

$$K_c = \frac{[SO_3]^2}{[SO_2]^2[O_2]}$$

A *heterogeneous equilibrium* is a reaction where one of the substances is in a different physical state, such as the reaction in the following example:

$$C \, (s) + H_2O \, (g) \rightleftarrows CO \, (g) + H_2 \, (g)$$

$$K_c = \frac{[CO] \cdot [H_2]}{[H_2O]}$$

Notice that the concentrations of liquids and solids do not change, and are therefore omitted from the equilibrium constant expression. This is a similar concept to the mass-action equilibrium.

The reaction quotient (Q_c) is calculated using the same method as K_c, but calculation of Q_c can be performed at any time during the reaction.

Q_c is a "snapshot" of the system, representing the ratio between products and reactants at a given time.

A comparison of Q_c and K_c can determine the direction of the reaction:

- If $Q_c > K_c$, reaction creates more reactants

- If $Q_c < K_c$, reaction creates more products

- If $Q_c = K_c$, reaction is at equilibrium

Application of Le Châtelier's principle

Le Châtelier's principle states that when a reversible reaction at equilibrium is stressed by a change in concentration, pressure, volume or temperature, the equilibrium shifts to relieve or counteract the effect of that change.

For the equilibrium between colorless N_2O_4 and brown NO_2:

$$N_2O_4\,(g) \rightleftarrows 2\,NO_2\,(g)$$

Effect of Concentration

If the amount of N_2O_4 reactant is increased, the reaction shifts to the right to produce more NO_2 product. If the amount of NO_2 product is increased, the reaction shifts to the left to produce more N_2O_4 reactant.

Effect of Pressure

In a gaseous equilibrium, increasing the pressure shifts the reaction to the side with fewer gas molecules. In the reaction $N_2O_4\,(g) \rightleftarrows 2\,NO_2\,(g)$, increasing the pressure shifts the reaction to the left, producing more N_2O_4. If there are the same moles of gases on both the reactant and product side, then changing the pressure does not shift the equilibrium.

Effect of Decreasing Volume on Equilibrium

A change in the volume of a gas mixture at equilibrium changes the concentration of the gases in the mixture.

Decreasing volume, shifts toward fewer moles

$$2\,CO_2\,(g) + O_2\,(g) \rightleftarrows 2\,CO_2\,(g)$$

Decreasing the volume increases the concentration of the gases. The system shifts in the direction of the smaller number of moles to compensate for the decrease in volume..

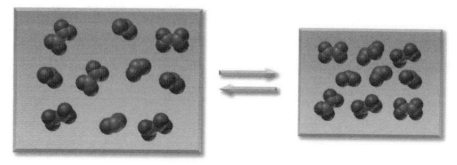

1.00 L at equilibrium   0.750 L at equilibrium

Effect of Increasing Volume on Equilibrium:

A change in the volume of a gas mixture changes the concentration of the gases.

Increasing volume, shifts toward more moles

$$2\ CO\ (g) + O_2\ (g) \rightleftarrows 2\ CO_2\ (g)$$

Increasing the volume decreases the concentration of the gases. The system shifts in the direction of the larger number of moles to compensate.

The effect of temperature on equilibrium depends on the ΔH of a reaction (i.e., endothermic or exothermic).

Endothermic Reaction Equilibrium and Temperature

Decreasing the temperature of an endothermic reaction ($+\Delta H$) causes the system to respond by shifting the reaction toward more heat; in this case it is toward the reactants, increasing heat in the system.

$$N_2O_4\ (g) + heat \rightleftarrows 2\ NO_2\ (g)$$

Decrease temperature

Increasing the temperature of an endothermic reaction causes the system to respond by shifting the reaction to remove heat; in this case it is towards the products, consuming the heat.

$$N_2O_4\,(g) + heat \rightleftarrows 2\,NO_2\,(g)$$

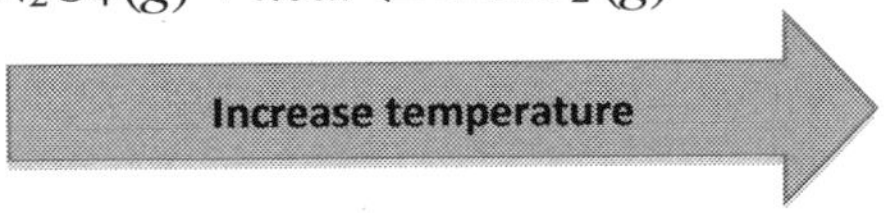

Increase temperature

Exothermic Reaction Equilibrium and Temperature

Decreasing the temperature of an exothermic reaction ($-\Delta H$) causes the system to respond by shifting the reaction toward more heat; it shifts the reaction toward the products, increasing heat in the system.

$$2\,SO_2\,(g) + O_2\,(g) \rightleftarrows 2\,SO_3\,(g) + heat$$

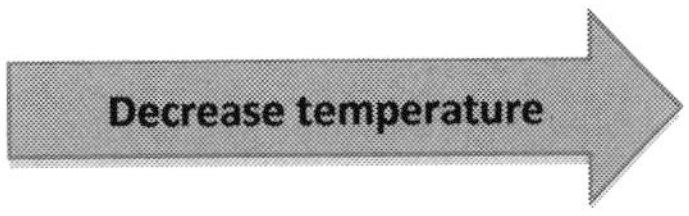

Decrease temperature

Increasing the temperature of an exothermic reaction causes the system to respond by shifting the reaction toward removing heat; it shifts the reaction toward the reactants, decreasing heat in the system.

$$2\,SO_2\,(g) + O_2\,(g) \rightleftarrows 2\,SO_3\,(g) + heat$$

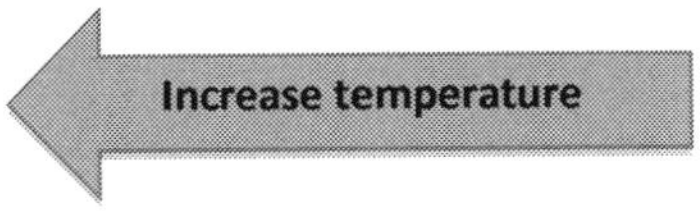

Increase temperature

Summary of changes in conditions and effect on equilibrium:

Condition	Change (Stress)	Equilibrium Shifts Towards…
Concentration	Add a reactant	Products (forward reaction)
	Remove a reactant	Reactants (reverse reaction)
	Add a product	Reactants (reverse reaction)
	Remove a product	Products (forward reaction)
Volume (container)	Decrease volume	Side with lower total coefficients (*aq* and *g*)*
	Increase volume	Side with higher total coefficients (*aq* and *g*)
Pressure	Decrease pressure	Side with higher total coefficients (*aq* and *g*)
	Increase pressure	Side with lower total coefficients (*aq* and *g*)
Temperature	**Endothermic Rxn**	
	Raise T	Products (forward reaction to remove heat)
	Lower T	Reactants (reverse reaction to add heat)
	Exothermic Rxn	
	Raise T	Reactants (reverse reaction to add heat)
	Lower T	Products (forward reaction to remove heat)
Catalyst	Increases rates equally	No effect

* Pure solids and pure liquids are not included in equilibrium expression.

Equilibrium is an important concept in many systems, including biological ones. For example, oxygen transport involves an equilibrium between hemoglobin (Hb), oxygen and oxyhemoglobin (HbO_2).

$$Hb\,(aq) + O_2\,(g) \rightleftarrows HbO_2\,(aq)$$

$$K_c = \frac{[HbO_2]}{[Hb] \cdot [O_2]}$$

When there is a high concentration of O_2 in the alveoli of the lungs, the reaction shifts to make more oxyhemoglobin. When the concentration of O_2 is low in the tissues, the reverse reaction releases O_2 from oxyhemoglobin.

At normal atmospheric pressure, oxygen diffuses into the blood because the partial pressure of oxygen in the alveoli is higher than that in the blood. At altitudes above 8,000 ft, a decrease in atmospheric pressure results in a lower pressure of O_2.

Hypoxia may occur at high altitudes where the oxygen concentration is lower. At an altitude of 18,000 ft, a person obtains 29% less oxygen and may experience hypoxia. According to Le Châtelier's principle, a decrease in oxygen shifts the equilibrium in the direction of the reactants and depletes the concentration of HbO_2, which can cause hypoxia.

$$Hb\ (aq) + O_2\ (g) \ \rightleftarrows \ HbO_2\ (aq)$$

Removing product

Here is another reaction to practice applying Le Châtelier's principle.

In the following example, indicate the shift in equilibrium caused by each change:

$$2\ NO_2\ (g)\ +\ heat\ \rightleftarrows\ 2\ NO\ (g) + O_2\ (g)$$

toward products or *toward reactants*

A. adding NO
B. lowering the temperature

C. removing O_2
D. increasing the volume
E. removing NO

Solution:

A. adding NO: *toward reactants*

B. lowering the temperature: *toward reactants*

C. removing O_2: *toward products*

D. increasing the volume: *toward products*

E. removing NO: *toward products*

Relationship of the Equilibrium Constant and Δ*G*°

Gibbs free energy (Δ*G*°) is an expression for the free energy of a system. In the previous chapter, the following equation, relating Gibbs free energy to the equilibrium constant, was given:

$$\Delta G^\circ = -RT \ln K$$

Taking the antilog (e^x) of both sides gives:

$$K = e^{-\Delta G^\circ / RT}$$

The Δ*G* and *K*$_c$ m only implies the direction and extent of a reaction, not the rate.

ΔG affects the position of equilibrium in the following ways:

- When Δ*G*° > 0 (positive):

Equilibrium is closer to reactants; reverse reaction (towards reactants) is spontaneous.

- When Δ*G*° < 0 (negative):

Equilibrium is closer to products; forward reaction (towards products) is spontaneous.

- When Δ*G*° = 0:

Reaction is at equilibrium; there is no net change to system or surroundings. Reaction appears spontaneous in either direction if some small change is made to some property of the system.

For example, consider the freezing of water at 0 °C:

$$H_2O \ (l) \rightarrow H_2O \ (s)$$

The system remains at equilibrium as long as no heat is added or removed. Both phases can exist together indefinitely.

Below 0 °C, Δ*G* < 0 and freezing is spontaneous. Above 0 °C, Δ*G* > 0 and freezing is nonspontaneous.

The energy profile below displays a reaction with positive ΔG (nonspontaneous).

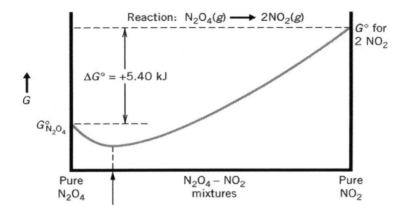

This energy profile below displays a reaction with negative ΔG (spontaneous).

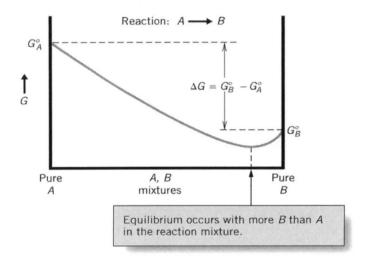

Example: Calculate the equilibrium constant at 25 °C for the decarboxylation of liquid pyruvic acid to form gaseous acetaldehyde (CH_3COH) and carbon dioxide (CO_2).

$$CH_3COCOOH \rightleftarrows CH_3COH + CO_2$$

Compound	$\Delta G°_f$ (kJ/mol)
CH_3COH	−133.30
$CH_3COCOOH$	−463.38
CO_2	−394.36

First, sum the $\Delta G°_f$ for each reaction to obtain the total $\Delta G°$.

$$\Delta G° = \Delta G°_f (CH_3COH) + \Delta G°_f (CO_2) - \Delta G°_f (CH_3COCOOH)$$

$$\Delta G° = -133.30 + (-394.36) - (-463.38)$$

$$\Delta G° = -64.28 \text{ kJ}$$

Use the $\Delta G°$ value to calculate K:

$$K = e^{-\Delta G° / RT}$$

$$\frac{\Delta G°}{RT} = \frac{-64.28 \text{ kJ}}{(8.314 \text{ J/K}) \times (298 \text{ K})} \times \frac{1,000 \text{ J}}{\text{kJ}} = -25.94$$

$$K = e^{-(-25.945)} = e^{25.945}$$

$$K = 1.85 \times 10^{11}$$

Relationship of the Equilibrium Constant and ΔH°, ΔS°

The previous section describes the relationship between the equilibrium constant and ΔG, however enthalpy H and entropy S are both also related to the equilibrium constant. It is known that:

$$\Delta G° = \Delta H° - T\Delta S°$$

and

$$\Delta G° = -RT \ln K$$

therefore,

$$-RT \ln K = \Delta H° - T\Delta S°$$

A rearrangement of that equation yields the following *point-slope formula*:

$$\ln K = -(\Delta H° / R)(1 / T) + (\Delta S° / R)$$

This equation is in the form of line equation, which means that on a plot of $\ln K$ vs. $1 / T$, the slope is $-\Delta H° / RT$, and the *y*-intercept is $\Delta S° / R$.

Practice Questions

1. Which statement is NOT a correct characterization for a catalyst?

    A. Catalysts are not consumed in a reaction
    B. Catalysts do not actively participate in a reaction
    C. Catalysts lower the activation energy for a reaction
    D. Catalysts can be either solids, liquids or gases

2. What is the rate law for the following reaction that was found to be first order in each of the two reactants and second order overall?

$$2 \, NO \, (g) + O_2 \, (g) \rightarrow 2 \, NO_2 \, (g)$$

    A. rate = $k[NO]^2 \cdot [O_2]^2$ C. rate = $k[NO] \cdot [O_2]$
    B. rate = $k[NO_2]^2 \cdot [NO]^{-2} \cdot [O_2]^{-\frac{1}{2}}$ D. rate = $k[NO]^2$

3. Which equilibrium constant applies to a reversible reaction involving a gaseous mixture at equilibrium?

    A. Ionization equilibrium constant, K_w C. Solubility product equilibrium constant, K_{sp}
    B. General equilibrium constant, K_p D. Ionization equilibrium constant, K_i

4. What is the equilibrium constant (K_{eq}) expression for the following reaction:

$$CaCO_3 \, (s) \leftrightarrow CaO \, (s) + CO_2 \, (g)$$

    A. $K_{eq} = [CO_2]$ C. $K_{eq} = [CaO] \cdot [CO_2] / [CaCO_3]$
    B. $K_{eq} = 1 / [CO_2]$ D. $K_{eq} = [CaO] \cdot [CO_2]$

5. Which of the following statements about catalysts is NOT true?

    A. A catalyst does not change the energy of the reactants or the products
    B. A catalyst increases the rate of slow reactions
    C. A catalyst is consumed in a reaction
    D. A catalyst alters the rate of a chemical reaction

6. Increasing the temperature of a chemical reaction increases the rate of reaction because:

    A. both the collision frequency and collision energies of reactant molecules increase
    B. the collision frequency of reactant molecules increases
    C. the activation energy increases
    D. the activation energy decreases

7. If $K_{eq} = 6.1 \times 10^{-11}$, which statement is true?

A. Slightly more products are present

B. The amount of reactants equals products

C. Mostly products are present

D. Mostly reactants are present

8. Which is true before a reaction reaches chemical equilibrium?

A. The amounts of reactants and products are equal

B. The amounts of reactants and products are constant

C. The amount of products is decreasing

D. The amount of products is increasing

9. Why might increasing temperature alter the rate of a chemical reaction?

A. The molecules combine with other atoms at high temperature to save space

B. The density decreases as a function of temperature that increases volume and decreases reaction rate

C. The molecules have a higher kinetic energy and have more force when colliding

D. The molecules are less reactive at higher temperatures

10. In the following reaction, how does increasing the pressure affect the equilibrium?

$$2 \, SO_2 \, (g) + O_2 \, (g) \leftrightarrow 2 \, SO_3 \, (g) + heat$$

A. Remains unchanged, but the reaction mixture gets warmer

B. Remains unchanged, but the reaction mixture gets cooler

C. Shifts to the right towards products

D. Shifts to the left towards reactants

11. According to Le Chatelier's principle, which changes shifts the equilibrium to the left for the following reactions?

$$N_2 \, (g) + 3 \, H_2 \, (g) \leftrightarrow 2 \, NH_3 \, (g) + heat$$

A. Decreasing the temperature

B. Increasing [H_2]

C. Increasing [N_2] the pressure

D. Decreasing the pressure on the system

12. What is the term for a dynamic state of a reversible reaction in which the rates of the forward and reverse reactions are equal?

A. chemical equilibrium

B. rate equilibrium

C. reversible equilibrium

D. concentration equilibrium

13. When a system is at equilibrium, the:

    A. reaction rate of the forward reaction is small compared to the reverse

    B. amount of products and reactants is exactly equal

    C. reaction rate of the forward reaction is equal to the rate of the reverse

    D. reaction rate of the reverse reaction is small compared to the forward

Solutions

1. B is correct.

Enzymes (i.e., biological catalysts) bind to substrates to form an enzyme-substrate complex. While in this complex, enzymes often align reactive chemical groups and hold them closer together. Enzymes can induce structural changes that strain substrate bonds. Therefore, catalysts can actively participate in reactions.

The main function of catalysts is lowering the reaction's activation energy (energy barrier), thus increasing its rate (k).

Although catalysts do decrease the amount of energy required to reach the rate-limiting transition state, they do *not* decrease the relative energy of the products and reactants.

Therefore, a catalyst has no effect on ΔG.

A catalyst provides an alternative pathway for the reaction to proceed to product formation. It lowers the energy of activation (i.e., relative energy between reactants and transition state) and therefore speed the rate of the reaction.

Catalysts have no effect on the Gibbs free energy (ΔG: stability of products vs. reactants) or the enthalpy (ΔH: bond breaking in reactants or bond making in products).

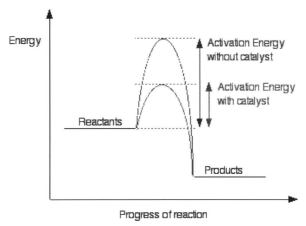

2. C is correct.

The rate law is calculated by comparing trials and determining how changes in the initial concentrations of the reactants affect the rate of the reaction.

$$\text{rate} = k[A]^x \cdot [B]^y$$

where k is the rate constant and the exponents x and y are the partial reaction orders (i.e., determined experimentally). They are not equal to the stoichiometric coefficients.

In order to write a complete rate law, the order of each reactant is required.

The order of each reactant has been provided by the problem (first order in each).

The total order is a sum of the individual orders: $1 + 1 = 2$. However, the total order is usually not expressed in the rate law.

3. B is correct.

To determine the amount of each compound at equilibrium, consider the chemical reaction written in the form:

$$aA + bB \leftrightarrow cC + dD$$

The equilibrium constant is:

$$K_{eq} = ([C]^c \times [D]^d / ([A]^a \times [B]^b)$$

K_w is the notation for the self-ionization (i.e., autoionization) constant for water.

K_{sp} is used for "solubility" and is only applicable for equilibriums for solids dissolving in liquids.

K_i is used for "ionization" and is only applicable for equilibrium systems that involve liquids.

For equilibria in the gas phase, the equilibrium equation (K_p) is a function of the partial pressures (P) of the reactants and products. Therefore:

$$K_p = ([P_C]^c \times [P_D]^d) / ([P_A]^a \times [P_B]^b)$$

Where P represents partial pressure, usually in atm.

4. A is correct.

General formula for the equilibrium constant of a reaction:

$$aA + bB \leftrightarrow cC + dD$$

$$K_{eq} = ([C]^c \times [D]^d) / ([A]^a \times [B]^b)$$

For equilibrium constant calculation, only include species in aqueous or gas phases:

$$K_{eq} = [CO_2]$$

5. C is correct. The main function of catalysts is lowering the reaction's activation energy (energy barrier), thus increasing its rate (k).

Although catalysts do decrease the amount of energy required to reach the rate-limiting transition state, they do *not* decrease the relative energy of the products and reactants. Therefore, a catalyst has no effect on ΔG.

A catalyst is never consumed in a reaction; reagents are consumed during the reaction.

A catalyst lowers the energy of the high-energy transition state (i.e., the activation energy), but it does not change the energy of the reactants of the reactants or the products.

Catalysts increases the rate of chemical reactions.

6. A is correct. Temperature is a measure of the average kinetic energy of the molecules. Increasing the temperature increase both the collision frequency (i.e., due to increased probability of molecules striking each other) and collision energies (kinetic energy = $\frac{1}{2}mv^2$) of reactant molecules.

7. D is correct.

For the general equation:

$$a\text{A} + b\text{B} \leftrightarrow c\text{C} + d\text{D}$$

The equilibrium constant is:

$$K_{eq} = ([\text{C}]^c \times [\text{D}]^d) / ([\text{A}]^a \times [\text{B}]^b)$$

or

$$K_{eq} = [\text{products}] / [\text{reactants}]$$

If K_{eq} is less than 1 (e.g., 6.1×10^{-11}), then the numerator (i.e., products) is smaller than the denominator (i.e., reactants) and fewer products have formed relative to the reactants.

If the reaction favors reactants compared to products, the equilibrium lies to the left.

8. D is correct.

A reaction proceeds with the formation of products.

Therefore, the rate of the forward reaction is greater than the rate of the reverse reaction until the reaction achieves equilibrium. At equilibrium, the rate (not relative concentrations of products and reactants) decreases for the forward reaction while the rate of the reverse reaction increases. At equilibrium, the rate of the forward reaction equals the rate of the reverse reaction.

An endergonic reaction (i.e., $+\Delta G$) has less products formed than reactants remaining (i.e., reaction is nonspontaneous) with the products higher in energy than the reactants.

An exergonic reaction (i.e., $-\Delta G$) has more products formed than reactants remaining (i.e., reaction is spontaneous) with the products lower in energy than the reactants.

The main function of catalysts is lowering the reaction's activation energy (energy barrier), thus increasing its rate (k).

Although catalysts do decrease the amount of energy required to reach the rate-limiting transition state, they do *not* decrease the relative energy of the products and reactants. Therefore, a catalyst has no effect on ΔG.

A catalyst provides an alternative pathway for the reaction to proceed to product formation. They lower the energy of activation (i.e., relative energy between reactants and transition state), and therefore speed the rate of the reaction.

Catalysts have no effect on the Gibbs free energy (ΔG: stability of products vs. reactants) or the enthalpy (ΔH: bond breaking in reactants or bond making in products).

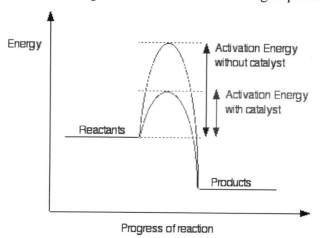

9. C is correct.

As the average kinetic energy (i.e., $KE = \frac{1}{2}mv^2$) *increases*, the particles move faster and collide more frequently per unit time and possess greater energy when they collide. This *increases* the *reaction rate*. Hence the *reaction rate* of most *reactions increases* with *increasing temperature*.

10. C is correct.

When changing the conditions of a reaction, Le Châtelier's principle states that the position of equilibrium shifts to counteract the change. If the reaction temperature, pressure or volume change, the position of equilibrium changes.

In general, increasing the pressure tends to favor the side of the reaction that has a lower molar coefficient sum (i.e., toward the products in this example).

11. D is correct.

When changing the conditions of a reaction, Le Châtelier's principle states that the position of equilibrium shifts to counteract the change. If the reaction temperature, pressure or volume is changed, the position of equilibrium will change.

Removing reactants or adding products shifts the equilibrium to the left.

In this reaction, reducing the pressure of the system favors the reactants because of their respective molar concentrations of reactants (i.e., 1 + 3) and products (i.e., 2).

All other modifications listed would shift the equilibrium toward products (i.e., to the right).

12. A is correct.

Equilibrium refers to the state when the rate of the forward reaction equals the rate of the reverse reaction. It does not describe the state when the relative energy of the reactants and products is the same nor does it describe the state when the relative amounts of reactants and products is the same.

13. C is correct.

Chemical equilibrium refers to a dynamic process whereby the rate at which a reactant molecule is being transformed into product is the same as the rate for a product molecule to be transformed into a reactant. Therefore, the reaction rate of the forward reaction is equal to the rate of the reverse.

Chapter 7

Acids and Bases

- **Acid–Base Equilibria**
- **Titration**

Acid–Base Equilibria

Before the twentieth century, acids, bases and salts were characterized by properties such as taste and their ability to change the color of *litmus* (a water soluble mixture of organic dyes). Acids taste sour (e.g., lemon juice), bases taste bitter (e.g., mustard), and salts, as their name suggests, taste salty (e.g., sodium chloride, or table salt).

Acids cause blue litmus paper to turn red, bases turn red litmus paper blue, while neutral compounds do not affect the color of litmus paper.

Bases are also recognized by their slippery feel (e.g., soap). In modern times, acids and bases are categorically classified by their position on the pH scale.

The chemistry of acids and bases has a very significant role in processes within nature, as well as industry. Some complex metabolic processes in the human body are controlled by physiological pH (~ 7.4); even a small change in this pH may lead to serious illness and death. Another example is the acidity of soil, which is essential to plant growth.

Additionally, acids and bases are very important in manufacturing industries. Sulfuric acid (H_2SO_4) is the most widely produced chemical. It is needed in the production of fertilizers, polymers, steel and many other materials. The extensive use of sulfuric acid has also led to environmental problems, such as the phenomenon of acid rain.

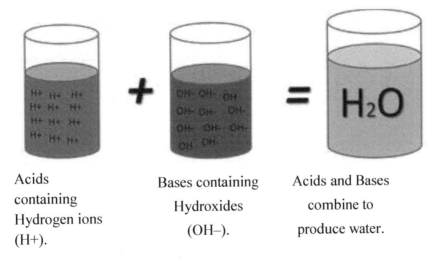

Acids containing Hydrogen ions (H+).

Bases containing Hydroxides (OH–).

Acids and Bases combine to produce water.

Acids have names that are slightly different from the ionic naming rules discussed earlier, while bases follow the naming rules. There are two types of acids: binary acids (acids that do not contain oxygen atoms) and oxoacids (those containing oxygen atoms). The names of binary acids start with *hydro-*, followed by the first syllable of the anion's name, and end with *-ic*:

HF - *hydro*fluor*ic* acid   HCl - *hydro*chlor*ic* acid   HBr - *hydro*brom*ic* acid

HI - *hydro*iod*ic* acid H_2S - *hydro*sulfur*ic* acid   HCN - *hydro*cyan*ic* acid

The names of oxoacids are derived from the name of the oxy-anion the acids contain. For an anion whose name ends with *-ate*, the acid's name starts with the first syllable of the anion and ends with   *-ic*.

If the anion's name ends with *-ite*, the name of acid starts with the first syllable of the anion's name and ends with *-ous*.

Anion	Name of Anion	Acid	Name of Acid
NO_3^-	nitrate ion	HNO_3	nitric acid
NO_2^-	nitrite ion	HNO_2	nitrous acid
SO_4^{2-}	sulfate ion	H_2SO_4	sulfuric acid
SO_3^{2-}	sulfite ion	H_2SO_3	sulfurous acid
PO_4^{3-}	phosphate ion	$H3PO4$	phosphoric acid
$C_2H_3O_2^-$	acetate ion	$HC_2H_3O_2$	acetic acid
ClO^-	hypochlorite	$HClO$	hypochlorous acid
ClO_2^-	chlorite	$HClO_2$	chlorous acid
ClO_3^-	chlorate	$HClO_3$	chloric acid
ClO_4^-	perchlorate	$HClO_4$	perchloric acid

Arrhenius definition of acids and bases

In 1884, Swedish chemist Svante Arrhenius proposed a definition for acids and bases. He stated that acids are substances that dissociate in water to produce hydrogen ions (H^+), and bases are substances that dissociate to produce hydroxide ions (OH^-). These are known as the Arrhenius definitions of acids and bases. For example:

- HCl is an acid: $HCl\ (aq) \rightarrow H^+\ (aq) + Cl^-\ (aq)$
- NaOH is a base: $NaOH\ (aq) \rightarrow Na^+\ (aq) + OH^-\ (aq)$

Arrhenius acids and bases can be described as:

An acid is a substance that increases the hydronium ion concentration $[H_3O^+]$ in aqueous solution.

A base is a substance that increases the hydroxide ion concentration $[OH^-]$ in aqueous solution.

Below are some examples, according to the Arrhenius concept.

Examples of acids:

1. $HCl\ (aq) + H_2O \rightarrow H_3O^+\ (aq) + Cl^-\ (aq)$

2. $HNO_3\ (aq) + H_2O \rightarrow H_3O^+\ (aq) + NO_3^-\ (aq)$

3. $CH_3COOH\ (aq) + H_2O \rightleftarrows H_3O^+\ (aq) + CH_3COO^-\ (aq)$

Examples of bases:

1. $NaOH\ (aq) \rightarrow Na^+\ (aq) + OH^-\ (aq)$

2. $Ba(OH)_2\ (aq) \rightarrow Ba^{2+}\ (aq) + 2\ OH^-\ (aq)$

3. $NH_3\ (aq) + H_2O \rightleftarrows NH_4^+\ (aq) + OH^-\ (aq)$

Lewis definition of acids and bases

The *Lewis definition* of acids and bases states that an acid is the reactant that is capable of sharing a pair of electrons from another reactant to form a covalent bond, while a base is the reactant that provides the pair of electrons to be shared to form a covalent bond.

According to the Lewis definition, the hydrogen ion (H^+) is a Lewis acid and water and ammonia are the Lewis bases in the following reactions:

$$H^+ + H_2O \rightarrow H_3O^+ \qquad\qquad H^+ + NH_3 \rightarrow NH_4^+$$

Lewis   Lewis   Lewis   Lewis

acid   base   acid   base

In reactions that involve the formation of new covalent bonds, the species with an incomplete octet (i.e., an electron-deficient molecule) may act as Lewis acids, and those with a lone pair of electrons may act as Lewis bases.

In the following reactions, BF_3, $AlCl_3$ and $FeBr_3$ are Lewis acids, while NH_3, Cl^- and Br^- are Lewis bases.

$$BF_3 + NH_3 \rightarrow F_3B{:}NH_3 \qquad AlCl_3 + Cl^- \rightarrow AlCl_4^- \qquad FeBr_3 + Br^- \rightarrow FeBr_4^-$$

In the formation of complex ions, the positive ions act as Lewis acids, and the ligands (anions or small molecules) are Lewis bases:

$$Cu^{2+}(aq) + 4\,NH_3(aq) \rightleftarrows Cu(NH_3)_4^{2+}(aq)$$

Lewis acid   Lewis base

$$Al^{3+}(aq) + 6\,H_2O \rightleftarrows [Al(H_2O)_6]^{3+}(aq)$$

Lewis acid   Lewis base

Note that the ionizable hydrogen in oxoacids is bonded to the oxygen in the molecule.

Brønsted–Lowry definition of acids and bases

The *Brønsted-Lowry theory* was proposed independently by Danish chemist Johannes Nicolaus Brønsted and British chemist Martin Lowry in 1923. It states that an acid is a substance that acts as a proton donor in a chemical reaction, and a base is a substance that acts as a proton acceptor in a chemical reaction. Through this exchange of protons, the acid forms its conjugate base and the base forms its conjugate acid.

The Brønsted-Lowry acid-base reaction can be represented as follows:

$$HA + B \rightleftarrows BH^+ + A^-$$
acid base   conjugate   conjugate
               acid   base

Some examples of Brønsted-Lowry acids, bases, conjugate acids and conjugate bases:

1. $HCl + H_2O \rightarrow H_3O^+ (aq) + Cl^- (aq)$
   acid   base   conjugate   conjugate
                 acid   base

2. $HC_2H_3O_2 + H_2O \rightleftarrows H_3O^+ (aq) + C_2H_3O_2^- (aq)$
   acid   base   conjugate   conjugate
                     acid   base

3. $NH_3 + H_2O \rightleftarrows NH_4^+ (aq) + OH^- (aq)$
   base   acid   conjugate   conjugate
                 acid   base

The transfer of protons in a Brønsted-Lowery acid-base reaction

$$HF\ (aq)\ +\ NH_3\ \rightleftharpoons\ F^-\ +\ NH_4\ (aq)$$

Acid donates H^+ to NH_3 Base accepts H^+ from HF   Conjugate base accepts H^+ from NH_4 Conjugate acid donates H^+ to F^-

Ionization of water

Water is an *amphoteric* substance – it can act as an acid or a base. One water molecule acting as a base can accept a hydrogen ion from a second water molecule acting as an acid. Therefore, ions form even in pure water. As they are formed, they react with each other to produce water again, and thus the following equilibrium occurs:

$$H_2O\ +\ H_2O\ \rightleftharpoons\ H_3O^+\ (aq)\ +\ OH^-\ (aq)$$

acid   base   conjugate acid   conjugate base

This is the *auto-ionization of water*.

Ions formed in the auto-ionization of water

$$H_2O\ (l)\ +\ H_2O\ (l)\ \rightleftharpoons\ H_3O^+\ (aq)\ +\ OH^-\ (aq)$$

H^+ acceptor base H^+ donor acid   Conjugate acid   Conjugate base

K_w, its approximate value ($K_w = [H^+] \cdot [OH^-] = 10^{-14}$ at 25 °C, 1 atm)

The equilibrium constant expression for the above equilibrium is:

$$K = \frac{[H_3O^+] \cdot [OH^-]}{[H_2O]^2}$$

At standard temperature and pressure (25 °C, 1 atm), the equilibrium constant for water K_w (the *ion-product constant* for water) = $[H_3O^+] \cdot [OH^-] = 1.0 \times 10^{-14}$.

If $[H_3O^+]$ increases ($> 1.0 \times 10^{-7}$ *M*), $[OH^-]$ decreases ($< 1.0 \times 10^{-7}$ M), and vice versa.

- If $[H_3O^+] = [OH^-] = 1.0 \times 10^{-7}$ M →

  the solution is neutral (such as in pure water)
- If $[H_3O^+] > 1.0 \times 10^{-7}$ M, $[OH^-] < 1.0 \times 10^{-7}$ M →

  the solution is acidic ($[H^+] > [OH^-]$)
- If $[H_3O^+] < 1.0 \times 10^{-7}$ M, $[OH^-] > 1.0 \times 10^{-7}$ M →

  the solution is basic ($[H^+] < [OH^-]$)

pH definition, pH of pure water

The pH scale is used to measure the acidity (or basicity) of a solution, especially when the hydrogen ion concentration is very low.

$$pH = -\log[H^+] \qquad pOH = -\log[OH^-]$$

Neutral solutions, $[H^+] = 1.0 \times 10^{-7}$ M → $pH = -\log(1.0 \times 10^{-7}) = 7.00$

Neutral solutions also contain $[OH^-] = 1.0 \times 10^{-7}$ M → $pOH = -\log(1.0 \times 10^{-7}) = 7.00$

Acidic solutions, $[H^+] > 1.0 \times 10^{-7}$ M, and pH < 7.00

Basic solutions, $[H^+] < 1.0 \times 10^{-7}$ M, and pH > 7.00

Thus, pH = 7 → a neutral solution

  pH < 7 → an acidic solution

  pH > 7 → a basic solution

Note: $K_w = [H^+]\cdot[OH^-] = 1.0 \times 10^{-14} \to pK_w = -\log(K_w) = -\log(1.0 \times 10^{-14}) = 14.00$

But, $pK_w = pH + pOH = 14.00 \to pOH = 14.00 - pH$, and $pH = 14.00 - pOH$

If $pH = 7 \to pOH = 7$, if $pH < 7 \to pOH > 7$, if $pH > 7 \to pOH < 7$

Thus, $pH < 7 \to [H^+] > [OH^-]$, and $pH > 7 \to [OH^-] > [H^+]$

For example: if $[H^+] = 1.0 \times 10^{-4}$ M, $pH = -\log(1.0 \times 10^{-4}) = 4.00$

When $[OH^-] = 1.0 \times 10^{-4}$ M,

$$[H^+] = \frac{1.0 \times 10^{-14}}{1.0 \times 10^{-4} M} = 1.0 \times 10^{-10} \text{ M}$$

$$pH = -\log(1.0 \times 10^{-10}) = 10.00$$

Alternatively, $[OH^-] = 1.0 \times 10^{-4}$ M

$$pOH = -\log[OH^-] = -\log(1.0 \times 10^{-4} \text{ M}) = 4.00$$

$$pH = 14.00 - 4.00 = 10.00$$

Reference for $[H^+]$ and pH

$[H^+]$, M	pH		$[H^+]$, M	pH
1.0×10^{-1}	1.00		1.0×10^{-8}	8.00
1.0×10^{-2}	2.00		1.0×10^{-9}	9.00
1.0×10^{-3}	3.00		1.0×10^{-10}	10.00
1.0×10^{-4}	4.00		1.0×10^{-11}	11.00
1.0×10^{-5}	5.00		1.0×10^{-12}	12.00
1.0×10^{-6}	6.00		1.0×10^{-13}	13.00
1.0×10^{-7}	7.00		1.0×10^{-14}	14.00

$$pH = -\log[H_3O^+]$$

For example, if $[H_3O^+] = 1.0 \times 10^{-2}$ M

$$pH = -\log(1.0 \times 10^{-2}) = -(-2.00) = 2.00 \quad (\to \text{acidic})$$

Basicity: $pOH = -\log[OH^-]$

If a solution has $[OH^-] = 1.0 \times 10^{-2}$ M, $pOH = -\log(1.0 \times 10^{-2})$

$pOH = -(2.00) = 2.00$ ($\rightarrow$ basic).

Since, at 25°C, $K_w = [H_3O^+] \cdot [OH^-] = 1.0 \times 10^{-14}$

$pK_w = -\log(K_w) = -\log[H_3O^+] + (-\log[OH^-]) = -\log(1.0 \times 10^{-14}) = -(-14.00) = 14.00$

$pK_w = pH + pOH = 14.00$;   and $pOH = 14.00 - pH$

Thus, in aqueous solutions, $pH = 2 \rightarrow pOH = 12$, and $pOH = 2 \rightarrow pH = 12$

Equilibrium constants K_a and K_b (pK_a and pK_b)

Equilibrium constants K_a and K_b measure the extent to which an acid or base dissociates (dissociation constants).

The strength of an acid is defined by its dissociation (ionization) in aqueous solution.

$$HX\,(aq) + H_2O \rightleftarrows H_3O^+\,(aq) + X^-\,(aq)$$

The equilibrium constant, K_a, for the acid ionization:

$$K_a = \frac{[H_3O^+][X^-]}{[HX]}$$

For K_a, the products (conjugate acid H_3O^+ and conjugate base X^-) of the dissociation are the numerator, while the parent acid (HX) is the denomenator.

The strength of a base is defined by its dissociation (ionization) in aqueous solution.

$$X^-\,(aq) + H_2O \rightleftarrows OH^-\,(aq) + HX\,(aq)$$
$$K_b = \frac{[HX][OH^-]}{[X]}$$

For K_b, the products (conjugate acid HX^+ and conjugate base OH^-) of the dissociation are the numerator, while the parent base (X) is the denominator.

The value of K_a measures the extent of acid dissociation, hence the relative strength of the acid. Stronger acids have larger K_a values. For strong acids (such as $HClO_4$, HCl, H_2SO_4 and HNO_3), their K_as are very large (not in tables of K_a values).

For weak acids, $K_a \ll 10^{-1}$. Likewise, stronger bases have larger K_b values, while weak bases have very small K_b values.

If the K_a value for a conjugate acid-base pair is known, K_b can be calculated (and vice versa), by using the following relationship:

$$K_a K_b = K_w$$

An example follows:

When sodium acetate is dissolved in water, it dissociates into sodium and acetate ions:

$$NaC_2H_3O_2\,(aq) \rightarrow Na^+\,(aq) \; + \; C_2H_3O_2^-\,(aq)$$

The K_a is 1.8×10^{-5} (provided in a reference table). What is the K_b?

The acetate ion reacts with water and the following equilibrium is established:

$$C_2H_3O_2^-\,(aq) \; + \; H_2O \rightleftarrows HC_2H_3O_2\,(aq) \; + \; OH^-\,(aq); \qquad K_b = \frac{[HC_2H_3O_2][OH^-]}{[C_2H_3O_2^-]}$$

For the dissociation of acetic acid:

$$HC_2H_3O_2\,(aq) \; + \; H_2O \rightleftarrows H_3O^+\,(aq) \; + \; C_2H_3O_2^-\,(aq); \qquad K_a = \frac{[H_3O^+][C_2H_3O^-]}{[HC_2H_3O_2]}$$

$$K_a \times K_b = \frac{[H_3O^+][C_2H_3O^-]}{[HC_2H_3O_2]} \times \frac{[HC_2H_3O_2][OH^-]}{[C_2H_3O_2^-]} = [H_3O^+]\cdot[OH^-] = K_w = 1.0 \times 10^{-14}$$

Thus, for $C_2H_3O_2^-$, $K_b = K_w / K_a$ (for $HC_2H_3O_2$)

$$K_b = (1.0 \times 10^{-14}) / (1.8 \times 10^{-5}) = 5.6 \times 10^{-10}$$

Thus, acetate ion in solution has $K_b = 5.6 \times 10^{-10}$ ($> K_w$). Aqueous solution of 0.10 M $NaC_2H_3O_2$ has $[OH^-] \sim 7.5 \times 10^{-6}$ M and pH $\sim$ 8.9.

pK_a and pK_b are also measures of acidity and basicity. The operator "p" means "take the negative logarithm of." Therefore,

$$pK_a = -\log K_a$$

As K_a gets larger, pK_a gets smaller.

The smaller the value of pK_a, the stronger the acid (e.g., pK_a for $H_2SO_4 = 1.92$).

$$pK_b = -\log K_b$$

As K_b gets larger, pK_b gets smaller.

The smaller the value of pK_b, the stronger the base.

Conjugate acids and bases

As previously mentioned, a *conjugate base* is what remains of the acid after it loses a proton (H^+), and a *conjugate acid* is what becomes of the base after it gains a proton. The pairs (acid₁−conjugate base₁ and acid₂−conjugate base₂) are *conjugate acid-base pairs*; these are pairs of substances that are related to each other only by the loss or gain of a single proton (H^+). Thus, H_2O and H_3O^+, and H_2O and OH^- are conjugate acid-base pairs, but H_3O^+ and OH^- are not conjugate acid-base pairs.

Strong acids have weak conjugate bases, while weak acids have strong conjugate bases; the weaker the acid, the stronger its conjugate base. Likewise, weak bases have strong conjugate acids; the weaker the base, the stronger the conjugate acid it produces. Some examples include HCl which is a strong acid and Cl^- which is a very weak base. Similarly, HF is a weak acid, and F^- is a stronger conjugate base than Cl^-.

A Brønsted-Lowry acid-base reaction involves a competition between two bases for a proton, in which the stronger base is the most protonated at equilibrium.

In the reaction: $HCl + H_2O \rightarrow H_3O^+$ (aq) $+ Cl^-$ (aq)

H_2O is a much stronger base than Cl^-. At equilibrium, HCl solution contains mostly H_3O^+ and Cl^- ions.

In the reaction: $HC_2H_3O_2\,(aq) + H_2O \rightleftarrows H_3O^+\,(aq) + C_2H_3O_2^-\,(aq)$

$C_2H_3O_2^-$ is the stronger base. At equilibrium, acetic acid contains mostly $HC_2H_3O_2$ and a small amount of H_3O^+ and $C_2H_3O_2^-$ ions.

In the reaction: $NH_3\,(aq) + H_2O \rightleftarrows NH_4^+\,(aq) + OH^-\,(aq)$

H_2O is an acid. Competition for protons occurs between NH_3 and OH^-, in which OH^- is the stronger base. The above equilibrium favors the reactants, and aqueous ammonia solution contains mostly NH_3 molecules and smaller amounts of NH_4OH, NH_4^+ and OH^-.

According to Brønsted-Lowry, the net acid-base reactions are favored in the direction from strong acid-strong base combinations to weak acid-weak base combinations:

The following acid-base reactions proceed in the forward direction:

1. $HCl\,(aq) + NH_3\,(aq) \rightarrow NH_4^+\,(aq) + Cl^-\,(aq)$

    (HCl is a strong acid)

2. $HSO_4^-\,(aq) + CN^-\,(aq) \rightarrow HCN\,(aq) + SO_4^{2-}\,(aq)$

    HSO_4^- ($pK_a = 6.91$) is a stronger acid than HCN ($pK_a = 9.21$).

Many acid-base reactions reach a state of equilibrium.

For the following acid-base reactions, the equilibrium may favor the products or the reactants, depending on the relative strength of the acid:

1. $H_2PO_4^-\,(aq) + C_2H_3O_2^-\,(aq) \rightleftarrows HC_2H_3O_2\,(aq) + HPO_4^{2-}\,(aq)$;

    Equilibrium shifts left; $HC_2H_3O_2$ ($pK_a = 4.75$) is the stronger acid and HPO_4^{2-} ($pK_a = 7.21$) is the stronger base.

2. $HNO_2\,(aq) + C_2H_3O_2^-\,(aq) \rightleftarrows HC_2H_3O_2\,(aq) + NO_2^-\,(aq)$;

    Equilibrium shifts right; HNO_2 ($pK_a = 3.39$) is the stronger acid and $C_2H_3O_2^-$ ($pK_a = 4.75$) is the stronger base.

As described previously, common ions are ions produced by more than one solute in the same solution. For example, in a solution containing sodium acetate and acetic acid, the acetate ion ($C_2H_3O_2^-$) is the common ion.

According to Le Châtelier's principle, the following equilibrium for acetic acid,

$$HC_2H_3O_2\,(aq)\ +\ H_2O\,(l)\ \leftrightharpoons\ H_3O^+\,(aq)\ +\ C_2H_3O_2^-\,(aq),$$

shifts to the left if $C_2H_3O_2^-$, from another source, is introduced. This effect reduces the degree of dissociation of the acid, decreases $[H_3O^+]$ and increases the pH of the solution.

Addition of ammonium chloride, NH_4Cl, causes a shift to the left in the following equilibrium of ammonia in aqueous solution:

$$NH_3\,(aq)\ +\ H_2O\,(l)\ \leftrightharpoons\ NH_4^+\,(aq)\ +\ OH^-\,(aq)$$

In solution, NH_4Cl dissociates to produce NH_4^+ and Cl^- ions, where the former is a common ion in the equilibrium of ammonia. The equilibrium shift caused by this ion reduces the extent of ionization of ammonia, which decreases $[OH^-]$ in the system and lowers the pH of the solution

Salts

Salts are the products of acid-base reactions. The general reaction for the production of a salt is:

$$Acid + Base \rightarrow Salt + Water$$

Both the acid and the base are neutralized, and the H^+ and OH^- reactions combine to form water. The nonmetallic ions of the acid and the metal ions of the base form the salt. For example, NaCl is a product of the following acid-base reaction:

$$HCl\,(aq)\ +\ NaOH\,(aq)\ \rightarrow\ NaCl\,(aq)\ +\ H_2O$$

In the chemical formula of a salt, the cation is contributed by the base (e.g., Na^+), while the anion is contributed by the acid (e.g., Cl^-).

There are four types of salts:

- Salts of strong acid-strong base reactions (e.g., NaCl, KNO$_3$, NaClO$_4$, etc.)

- Salts of weak acid-strong base reactions (e.g., NaC$_2$H$_3$O$_3$, K$_2$CO$_3$, KCN, NaCHO$_2$, etc.)

- Salts of strong acid-weak base reactions (e.g., NH$_4$Cl, NH$_4$NO$_3$, HONH$_3$Cl, etc.)

- Salts of weak acid-weak base reactions (e.g., NH$_4$C$_2$H$_3$O$_2$, NH$_4$CN, NH$_4$HS, etc.)

These salts, when dissolved in water, produce acidic, basic or neutral solutions.

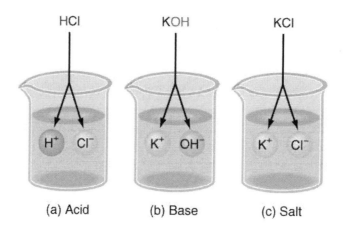

Strength of acids and bases

A *strong acid* ionizes completely in aqueous solutions (examples include HClO$_4$, HCl, H$_2$SO$_4$, HNO$_3$, HBr and HI). For these acids, the equilibrium lies far to the right. *Weak acids* only partially ionize and their ionization equilibriums lie far to the left. Weak acids include HC$_2$H$_3$O$_2$, HNO$_2$, H$_2$SO$_3$, H$_3$PO$_4$ HClO and others.

Consider the reversible process when an acid is dissolved in water:

$$HA \ (aq) \ + \ H_2O \ \leftrightarrow \ H_3O^+ \ (aq) \ + \ A^- \ (aq)$$

In the forward reaction, the acid HA donates a proton to the water molecule to form the hydronium ion (H_3O^+) and the conjugate base (A^-). Water acts as a Brønsted-Lowry base. The acid strength is measured by their degree of ionization (or dissociation) in water. If an acid ionizes completely, it is a strong acid. A strong acid has a weak conjugate base (i.e., the conjugate base loses its proton to water quite readily). Cl^-, Br^-, I^-, ClO_4^-, HSO_4^-, and NO_3^- are weak conjugate bases. A strong acid is less able to compete with water for a proton. The ionization constant K_a for a strong acid is very large and equilibrium shifts far to the right.

A weak acid does not readily give up its proton to water, and it has a strong conjugate base. ($C_2H_3O_2^-$, F^-, CN^-, NO_2^-, HSO_3^-, SO_3^{2-}, $H_2PO_4^-$, HPO_4^{2-} and PO_4^{3-} are strong conjugate bases.) The weaker the acid, the stronger its conjugate base. The ionization equilibrium for weak acids shifts far to the left.

An aqueous solution of a strong acid contains only hydronium ions (H_3O^+) and the acid's conjugate base. For example, in aqueous HCl solution there are only H_3O^+ and Cl^- ions, but no HCl molecules.

Conversely, an aqueous solution of weak acid, such as acetic acid, contains mainly the undissociated molecules, $HC_2H_3O_2$, with a small fraction (~1%) of H_3O^+ and $C_2H_3O^-$ ions.

The strength of acids is determined by a combination of various factors, such the strength and polarity of the X−H bond in the molecule, and the hydration energy of the ionic species in aqueous solution.

For inorganic binary acids, such as HF, HCl, HBr, and HI, H−X bond strength decreases down the group. The weaker the bond, the easier the molecule ionizes in aqueous solution. Hence, the stronger bond is the acid. For this group of acids, their strength increases down the group: HF < HCl < HBr < HI.

Among the hydrohalic acids, HF is the only weak acid; the others are strong acids. The relative strength of HCl, HBr and HI cannot be differentiated in aqueous solution, because each of them dissociates almost completely. Less polar solvents are used to determine their relative strength. For example, HCl, HBr and HI ionize only partially in acetone or methanol, which have a weaker ionizing strength than water. The ionization of HCl in acetone can be represented by the following equilibrium:

$$(CH_3)_2CO \ (l) \ + \ HCl \ (acetone) \ \rightleftarrows \ (CH_3)_2COH^+ \ (acetone) \ + \ Cl^- \ (acetone)$$

The degree of ionization in acetone increases in the order of HCl < HBr < HI. The acidity of hydrogen halides increases down the group, as stated previously.

A similar trend of relative acidity is also observed for the hydrides of Group VIA elements: $H_2O < H_2S < H_2Se < H_2Te$.

For the same period hydrides, the relative acidity increases from left to right, such that:

$$CH_4 < NH_3 < H_2O < HF; \qquad PH_3 < H_2S << HCl$$

Water is a stronger acid than ammonia, and in an acid-base reaction, H_2O acts as a Brønsted-Lowry acid, which donates a proton to NH_3:

$$H_2O + NH_3\,(aq) \rightleftarrows NH_4^+\,(aq) + OH^-\,(aq)$$

In reaction with HF, water acts as a Brønsted-Lowry base, which accepts a proton:

$$HF\,(aq) + H_2O \rightleftarrows H_3O^+\,(aq) + F^-\,(aq)$$

Oxoacids are acids that contain one or more ~OH groups covalently bonded to a central atom, which can be a metal or a nonmetal. The ~OH group ionizes completely or partially in an aqueous solution, producing hydrogen ions.

Some examples of oxoacids are H_2CO_3, HNO_3, H_3PO_4, H_2SO_4, $HClO_4$ and $HC_2H_3O_2$.

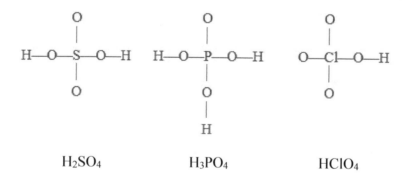

H_2SO_4 $\qquad$ H_3PO_4 $\qquad$ $HClO_4$

For these type of acids, their relative strengths depend on the *electronegativity* of the central atoms. The more electronegative the central atom, the more polarized the O−H bond and the more readily it ionizes in aqueous solution to release the H^+ ion.

For example, N, S and Cl are more electronegative than P; and HNO_3, H_2SO_4 and $HClO_4$ are stronger acids, whereas H_3PO_4 is a weak acid.

The order of electronegativity of the atoms and that of the relative acid strength are as follows:

Electronegativity: $Cl \sim N > S > P$;   Acid strength: $HClO_4 > HNO_3 > H_2SO_4 > H_3PO_4$.

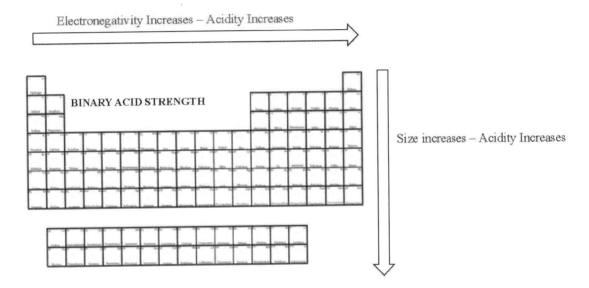

For oxoacids that have the central atoms with elements of the same group in the periodic table, their relative strength decreases from top to bottom (as the electronegativity of the central atom decreases):

HOCl > HOBr > HOI $HClO_2 > HBrO_2 > HIO_2$ $HClO_4 > HbrO_4 > HIO_4$

For oxoacids containing identical central atoms, their acidity increases as more oxygen atoms are bonded. For example, acidity increases as follows:

HOCl < $HClO_2$ < $HClO_3$ < $HClO_4$ H_2SO_3 < H_2SO_4 HNO_2 < HNO_3

When more oxygen atoms are bonded to the central atom, the O–H bond in the molecule becomes highly polarized (due to the inductive electronegative effect) and ionizes more readily to release an H^+ ion.

Acetic acid (CH_3COOH) is an organic acid, which contains the carboxyl (−COOH) group. In an aqueous solution, ionization of an acetic acid only involves the breaking of O–H bond of the carboxyl group, but not the C–H bonds in the methyl group (CH_3). However, if one or more of the hydrogen atoms in the methyl group is substituted with a more electronegative atom, the inductive effect causes the electron cloud to be drawn away from the carbonyl group. The O–H bond becomes more polarized and ionizes more readily, increasing the acidity.

The following K_a values illustrate the effect on the acidity of acetic acid and its derivatives when methyl hydrogens are substituted with electronegative atoms. The stronger the acid, the higher the K_a value:

CH_3COOH (*aq*) + H_2O ⇌ CH_3COO^- (*aq*) + H_3O^+ (*aq*) $K_a = 1.8 \times 10^{-5}$
   acetic acid

$ClCH_2COOH$ (*aq*) + H_2O ⇌ $ClCH_2COO^-$ (*aq*) + H_3O^+ (*aq*) $K_a = 1.4 \times 10^{-3}$
   chloroacetic acid

FCH_2COOH (*aq*) + H_2O ⇌ FCH_2COO^- (*aq*) + H_3O^+ (*aq*) $K_a = 2.6 \times 10^{-3}$
   fluoroacetic acid

CCl_3COOH (*aq*) + H_2O ⇌ CCl_3COO^- (*aq*) + H_3O^+ (*aq*) $K_a = 3.0 \times 10^{-1}$
   trichloroacetic acid

Acids such as HCl, HF, HOCl, HNO_2 and $HC_2H_3O_2$ are called *monoprotic acids* because each contains a single ionizable hydrogen ion. Some acids contain more than one ionizable hydrogen, and they are *polyprotic acids*. Examples of polyprotic acids are H_2SO_4, H_2SO_3, $H_2C_2O_4$ and H_3PO_4. In each case, the hydrogen ionizes in stages and with different ionization constants, such as the following example with H_3PO_4:

H_3PO_4 (*aq*) ⇌ H^+ (*aq*) + $H_2PO_4^-$ (*aq*); $K_{a1} = 7.5 \times 10^{-3}$

$H_2PO_4^-$ (*aq*) ⇌ H^+ (*aq*) + HPO_4^{2-} (*aq*); $K_{a2} = 6.2 \times 10^{-8}$

HPO_4^{2-} (*aq*) ⇌ H^+ (*aq*) + PO_4^{3-} (*aq*); $K_{a3} = 4.8 \times 10^{-13}$

As seen above, acid strength decreases in the order: $H_3PO_4 \gg H_2PO_4^- \gg HPO_4^{2-}$.

Sulfuric acid (H_2SO_4) is a strong acid, but only the first hydrogen ionizes completely:

$$H_2SO_4\,(aq)\ \rightarrow\ H^+\,(aq)\ +\ HSO_4^-\,(aq) \qquad K_{a1} = \text{very large}$$

The second hydrogen does not dissociate complete and HSO_4^- is a weak acid:

$$HSO_4^-\,(aq)\ \rightleftarrows\ H^+\,(aq)\ +\ SO_4^{2-}\,(aq) \qquad K_{a2} = 1.2 \times 10^{-2}$$

Strong bases, like strong acids, (e.g., NaOH, KOH and Ba(OH)$_2$) ionize completely when dissolved in water. A strong base has a tendency to accept a proton. *Weak bases* do not ionize completely when dissolved in water, and show very little tendency to accept a proton. Examples of weak bases are NH_3 (or NH_4OH), NH_2OH, $Mg(OH)_2$ and all hydroxides and oxides that are only slightly soluble in water.

Hydroxides of Group IA metals (LiOH, NaOH, KOH, RbOH and CsOH) are strong bases, but only NaOH and KOH are commercially-important and commonly used laboratory bases. These bases are soluble in water and they completely dissociate in aqueous solution, producing a high concentration of hydroxide ions. A moderately dilute solution of NaOH contains [OH$^-$]: initial [NaOH].

Among the hydroxides of the alkaline earth metals, Ba(OH)$_2$ is a relatively strong base. The other metal hydroxides are only sparingly soluble in water, which limits their basicity. A saturated solution of these hydroxides contains a very low concentration of OH$^-$. These hydroxides can react with strong acids:

$$Na_2O\,(s)\ +\ H_2O\ \rightarrow\ 2\,NaOH\,(aq)$$

$$BaO\,(s)\ +\ H_2O\ \rightarrow\ Ba(OH)_2\,(aq)$$

$$MgO\,(s)\ +\ 2\,HCl\,(aq)\ \rightarrow\ MgCl_2\,(aq)\ +\ H_2O$$

Hydroxides of some metals (e.g., $Al(OH)_3$, $Cr(OH)_3$, $Zn(OH)_2$, $Sn(OH)_2$ and $Pb(OH)_2$) exhibit amphoteric properties (i.e., can act as an acid or a base). For example:

$$Al(OH)_3\,(s)\ +\ OH^-\,(aq)\ \rightleftarrows\ Al(OH)_4^-\,(aq)$$

$$Al(OH)_3\,(s)\ +\ 3\,H_3O^+\,(aq)\ \rightleftarrows\ [Al(H_2O)_6]^{3+}\,(aq)$$

Hydrides of reactive metals (e.g., NaH, MgH_2 and CaH_2) form strong basic solutions when dissolved in water. The hydride ion reacts with water to produce hydroxide ions and hydrogen gas:

$$H^- (aq) + H_2O \rightarrow H_2 (g) + OH^- (aq)$$

The oxide ion O^{2-} has a very strong affinity for protons and reacts with water to produce hydroxide ions.

$$O^{2-} (aq) + H_2O \rightarrow 2\,OH^- (aq)$$

Oxides of nonmetals are acidic. They form acidic solutions when dissolved in water.

$$CO_2 (g) + H_2O \rightleftarrows H_2CO_3 (aq) \rightleftarrows H^+ (aq) + HCO_3^- (aq)$$

$$SO_2 (g) + H_2O \rightleftarrows H_2SO_3 (aq) \rightleftarrows H^+ (aq) + HSO_3^- (aq)$$

Ammonia is the only weak base that is of commercial importance. It does not contain hydroxide ions, but it reacts with water, and ionizes as follows:

$$NH_3 (aq) + H_2O \rightleftarrows NH_4^+ (aq) + OH^- (aq)$$

The base dissociation constant K_b is given by the expression:

$$K_b = \frac{[NH_4^+][OH^-]}{[NH_3]} = 1.8 \times 10^{-5}$$

Dissociation of acids and bases without added salt

The *percent dissociation* (or *degree of ionization*) of a weak acid is:

$$\text{Percent dissociation} = \frac{\text{Concentration of acid ionized}}{\text{Initial concentration of acid}} \times 100\%$$

For strong acids, the percent dissociation at equilibrium is almost 100%.

For weak acids, the percent dissociation depends on K_a of the acid and its initial concentration. For example, the percent dissociation of acetic acid ($HC_2H_3O_2$, $K_a = 1.8 \times 10^{-5}$) at 0.10 M concentration is:

$$(1.3 \times 10^{-3}\,M \,/\, 0.10\,M) \times 100\% = 1.3\,\%$$

The stronger the acid, the larger its K_a and the greater its percent ionization. Thus, the percent ionization of a weak acid depends on its K_a value and also on the extent of dilution. The more an acid solution is diluted, the higher its percentage ionization.

Consider a solution of 0.010 M acetic acid and its ionization products. Use an ICE table (Initial, Change, Equilibrium), which is a method used to simplify the calculations in reversible equilibrium reactions. Once the equilibrium row is completed (by summing the initial and change rows), its contents can be substituted into the equilibrium constant expression to solve for K_a.

$$HC_3H_3O_2\,(aq) \rightleftarrows H^+\,(aq) + C_2H_3O_2^-\,(aq)$$

Initial [ ], M:	0.010	0.00	0.00
Change, Δ[ ], M:	$-x$	$+x$	$+x$
Equilibrium [ ], M :	$(0.010 - x)$	x	x

The acid ionization constant, K_a, is given by the expression:

$$K_a = \frac{[H_3O^+][C_2H_3O^-]}{[HC_2H_3O_2]} = x^2 / (0.010 - x) = 1.8 \times 10^{-5}$$

Since $K_a \ll 0.010$, approximate that $x \ll 0.010$, and $(0.010 - x) \sim 0.010$

Then, $K_a = x^2 / (0.010 - x) \sim x^2 / 0.010 = 1.8 \times 10^{-5}$

$x^2 = 1.8 \times 10^{-7}$, and $x = \sqrt{(1.8 \times 10^{-7})} = 4.2 \times 10^{-4}$

$x = [H_3O^+] = 4.2 \times 10^{-4}$ M

The degree of ionization of acetic acid at this concentration is

$$(4.2 \times 10^{-4}\,M / 0.010\,M) \times 100\% = 4.2\%$$

Note that the degree of ionization of the acid increases as the solution is more diluted. In fact, in 1.0 M acetic acid, the degree of ionization is only 0.42%, which is a 10-fold lower than in 0.010 M acid solution.

Like weak acids, the percent dissociation of weak bases depends on the K_b value and dilution of the base solution; larger K_b and greater extent of dilution results in higher percent dissociation.

Hydrolysis of salts

The presence of salt affects the dissociation of acids and bases. For example, CH_3COOH dissociates less in a solution containing CH_3COONa salt, while NH_4OH dissociates less in a solution containing NH_4Cl salt. This is due to the *hydrolysis* of salts.

When salts (ionic compounds) dissolve in water, it is generally assumed that they completely dissociate into separate ions. Some of these ions can react with water and behave as acids or bases. The acidic or basic nature of a salt solution depends on whether it is a product of a strong acid-strong base reaction, a weak acid-strong base reaction, a strong acid-weak base reaction or a weak acid-weak base reaction.

Salts of Strong Acid-Strong Base Reactions: (e.g., NaCl, NaNO$_3$, KBr, etc.)

- Salts of this type form neutral solution, because neither the cation nor the anion reacts with water and offsets the equilibrium concentrations of H_3O^+ and OH^- in the solution.

Salts of Weak Acid-Strong Base Reactions: (e.g., NaF, NaNO$_2$, NaC$_2$H$_3$O$_2$, etc.)

- Salts that are products of reactions between weak acids and strong bases form basic solutions when dissolved in water. The anions of such salts react with water that increases $[OH^-]$.

- Sodium acetate ($NaC_2H_3O_2$) is a product of reaction between acetic acid ($HC_2H_3O_2$), which is a weak acid, and a strong base (NaOH).

$$HC_2H_3O_2\,(aq)\ +\ NaOH\,(aq)\ \rightarrow\ NaC_2H_3O_2\,(aq)\ +\ H_2O$$

Salts of Strong Acid-Weak Base Reactions: (e.g., NH$_4$Cl, NH$_4$NO$_3$, (CH$_3$)$_2$NH$_2$Cl, C$_5$H$_5$NHCl, etc.)

- Aqueous solutions of salts that are products of strong acid-weak base reactions are acidic.

- The cations react with water and increase $[H_3O^+]$ in solutions.

- Example: NH_4Cl is produced when HCl (strong acid) reacts with NH_3 (weak base):

$$HCl\ (aq)\ +\ NH_3\ (aq)\ \rightarrow\ NH_4Cl\ (aq)\ \rightarrow\ NH_4^+\ (aq)\ +\ Cl^-\ (aq)$$

In an aqueous solution, NH_4^+ establishes the following equilibrium that increases $[H_3O^+]$, and creates an acidic solution:

$$NH_4^+\ (aq)\ +\ H_2O\ \rightleftarrows\ H_3O^+\ (aq)\ +\ NH_3\ (aq);$$

$$K_a = \frac{[H_3O^+][NH_3]}{[NH_4^+]}$$

While in a solution of NH_3, the following equilibrium occurs:

$$NH_3\ (aq)\ +\ H_2O\ \rightleftarrows\ NH_4^+\ (aq)\ +\ OH^-\ (aq);$$

$$K_b = \frac{[NH_4^+][OH^-]}{[NH_3]}$$

$$K_a \times K_b = \frac{[H_3O^+][NH_3]}{[NH_4^+]} \times \frac{[NH_4^+][OH^-]}{[NH_3]}$$

$$K_a \times K_b = [H_3O^+][OH^-] = K_w = 1.0 \times 10^{-14}$$

For NH_4^+, $K_a = K_w\ /\ K_{b(for\ NH3)}$

$$K_a = (1.0\ x\ 10^{-14})\ /\ (1.8\ x\ 10^{-5}) = 5.6 \times 10^{-10}$$

Thus, aqueous solution of NH_4^+ has a $K_a = 5.6 \times 10^{-10}$ at 25 °C (which is $> K_w$). Then, a 0.10 M solution of NH_4Cl or NH_4NO_3 has $[H_3O^+] \sim 7.5 \times 10^{-6}$ M and pH $\sim$ 5.1

Salts of Weak Acid-Weak Base Reactions: (e.g., $NH_4C_2H_3O_2$, NH_4CN, NH_4NO_2, etc.)

- Solutions of salts that are products of weak acid-weak base reactions can be neutral, acidic, or basic, depending on the relative magnitude of the K_a of the weak acid and the K_b of the weak base.

If $K_a \sim K_b$, the salt forms an approximately neutral solution.

Example: K_a of $HC_2H_3O_2 = 1.8 \times 10^{-5}$, and K_b of $NH_3 = 1.8 \times 10^{-5}$

When $NH_4C_2H_3O_2$ dissolves in water and dissociates, the following equilibria exists:

$$NH_4C_2H_3O_2\,(aq) \rightarrow NH_4^+\,(aq) + C_2H_3CO_2^-\,(aq)$$

$$NH_4^+\,(aq) + H_2O \rightleftarrows H_3O^+\,(aq) + NH_3\,(aq) \qquad K_a = 5.6 \times 10^{-10}$$

$$C_2H_3O_2^-\,(aq) + H_2O \rightleftarrows HC_2H_3O_2\,(aq) + OH^-\,(aq) \qquad K_b = 5.6 \times 10^{-10}$$

Since K_a(for NH_4^+) = K_b(for $C_2H_3O_2^-$), at equilibrium $[H_3O^+] = [OH^-]$, $NH_4C_2H_3O_2$ solution is neutral.

- If $K_a > K_b$, the salt solution is acidic.

For NH_4NO_2, K_a(HNO_2) $= 4.0 \times 10^{-4}$, and K_b(NH_3) $= 1.8 \times 10^{-5}$; according to the following equilibria:

$$NH_4NO_2\,(aq) \rightarrow NH_4^+\,(aq) + NO_2^-\,(aq)$$

$$NH_4^+\,(aq) + H_2O \rightleftarrows H_3O^+\,(aq) + NH_3\,(aq) \qquad K_a = 5.6 \times 10^{-10}$$

$$NO_2^-\,(aq) + H_2O \rightleftarrows HNO_2\,(aq) + OH^-\,(aq) \qquad K_b = 2.5 \times 10^{-11}$$

$K_a > K_b \rightarrow$ acidic solution, because the hydrolysis results in a solution with $[H_3O^+] > [OH^-]$.

- If $K_a < K_b$, the salt solution is basic.

For NH_4CN in solution, K_a(HCN) $= 6.2 \times 10^{-10}$, and K_b(NH_3) $= 1.8 \times 10^{-5}$, the following equilibria exist:

$$NH_4CN\,(aq) \rightarrow NH_4^+\,(aq) + CN^-\,(aq)$$

$$NH_4^+\,(aq) + H_2O \rightleftarrows H_3O^+\,(aq) + NH_3\,(aq) \qquad K_a = 5.6 \times 10^{-10}$$

$$CN^-\,(aq) + H_2O \rightleftarrows HCN\,(aq) + OH^-\,(aq) \qquad K_b = 1.6 \times 10^{-5}$$

Since K_b (CN^-) $> K_b$ (NH_4^+), at equilibrium $[OH^-] > [H_3O^+]$ and an aqueous solution of NH_4CN is basic.

Calculation of pH

Calculating the pH of Strong Acid and Strong Base Solutions

Strong acids are assumed to ionize completely in aqueous solution. For monoprotic acids (that is, acids with a single ionizable hydrogen atom) such as HCl and HNO_3, the concentration of hydronium ion in solution is the same as the molar concentration of the acid:

$$[H_3O^+] = [HX]$$

Example: in 0.10 M HCl (*aq*), $[H_3O^+]$ = 0.10 M,

$$pH = -\log(0.10) = 1.00.$$

A strong base such as NaOH has $[OH^-]$ equal to the molar concentration of dissolved NaOH. That is, a solution of 0.10 M NaOH (*aq*) has $[OH^-]$ = 0.10 M.

$$pOH = -\log[OH^-] = -\log(0.10) = 1.00$$

$$pH = 14.00 - 1.00 = 13.00$$

A strong base such as $Ba(OH)_2$ produces twice the concentration of OH^- as the molar concentration of $Ba(OH)_2$ in solution:

$$Ba(OH)_2 \ (aq) \ \rightarrow \ Ba^{2+} \ (aq) + 2OH^- \ (aq); \qquad [OH^-] = 2 \times [Ba(OH)_2]$$

In a solution of 0.010 M $Ba(OH)_2$, $[OH^-]$ = 0.020 M,

$$pOH = 1.70, \text{ and } pH = 12.30.$$

Calculating the pH of Weak Acid Solutions

Unlike strong acids, weak acids do not ionize completely. At equilibrium, $[H^+]$ is much less than the concentration of the acid. The concentration of H^+ in a weak acid solution depends on the initial acid concentration and the K_a of the acid.

To determine [H$^+$] of a weak acid. the "ICE" table be set up as follows:

Consider a solution of 0.10 M acetic acid and its ionization products.

$$HC_3H_3O_2\,(aq) \rightleftarrows H^+\,(aq) + C_2H_3O_2^-\,(aq)$$

Initial [ ], M:	0.10	0.00	0.00
Change, Δ[ ], M:	$-x$	$+x$	$+x$
Equilibrium [ ], M :	$(0.10-x)$	x	x

The acid ionization constant, K_a, is given by the expression:

$$K_a = \frac{[H_3O^+][C_2H_3O^-]}{[HC_2H_3O_2]} = x^2 / (0.10-x) = 1.8 \times 10^{-5}$$

Since $K_a \ll 0.10$, approximate that $x \ll 0.10$, and $(0.10-x) \sim 0.10$

Then, $K_a = x^2 / (0.10-x) \sim x^2 / 0.10$

$K_a = 1.8 \times 10^{-5}$

$x^2 = 1.8\ x\ 10^{-6}$

$x = \sqrt{(1.8\ x\ 10^{-6})} = 1.3 \times 10^{-3}$

Note that $x = [H_3O^+] = 1.3 \times 10^{-3}$ M

$$pH = -\log(1.3 \times 10^{-3}) = 2.89$$

Calculating the pH of Weak Base Solutions

The concentration of OH^- in a weak base, such as NH_3 *(aq)*, depends on its K_b value and the initial concentration of the base.

To determine $[OH^-]$ and pH of 0.10 M NH_3 *(aq)*, set the following "ICE" table:

Concentration: $NH_3\,(aq) + H_2O \rightleftharpoons NH_4^+\,(aq) + OH^-\,(aq)$

	NH_3	NH_4^+	OH^-
Initial [ ], *M*:	0.10	0.00	0.00
Change, Δ[ ], *M*:	$-x$	$+x$	$+x$
Equilibrium [ ], *M* :	(0.10 - x)	x	x

$$K_b = \frac{[NH_4^+][OH^-]}{[NH_3]} = x^2 / (0.10 - x)$$

$$K_b = 1.8 \times 10^{-5}$$

Using the approximation method:

$$K_b = x^2 / (0.10 - x)$$

$$\sim x^2 / 0.10 = 1.8 \times 10^{-5}$$

$$x^2 = 1.8 \times 10^{-6}$$

$$x = \sqrt{(1.8 \times 10^{-6})}$$

$$x = 1.3 \times 10^{-3}$$

where, $x = [OH^-] = 1.3 \times 10^{-3}$ *M*

$pOH = -\log(1.3 \times 10^{-3}) = 2.87$

$pH = 11.13$

Calculating the pH of basic or acidic salt solutions

1. Consider a solution of 0.050 M sodium acetate, which dissociates completely and establishes the following equilibirium:

$$NaC_2H_3O_2 \, (aq) \rightarrow Na^+ \, (aq) \; + \; C_2H_3O_2^- \, (aq)$$

The acetate ion establishes the equilibrium in aqueous solution:

$$C_2H_3O_2^- \, (aq) \; + \; H_2O \rightleftarrows HC_2H_3O_2 \, (aq) \; + \; OH^- \, (aq)$$

$$K_b = \frac{[HC_2H_3O_2][OH^-]}{[C_2H_3O_2^-]} = 5.6 \times 10^{-10}$$

By approximation, $[OH^-] = \sqrt{(K_b[C_2H_3O_2^-])}$

$$[OH^-] = \sqrt{\{(5.6 \times 10^{-10}) \cdot (0.050)\}} = 5.3 \times 10^{-6} \text{ M}$$

$$pOH = -\log(5.3 \times 10^{-6}) = 5.28$$

$$pH = 8.72 \text{ (solution is basic)}$$

2. Consider a solution of 0.050 M NH$_4$Cl, which dissociates and establishes the following equilibrium:

$$NH_4Cl \, (aq) \rightarrow NH_4^+ \, (aq) \; + \; Cl^- \, (aq)$$

$$NH_4^+ \, (aq) \; + \; H_2O \rightleftarrows H_3O^+ \, (aq) \; + \; NH_3 \, (aq)$$

$$K_a = \frac{[H_3O^+][NH_3]}{[NH_4^+]} = 5.6 \times 10^{-10}$$

By approximation, $[H_3O^+] = \sqrt{(K_a[NH_4^+])}$

$$[H_3O^+] = \sqrt{\{(5.6 \times 10^{-10}) \cdot (0.050)\}} = 5.3 \times 10^{-6} \text{ M}$$

$$pH = -\log(5.3 \times 10^{-6}) = 5.28, \text{ (solution is acidic)}$$

Buffers

A *buffer* is a solution that maintais its pH (with very little change) even when a small amount of strong acid or strong base is added. A buffer solution contains a weak acid and the "salt" of its conjugate base, or a weak base and the "salt" of its conjugate acid. A given buffer is effective within a range of pH that is typically within approximately ±1 of the pK_a of its acid component.

Below are some examples of some common buffer systems:

Buffer	pK_a	pH Range
$HCHO_2 - NaCHO_2$	3.74	2.75–4.75
$HC_2H_3O_2 - NaC_2H_3O_2$	4.74	3.75–5.75
$KH_2PO_4 - K_2HPO_4$	7.21	6.20–8.20 (a buffer system in blood)
$CO_2/H_2O - NaHCO_3$	6.37	5.40–7.40 (a buffer system in blood)
$NH_3 - NH_4Cl$	9.25	8.25–10.25

Buffered solutions are vital to living organisms. All metabolic reactions are controlled or accelerated by biological catalysts called *enzymes*, which are often proteins that function only within a narrow pH range.

For example, it is important that the fluid of the human body be maintained at a certain (narrow) pH range. Human blood is maintained at the pH range of 7.30 - 7.40. A drop below pH 7 or a rise above pH 7.5 can be fatal.

Consider the following statements:

When 0.01 mol of HCl is added to 1 L of pure water, $[H^+]$ increases from 10^{-7} to 10^{-2} M, and the pH changes from about 7 to 2, which indicates that water is not a buffer.

When the same amount of HCl is added to a solution containing a mixture of 1 M acetic acid ($HC_2H_3O_2$) and 1 M sodium acetate ($NaC_2H_3O_2$), the pH of the solution changes very little – it goes from 4.74 to 4.66. Therefore, a solution that is composed of acetic acid and sodium acetate is a buffer solution.

Consider a buffered solution composed of KH_2PO_4 and K_2HPO_4. The species present in solution are primarily K^+, $H_2PO_4^-$ and HPO_4^{2-}. (K^+ is a spectator ion and not involved in the buffering reaction.)

When a small amount of strong acid is added to this solution, the H^+ ions from the acid reacts with the base component of the buffer (HPO_4^{2-}):

$$H^+ (aq) + HPO_4^{2-} (aq) \rightarrow H_2PO_4^- (aq) \quad ....\text{(buffering reaction 1)}$$

When a strong base such as NaOH is added, the OH^- reacts with the acid component of the base ($H_2PO_4^-$):

$$OH^- (aq) + HC_2H_3O_2 (aq) \rightarrow H_2O + C_2H_3O_2^- (aq) \quad ....\text{(buffering reaction 2)}$$

Reactions (1) and (2) are important buffering reactions that maintain the pH of the solution. Two buffer systems – the phosphate buffer ($H_2PO_4^-$-HPO_4^{2-}) and carbonic acid-bicarbonate buffer, (H_2CO_3-HCO_3^-) are important to maintain the normal blood pH. The buffering reactions of bicarbonate buffer are:

$$H^+ (aq) + HCO_3^- (aq) \rightarrow H_2O + CO_2 (aq)$$

$$OH^- (aq) + CO_2 (aq) + H_2O \rightarrow 2 HCO_3^- (aq)$$

Consider a buffer made up of acetic acid and sodium acetate, in which the major species present in solution are $HC_2H_3O_2$ and $C_2H_3O_2^-$.

If a small amount of HCl (*aq*) is added to this solution, most of H^+ (from HCl) is absorbed by the conjugate base, $C_2H_3O_2^-$, in the following reaction:

$$H^+ (aq) + C_2H_3O_2^- (aq) \rightarrow HC_2H_3O_2^- (aq)$$

Since $C_2H_3O_2^-$ is present in a much larger quantity than the added H^+, the reaction shifts almost completely to the right. This buffering reaction prevents a significant increase in $[H^+]$ and minimizes the change in its pH.

If a strong base, such as NaOH (*aq*), is added, most of the OH^- ions (from NaOH) are reacted on by the acid component of the buffer as follows:

$$OH^- (aq) + HC_2H_3O_2 (aq) \rightarrow H_2O + C_2H_3O_2^- (aq)$$

Again, because of the larger concentration of $HC_2H_3O_2$ compared to OH^-, this reaction also goes almost to completion. This buffering reaction prevents a large increase in the $[OH^-]$, and minimizes any change in the pH of the solution.

For a buffer containing the weak acid HB and the salt NaB, such that B^- is the conjugate base to the acid, the concentration $[H^+]$ and pH of the buffer depend on the dissociation constant, K_a, of the acid component and the concentration ratio $[B^-] / [HB]$ in the buffer solution.

Consider the equilibrium: HB (*aq*) $\leftrightarrows$ H^+ (*aq*) $+$ B^- (*aq*)

$$K_a = \frac{[H^+] \cdot [B^-]}{[HB]}$$

Rearranging obtains $[H^+] = K_a \times ([HB] / [B^-])$

$$pH = pK_a + \log([B^-] / [HB])$$

The last expression is called the *Henderson-Hasselbalch equation*, which is useful for calculating the pH of solutions when both the K_a and the ratio $[B^-] / [HB]$ are known.

The *buffering capacity* of a buffered solution represents the amount of H^+ ion or OH^- ion the buffer can absorb without significantly altering its pH. A buffer that contains large concentrations of buffering components and is able to absorb significant quantities of strong acid or strong base, with little change in its pH, has a large buffering capacity.

Whereas the pH of a buffered solution is determined by the ratio $[B^-] / [HB]$, the capacity of a buffer is determined by the sizes of $[AB]$ and $[B^-]$.

The following example illustrates how to calculate the change in pH and the buffering capacity of a buffered solution after a strong acid is added.

Calculate the change in pH when 0.010 mol of HCl is added to 1.0 L of each of the following buffers:

Buffer A: 1.0 M $HC_2H_3O_2$ + 1.0 M $NaC_2H_3O_2$

Buffer B: 0.020 M $HC_2H_3O_2$ + 0.020 M $NaC_2H_3O_2$

Solution: For both buffers, the pH can be calculated using the Henderson-Hasselbalch equation:

$$pH = pK_a + \log([B^-] / [HB])$$

$$pH = pK_a + \log([C_2H_3O_2^-] / [HC_2H_3O_2])$$

$$pH = -\log(1.8 \times 10^{-5}) + \log(1) = 4.74$$

When 0.010 mol HCl is added to Buffer A, the following reaction takes place:

$$H^+(aq) + C_2H_3O_2^-(aq) \rightarrow HC_2H_3O_2(aq)$$

[ ] before reaction:	0.010 M	1.0 M	1.0 M
[ ] after reaction:	0	0.99 M	1.01 M

The new pH = $4.74 + \log(0.99 / 1.01) = 4.74 - 0.010 = 4.73$. (pH is changed ~ 0.21%.)

When 0.010 mol HCl is added to Buffer B, the following reaction takes place:

$$H^+(aq) + C_2H_3O_2^-(aq) \rightarrow HC_2H_3O_2(aq)$$

[ ] before reaction:	0.010 M	0.020 M	0.020 M
[ ] after reaction:	0	0.010 M	0.030 M

The new pH = $4.74 + \log(0.010 / 0.030) = 4.74 - 0.48 = 4.26$ (pH decreases by 10%).

From above, Buffer A, which contains larger quantities of buffering components, has a much higher buffering capacity than Buffer B.

For Buffer A to decrease its pH by 0.48 unit (or 10%), it has to absorb the equivalent of 0.50 mol of HCl.

In summary, buffer solutions have the following characteristics:

1. The solution contains a weak acid HX and its conjugate base X⁻, or a weak base B and its conjugate acid BH⁺, in appreciable amounts.

2. A buffer solution maintains its pH by absorbing H⁺ or OH⁻ produced by a strong acid or strong base, so these ions do not accumulate.

3. The buffering reactions involve the reaction of H⁺ with the conjugate base **X⁻** in the buffer, or the reaction of OH⁻ with the acid component (HX) of the buffer:

$$H^+ (aq) \ + \ \mathbf{X^-} (aq) \ \rightarrow \ HX (aq)$$

$$OH^- (aq) + \mathbf{HX} (aq) \rightarrow H_2O + X^-$$

These two reactions prevent a significant increase in [H⁺] or [OH⁻] in the solution.

4. The *buffering capacity* of a solution implies the amount of H⁺ or OH⁻ it can absorb without significantly changing its pH. This depends on the concentration of the weak acid and its conjugate base in the solution.

5. The *buffering range* of a solution depends on the pK_a of the acid component of the buffer. A given buffer is most effective when the pH range = pK_a ± 1.

Neutralization

As discussed previously, the products of acid-base reactions are salt and water. *Neutralization* is a chemical reaction where an acid and a base react quantitatively with each other, resulting in there being no excess of hydrogen or hydroxide ions in the aqueous solution.

The following are examples of acid-base reactions:

$$HCl\ (aq)\ +\ NaOH\ (aq)\ \rightarrow\ H_2O\ (l)\ +\ NaCl\ (aq)$$

$$HClO_4\ (aq)\ +\ KOH\ (aq)\ \rightarrow\ H_2O\ (l)\ +\ KClO_4\ (aq)$$

$$HC_2H_3O_2\ (aq)\ +\ NaOH\ (aq)\ \rightarrow\ H_2O\ (l)\ +\ NaC_2H_3O_2\ (aq)$$

Note that the substances involved in these reactions are subject to dissociation.

Listed below are examples of molecular, complete (or total) ionic and net ionic equations for strong acid-strong base reactions:

Molecular:

$$HCl\ (aq)\ +\ NaOH\ (aq)\ \rightarrow\ H_2O\ (l)\ +\ NaCl\ (aq)$$

Complete ionic:

$$H^+\ (aq)\ +\ Cl^-\ (aq)\ +\ Na^+\ (aq)\ +\ OH^-\ (aq)\ \rightarrow\ H_2O\ (l)\ +\ Na^+\ (aq)\ +\ Cl^-\ (aq)$$

Net ionic:

$$H^+\ (aq)\ +\ OH^-\ (aq)\ \rightarrow\ H_2O\ (l)$$

Spectator ions:

$$Na^+\ \text{and}\ Cl^-$$

Weak acids and weak bases only ionize partially. In fact, most remain in the molecular form in solution. Therefore, they should NOT be written in the ionized forms, even when writing the ionic equations.

For example, the three equations for the reaction between acetic acid (a weak acid) and sodium hydroxide (a strong base) are as follows:

Molecular:

$$HC_2H_3O_2\,(aq) \;+\; NaOH\,(aq) \;\rightarrow\; H_2O\,(l) \;+\; NaC_2H_3O_2\,(aq)$$

Complete ionic:

$$HC_2H_3O_2\,(aq) \;+\; Na^+\,(aq) \;+\; OH^-\,(aq) \;\rightarrow\; H_2O\,(l) \;+\; Na^+\,(aq) \;+\; C_2H_3O_2^-\,(aq)$$

Net ionic:

$$HC_2H_3O_2\,(aq) \;+\; OH^-\,(aq) \;\rightarrow\; H_2O\,(l) \;+\; C_2H_3O_2^-\,(aq)$$

Spectator ion:

$$Na^+$$

The following illustrate the stoichiometry of acid-base neutralization reactions.

1. How many mL of 0.1500 M NaOH (*aq*) are needed to neutralize 25.00 mL of 0.2040 M HCl (*aq*)?

    According to the equation:

    $$HCl\,(aq) \;+\; NaOH\,(aq) \rightarrow H_2O\,(l) \;+\; NaCl\,(aq)$$

    Moles of NaOH needed = Moles of HCl present

    (Liters of NaOH × Molarity of NaOH) = (Liters of HCl × Molarity of HCl)

    (Liters of NaOH × 0.1725 mol/L) = (0.02500 L × 0.2040 mol/L)

Divide both side by 0.1725 mol/L:

Liters of NaOH = $\dfrac{0.02500\ L \times 0.2040\ mol/L}{0.1725\ mol/L}$ = 0.02957 L (= 29.57 mL)

2. If 10.00 mL of acetic acid of unknown concentration requires 38.64 mL of 0.2250 M KOH to neutralize, what is the molarity of the acetic acid?

From the reaction:

$HC_2H_3O_2\ (aq) +\ NaOH\ (aq) \rightarrow H_2O\ (l)\ +\ NaC_2H_3O_2\ (aq)$

Moles of acetic acid = Moles of NaOH

(Liter of acid × Molarity of acid) = (Liter of base × Molarity of base)

(0.01000 L × Molarity of $HC_2H_3O_2$) = (0.03864 L × 0.2250 M of NaOH)

Divid both side by 0.01000 L:

Molarity of $HC_2H_3O_2$ = $\dfrac{0.03864\ L \times 0.2250\ M}{0.01000\ L}$ = 0.8694 M

Titration

Titration (*volumetric analysis*) is an important application of neutralization reactions. It involves adding an exact amount of one reactant (*titrant*) from a buret to another reactant (*analyte*) in a flask or beaker.

The primary objective of titration is to determine the molar concentration of one solution (the analyte) using the volume and concentration of another solution (titrant). In the process, the titrant is carefully added from a buret until the *equivalence point* is reached (i.e., the point of neutralization).

The *end-point* of a titration is marked by the change in the color of the *indicator*, a substance that changes color when a solution transitions from being acidic to slightly basic. In a good titration, the equivalence point should match the *end-point*. If the volume and concentration of the titrant are known, its number of moles can be calculated. From the reaction stoichiometry (the balanced equation), the number of moles of the analyte and its concentration can be determined.

A successful titration experiment depends on the following factors:

1. The reaction between titrant and analyte occurs rapidly.

2. The balanced equation is known.

3. The end-point occurs exactly at or very close to the equivalence point.

4. The volume of titrant to reach the equivalence point is accurately measurable.

When an acid (e.g., HCl (*aq*)) is titrated with aqueous NaOH as follows:

$$HCl\ (aq)\ +\ NaOH\ (aq)\ \rightarrow\ NaCl\ (aq)\ +\ H_2O$$

The stoichiometric ratio of HCl to NaOH is 1 mole HCl to 1 mole NaOH. In titration, the volume and concentration of the standard solution (acid or base) are known, but only the volume of the other solution (acid or base), whose concentration to be determined, is known.

In the following example, the above stoichiometry enables the calculation of the unknown concentration.

Suppose that 25.00 mL of 0.2250 M HCl (*aq*) is required to neutralize 27.45 mL of aqueous NaOH solution, whose concentration is not known. The moles of each reactant and the concentration of NaOH can be calculated as follows:

No. of mol of HCl reacted:

$$25.0 \text{ mL} \times (1 \text{ L}/1{,}000 \text{ mL}) \times (0.2250 \text{ mol/L}) = 0.005625 \text{ mol}$$

Since HCl and NaOH react in a 1:1 ratio,

$$\text{No. of mol of NaOH} = \text{No. of mol of HCl} = 0.005625 \text{ mol}$$

$$\text{Molarity of NaOH} = (0.005625 \text{ mol} / 0.02745 \text{ L}) = 0.2049 \text{ M}$$

Sometimes, the stoichiometric ratio is not 1 to 1, as in the example below.

20.0 mL H_2SO_4 of unknown concentration requires 32.0 mL of 0.205 M NaOH. Calculate the concentration of H_2SO_4 solution.

$$H_2SO_4 \, (aq) \; + \; 2 \, NaOH \, (aq) \; \rightarrow \; Na_2SO_4 \, (aq) \; + \; 2 \, H_2O$$

The stoichiometric ratio above is 1 mole of H_2SO_4 to 2 moles of NaOH.

$$\text{No. of mol of NaOH reacted} = \frac{0.205 \text{ mol. NaOH}}{1 \text{ L solution}} \times 32.0 \text{ mL} \times \frac{1 \text{ L}}{1{,}000 \text{ mL}} = 0.00656 \text{ mol}$$

$$\text{No. of mol of } H_2SO_4 = \text{Mol NaOH} \times (1 \text{ mol } H_2SO_4 / 2 \text{ mol NaOH})$$

$$= 0.00656 \text{ mol NaOH} \times (1 \text{ mol } H_2SO_4 / 2 \text{ mol NaOH}) = 0.00328 \text{ mol}$$

$$\text{Molarity of } H_2SO_4 = \frac{0.00328 \text{ mol } H_2SO_4}{0.0200 \text{ L}} = 0.164 \text{ M}$$

Consider the strong acid-strong base titration of 20.0 mL of 0.100 M HCl (*aq*) with 0.100 M NaOH (*aq*) solution. Calculate the pH of the acid solution: (a) before any of the NaOH is added, (b) after 15.0 mL of NaOH is added, (c) after 19.5 mL of NaOH is added, (d) after 20.0 mL of NaOH is added, (e) after 21.0 mL of NaOH is added and (f) after 25.0 mL of NaOH is added.

(a) Before titration, $[H^+] = 0.100$ M,

pH = 1.000

(b) When 15.0 mL of NaOH is added, the following reaction occurs:

$$H^+ (aq) + OH^- (aq) \rightarrow H_2O$$

[ ] before mixing:　　　0.100 M　0.100 M

[ ] after mixing, but before reaction:

0.0571 M　0.0429 M

[ ] after reaction:

0.0142 M　　0

$[H^+] = 0.0142$ M,

$pH = -\log(0.0142) = 1.848$

(c) After 19.5 mL of NaOH is added, calculation of $[H^+]$ is as follows:

$$H^+ (aq) + OH^- (aq) \rightarrow H_2O$$

[ ] before mixing:　　　0.100 M　0.100 M

[ ] after mixing, but before reaction:

0.0506 M　0.0494 M

[ ] after reaction:

0.0012 M　　0

$[H^+] = 0.0012$ M,

$pH = -\log(0.0012) = 2.92$

Note that before the equivalent point, [H$^+$] can be calculated:

[H$^+$] = (initial mol of H$^+$ – mol of OH$^-$ added) / (L of HCl titrated + L of NaOH added)

[H$^+$] = (0.00200 mol H$^+$ – 0.00195 mol OH$^-$) / (0.0200 L of HCl + 0.0195 L NaOH)

[H$^+$] = (0.000050 mol / 0.0395 L) = 0.0013 M

pH = 2.90

(d) When 20.0 mL of 0.100 M NaOH has been added,

$$H^+ (aq) \ + \ OH^- (aq) \ \rightarrow \ H_2O$$

[ ] after mixing, but before reaction:

0.0500 M   0.0500 M

[ ] after reaction: 0   0

This point of the titration is the equivalence point, whereby only Na$^+$ and Cl$^-$ occur in the solution. Since neither of them reacts with water, the solution has a pH = 7.00.

(e) When 21.0 mL of 0.100 M NaOH has been added, there is excess OH$^-$:

$$H^+ (aq) \ + \ OH^- (aq) \ \rightarrow \ H_2O$$

[ ] after mixing, but before reaction:

0.0488 M   0.0512 M

[ ] after reaction:

0   0.0024 M

[OH$^-$] = 0.0024 M

pOH = 2.62 and pH = 11.38

(f) When 25.0 mL of NaOH is added,

$$H^+ (aq) + OH^- (aq) \rightarrow H_2O$$

[ ] after mixing, but before reaction:

0.0444 M   0.0556 M

[ ] after reaction:

0   0.0112 M

$[OH^-] = 0.0112$ M

pOH = 1.953 and pH = 12.047

Note that in strong acid-strong base titrations, an abrupt change from about pH 3 to 11 occurs within ±0.5 mL of NaOH, added near the equivalent point.

This next example is of a weak acid-strong base titration.

General reaction: $HA (aq) + OH^- (aq) \rightarrow H_2O + A^- (aq)$

When acetic acid (weak) is titrated with sodium hydroxide (strong), the net reaction is:

$$HC_2H_3O_2 (aq) + OH^- (aq) \rightarrow C_2H_3O_2^- (aq) + H_2O$$

Consider the titration of 20.0 mL of 0.100 M $HC_2H_3O_2$ (aq) with 0.100 M NaOH (aq) solution. Calculate the pH of the solution: (a) before any of the NaOH is added; (b) after 10.0 mL of NaOH is added; (c) after 15.0 mL of NaOH is added; (d) after 20.0 mL of NaOH is added; (e) after 25.0 mL of NaOH is added.

(a) Before titration, $[H^+] = \sqrt{(0.100 \text{ M}) \cdot (1.8 \times 10^{-5})} = 1.34 \times 10^{-3}$ M,

$$pH = -\log(1.34 \times 10^{-3}) = 2.873$$

(b) After adding 10.0 mL of 0.100 M NaOH, $[H^+]$ is calculated as follows:

$$HC_2H_3O_2 (aq) + OH^- (aq) \rightarrow C_2H_3O_2^- (aq) + H_2O$$

Before mixing: 0.100 M   0.100 M   0.000 M

After mixing (before rxn):

0.0667 M   0.0333 M   0.000 M

After reaction: 0.0333 M   0.000 M   0.0333 M

Using the Henderson-Hasselbalch equation,

$$pH = pK_a + \log([B^-] / [HB])$$

$$[H^+] = K_a \times \frac{[HC_2H_3O_2]}{[C_2H_3O_2^-]} = 1.8 \times 10^{-5} \times (0.0333 \text{ M} / 0.0333 \text{ M}) = 1.8 \times 10^{-5} \text{ M}$$

$$pH = pK_a + \log([C_2H_3O_2^-] / [HC_2H_3O_2]) = 4.74 + \log(1) = 4.74$$

Therefore, when a weak acid is half-neutralized, 50% of the acid is converted to its conjugate base. That is, at halfway to the equivalence point of the titration, $[C_2H_3O_2^-] = [HC_2H_3O_2]$. Under this condition, $[H^+] = K_a$, and $pH = pK_a$.

(c) After adding 15.0 mL of 0.100 M NaOH, $[H^+]$ is calculated as follows:

$$HC_2H_3O_2\,(aq) + OH^-\,(aq) \rightarrow C_2H_3O_2^-\,(aq) + H_2O$$

Before mixing:	0.100 M	0.100 M	0.000 M
After mixing (before rxn):	0.0571 M	0.0429 M	0.000 M
After reaction:	0.0142 M	0.000 M	0.0429 M

Using the Henderson-Hasselbalch equation:

$$pH = pK_a + \log([B^-] / [HB])$$

$$[H^+] = K_a \times \frac{[HC_2H_3O_2]}{[C_2H_3O_2^-]}$$

$$[H^+] = 1.8 \times 10^{-5} \times (0.0142 \text{ M} / 0.0429 \text{ M}) = 6.0 \times 10^{-6} \text{ M}$$

$$pH = pK_a + \log([C_2H_3O_2^-] / [HC_2H_3O_2])$$

$$pH = 4.74 + \log(3.02) = 4.74 + 0.48 = 5.22$$

(d) At the equivalent point, when 20.0 mL of 0.100 M NaOH has been added, all of the acid has been reacted and converted to its conjugate base. The latter undergoes hydrolysis (reacts with water) as follows:

$$C_2H_3O_2^- (aq) + H_2O (l) \leftrightarrows HC_2H_3O_2 (aq) + OH^- (aq)$$

	$C_2H_3O_2^-$	$HC_2H_3O_2$	OH^-
Initial [ ], M:	0.0500	0.000	0.000
Change, Δ[ ], M:	$-x$	$+x$	$+x$
Equilibrium [ ], M:	$(0.0500 - x)$	x	x

By approximation, $[OH^-] = x = \sqrt{(K_b \times [C_2H_3O_2^-]_0)}$

$[OH^-] = \sqrt{(5.6 \times 10^{-10}) \cdot (0.0500)} = 5.3 \times 10^{-6}$ M

$pOH = -\log(5.3 \times 10^{-6}) = 5.28$

$pH = 8.72$

Since the conjugate base of a weak acid undergoes hydrolysis (reacts with water), the pH of the solution at equivalence point is greater than 7.00. In the case of acetic-NaOH titration, the pH at the equivalence point is about 8.72.

For weak acids with larger K_as, the pH at equivalence point is closer to the neutral pH; for those with smaller K_as, the pH at equivalence point is much greater than the neutral pH.

Indicators

An *indicator* is a substance that changes color to mark the *end-point* of a titration. Most indicators used in acid-base titration are weak organic acids. Indicators exhibit one color in the acid or protonated form (HIn) and another in the base or deprotonated form (In$^-$). Each indicator has a range of pH = $pK_a \pm 1$, where the change of colors occurs. A suitable indicator gives the *end-point* that corresponds to the equivalence point of the titration; this is one with a range of pH that falls within the sharp increase (or decrease) of pH in the titration curves.

Like a weak acid, an indicator exhibits the following equilibrium in aqueous solution:

$$HIn (aq) \leftrightarrows H^+ (aq) + In^- (aq)$$

$$K_a = \frac{[H^+] \cdot [In^-]}{[HIn]}$$

Rearranging obtains: $[H^+] = K_a \times ([HIn] / [In^-])$

$$pH = pK_a + \log([In^-] / [HIn])$$

When $[HIn] = 10 \times [In^-]$,

$$pH = pK_a + \log([In^-] / 10[In^-])$$

$pH = pK_a - 1.0$; the indicator assumes the color of acid form.

When $[In^-] = 10 \times [HIn]$,

$$pH = pK_a + \log(10[HIn] / [HIn])$$

$pH = pKa + 1.0$; the indicator assumes the color of base form.

Phenolphthalein, which is the most common acid-base indicator, has $K_a \sim 10^{-9}$. Its acid form (HIn) is colorless and the conjugate base form (In$^-$) is pink. It is colorless when the solution's pH $\leq$ 8, when 90% or more of the species are in the acid form (HIn) and pink at pH $\geq$ 10, when 90% or more of the species are in the conjugate base form (In$^-$). The pH range at which an indicator changes depends on the K_a. For phenolphthalein, which has K_a $\sim 10^{-9}$, its color changes in the pH range 8–10. It is a suitable indicator for strong acid-strong base titrations and weak acid-strong base titrations. The pH ranges for other common acid-base indicators are listed below.

Indicators	Acid color	Base color	pH Range	Type of Titrations
Methyl orange	orange	yellow	3.2–4.5	strong acid-strong base strong acid-weak base
Bromocresol green	yellow	blue	3.8–5.4	strong acid-strong strong acid-weak base
Methyl red	red	yellow	4.5–6.0	strong acid-strong base strong acid-weak base
Bromothymol blue	yellow	blue	6.0–7.6	strong acid-strong base
Phenol Red	orange	red	6.8–8.2	strong acid-strong base weak acid-strong base

Interpretation of titration curves

A *pH curve* is a graph of the pH of solution against the volume of titrant in an acid-base titration. The data used to plot a pH curve may be obtained either by computation or by measuring the pH directly with a pH meter during titration.

There are four types of pH curves for the different types of acid-base titrations. The acid is incrementally added to the alkali (how titrations are normally carried out).

1. Strong acid - strong base titration

$$NaOH \ (aq) \ + \ HCl \ (aq) \ \rightarrow \ NaCl \ (aq) \ + \ H_2O \ (l).$$

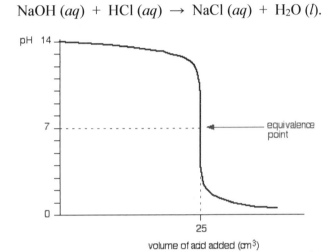

Notice that the pH falls only a very small amount until near the equivalence point. Then there is a very steep drop.

2. Strong acid - weak base titration

$$NH_3\,(aq)\ +\ HCl\,(aq)\ \rightarrow\ NH_4Cl\,(aq).$$

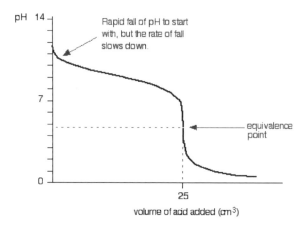

Since it is a weak base, rather than a strong base, the beginning of the titration curve is very different. The pH decreases steeply as the acid is added, but the curve soon becomes less steep. This is because a buffer solution, composed of excess ammonia and formed ammonium chloride, is being created. (The pH of the buffering region is usually $14 - pK_b \pm 1$).

Notice that the equivalence point is now acidic (pH ~ 5), but is still on the steepest part of the curve.

3. Weak acid - strong base titration

$$CH_3COOH\,(aq)\ +\ NaOH\,(aq)\ \rightarrow\ CH_3COONa\,(aq)\ +\ H_2O\,(aq)$$

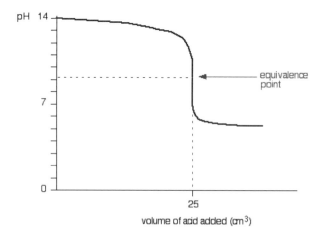

In the first part of the graph, there is an excess of sodium hydroxide, and this part of the curve is similar to the strong acid-strong base titration. However, once the acid is in excess there is a difference, due to the formation of a buffer solution that contains sodium ethanoate and ethanoic acid. The pH of the buffering region is usually $pK_a \pm 1$, which resists changes in pH before the smooth (horizontal) portion of the curve is reached.

4. Weak acid - weak base titration.

The following titration curve is for the reaction:

$$CH_3COOH\ (aq)\ +\ NH_3\ (aq)\ \rightarrow\ CH_3COONH_4\ (aq)$$

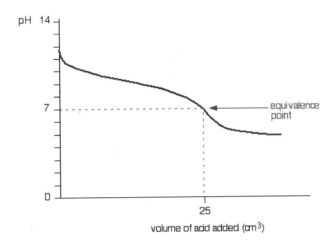

In this example, the acid and the base are equally weak, so the equivalence point is around pH 7. This titration curve is essentially a combination of the two previous graphs. Before the equivalence point, it is similar to the strong acid-weak base case. After the equivalence point, it is similar to the end of the weak acid-strong base case. There is no steep portion of this graph; the lack of a steep portion is an important identifying factor of a weak acid-weak base titration curve.

The image shows all four titration curves for comparison.

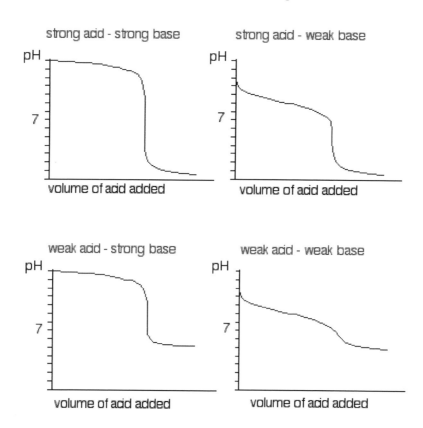

Redox titration

A redox titration is a type of titration based on the transfer of electrons. In redox titration, standard solutions of oxidizing agents are usually used because solutions of reducing agents may react with oxygen in the air. It is important that the species being analyzed is in a single oxidation state before titration.

For example, when iron ore is dissolved in hydrochloric acid solution, both Fe^{2+} and Fe^{3+}, known as iron(II) and iron(III), are present in solution. However, since it must be in a single oxidation state before titration with standard $KMnO_4$ solution, iron(III) is reduced to iron(II) by reaction with excess zinc:

$$2\ Fe^{3+}(aq) + Zn\ (s) \rightarrow 2\ Fe^{2+}(aq) + Zn^{2+}(aq)$$

$$MnO_4^-(aq) + 5\ Fe^{2+}(aq) + 8\ H^+(aq) \rightarrow Mn^{2+}(aq) + 5\ Fe^{3+}(aq) + 4\ H_2O\ (l)$$

$KMnO_4$ and $K_2Cr_2O_7$ are the most commonly used oxidizing agents in redox titration, because the solutions change color as they are being reduced; this color change serves as the titration indicator. $KMnO_4$ is purple, but becomes colorless when MnO_4^- is reduced to Mn^{2+}. The bright orange color of $K_2Cr_2O_7$ changes to purplish-blue when $Cr_2O_7^{2-}$ is reduced to Cr^{3+}.

An example problem of a redox titration.

A solution contains both iron(II) and iron(III) ions. A 50.0 mL sample of the solution is titrated with 35.0 mL of 0.00280 M $KMnO_4$, which oxidizes Fe^{2+} to Fe^{3+}. The permanganate ion is reduced to manganese(II) ion. Another 50.0 mL sample of solution is treated with zinc metal, which reduces all the Fe^{3+} to Fe^{2+}. The resulting solution is again titrated with 0.00280 M $KMnO_4$. Therefore, 48.0 mL is required. What are the concentrations of Fe^{2+} and Fe^{3+} in the solution?

To solve this problem, several steps are required.

1) The stoichiometric relationship of Fe(II) to permanganate is five to one:

$$MnO_4^-(aq) + 5\ Fe^{2+}(aq) + 8\ H^+(aq) \rightarrow Mn^{2+}(aq) + 5\ Fe^{3+}(aq) + 4\ H_2O\ (l)$$

2) Calculate moles of Fe(II) reacted:

$$(0.00280 \text{ mol/L}) \, (0.0350 \text{ L}) = 0.000098 \text{ mol of MnO}_4^-$$

$$(0.0000980 \text{ mol Mn}) \cdot (5 \text{ mol Fe} / 1 \text{ mol Mn}) = 0.000490 \text{ mol Fe(II)}$$

3) Determine the total iron content:

$$(0.00280 \text{ mol/L}) \cdot (0.0480 \text{ L}) = 0.0001344 \text{ mol of MnO}_4^-$$

$$(0.0000980 \text{ mol Mn}) \, (5 \text{ mol Fe} / 1 \text{ mol Mn}) = 0.000672 \text{ mol of total Fe}$$

4) Determine Fe(III) in solution and its molarity:

$$0.000672 \text{ mol} - 0.000490 \text{ mol} = 0.000182 \text{ mol}$$

$$0.000182 \text{ mol} / 0.050 \text{ L} = 0.00364 \text{ M}$$

5) Determine molarity of Fe(II):

$$0.000490 \text{ mol} / 0.050 \text{ L} = 0.0098 \text{ M}$$

Practice Questions

1. Which of the following indicators is green at pH 7?

       I. phenolphthalein   II. bromothymol blue   III. methyl red

   A. I only   **C.** III only
   B. II only   **D.** I and II only

2. Which of the following is NOT a strong acid?

   A. $HClO_3$ **B.** HF   **C.** HBr   **D.** HCl

3. Which of the following compounds is the strongest base?

   A. ClO_3^- **B.** NH_3 **C.** ClO^- **D.** ClO_2^-

4. A Brønsted-Lowry acid is defined as a substance that:

   A. acts as a proton donor in any system   **C.** increases $[H^+]$ when placed in water
   B. acts as a proton acceptor in any system   **D.** decreases $[H^+]$ when placed in water

5. Which of the following acts as the best buffer solution?

   A. Strong acids or bases   **C.** Salts
   B. Strong acids and their salts   **D.** Weak acids or bases and their salts

6. Which of the following is true if a drain cleaner solution is a strong electrolyte?

       I. Slightly reactive   II. Highly reactive   III. Highly ionized

   A. I only   **C.** III only
   B. II only   **D.** I and III only

7. Which of the following statements describes a basic solution?

   A. $[H_3O^+] \times [^-OH] \neq 1 \times 10^{-14}$ **C.** $[H_3O^+] > [^-OH]$
   B. $[H_3O^+] / [^-OH] = 1 \times 10^{-14}$ **D.** $[H_3O^+] < [^-OH]$

8. Which of the following is a general property of an acidic solution?

       I. Neutralizes bases   II. Tastes sour   III. Turns litmus paper red

   A. I only   **C.** III only
   B. II only   **D.** I, II and III

9. Compared to a solution with a higher pH, a solution with a lower pH has a(n):

A. decreased K_a

B. increased [$^-$OH]

C. increased pK_a

D. increased [H^+]

10. Which of the following statements is a correct definition for an Arrhenius acid?

A. Decreases [H^+] when placed in aqueous solutions

B. Increases [H^+] when placed in aqueous solutions

C. Acts as a proton acceptor in any system

D. Acts as a proton donor in any system

11. A Brønsted-Lowry base is a(n):

A. electron acceptor

B. proton acceptor

C. electron donor

D. proton donor

12. Which of the following is the conjugate base of water?

A. $^-$OH (*aq*)   **B.** H^+ (*aq*)   **C.** H_2O (*l*)   **D.** H_3O^+ (*aq*)

13. Which of the following explains why distilled H_2O is neutral?

A. [H^+] = [OH^-]

B. Distilled H_2O has no OH^-

C. Distilled H_2O has no H^+

D. Distilled H_2O has no ions

14. In the reaction below, what does the symbol $\rightleftharpoons$ indicate?

$^-$OH + NH_4^+ $\rightleftharpoons$ H_2O + NH_3

A. The rate of the reverse reaction is the same as the forward reaction

B. The forward reaction does not proceed

C. The reaction does not produce an equilibrium

D. The reverse reaction does not proceed

15. What is the [H_3O^+] of a solution that has a pH = 2.34?

A. 1.3×10^1 M

B. 2.3×10^{-10} M

C. 4.6×10^{-3} M

D. 2.4×10^{-3} M

Solutions

1. B is correct.

Bromothymol blue is a pH indicator that is often used for solutions with neutral pH near 7 (e.g., managing the pH of pools and fish tanks). Bromothymol blue acts as a weak acid in solution that can be protonated or deprotonated. It appears yellow when protonated (lower pH), blue when deprotonated (higher pH) and bluish green in neutral solution.

Phenolphthalein is used as an indicator for acid-base titrations. It is a weak acid, which can dissociate protons (H^+ ions) in solution. The phenolphthalein molecule is colorless, and the phenolphthalein ion is pink. It turns colorless in acidic solutions and pink in basic solutions. With basic conditions, the phenolphthalein (neutral) $\rightleftharpoons$ ions (pink) equilibrium shifts to the right, leading to more ionization as H^+ ions are removed.

Methyl red has a pK_a of 5.1 and is a pH indicator dye that changes color in acidic solutions: turns red in pH under 4.4, orange in pH 4.4-6.2 and yellow in pH over 6.2.

2. B is correct.

Strong acids dissociate a proton to produce the weakest conjugate base (i.e., most stable anion).

Weak acids dissociate a proton to produce the strongest conjugate base (i.e., least stable anion).

Hydrofluoric (HF) acid has a pK_a of about 3.8 and is considered a weak acid because it does not dissociate completely. The F– anion is the least stable of the halogen anions (due to its small valence shell).

3. C is correct.

Perchloric acid ($HClO_4$) is the strongest acid listed and therefore is the weakest conjugate base (i.e., most stable anion).

Hypochlorite (ClO^-) is the strongest base (i.e., least stable anion).

In oxy acids, the more oxygen present, the greater is the acid strength.

Weakest conjugate bases of oxy acids (containing more than one oxygen) are is stabilized by resonance.

4. A is correct.

The Brønsted-Lowry acid-base theory focuses on the ability to accept and donate protons (H^+).

A Brønsted-Lowry acid is the term for a substance that donates a proton in an acid-base reaction, while a Brønsted-Lowry base is the term for the substance that accepts the proton.

5. D is correct.

A buffer is an aqueous solution that consists of a weak acid and its conjugate base, or vice versa.

Buffered solutions resist changes in pH, and are often used to keep the pH at a nearly constant value in many chemical applications. It does this by readily absorbing or releasing protons (H^+) and ^-OH.

When an acid is added to the solution, the buffer releases ^-OH and accepts H^+ ions from the acid.

Weak acids or bases and their salts are the best buffer systems.

6. C is correct.

An electrolyte is a substance that dissociates into cations (i.e., positive ions) and anions (i.e., negative ions) when placed in solution.

7. D is correct.

In a basic solution, the concentration of ^-OH is higher than H^+ or H_3O^+.

8. D is correct.

An acid can neutralize a base (i.e., a substance with a pH above 7) to form salt.

Acids have a sour taste (e.g., lemon juice has a pH of about 2).

An acid is a chemical substance with a pH less than 7.

Litmus paper is red under acidic conditions and blue under basic conditions.

Acids are known to have a sour taste (e.g., lemon juice) because the sour taste receptors on the tongue detect the dissolved hydrogen (H^+) ions.

A pH greater than 7 and feels slippery are all qualities of bases, not acids. An acid is a chemical substance with a pH less than 7 which produces H^+ ions in water. An acid can be neutralized by a base (i.e., a substance with a pH above 7) to form salt.

Litmus paper is red under acidic conditions and blue under basic conditions.

However, acids are not known to have a slippery feel; this is a characteristic of bases. Bases feels slippery because they dissolve the fatty acids and oils from skin and therefore reduce the friction between the skin cells.

9. D is correct.

Acidic solutions contain hydronium ions (H_3O^+). These ions are in the aqueous form because they are dissolved in water.

Although chemists often write H^+ (*aq*), referring to a single hydrogen nucleus (a proton), it actually exists as the hydrogen atom.

10. B is correct.

An Arrhenius acid increases the concentration of H^+ ions in an aqueous solution. Since pH is the negative log of the activity of H^+ ions in an aqueous solution, this is why acids have a low pH.

An acid can act as a proton donor, but this is the Brønsted-Lowry definition of an acid, not Arrhenius.

11. B is correct.

Brønsted-Lowry acids are proton donors (e.g., HCl, H_2SO_4).

Brønsted-Lowry bases are proton acceptors (e.g., HSO_4^-, NO_3^-).

Lewis acids are electron pair acceptors, whereas Lewis bases are electron pair donors.

12. A is correct.

By the Brønsted-Lowry acid-base theory:

An acid (reactant) dissociates a proton to become the conjugate base (product).

A base (reactant) gains a proton to become the conjugate acid (product).

The definition is expressed in terms of an equilibrium expression

acid + base ↔ conjugate base + conjugate acid.

13. A is correct.

If the $[H_3O^+] = [^-OH]$, it has a pH of 7 and the solution is neutral.

14. D is correct.

The symbol ⇌ indicates that the reaction is in equilibrium whereby the rate of the forward reaction is equal to the rate of the reverse reaction. It refers to the rate and not the relative magnitude of the remaining reactants nor the formed products during the reaction.

15. C is correct.

The formula for pH is:

$$pH = -\log[H_3O^+]$$

Rearrange to solve for $[H_3O^+]$:

$$[H_3O^+] = 10^{-pH}$$

$$[H_3O^+] = 10^{-2.34}$$

$$[H_3O^+] = 4.6 \times 10^{-3} \text{ M}$$

Chapter 8

Thermochemistry and Thermodynamics

Thermochemistry
- **Thermodynamic System, State Function**
- **Endothermic and Exothermic Reactions**
- **Bond Dissociation Energy as Related to Heats of Formation**
- **Measurement of Heat Changes (Calorimetry), Heat Capacity, Specific Heat Capacity**
- **Gibbs Free Energy (G)**
- **Spontaneous Reactions and ΔG°**

Thermodynamics
- **Zeroth Law (Concept of Temperature)**
- **First Law (ΔE = q + w, Conservation of Energy in Thermodynamic Processes)**
- **Equivalence of Mechanical, Chemical, Electrical and Thermal Energy Units**
- **Second Law (Concept of Entropy)**
- **Third Law**
- **Temperature Scales, Conversions**
- **Heat Transfer (Conduction, Convection, Radiation)**
- **Heat of Fusion, Heat of Vaporization**
- **PV Diagram (Work Done = Area Under or Enclosed by Curve)**
- **Coefficient of Expansion**
- **Phase Diagram: Pressure and Temperature**

Thermochemistry: Energy Changes in Chemical Reactions

Thermochemistry studies energy and heat associated with chemical reactions and physical transformations. A reaction may release energy (exothermic reactions) or absorb energy (endothermic reactions), and a phase change may do the same (e.g., boiling, melting). Thermochemistry explains these energy changes, particularly in the context of the energy exchange between the system and its surroundings. Thermochemistry is applied to predict reactant and product quantities throughout the reaction. It is also used to predict whether a reaction is spontaneous or non-spontaneous, favorable or unfavorable.

Thermochemistry combines the concepts of thermodynamics and energy of chemical bonds. The subject commonly includes calculations of such quantities as heat capacity, heat of combustion, heat of formation, enthalpy, entropy, free energy and calories.

Thermodynamic System, State Function

Thermodynamics deals with the energy requirements of physical and chemical changes. It defines many variables related to energy. Some typical variables are listed below:

ΔE or ΔU measures the total internal energy of a system

q measures the heat of a system

W measures the work of a system

ΔH measures the enthalpy change of a system – whether a process is exothermic or endothermic

ΔG measures the Gibbs free energy change of a system – whether a process is spontaneous or nonspontaneous

ΔS measures the entropy change of a system or surroundings – whether the randomness of a system or surroundings is increasing or decreasing

A *state function* is a quantity whose value does not depend on the path used to measure the value. State functions such as $\Delta E°$, $\Delta H°$, $\Delta S°$ and $\Delta G°$ depend only on the initial and final states of the system.

Quantities, such as work (W) and heat (q), which are not state functions, are *path functions* and are generally represented by lowercase letters. The term *system* defines the part of the universe being studied, such as the substances involved in a chemical reaction or a phase change. The *surroundings* are everything other than the system that is being studied.

There are different types of systems that can be studied:

- An *isolated system* has no exchange of heat, work or matter between the system and surroundings.

- A *closed system* has an exchange of heat and work but not exchange of matter between the system and surroundings.

- An *open system* has heat, work and matter exchanged between the system and surroundings.

Note that heat and temperature are different quantities.

Heat is a specific form of thermal energy that can leave or enter a system.

Temperature is a measure of the average kinetic energy of the particles in a system.

Endothermic and Exothermic Reactions

Some chemical reactions produce energy, while others require energy in the form of heat. This is the energy used to form or break chemical bonds, which is known as the bonding energy. The term that describes the energy change associated with the formation or destruction of a chemical bond is called the *enthalpy change* (ΔH). The unit for enthalpy is Joules (J), the same as for energy; it can also be expressed as energy per mol (J/mol).

An *exothermic reaction* releases heat. Energy is released into the surroundings because stronger, more stable bonds are formed in the products compared to the bonds in the reactants. Therefore, the energy that is needed to initiate the reaction is less than the energy that is released, leading to the liberation of heat. This can be represented in a chemical reaction in the following way, with heat on the product side:

$$4 \text{ Fe } (s) + 3 \text{ O}_2 (g) \rightarrow 2 \text{ Fe}_2\text{O}_3 (s) + \text{heat}$$

An example of an exothermic reaction is fuel burning. In an exothermic reaction, heat is released and the sign of ΔH is (−), meaning that the energy of the products is less than the energy of the reactants. The amount of energy released can be calculated using bond-dissociation energies, which is explained in a later section.

Exothermic reaction → energy is released → $\Delta H < 0$ → enthalpy decreases

For example, the chemical reaction between hydrogen gas and chloride gas:

$$H_2\,(g) + Cl_2\,(g) \rightarrow 2\,HCl\,(g) + 185\,kJ$$

$$\Delta H = -185\,kJ/mol\ (\text{heat released})$$

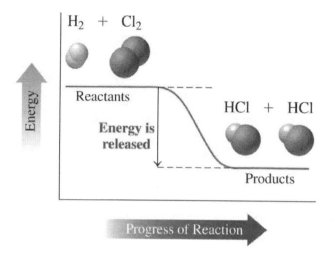

Heat is released, indicating that the reaction is exothermic and ΔH is negative.

Endothermic reactions require energy to break bonds. In endothermic reactions, weaker bonds are formed in the products compared to the bonds in the reactants. This can be represented in a chemical reaction, with heat on the reactant side:

$$\text{Heat} + NH_4NO_3\,(s) \rightarrow NH_4NO_3\,(aq)$$

The above reaction is the ionic compound ammonium nitrate dissolving in water, which means that it is breaking up into its constituent ions, NH_4 and NO_3.

A few examples of endothermic reactions are melting ice and cooking an egg (heat is required for both of these processes). In an endothermic reaction, heat is absorbed and the sign of ΔH is (+), meaning that the energy of the products is greater than the energy of the reactants.

The amount of energy absorbed can be calculated using bond-dissociation energies.

Endothermic reaction $\rightarrow$ energy is absorbed $\rightarrow$ $\Delta H > 0$ $\rightarrow$ enthalpy increases

For example, the chemical reaction between nitrogen gas (N_2) and oxygen gas (O_2) to form nitrogen monoxide (NO):

$$N_2\ (g) + O_2\ (g) + 181\ kJ \rightarrow 2\ NO\ (g)$$

$$\Delta H = +181\ kJ\ \text{(heat added)}$$

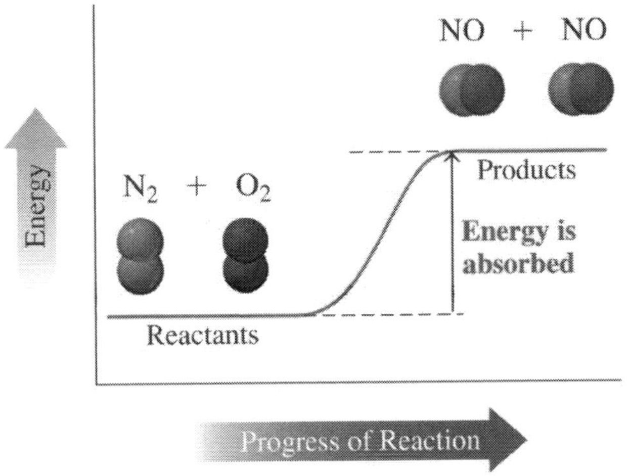

Heat is absorbed, indicating that the reaction is endothermic and ΔH is positive.

Below is a table that summarizes exothermic and endothermic reactions.

Reaction	Energy Change	Heat in the Equation	Sign of ΔH
Endothermic	Heat absorbed	Reactant side	Positive sign (+)
Exothermic	Heat released	Product side	Negative sign (−)

Example: Is the following reaction endothermic or exothermic?

$$O_2N\text{–}NO_2 \rightarrow O_2N + NO_2$$

Solution: This reaction is endothermic because it involves the formation of two products from a single reactant and the breaking of a chemical bond, which requires energy.

Enthalpy (H), standard heats of reaction and formation

Enthalpy changes can occur at standard temperatures and pressures.

The *standard state* refers to substances in their most stable form (i.e., the lowest-energy state). Standard state in thermodynamics also refers to one atmosphere pressure (1 atm) and a temperature of 25 °C (298 K). For example, at standard state, oxygen naturally occurs as O_2 (diatomic gas) and carbon exists as C (solid graphite).

The *standard heat of reaction* (*standard enthalpy of reaction* ΔH°_{rxn}) is the change in heat content when one mole of matter is transformed by a chemical reaction under standard conditions (1 atm and 298 K).

The *standard heat of formation* (*standard enthalpy of formation* ΔH°_f) is the change in heat content associated with the formation of one mole of a compound or molecule from its constituent elements in their standard states.

The standard enthalpy of formation has been determined for many molecules, and the ΔH_f° for the most common molecules are generally listed in a tabulated data chart. When choosing ΔH°_f values from a table, choose the value corresponding to the appropriate state of matter (solid, liquid, aqueous, gas). The standard heat of formation for an element in its standard state always has a value of 0 kJ/mol.

The enthalpy change of a chemical reaction can be calculated using both theoretical and experimental methods. The general equation for calculating the heat of a reaction from the difference in the energy of the reactants and the products is as follows:

$$\Delta H = H_{products} - H_{reactants}$$

Example: For the following balanced chemical equation, calculate the heat of reaction from the heats of formation and determine if the process is exothermic or endothermic:

$$16\ H_2S\ (g) + 8\ SO_2\ (g) \rightarrow 16\ H_2O\ (l) + 3\ S_8\ (s)$$

From the table of thermodynamic quantities, use the values for the heats of formation of each the components in the reaction, and set the equation to calculate the heat of reaction:

$$\Delta H = H_{products} - H_{reactants}$$

$$\Delta H^{\circ}_{rxn} = [16 \text{ mol}(\Delta H^{\circ}_f \text{ of } H_2O \ (l)) + 3 \text{ mol}(\Delta H^{\circ}_f \text{ of } S_8 \ (s))] -$$
$$[16 \text{ mol}(\Delta H^{\circ}_f \text{ of } H_2S \ (g)) + 8 \text{ mol}(\Delta H^{\circ}_f \text{ of } SO_2 \ (g))]$$

$$\Delta H^{\circ}_{rxn} = [16 \text{ mol}(-285.8 \text{ kJ/mol}) + 3 \text{ mol}(0 \text{ kJ/mol})] -$$
$$[16 \text{ mol}(-20.2 \text{ kJ/mol}) + 8 \text{ mol}(-296.8 \text{ kJ/mol})]$$

$$\Delta H^{\circ}_{rxn} = [-4{,}573 \text{ kJ} + 0 \text{ kJ}] - [-323 \text{ kJ} + (-2{,}374 \text{ kJ})]$$

$$\Delta H^{\circ}_{rxn} = -4{,}573 \text{ kJ} + 323 \text{ kJ} + 2374 \text{ kJ}$$

$$\Delta H^{\circ}_{rxn} = -1{,}876 \text{ kJ}$$

Since ΔH_{rxn}° is negative, the reaction is exothermic, whereby heat is released by the system to the surroundings.

Follow the steps when calculating the heat of reaction (ΔH):

1) Identify the given and needed quantities.
2) Write an expression using the heat of reaction and any molar mass needed.
3) Write the conversion factors including heat of reaction.
4) Set the expression to calculate heat.

Example: In the following reaction, how much heat (kJ) is absorbed when 1.65 grams of nitrogen monoxide gas is produced?

$$N_2 \ (g) + O_2 \ (g) \rightarrow 2 \ NO \ (g) \quad \Delta H = +181 \text{ kJ/mol}$$

Step 1: State the given and needed quantities.

Given: 1.65 grams of NO

$$\Delta H = +181 \text{ kJ/mol}$$

Solve: Heat absorbed in kJ.

$$N_2(g) + O_2(g) \rightarrow 2\,NO(g) \qquad \Delta H = +181 \text{ kJ/mol}$$

$$1.65 \text{ g} \qquad\qquad\qquad ? \text{ kJ}$$

Step 2: Write an expression using the heat of reaction and any molar mass needed.

grams of NO → moles of NO → kilojoules of energy

molar mass   heat of reaction

Step 3: Write the conversion factors, including heat of reaction.

1 mole of NO = 30.01 g of NO:

30.01 g NO / 1 mol NO   or   1 mol NO / 30.01 g NO

ΔH for 2 moles of NO = +181 kJ/mol, therefore:

2 mol NO / +181 kJ/mol   or   +181 kJ/mol / 2 mol NO

Step 4: Set the expression to calculate the heat.

1.65 g NO × (1 mol NO / 30.01 g NO) × (+181 kJ/mol / 2 mol NO) = 4.98 kJ/mol

4.98 kJ/mol of nitrogen gas is absorbed when 1.65 g of nitrogen monoxide is produced from nitrogen and oxygen.

Below is a chart to help determine when to use different chemical quantities.

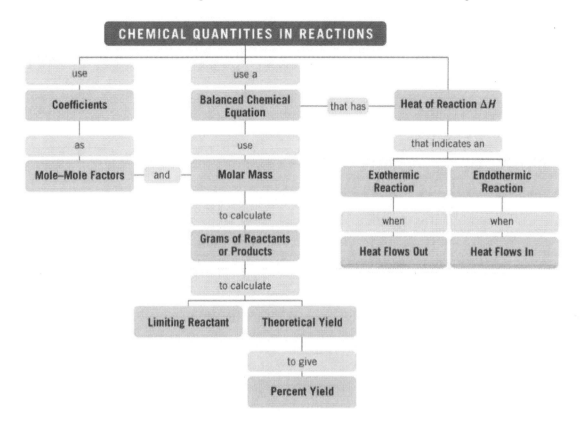

Hess' law of heat summation

Hess' law of constant heat summation is an important relationship in physical chemistry. Enthalpy is a state function (i.e., depends only on initial and final states; it does not depend on the path).

The equation for *Hess' Law of Heat Summation* is given by:

$$\Delta H°_{rxn} = \Sigma \, n(\Delta H°_f \text{ of products}) - \Sigma \, n(\Delta H°_f \text{ of reactants})$$

where *n* represents the moles of each reactant or product in the balanced chemical equation. The Greek letter Σ means the sum of the variables.

Essentially, Hess' law states that the total energy change over the complete course of a reaction is the same, regardless of whether the reaction occurs in one step or several steps.

In addition to applying Hess' law of summation equation, enthalpy can be calculated using alternative means. For example, if a series of reactions whose enthalpies are known create an overall reaction that gives the reaction sought, then the sum of those enthalpies is the enthalpy of the entire reaction. This method of calculating the enthalpy change is the *thermochemical systems of equations* method.

Example: From Hess' Law, determine the enthalpy of reaction for the reaction:

$$2 N_2 (g) + 5 O_2 (g) \longrightarrow 2 N_2O_5 (g) \qquad \Delta H = ?$$

Use the following heats of reaction:

Equation (1) $2 H_2 (g) + O_2 (g) \longrightarrow 2 H_2O (l)$ $\quad \Delta H = -571.7 \text{ kJ}$

Equation (2) $N_2O_5 (g) + H_2O (l) \longrightarrow 2 HNO_3 (l)$ $\quad \Delta H = -92 \text{ kJ}$

Equation (3) $N_2 (g) + 3 O_2 (g) \longrightarrow 2 HNO_3 (l)$ $\quad \Delta H = -348.2 \text{ kJ}$

Manipulate the above equations so that the overall equation sums to the desired equation. First, inspect the compounds in each equation and choose an equation which contains a compound that only appears once in the given equations. Nitrogen, N_2, is found only in equation (3), so start with this equation. Dinitrogen pentoxide, N_2O_5, is found only in equation (2), so equation (2) could also be used to start solving the problem. Oxygen, O_2, is found in both equations (1) and (3), so it is not a good compound by which to begin solving the problem.

Continue solving the problem using the compound nitrogen and equation (3). Equation (3) is written containing only one mole of nitrogen as a reactant. Two moles of nitrogen are needed as a reactant. Since nitrogen is a reactant in both instances, the equation does not need to be reversed, but equation (3) must be multiplied by two in order to obtain the required two moles of nitrogen. Whatever is done to manipulate the chemical equation is also applied to the heat of reaction; thus, the given heat of reaction is also multiplied by two:

$$2 \times \text{Equation (3): } 2 N_2 (g) + 6 O_2 (g) + 2 H_2O (g) \longrightarrow 4 HNO_3 (l)$$

$$\Delta H = 2(-348.7 \text{ kJ}) = -696.4 \text{ kJ}$$

Next, dinitrogen pentoxide is introduced into the problem, since only equation (2) contained the compound. In the equation sought, N_2O_5 appears as two moles of product. In equation (2), N_2O_5 appears as one mole of reactant. Reverse the equation and multiply by two. This means the sign of the heat of reaction is also changed, in addition to the equation being reversed and doubled:

$-2 \times$ Eqn(2): $4\ HNO_3\ (l) \longrightarrow 2\ N_2O_5\ (g) + 2\ H_2O\ (l)$

$$\Delta H = -2(-92\ kJ) = +184\ kJ$$

The four moles of nitric acid cancel. This is convenient, since this compound is not found in the sought equation.

$2 \times$ Eqn(3): $2\ N_2\ (g) + 6\ O_2\ (g) + 2\ H_2O\ (g) \longrightarrow$ ~~$4\ HNO_3\ (l)$~~

$$H = 2(-348.7\ kJ) = -696.4\ kJ$$

$-2 \times$ Eqn(2): ~~$4\ HNO_3\ (l)$~~ $\longrightarrow 2\ N_2O_5\ (g) + 2\ H_2O\ (l)$

$$\Delta H = -2(-92\ kJ) = +184\ kJ$$

Cancel two moles of H_2, two moles of H_2O and one mole of O_2 by using equation (1) in reverse. Remember to reverse the sign for the heat of reaction:

$2 \times$ Eqn(3): $2\ N_2\ (g) +$ ~~6~~ $O_2\ (g) + 2\ H_2O\ (g) \longrightarrow$ ~~$4\ HNO_3\ (l)$~~

$$\Delta H = 2(-348.7\ kJ) = -696.4\ kJ$$

$-2 \times$ Eqn(2): ~~$4\ HNO_3\ (l)$~~ $\longrightarrow 2\ N_2O_5\ (g) + 2\ H_2O\ (l)$

$$\Delta H = -2(-92\ kJ) = +184\ kJ$$

$-1 \times$ Eqn(1) $2\ H_2O\ (l) \longrightarrow$ ~~$2\ H_2\ (g) + O_2\ (g)$~~

$$\Delta H = -1(571.7\ kJ) = +571.1\ kJ$$

Summing the chemical equations gives the sought reaction. Summing the heats of reaction gives the heat of reaction for the overall process:

$2\ N_2\ (g) + 5\ O_2\ (g) \longrightarrow 2\ N_2O_5\ (g)$ $\Delta H = +59\ kJ$

The various ΔH values used in calculations need not be for actual, measurable processes. Often, values from the table of heats of formation have been calculated via Hess' Law, and can now be used for further calculations.

Bond-Dissociation Energy as Related to Heats of Formation

Bond-dissociation energy is the standard enthalpy change when a bond is cleaved, and is thus a measure of the strength of a chemical bond.

Bond energy is a more specific term that refers to the heat required to break the chemical bonds of one mole of gaseous molecules to give separate gaseous atoms. Since energy input is always required to pull two atoms apart, bond-dissociation energy and bond energy are always positive quantities associated with an endothermic process.

Bond dissociation is the reverse process of *bond formation*, for which the energy is always a negative quantity and is associated with an exothermic process.

Bond energy depends on the types of atoms bonding. The H–H single bond, for example, has a bond energy of 436 kJ per mole, but the H–O single bond has a bond energy of 464 kJ per mole.

The following chart shows the energies for some common bonds:

Bond	Bond Energy (kJ/mole)	Bond	Bond Energy (kJ/mole)
H–H	436	N–N	159
H–C	414	O–O	138
H–N	389	Cl–Cl	243
H–O	464	C=O	803
H–F	569	N=O	631
H–Cl	431	O=O	498
C–O	351	C≡C	837
C–C	347	N≡N	946

The bond energies in the above chart can be used to estimate ΔH°_{f}.

Example: Calculate ΔH_f^o for CH_3OH (g) (the bottom reaction in the figure below)

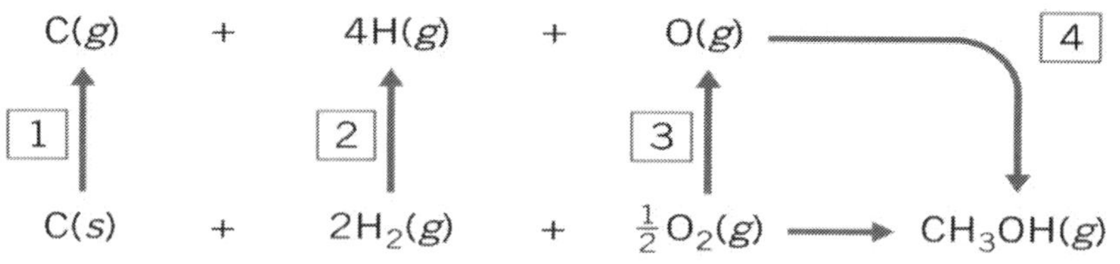

C (g)   +   4 H (g)   +   O (g)   Step 4

Step 1 ↑   Step 2 ↑   Step 3 ↑

C (s)   +   2 H$_2$ (g)   + ½ O$_2$ (g)   → CH_3OH (g)

Use four step path-

Step 1: break C–C bonds (positive energy)

Step 2: break H–H bonds (positive energy)

Step 3: break O–O bond (positive energy)

Step 4: form four C–H bonds (negative energy)

$$\Delta H_f^o\, CH_3OH\,(g) = \Delta H_f^o\, C\,(g) + 4 \times \Delta H_f^o\, H\,(g) + \Delta H_f^o\, O\,(g) - \Delta H_{atom}\, CH_3OH\,(g)$$

$$\Delta H_f^o\, CH_3OH\,(g) = [716.7 + (4 \times 217.9) + 249.2]\ kJ - \Delta H_{atom}\, CH_3OH\,(g)$$

$$\Delta H_f^o\, CH_3OH\,(g) = 1{,}837.5\ kJ - \Delta H_{atom}\, CH_3OH\,(g)$$

$$\Delta H_f^o\, CH_3OH\,(g) = 1{,}837.5\ kJ - 3D_{C-H} + D_{C-O} + D_{O-H}$$

$$\Delta H_f^o\, CH_3OH\,(g) = 1{,}837.5\ kJ - (3 \times 412) + 360 + 463 = 2{,}059\ kJ$$

$$\Delta H_f^o\, CH_3OH\,(g) = 1{,}837.5\ kJ - 2{,}059\ kJ$$

$$= -222\ kJ$$

The ΔH_f^o of CH_3OH (g) is calculated to be –222 kJ using bond energies. According to the chart on the previous page, ΔH_f^o of CH_3OH (g) was experimentally determined to equal –201 kJ/mol (experimentally determined).

Therefore, bond energies give an estimate within 10% of the actual quantity.

Measurement of Heat Changes, Heat Capacity, Specific Heat Capacity

One of the experimental methods enthalpy change may be calculated is by using *calorimetry*. The basic principle behind calorimetry involves heat flow. Heat lost by the system equals the heat gained by the surroundings during an *exothermic* process. Conversely, heat gained by the system from the surroundings equals the heat lost by the surroundings in an *endothermic* process.

The apparatus used in calorimetry experiments is a *calorimeter*, which measures the amount of energy in food. The food is placed inside a closed container surrounded by water and burned in the presence of oxygen. The change in the temperature of the water is directly related to the amount of energy released. The energy is commonly reported in units of nutritional Calories, or kilojoules. A nutritional Calorie (Cal) is an energy unit equal to 1000 calories (cal) and a kilocalorie (kcal).

Nutrient Molecule in Food	Example	Cal/g	kJ/g
Carbohydrate	Table sugar, potatoes, flour	4	17
Protein	Meats, fish, beans	4	17
Fat	Oil, butter	9	38

Even though cells within the body combust the molecules differently, the calorimeter provides an accurate *caloric value* because the end products of the two reactions are the same. Different forms of food contain different amounts of energy, as shown in the table.

Heat capacity (*thermal capacity*) is a physical property relating the ability of a substance to hold heat. Heat capacity is the amount of heat energy required to raise a substance by one degree Celsius.

Specific heat capacity is often used instead of heat capacity. The specific heat capacity differs from heat capacity in that it relates the amount of heat energy required to raise one gram of a substance by one degree Celsius.

A comparison of heat capacities between metals and water demonstrates how heat capacities of substances can vary over a wide range. Metals tend to have low specific heat capacities. Water has a relatively high specific heat capacity; it takes 4.2 J of heat energy to raise the temperature of one gram of water by 1 °C. It is this property of water that helps control global temperatures. Temperature fluctuations during day and night would be much larger if the heat capacity of water was a lower value. This is evident in a desert where water is scarce. Daytime temperatures are very high, yet nighttime temperatures can drop to near freezing.

The heat capacity (mC) of an object is given by the product of the mass m of the object and the specific heat capacity (c) of the substance.

The equation that relates specific heat to heat and temperature is:

$$q = mc\Delta T$$

where q is the heat flow, m is the mass measured in units grams, c is the specific heat capacity of the substance and ΔT is the change in temperature.

There are several different types of heat capacities measured in chemistry, including:

Molar heat capacity = heat capacity per mole = J/mol·°C

Specific heat capacity (c) = heat capacity per mass = J/g·°C

In solving calorimetry problems it is useful to know that one unit degree Celsius (1 °C) is the same as a change in one Kelvin (1 K).

Some useful conversion factors:

1 calorie = 4.2 J

1 Calorie (with capital C) = 1,000 calorie = 1 kilocalorie

1 Calorie = 4200 J.

For water, 1 gram = 1 cubic centimeter = 1 mL

In a typical calorimetry experiment, a hot substance (the system) is introduced to a cold substance (the surroundings). The system and surroundings are allowed to reach thermal equilibrium at some final temperature. Heat dissipates from the hotter substance to the cooler substance. The heat lost by the hot substance (the system) must be equal in magnitude to the heat gained by the cooler substance (the surroundings) but opposite in sign.

$$q_{sys} = -q_{surr}$$

There are two types of calorimeters. The *constant-pressure calorimeter* is where heat flow is measured at constant atmospheric pressure. In the real world, a perfect calorimeter does not exist; no calorimeter can completely insulate heat flow. The calorimeter itself, as part of the surroundings, absorbs some heat. Therefore, the calorimeter must be calibrated to obtain the most accurate result. The simplest type of constant-pressure calorimeter is a Styrofoam cup, which is often used in introductory chemistry classes. Although the temperature insulating properties of a Styrofoam cup are fairly good, the cup still absorbs some heat. Calibration is often performed as an experiment in which hot water of known mass and temperature is poured into a coffee cup containing cool water of known mass and temperature. The combined water samples are allowed to equilibrate to a final maximum temperature, and a calorimeter constant can be determined, as shown in the example below.

Example: Suppose 60.1 g of water at 97.6 °C is poured into a coffee cup calorimeter containing 50.3 g of water at 24.7 °C. The final temperature of the combined water samples reaches 62.8 °C. What is the calorimeter constant?

Solution: Consider the basic principle of calorimetry:

heat lost by the hot water = heat gained by the cool water + heat gained by the calorimeter

Determine the mathematical equations corresponding to the premise described:

heat lost by the hot water = heat gained by the cool water + heat gained by the calorimeter

$$-m_{hot}C_{water}(T_{final} - T_{intial, hot}) = m_{cool} \, c_{water}(T_{final} - T_{initial, cool}) + K_{cal} (T_{final} - T_{initial, cool})$$

Notice the negative sign for the heat lost by the hot water because heat loss is negative. Substitute the proper masses and temperatures into the expression. Note that since the cool water was contained in the cup, the initial temperature of the calorimeter and the cool water are the same.

The specific heat capacity of water, $c_{water} = 4.184$ J/g°C.

$$-(60.1 \text{ g}) \cdot (4.184 \text{ J/g°C}) \cdot (62.8 \text{ °C} - 97.6 \text{ °C})$$

$$= (50.3 \text{ g}) \cdot (4.184 \text{ J/°C}) \cdot (62.8 \text{ °C} - 24.7 \text{ °C}) + K_{cal} (62.8 \text{ °C} - 24.7 \text{ °C})$$

Combining terms: $8.75 \times 10^3 \text{ J} = 8.02 \times 10^3 \text{ J} + K_{cal} (38.1 \text{ °C})$

Solving for K_{cal}: $K_{cal} = \dfrac{8.75 \times 10^3 \text{ J} - 8.02 \times 10^3 \text{ J}}{38.1 \text{°C}} = 19.2 \text{ J/°C}$

Now that the calorimeter has been calibrated, use it to determine the specific heat capacity of a metal. In this experiment, a known quantity of a metal is heated to a known temperature. The heat metal sample is placed into a coffee cup calorimeter containing a known quantity of water at a known temperature. The temperature is allowed to equilibrate, and a final temperature is measured.

Example: Suppose 28.2 g of an unknown metal is heated to 99.8 °C and placed into a coffee cup calorimeter containing 150.0 g of water at a temperature of 23.5 °C. The temperature of the water equilibrates at a final temperature of 25.0 °C. The calorimeter constant has been determined to be 19.2 J/°C. What is the specific heat capacity of the metal?

This problem is based on the heat flow:

heat lost by the hot metal = heat gained by the water + heat gained by the calorimeter

$$-(28.2 \text{ g}) \cdot (C_{metal}) \cdot (25.0 \text{ °C} - 99.8 \text{ °C}) = (150.0 \text{ g}) \cdot (4.184 \text{ J/g°C}) \cdot (25.0 \text{ °C} - 23.5 \text{ °C})$$

$$+ 19.2 \text{ J/°C}(25.0 \text{ °C} - 23.5 \text{ °C})$$

Combining terms:

$$2.11 \times 10^3 \text{ g°C } (C_{metal}) = 9.4 \times 10^2 \text{ J} + 29 \text{ J}$$

$$2.11 \times 10^3 \text{ J } (C_{metal}) = 969 \text{ J}$$

Solving for specific heat capacity:

$$C_{metal} = \frac{969\,J}{2.11 \times 10^3\,g\,°C} = 0.459\,J/g\,°C$$

The second type of calorimeter is the *constant-volume calorimeter*, where heat flow is measured at constant volume. The most commonly used constant-volume calorimeter is the bomb calorimeter, also known as a decomposition vessel.

When oxygen reacts with molecules to produce carbon dioxide, water and energy, the process is called combustion. Bomb calorimeters are most frequently used for the combustion of hydrocarbons.

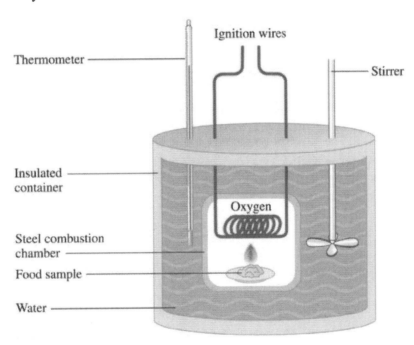

A common setup for a bomb calorimeter

Free Energy *G*

The *Gibbs free energy* (*G*) is the amount of energy present in molecules available to do work. The *free energy change* Δ*G* is the energy difference between the free energy present in the product and reactant molecules. When molecules react, some chemical bonds are broken and others are formed in the products. Recall that breaking a bond is a process that requires input of energy, and that making a bond releases energy, so free energy is exchanged during a chemical reaction. Not all chemical bonds have the same strength, and therefore do not require the same amount of energy.

The Gibbs free energy change is also equal to the maximum amount of energy produced during a reaction that can theoretically be harnessed as work. More specifically, the Gibbs free energy change equals the amount of work that a *reversible reaction* can produce.

Recall that reactions that give off heat are exothermic, and those that absorb heat are endothermic. For a chemical reaction to occur, the reactants must collide with enough energy to react. The energy necessary to align the reactant molecules and to cause them to collide with enough energy to form products is the *activation energy*. If the energy in the reactant molecules is less than the activation energy, the molecules bounce off each other without forming products, and a chemical reaction does not occur.

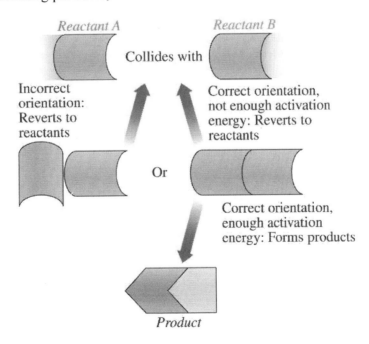

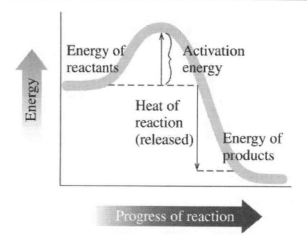

The thermodynamics of a chemical reaction can be represented on a *reaction energy diagram* showing the energy of the reactants, products, the activation energy and the free energy change ΔG. Energy appears on the *y*-axis, and the reaction progress from reactants to products appears on the *x*-axis. Notice that each reaction has an activation energy hill or *energy barrier* before the reactant forms products.

There are numerous ways to calculate Gibbs free energy. Since Gibbs free energy is a state function, one of the methods is analogous to previous methods discussed for enthalpy and entropy. The equation is shown below:

$$\Delta G°_{rxn} = \Sigma\, n(\Delta G°_f \text{ of products}) - \Sigma\, n(\Delta G°_f \text{ of reactants})$$

where *n* represents the moles of each product or reactant, and is given by the coefficient in the balanced chemical equation.

As with enthalpy, the standard Gibbs free energy of formation of elements in their standard states is 0 kJ/mol. Notice the similarity of this equation to Hess' law of heat summation.

Spontaneous Reactions and ΔG°

The term *spontaneous* describes a process that occurs independently without any input of energy from outside the system. If ΔG of the reaction is negative, the reaction is spontaneous (or exergonic). If ΔG of the reaction is positive, the reaction is *nonspontaneous* (or endergonic). This is related to the second law of thermodynamics.

Two reaction energy diagrams for an exergonic and endergonic process are shown:

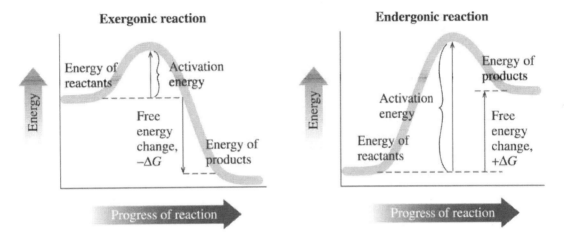

Gibbs free energy ΔG determines whether a reaction is spontaneous or nonspontaneous.

If $\Delta G < 0$, then the reaction is spontaneous in the forward reaction

If $\Delta G = 0$, the reaction is at equilibrium.

If $\Delta G > 0$, then the reaction is spontaneous in the reverse direction

Entropy (S) is a thermodynamic quantity that measures the spreading of energy or disorder of a system. An increase in entropy of a system corresponds to an increase in the randomness or disorder of the system. $\Delta S° < 0$ represents a decrease in entropy.

$\Delta S° > 0$ represents an increase in entropy.

For instance, crystals form naturally within a supersaturated solution of sugar water. The formation of these sugar crystals results in an increase in entropy. An increase in entropy occurs because the crystals form "on their own" in a spontaneous process and thus must result in an entropy increase.

Enthalpy, temperature and entropy are all related to the free energy by the following equation:

$$\Delta G^{\circ} = \Delta H^{\circ} - T\Delta S^{\circ}$$

where ΔG° is change in free energy, ΔH° is change in enthalpy, T is temperature and ΔS° is change in entropy.

The table displays how ΔH, ΔS and T affect the spontaneity of a reaction.

ΔH	ΔS	Sign of ΔG	Spontaneous?
–	+	$\Delta G = (-) - [T\,(+)] = -$	Always, regardless of T
+	–	$\Delta G = (+) - [T\,(-)] = +$	Never, regardless of T
+	+	$\Delta G = (+) - [T\,(+)] = ?$	Depends; spontaneous at high T, $-\Delta G$
–	–	$\Delta G = (-) - [T\,(-)] = ?$	Depends; spontaneous at low T, $-\Delta G$

This table demonstrates that it is not correct to assume that an endothermic reaction is nonspontaneous, because a large, positive ΔS can make it spontaneous.

It is also not correct to assume that an exothermic reaction is spontaneous, because a large, negative ΔS can cause it to become nonspontaneous.

Temperature-controlled reactions are the reactions that are spontaneous at one temperature and not at another. These are the reactions in the bottom left and top right quadrants of the pie chart.

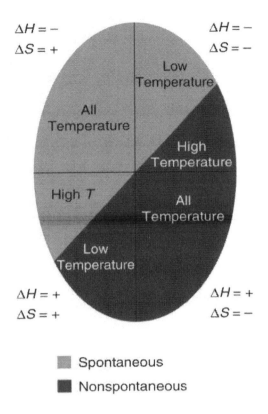

Example: If the enthalpy change of a reaction is –1,876 kJ, the entropy change is –3.375 kJ/K, and the temperature has a value of 298 K (standard temperature), is the reaction spontaneous? It is important to make sure the units are consistent. Entropy, which is often expressed in units of J/K has been converted to kJ/K for this question.

Substituting these quantities into the equation for Gibbs Free Energy:

$$\Delta G^\circ = \Delta H - T\Delta S$$

$$\Delta G^\circ = -1876 \text{ kJ} - (298 \text{ K}) \cdot (-3.375 \text{ kJ/K})$$

$$= -870.2 \text{ kJ}$$

Since ΔG° is negative, this is a spontaneous reaction.

There are two other equations to calculate ΔG°. The first of these equations is related to *chemical equilibrium*:

$$\Delta G^{\circ} = -RT\ln K$$

$$\Delta G = -2.303RT\log K$$

where R is the ideal gas law constant ($R = 8.314$ J/mol·K), T is temperature in Kelvin and K is the equilibrium constant for the chemical equilibrium.

Remember that ΔG only implies the direction and extent of a chemical reaction, but it does NOT imply rate of a reaction. Do not assume that a spontaneous reaction will occur quickly, because it may take a million years for it to happen, depending on its kinetics.

Another equation is used to calculate ΔG° in calculations in *electrochemistry*:

$$\Delta G^{\circ} = -nF\mathrm{E}^{\circ}$$

where n represents the moles of electrons transferred, F is Faraday's constant (96,485 C/mol) and E° is the standard potential for an electrochemical cell.

Calculations of the Gibbs free energy from these equations simply involves substitution of the appropriate quantities into the expression.

Thermodynamics

Thermodynamics answers several fundamental questions regarding whether a given reaction will occur, to what extent and whether the reaction will release or absorb heat. Thermodynamics states a set of four laws that characterize thermodynamic systems by describing the behavior of physical quantities such as temperature, energy and entropy.

Zeroth Law: Concept of temperature

The *zeroth law* of thermodynamics states that when two bodies are placed into contact, heat flows from the hotter body to the colder body until *thermal equilibrium* is reached. After thermal equilibrium is achieved, there is no more heat transfer. This law helps to define the concept of temperature.

If two systems are each in thermal equilibrium with a third system, then each is in thermal equilibrium with the other.

This can be expressed in equation form is as follows:

$$T_A = T_B, \text{ and } T_C = T_B, \text{ then } T_A = T_C$$

Two systems are in thermal equilibrium when they are separated by a barrier permeable to heat and no heat is transferred. The law is crucial for the mathematical formulation of thermodynamics.

The zeroth law of thermodynamics establishes that temperature is a core, measurable property of matter.

First Law

The *first law of thermodynamics* states that energy can neither be created nor destroyed, and the total energy in a system remains constant. Energy is always conserved in a chemical reaction; this is also known as the law of conservation of energy.

Essentially, the first law states that the change in total internal energy of a system is equal to the contributions from heat and work, as in the equation:

$$\Delta E = q - W$$

where ΔE is the change in internal energy (also represented as ΔU), q is the contribution from heat and W is the contribution from work.

In the above expression, use the following sign conventions:

- q is positive when heat is absorbed into the system (i.e., heating it).

- q is negative when heat is released from the system (i.e., cooling it).

- W is positive when work is done by the system (i.e., compression).

- W is negative when work is done on the system (i.e., expansion).

An alternative expression for the first law of thermodynamics is $\Delta E = q + W$, where work is positive if done *on* the system, or negative if done *by* the system. For this form of the equation, use the sign conventions given in the chart below:

q	+	Heat **absorbed** by system	E_{system} increases
q	−	Heat **released** by system	E_{system} decreases
W	+	Work done **on** system	E_{system} increases
W	−	Work done **by** system	E_{system} decreases

Important Note: Relate the sign to what is happening to the system. Heat or energy flowing out of the system is negative; heat or energy flowing into the system is positive.

Unfortunately, some disciplines of science choose to follow the opposite sign convention. It is important to note which sign convention is used.

Example: Consider a problem involving internal energy, heat and work. Suppose there is a process in which 3.4 kJ of heat flows out of the system while 4.8 kJ of work is done by the system on the surroundings. What is the internal energy?

Applying the equation, $\Delta E = q + W$ to calculate the internal energy:

$$\Delta E = q + W$$

$$\Delta E = -3.4 \text{ kJ} + (-4.8 \text{ kJ}) = -8.2 \text{ kJ}$$

Use the appropriate signs for heat and work.

Overall, energy has flowed out of the system to the surroundings by –8.2 kJ.

Equivalence of Mechanical, Chemical, Electrical and Thermal Energy Units

The units for mechanical, chemical, electrical and thermal energy are equivalent. If it is energy, it can be measured in Joules (J).

For example, 1 J of mechanical energy can be converted into 1 J of electrical energy

---

Second Law: Concept of Entropy

The *second law of thermodynamics* states that the natural order of the universe favors a net increase in the overall entropy. An isolated system increases in entropy over time, and never decreases. An open system, however, can decrease in entropy, but only at the expense of a greater increase in entropy of its surroundings.

There are two types of thermodynamic process: reversible and irreversible. The reversible process is an idealized process, while the irreversible process does frequently occur in nature.

$$\text{For reversible processes } \Delta S = q \,/\, T$$

$$\text{For irreversible processes } \Delta S > q \,/\, T$$

Essentially, all real processes that occur in the world are irreversible, so entropy change is always greater than the heat transfer over temperature. Due to the irreversible nature of real processes, the entropy of the universe is always increasing.

Reactions that are at an equilibrium condition are *reversible processes* since there is no net change to the system or surroundings and they proceed in both directions. Reversible processes are those that reverse direction whenever some infinitesimally small change is made to some property of the system. This can be written as follows:

$$\Delta S_{\text{total}} = \Delta S_{\text{system}} + \Delta S_{\text{surroundings}}$$

The change in entropy of the system is always equal in magnitude, but opposite in sign, of the change in entropy of the surroundings. This can be written as follows:

$$\Delta S_{\text{surr}} = - \, q \,/\, T$$

$$\Delta S_{\text{surr}} = - \, \Delta H \,/\, T \text{ (at constant pressure)}$$

Combining these two equations:

$$\Delta S_{\text{total}} = \Delta S_{\text{system}} - \frac{\Delta H_{\text{system}}}{T}$$

One way to calculate entropy change for a reaction is to use tabulated values for the standard molar entropies. This calculation follows the same format as the calculations for the enthalpy change and Gibbs free energy change for the heats of formation. The equation is described below:

$$\Delta S^\circ_{rxn} = \Sigma\, n(\Delta S^\circ_f \text{ of products}) - \Sigma\, n(\Delta S^\circ_f \text{ of reactants})$$

where n represents the moles of each reactant or product, as in the balanced chemical equation.

Example: Determine the entropy change for this chemical equation. (It is the same chemical equation for which change in enthalpy ΔH was calculated in a previous section of this chapter.)

$$16\ H_2S\ (g) + 8\ SO_2\ (g) \ \rightarrow\ 16\ H_2O\ (l) + 3\ S_8\ (s)$$

Set up the equation:

$$\Delta S^\circ_{rxn} = [(16\text{ mol}){\cdot}(S^\circ_f \text{ of } H_2O\ (l)) + (3\text{ mol}){\cdot}(S^\circ_f \text{ of } S_8\ (s))]$$

$$-[(16\text{ mol}){\cdot}(S^\circ_f \text{ of } H_2S\ (g)) + (8\text{ mol}){\cdot}(S^\circ_f \text{ of } SO_2\ (g))]$$

From the table of standard entropies of formation, substitute the quantities for the standard entropies of formation:

$$\Delta S^\circ_{rxn} = \Sigma\, n(\Delta S^\circ_f \text{ of products}) - \Sigma\, n(\Delta S^\circ_f \text{ of reactants})$$

$$\Delta S^\circ_{rxn} = [(16\text{ mol}){\cdot}(69.91\text{ J/mol}{\cdot}K) + (3\text{ mol}){\cdot}(31.80\text{ J/mol}{\cdot}K)]$$

$$-\,[(16\text{ mol}){\cdot}(205.79\text{ J/mol}{\cdot}K) + (8\text{ mol}){\cdot}(161.92\text{ J/mol}{\cdot}K)]$$

Collect terms, and make sure that the mathematical signs are accounted for:

$$\Delta S^\circ_{rxn} = [1{,}118\text{ J/K} + 95.40\text{ J/K}] - [3{,}292.6\text{ J/K} - 1{,}295.4\text{ J/K}]$$

$$\Delta S^\circ_{rxn} = -3{,}375\text{ J/K}$$

In this example, ΔS°_{rxn} is a measure of the entropy change of a system. The entropy change of the surroundings is related to the heat flow and the temperature as shown:

$$\Delta S_{surr} = -q / T \text{ or } - \Delta H / T \text{ (at constant pressure)}$$

The negative sign in this equation accounts for the fact that the heat of the surroundings is opposite in sign to the heat of the system. From the previous example, the enthalpy of reaction was calculated at –1,876 kJ at standard temperature, 298 K. The entropy change of this system was calculated to be –3,375 J/K (or –3.375 kJ/K). What is the entropy change of the surroundings?

Using the above equation:

$$\Delta S_{surr} = - (- 1{,}876 \text{ kJ}) / 298 \text{ K}$$

$$\Delta S_{surr} = 6.30 \text{ kJ/K or } 6.30 \times 10^3 \text{ J/K}$$

The entropy of the surroundings increased. The total entropy change is the sum of the entropy change of the system and the entropy change of the surroundings:

$$\Delta S_{total} = \Delta S_{sys} + \Delta S_{surr}$$

$$\Delta S_{total} = -3.375 \times 10^3 \text{ J/K} + 6.30 \times 10^3 \text{ J/K}$$

$$\Delta S_{total} = 2.92 \times 10^3 \text{ J/K}$$

Entropy as a measure of "disorder"

Entropy (*S*) measures randomness or disorder. More specifically, entropy is a measure of the number of specific ways in which a thermodynamic system can be arranged.

To understand entropy, imagine the following situation. Someone decides to take a piece of paper, tear it up into small pieces and throw the pieces into the air. The pieces of paper will randomly scatter about them. The pieces would not fly back together into the original piece of paper. They just increased the entropy of the universe. It did not take much energy to tear of the piece of paper and toss the pieces in the air.

Now, how much energy would it take to restore this piece of paper into its original form? First, some energy has to be expended to go around the room and pick up the pieces of paper. The paper is still not restored to its original state. Next, they have to take the pieces of paper to a pulp mill and have the paper turned back into pulp and pressed again into the original piece. These processes would take much more energy than the energy required to rip up the paper and toss it in the air. Imagine tearing up the paper as a spontaneous process and putting it back together as a nonspontaneous process. Thus, the entropy (or disorder) of the universe is always increasing.

The higher the entropy and lower the energy, the more stable the system.

Higher entropy + lower energy → more stability

Lower entropy + higher energy → less stability

Entropy has the dimension of energy divided by temperature, and the unit is Joules per Kelvin (J/K). However, it can also be expressed as entropy per unit mass (J/K·kg) or entropy per unit amount of substance (J/K·mol).

Relative entropy for gas, liquid and crystal states

As temperature increases, entropy increases as follows:

(*a*) $T = 0$ K, particles are in equilibrium lattice positions and S relatively low

(*b*) $T > 0$ K, molecules vibrate, S increases

(*c*) T increases further, more violent vibrations occur and S higher than in (*b*)

This may seem analogous to the molecules of a substance in different phases (i.e., solid, liquid, gas). The relative differences in entropies between the phases of matter can be understood in terms of the relative degrees of freedoms of forms of kinetic energy.

Solids have low entropy because the particles forming a solid are packed in an orderly matrix in the crystal. Particles of a solid are confined to vibrating in fixed positions and are limited in their freedom of forms of kinetic energy.

Liquids are intermediate in entropy. Intermolecular forces still hold the particles in a liquid together, but have increased freedom to slide past one another .

Gases are high in entropy, because the gas particles have complete freedom to randomly move around in their container with very few particles arranged in any orderly fashion. Essentially, at low pressure gas particles experience little to no intermolecular forces of attraction or repulsion.

The entropy changes accompanying phase changes can be estimated, at least qualitatively. Freezing is accompanied by a decrease in entropy as the relatively disordered liquid becomes a well-ordered solid. Boiling is accompanied by a large increase in entropy as the liquid becomes a much more highly-disordered gas.

For any substance, sublimation (phase change from a solid to a gas) is the phase transition with the greatest entropy change.

The figure displays gas, liquid and crystalline states ordered by increasing entropy.

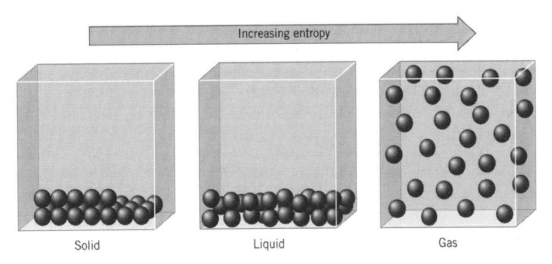

For gases, entropy increases as volume increases. Take the example in the image below, where a gas is separated from a vacuum by a partition (figure *a*). When the partition is removed (figure *b*), there are more ways to distribute energy. Gas expands to achieve a more probable particle distribution (figure *c*). The configuration of figure *c* is more random, has a higher probability and a more positive *S*.

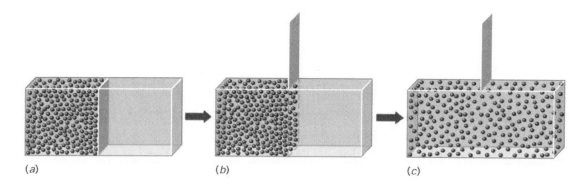

Entropy is also affected by the number of particles. By adding particles to a system, one increases the number of ways that energy can be distributed in that system.

Similarly, a reaction that produces more particles has a more positive Δ*S*.

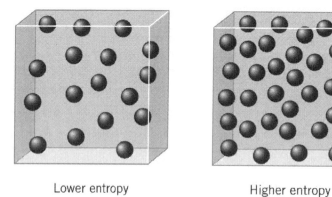

Lower entropy   Higher entropy

Third Law

The *third law of thermodynamics* states that the entropy of a perfectly ordered, pure crystalline solid is zero at absolute zero temperature (in Kelvin). At *absolute zero* (coldest temperature possible on Kelvin scale), the average kinetic energy of the particles equals zero; they essentially possess no kinetic energy.

As the entropy increases, the average kinetic energy of the particles increase and a substance transitions to liquid and ultimately gas states.

For a given substance, the gas state always has the highest entropy.

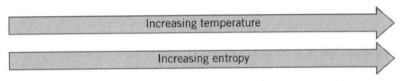

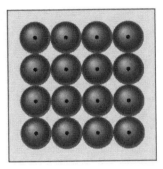 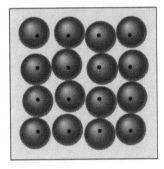 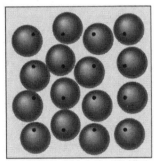

As a crystalline solid, there is minimal kinetic energy.

At a higher temperature, the particles vibrate. They have more kinetic energy and more ways to distribute it, so they have a higher entropy.

At a still higher temperature, the particles have even more kinetic energy and a higher entropy.

Example: For the following reaction, determine the sign of ΔS.

$$CaCO_3\,(s) + 2\,H^+\,(aq) \rightarrow Ca^{2+}\,(aq) + H_2O + CO_2\,(g)$$

$$\Delta n_{gas} = 1\ \text{mol} - 0\ \text{mol} = 1\ \text{mol}$$

since Δn_{gas} is positive, ΔS is positive

Example: For the following reaction, determine the sign of ΔS.

$$2\,N_2O_5\,(g) \longrightarrow 4\,NO_2\,(g) + O_2\,(g)$$

$$\Delta n_{gas} = 4\ \text{mol} + 1\ \text{mol} - 2\ \text{mol} = 3\ \text{mol}$$

since Δn_{gas} is positive, ΔS is positive

Example: For the following reaction, determine the sign of ΔS.

$$OH^-\,(aq) + H^+\,(aq) \longrightarrow H_2O$$

$$\Delta n_{gas} = 0\ \text{mol}$$

$$\Delta n = 1\ \text{mol} - 2\ \text{mol} = -1\ \text{mol}$$

since Δn is negative, ΔS is negative

Temperature Scales, Conversions

There are three commonly used temperature scales. Fahrenheit is the classic English system of measuring temperature, and was developed by dividing the difference between the boiling and freezing point of water into 180 equal degrees. Celsius is the modern metric way of measuring temperature; it divides the difference between the boiling and freezing point of water into 100 equal agrees. The expression to convert between Fahrenheit and Celsius is:

$$°F = (1.8 × °C) + 32$$

Kelvin is the third temperature scale; unlike the Fahrenheit and Celsius scales, it is not commonly used on a day-to-day basis (e.g., when talking about the weather), but it is the most important scale in science. It is based on the concept of absolute zero. The size of the units on the Kelvin scale are the same as the size of degrees on the Celsius scale. The way to convert between Kelvin and Celsius is:

$$K = °C + 273$$

The following chart lists the temperatures among the three different scales:

	K	°C	°F
Absolute zero	0	–273	–460
Freezing point of water / melting point of ice	273	0	32
Room temperature	298	25	77
Body temperature	310	37	99
Boiling point of water / condensation of steam	373	100	212

Heat Transfer: Conduction, Convection, Radiation

As described by the first law of thermodynamics, heat always flows from a hotter system to a colder system until the two systems are in thermal equilibrium.

There are three ways in which heat can be transferred: conduction, convection or radiation.

Conduction is heat transfer between substances that are in direct contact with each other (i.e., they must be touching). When particles of a hotter substance are vibrating, these molecules bump into nearby particles and transfer some energy to them. Conduction is the most significant means of heat transfer for solids. Metals are especially conductive.

Convection occurs when warmer areas of a liquid or gas rise to cooler areas of the liquid or gas, and the cooler liquid or gas takes the place of the warmer areas. It refers to the physical flow of matter. Convective heat transfer takes place by diffusion (the random Brownian motion of particles) and by advection (in which matter or heat is transported by larger scale flowing currents).

Radiation is a method of heat transfer that does not require contact between the heat source and the heated object. Radiation consists of electromagnetic waves traveling at the speed of light; no mass is exchanged and no medium is required (i.e., it can occur in a vacuum). An example is thermal radiation emitted by the sun, which warms Earth.

Heat of Fusion, Heat of Vaporization

Energy is released when a gas changes phase into a liquid (*condensation*), when a liquid turns into a solid (*freezing*), or when a gas changes phase directly into a solid (*deposition*). The energy released is the same as the energy of their reverse processes. *Vaporization* is the reverse of condensation. *Melting* is the reverse of freezing and *sublimation* is the reverse of deposition.

Heat of fusion (ΔH_{fus}) is the energy input needed to melt a given quantity of a solid substance to the liquid phase at constant temperature. The energy it takes to melt a solid is ΔH_{fus} times the number of moles of that solid, represented by the equation:

$$q = n \times \Delta H_{fus}$$

where q is heat energy and n is number of moles.

Heat of vaporization (ΔH_{vap}) is the energy input needed to vaporize a given quantity of a liquid substance to the gas phase at constant temperature. The energy it takes to vaporize a liquid is ΔH_{vap} times the number of moles of that liquid, represented by the equation:

$$q = n \times \Delta H_{vap}$$

where q is heat energy and n is number of moles.

Heat of fusion and heat of vaporization generally have the unit kJ/mol, but can also be expressed as J/g, where energy can be obtained by multiplying the latent heats by the mass of the substance, rather than the moles.

Example: 31.5 g of H_2O is being melted at its melting point of 0 °C. How many kJ is required? The molar heat of fusion for water is 6.02 kJ/mol.

Solution: Find the number of moles by using the molar mass = 18 g/mol.

$$31.5 \text{ g} / 18 \text{ g/mol} = 1.75 \text{ mol}$$

Use the equation given above.

$$q = 1.75 \text{ mol} \times 6.02 \text{ kJ/mol}$$

$$q = 10.54 \text{ kJ}$$

10.54 kJ heat is required to melt 31.5 g of water.

PV Diagram

A pressure vs. volume diagram (*PV diagram*) describes corresponding changes in pressure and volume in a system. The area under or enclosed by the curve on a *PV* diagram is equal to the work done.

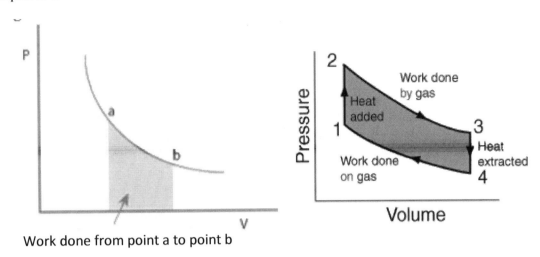

Work done from point a to point b

Note that the figure on the right clarifies that expansion is work done *by* the system ($\Delta E = q - W$) and compression is work done *on* the system ($\Delta E = q + W$).

For a gas phase system that consists of the gas and its container, work can calculated. Since gases may be expanded or compressed, work may be related by the pressure of the gas and the change in volume of the gas:

$$W = -P\Delta V$$

The change in volume, ΔV, is the final volume of the gas, minus the initial volume of the gas:

$$\Delta V = V_{final} - V_{initial}$$

To expand a gas, the volume of the gas is increased (ΔV is positive). The gas (part of the system) has to do work on the surroundings; thus, the work must be negative.

Similarly, to compress a gas, the volume of the gas is decreased (ΔV is negative). The surroundings must do work on the system; thus, the work must be positive.

There are four types of thermodynamic processes often depicted by *PV* diagrams:

o   *Adiabatic process*: no heat exchange

$$q = 0 \quad \Delta E = W$$

o   *Isothermal process*: no change in temperature

$$\Delta T = 0$$

o   *Isobaric process*: pressure is constant

$$W = P\Delta V$$

o   *Isovolumetric (isochoric) process*: volume is constant

$$W = 0 \quad \Delta E = q$$

Coefficient of Expansion

Thermal expansion is the tendency of matter to change in volume in response to changes in temperature. This occurs through heat transfer. In general, when a substance is heated, its molecules increase in kinetic energy and begin moving more; thus, a greater average separation is maintained, leading to an increase in volume (expansion). The degree of expansion divided by the change in temperature is the material's *coefficient of thermal expansion*, α.

There are different expansion relationships for linear expansion, area expansion and volume expansion, shown below.

Linear expansion: $\Delta L / L_0 = \alpha \Delta T$

Area expansion: $\Delta A / A_0 = 2\alpha \Delta T$

Volume expansion: $\Delta V / V_0 = 3\alpha \Delta T$

The value of the coefficient α depends on the type of expansion.

Example: A metal rod of length 7.00 m is being heated to 35° C. If the length of the rod expands to 7.12 m after some time, calculate the linear expansion coefficient (the temperature of the room is 27° C).

Solution: Calculate change in length ΔL from the initial length $L_0 = 7.00$ m and expanded length $L = 7.12$ m.

$$\Delta L = 7.12 \text{ m} - 7.00 \text{ m} = 0.12 \text{ m}$$

Calculate the change in temperature ΔT from the initial room temperature $T_0 = 27$ °C and the heated temperature $T = 35$ °C.

$$\Delta T = 35 \text{ °C} - 27 \text{ °C} = 8 \text{ °C}$$

Convert ΔT to Kelvin.

$$8 + 273 = 281 \text{ K}$$

Manipulate the formula for linear thermal expansion to isolate α.

$$\alpha = \Delta L / (L_0 \times \Delta T)$$

$$\alpha = 0.12 \text{ m} / (7 \text{ m} \times 281 \text{ K}) = 6.1 \times 10^{-5}$$

Phase Diagram: Pressure and Temperature

The phase of a substance (i.e., solid, liquid or gas) largely depends on the temperature and pressure. For example, if the pressure is very high, a substance is less likely to be in a gas phase because the pressure would bring the molecules so close together that the substance either liquefies or sublimes.

A phase diagram indicates the relationship between temperature, pressure and the associated phases.

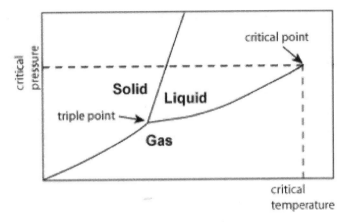

Phase Diagram

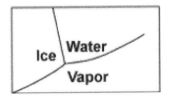

Phase Diagram for Water

The *solid-liquid boundary* is where solid and liquid exist in equilibrium, the *solid-gas boundary* is where solid and gas exist in equilibrium and the *liquid-gas boundary* is where liquid and gas exist in equilibrium. *Triple point* is the temperature and pressure at which all three phases of matter coexist in an equilibrium. *Critical point* is the temperature and pressure at which liquids and gases become indistinguishable. *Critical temperature* is the temperature above which a liquid cannot form, no matter how much pressure is put on it.

The water phase diagram is different from others because the solid-liquid boundary is slanted to the left. This is because water (liquid) is denser than ice (solid), and if the pressure at a given temperature is increased, ice is turned into water.

Practice Questions

1. If a stationary gas has a kinetic energy of 500 J at 25 °C, what is its kinetic energy at 50 °C?

A. 125 J

C. 540 J

B. 450 J

D. 1,120 J

2. What is the purpose of the hollow walls in a closed hollow-walled container that is effective at maintaining the temperature inside?

A. Traps air trying to escape from the container, which minimizes convection

B. Act as an effective insulator, which minimizes convection

C. Acts as an effective insulator, which minimizes conduction

D. Provides an additional source of heat for the container

3. How much heat energy (in Joules) is required to heat 21.0 g of copper from 21.0 °C to 68.5 °C? (Use specific heat c of Cu = 0.382 J/g·°C)

A. 462 J

B. 381 J

C. 522 J

D. 662 J

4. The species in the reaction $KClO_3$ (s) → KCl (s) + 3/2O_2 (g) have the values for standard enthalpies of formation at 25 °C. At constant physical states, assume that the values of $\Delta H°$ and $\Delta S°$ are constant throughout a broad temperature range. Which of the following conditions may apply for the reaction? (Use $KClO_3$ (s) with $\Delta H_f° = -391.2$ kJ mol^{-1} and KCl (s) with $\Delta H_f° = -436.8$ kJ mol^{-1})

A. Nonspontaneous at low temperatures, but spontaneous at high temperatures

B. Spontaneous at low temperatures, but nonspontaneous at high temperatures

C. Nonspontaneous at all temperatures over a broad temperature range

D. Spontaneous at all temperatures over a broad temperature range

5. Determine the value of $\Delta E°_{rxn}$ for this reaction, whereby the standard enthalpy of reaction ($\Delta H°_{rxn}$) is -311.5 kJ mol^{-1}:

$$C_2H_2 (g) + 2 H_2 (g) \rightarrow C_2H_6 (g)$$

A. -306.5 kJ mol^{-1}

C. $+346.0$ kJ mol^{-1}

B. -318.0 kJ mol^{-1}

D. $+306.5$ kJ mol^{-1}

6. The process of H_2O (g) → H_2O (l) is nonspontaneous under pressure of 760 torr and temperatures of 378 K because:

A. $\Delta H = T\Delta S$

C. $\Delta H > 0$

B. $\Delta G < 0$

D. $\Delta H > T\Delta S$

7. A fuel cell contains hydrogen and oxygen gas that react explosively and the energy converts water to steam which drives a turbine to turn a generator that produces electricity. The fuel cell and the turbine represent which forms of energy, respectively?

A. Electrical and mechanical energy

B. Electrical and heat energy

C. Chemical and mechanical energy

D. Chemical and heat energy

8. The thermodynamic systems that have high stability tend to demonstrate:

A. maximum ΔH and maximum ΔS

B. maximum ΔH and minimum ΔS

C. minimum ΔH and maximum ΔS

D. minimum ΔH and minimum ΔS

9. Which is true for the thermodynamic functions *G*, *H* and *S* in $\Delta G = \Delta H - T\Delta S$?

A. *G* refers to the universe, *H* to the surroundings and *S* to the system

B. *G*, *H* and *S* refer to the system

C. *G* and *H* refers to the surroundings and *S* to the system

D. *G* and *H* refer to the system and *S* to the surroundings

10. Whether a reaction is endothermic or exothermic is determined by:

A. an energy balance between bond breaking and bond forming, resulting in a net loss or gain of energy

B. the presence of a catalyst

C. the activation energy

D. the physical state of the reaction system

11. What is the term for a reaction that proceeds by releasing heat energy?

A. Endothermic reaction

B. Isothermal reaction

C. Exothermic reaction

D. Nonspontaneous

12. The bond dissociation energy is:

 I. useful in estimating the enthalpy change in a reaction

 II. the energy required to break a bond between two gaseous atoms

 III. the energy released when a bond between two gaseous atoms is broken

A. I only

B. II only

C. I and II only

D. I and III only

13. Which of the following statements is true for the following reaction? (Use the change in enthalpy, $\Delta H° = -113.4$ kJ/mol and the change in entropy, $\Delta S° = -145.7$ J/K mol)

$$2\,NO\,(g) + O_2\,(g) \rightarrow 2\,NO_2\,(g)$$

  A. Reaction is at equilibrium at 25 °C under standard conditions
  B. Reaction is spontaneous at only high temperatures
  C. Reaction is spontaneous only at low temperatures
  D. Reaction is spontaneous at all temperatures

14. Which law explains the observation that the amount of heat transfer accompanying a change in one direction is equal in magnitude but opposite in sign to the amount of heat transfer in the opposite direction?

  A. Law of Conservation of Mass
  B. Law of Definite Proportions
  C. Avogadro's Law
  D. Law of Conservation of Energy

15. Calculate the value of $\Delta H°$ of reaction using provided bond energies.

$$H_2C = CH_2\,(g) + H_2\,(g) \rightarrow H_3C–CH_3\,(g)$$

C–C: 348 KJ   C≡C: 960 kJ

C=C: 612 kJ   C–H: 412 kJ   H–H: 436 kJ

  A. −348 kJ   **C.** −546 kJ
  B. +134 kJ   **D.** −124 kJ

Solutions

1. C is correct.

Temperature is a measure of the average kinetic energy of the molecules.

Kinetic energy is proportional to temperature.

In most thermodynamic equations, temperatures are expressed in Kelvin, so convert the Celsius temperatures to Kelvin:

25 °C + 273.15 = 298.15 K

50 °C + 273.15 = 323.15 K

Calculate the kinetic energy using simple proportions:

KE = (323.15 K / 298.15 K) × 500 J

KE = 540 J

2. C is correct.

Conduction (i.e., transfer of thermal energy through matter) is reduced by an insulator.

Air and vacuum are the excellent insulators. Storm windows, which have air wedged between two glass panes, work by utilizing this principle of conduction.

3. B is correct.

Heat capacity is amount of heat required to increase temperature of *the whole sample* by 1 °C.

Specific heat is the heat required to increase temperature of *1 gram* of sample by 1 °C.

Heat = mass × specific heat × change in temperature:

$q = m \times c \times \Delta T$

$q = 21.0 \text{ g} \times 0.382 \text{ J/g·°C} \times (68.5 \text{ °C} - 21.0 \text{ °C})$

$q = 21.0 \text{ g} \times 0.382 \text{ J/g·°C} \times (47.5 \text{ °C})$

$q = 381 \text{ J}$

4. D is correct.

Calculate the value of $\Delta H_f = \Delta H_{f \text{ product}} - \Delta H_{f \text{ reactant}}$

$\Delta H_f = -436.8 \text{ kJ mol}^{-1} - (-391.2 \text{ kJ mol}^{-1})$

$\Delta H_f = -45.6 \text{ kJ mol}^{-1}$

To determine spontaneity, calculate the Gibbs free energy:

$\Delta G = \Delta H° - T\Delta S$

The reaction is spontaneous if ΔG is negative:

$\Delta G = -45.6 \text{ kJ} - T\Delta S$

Typical ΔS values are around 100–200 J.

If the ΔH value is –45.6 kJ or –45,600 J, the value of ΔG would still be negative unless $T\Delta S$ is less than –45,600.

Therefore, the reaction would be spontaneous over a broad range of temperatures.

5. A is correct.

Relationship between enthalpy (ΔH) and internal energy (ΔE):

Enthalpy = Internal energy + work (for gases, work = PV)

$\Delta H = \Delta E + \Delta(PV)$

Solving for ΔE:

$$\Delta E = \Delta H - \Delta(PV)$$

According to ideal gas law:

$$PV = nRT$$

Substitute ideal gas law to the previous equation:

$$\Delta E = \Delta H - \Delta(nRT)$$

R and T are constant, which leaves Δn as the variable.

The reaction is C_2H_2 (g) + $2H_2$ (g) $\rightarrow$ C_2H_6 (g).

There are three gas molecules on the left and one on the right, which means $\Delta n = 1 - 3 = -2$.

In this problem, the temperature is not provided. However, the presence of degree symbols ($\Delta G°$, $\Delta H°$, $\Delta S°$) indicates that those are standard values, which are measured at 25 °C or 298.15 K.

Always double check the units before performing calculations; ΔH is in kilojoules, while the gas constant (R) is 8.314 J/mol K. Convert ΔH to Joules before calculating.

Use the Δn and T values to calculate ΔE:

$$\Delta E = \Delta H - \Delta nRT$$

$$\Delta E = -311{,}500 \text{ J/mol} - (-2 \times 8.314 \text{ J/mol K} \times 298.15 \text{ K})$$

$$\Delta E = -306{,}542 \text{ J} \approx -306.5 \text{ kJ}$$

6. D is correct.

Spontaneity of a reaction is determined by evaluating the Gibbs free energy, or ΔG.

$$\Delta G = \Delta H - T\Delta S$$

A reaction is spontaneous if $\Delta G < 0$ (or ΔG is negative).

For ΔG to be negative, ΔH has to be less than $T\Delta S$.

A reaction is nonspontaneous if $\Delta G > 0$ (or ΔG is positive and ΔH is greater than $T\Delta S$).

7. C is correct.

Potential Energy Stored energy and the energy of position (gravitational)	Kinetic Energy Energy of motion: motion of waves, electrons, atoms, molecules and substances.
Chemical Energy Chemical energy is the energy stored in the bonds of atoms and molecules. Biomass, petroleum, natural gas, propane and coal are examples of stored chemical energy. **Nuclear Energy** Nuclear energy is the energy stored in the nucleus of an atom. It is the energy that holds the nucleus together. The nucleus of the uranium atom is an example of nuclear energy. **Stored Mechanical Energy** Stored mechanical energy is energy stored in objects by the application of a force. Compressed springs and stretched rubber bands are examples of stored mechanical energy. **Gravitational Energy** Gravitational Energy is the energy of place or position. Water in a reservoir behind a hydropower dam is an example of gravitational potential energy. When the water is released to spin the turbines, it becomes kinetic energy.	**Radiant Energy** Radiant energy is electromagnetic energy that travels in transverse waves. Radiant energy includes visible light, x-rays, gamma rays and radio waves. Solar energy is an example of radiant energy. **Thermal Energy** Thermal energy (or heat) is the internal energy in substances; it is the vibration and movement of atoms and molecules within substances. Geothermal energy is an example of thermal energy. **Motion** The movement of objects or substances from one place to another is motion. Wind and hydropower are examples of motion. **Sound** Sound is the movement of energy through substances in longitudinal (compression/rarefaction) waves. **Electrical Energy** Electrical energy is the movement of electrons. Lightning and electricity are examples of electrical energy.

8. C is correct.

Gibbs free energy:

$$\Delta G = \Delta H - T\Delta S$$

Stable molecules are non-spontaneous because they have a negative (or relatively low) ΔG.

ΔG is most negative (most stable) when ΔH is smallest and ΔS is largest.

9. B is correct.

All thermodynamic functions in $\Delta G = \Delta H - T\Delta S$ refer to the system.

10. A is correct.

ΔH refers to enthalpy (or heat).

Endothermic reactions have heat as a reactant.

Exothermic reactions have heat as a product.

Endothermic reactions absorb energy to break strong bonds to form a less stable state (i.e., positive enthalpy).

Exothermic reactions release energy during the formation of stronger bonds to produce the more stable state (i.e., negative enthalpy).

The reaction is nonspontaneous (i.e., endergonic) if the products are less stable than the reactants and ΔG is positive.

The reaction is spontaneous (i.e., exergonic) if the products are more stable than the reactants and ΔG is negative.

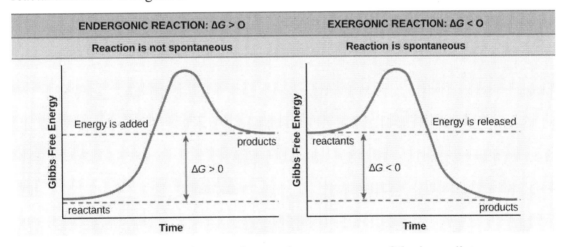

Exothermic reactions release heat, and cause the temperature of the immediate surroundings to rise (i.e., net loss of energy) while an endothermic process absorbs heat and cools the surroundings (i.e., net gain of energy).

11. C is correct.

ΔH refers to enthalpy (or heat).

Endothermic reactions have heat as a reactant.

Exothermic reactions have heat as a product.

Exothermic reactions release heat, and cause the temperature of the immediate surroundings to rise (i.e., net loss of energy) while an endothermic process absorbs heat and cools the surroundings (i.e., net gain of energy).

Endothermic reactions absorb energy to break strong bonds to form a less stable state (i.e., positive enthalpy).

Exothermic reactions release energy during the formation of stronger bonds to produce the more stable state (i.e., negative enthalpy).

The reaction is nonspontaneous (i.e., endergonic) if the products are less stable than the reactants and ΔG is positive.

The reaction is spontaneous (i.e., exergonic) if the products are more stable than the reactants and ΔG is negative.

12. C is correct.

Bond dissociation energy is the energy required to break a bond between two gaseous items and is useful in estimating the enthalpy change in a reaction.

13. C is correct.

To predict spontaneity of reaction, use the Gibbs free energy equation:

$$\Delta G = \Delta H^\circ - T\Delta S$$

The reaction is spontaneous if ΔG is negative.

Substitute the given values to the equation:

$$\Delta G = -113.4 \text{ kJ/mol} - [T \times (-145.7 \text{ J/K mol})]$$

$$\Delta G = -113.4 \text{ kJ/mol} + (T \times 145.7 \text{ J/K mol})$$

Important: note that the units aren't identical, ΔH° is in kJ and ΔS° is in J. Convert kJ to J (1 kJ = 1,000 J):

$$\Delta G = -113,400 \text{ J/mol} + (T \times 145.7 \text{ J/K mol})$$

It can be predicted that the value of ΔG would be negative if the value of T is small.

If T increases, ΔG approaches a positive value and the reaction is nonspontaneous.

14. D is correct.

The Law of Conservation of Energy states that the total energy (e.g., potential or kinetic) of an isolated system remains constant and is conserved. Energy can be neither created nor destroyed, but is transformed from one form to another. For instance, chemical energy can be converted to kinetic energy in the explosion of a firecracker.

The Law of Conservation of Mass states that for any system closed to all transfers of matter and energy, the mass of the system must remain constant over time.

Law of Definite Proportions (Proust's law) states that a chemical compound always contains exactly the same proportion of elements by mass. The law of definite proportions forms the basis of stoichiometry (i.e., from the known amounts of separate reactants, the amount of the product can be calculated).

Avogadro's Law is an experimental gas law relating volume of a gas to the amount of substance of gas present. It states that equal volumes of all gases, at the same temperature and pressure, have the same number of molecules.

Boyle's law is an experimental gas law that describes how the pressure of a gas tends to increase as the volume of a gas decreases. It states that the absolute pressure exerted by a given mass of an ideal gas is inversely proportional to the volume it occupies, if the temperature and amount of gas remain unchanged within a closed system

15. D is correct.

In a chemical reaction, bonds within reactants are broken down and new bonds will be formed to create products. Therefore, in bond dissociation problems,

ΔH reaction = sum of bond energy in reactants – sum of bond energy in products

For $H_2C=CH_2 + H_2 \rightarrow CH_3–CH_3$:

$\Delta H_{reaction}$ = sum of bond energy in reactants – sum of bond energy in products

$\Delta H_{reaction} = [(C=C) + 4(C–H) + (H–H)] – [(C–C) + 6(C–H)]$

$\Delta H_{reaction} = [612 \text{ kJ} + (4 \times 412 \text{ kJ}) + 436 \text{ kJ}] – [348 \text{ kJ} + (6 \times 412 \text{ kJ})]$

$\Delta H_{reaction} = –124 \text{ kJ}$

Remember that this is the opposite of ΔH_f problems, where:

$\Delta H_{reaction}$ = (sum of ΔH_f products) – (sum of ΔH_f reactants)

Chapter 9

Electrochemistry

Electrochemistry is a branch of chemistry that deals with the interconversion of electrical energy and chemical energy. Electrochemistry utilizes spontaneous oxidation-reduction reactions to obtain electrical energy and the use of electrical energy to drive nonspontaneous reactions. Electrochemistry always involves an oxidation-reduction process. There are many important applications in everyday life, such as batteries, control of corrosion, metallurgy and electrolysis are just a few examples of the applications of electrochemistry.

Electrolytic Cell

- **Anode, Cathode**

- **Electrolysis**

- **Electrolytes**

- **Faraday's Law Relating Amount of Elements Deposited (or Gas Liberated) at an Electrode to Current**

- **Electron Flow; Oxidation and Reduction at the Electrodes**

Galvanic (Voltaic) Cell

- **Half-Reactions**

- **Reduction Potentials; Cell Potential**

- **Direction of Electron Flow**

- **Concentration Cell**

- **Batteries**

Electrolytic Cell

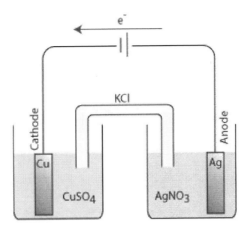

Electrolytic Cell

Anode, cathode

For any electrochemical cell, oxidation always occurs at the *anode* and reduction always occurs at the *cathode*.

Designation of Anode and Cathode

Write a balanced net ionic equation for the spontaneous cell reaction.

- The oxidizing agent (one with the more positive or less negative reduction potential E°) is the cathode and the other is the anode.

- Oxidation occurs in the anode half-cell and reduction in the cathode half-cell.

- Anode is negative (-) and cathode is positive (+).

Mnemonic: An Ox = ANode Oxidation   Red Cat = REDuction CAThode

Also, when drawing a galvanic cell, by convention the anode is on the left and the cathode is on the right. Use the mnemonic **ABC** to remember this convention (**A**node / **B**ridge / **C**athode).

Electrolysis

Electrolysis requires potential (voltage) input. On the diagram, this is represented by a battery in the circuit.

A galvanic (voltaic) cell has either a resistor or a voltmeter in place of a battery.

The potential (voltage) input + the cell potential must be > 0 for the reactions to occur.

For electrolytic cells, the cell potential is negative, so a potential input greater than the magnitude of the cell potential must be present for electrolysis to occur.

In contrast, galvanic (voltaic) cells already have a positive cell potential. Thus, no input is required for galvanic (voltaic) cells.

In the diagram, arrows show how the battery is forcing the flow of electrons. Without energy, the electrons would flow in the other direction (or not at all).

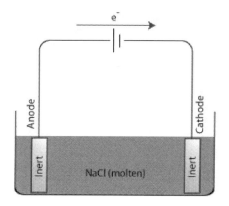
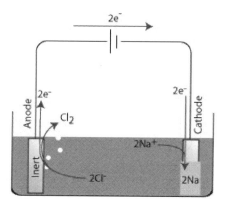

Electrolysis of Salt   *Salt Electrolysis Charge Flow*

The electrolysis process is often used to extract and purify metals from their molten salt form. A current is applied to the molten salt for a period of time.

Current is measured in amperes (A).

$$1 \text{ ampere} = \frac{1 \text{ coulomb}}{1 \text{ second}}$$

A galvanic (voltaic) cell produces current from a spontaneous oxidation-reaction. An *electrolytic cell* uses electrical energy to drive nonspontaneous oxidation-reduction reactions. *Electrolysis* involves forcing a current through a cell to produce a chemical change, which has a negative cell potential.

For example, the following spontaneous reaction occurs in a galvanic (voltaic) cell that consists of $Zn|Zn^{2+}$ (*aq*) and $Cu|Cu^{2+}$ (*aq*) half-cells:

$$Zn\ (s) + Cu^{2+}\ (aq) \rightarrow Zn^{2+}\ (aq) + Cu\ (s); \qquad E°_{cell} = 1.10\ V$$

In an electrolytic cell, the reverse reaction occurs if a voltage greater than the E° cell is applied. A higher voltage than E° is needed to cause the reverse reaction. The excess voltage is referred to as *overpotential* or overvoltage.

Three types of reactions occur in electrolytic cells when a sufficient voltage is applied:

- Solute ions or molecules may be oxidized or reduced.

- The solvent can be oxidized or reduced.

- Metal electrode that forms the anode can be oxidized.

Which of these reactions will actually occur depends both on the thermodynamic and kinetic properties of each reaction. In general, the half-reactions with the most positive (or the least negative) reduction potential occurs before others. The kinetic factor drives the reaction if the difference in the standard reduction potentials between two half-cell reactions is small, then concentration may determine the outcome of electrolysis.

Example: the following reactions are possible for the electrolysis of 1 M NaCl (*aq*):

At anode: $2\ Cl^-\ (aq) \rightarrow Cl_2\ (g) + 2e^-$ $E° = -1.36\ V$

                       $2\ H_2O \rightarrow O_2\ (g) + 4\ H^+\ (aq) + 4e^-$ $E° = -1.23\ V$

At cathode: $2\ H_2O + 2\ e^- \rightarrow H_2\ (g) + 2\ OH^-\ (aq)$ $E° = -0.83\ V$

                       $Na^+\ (aq) + e^- \rightarrow Na\ (s)$ $E° = -2.71\ V$

In an actual electrolysis of aqueous sodium chloride, Cl_2 is formed at the anode instead of O_2, although E^o for the formation of O_2 from H_2O is less negative than for the formation of Cl_2 from Cl^-. This is because the formation of O_2 involves a higher activation energy (overvoltage), thus it is kinetically less favorable. At the cathode, H_2 is formed, since it requires less voltage than the reduction of $Na^+(aq)$.

If a solution containing metal cations that require lower potential (or one that has a positive reduction potential) is electrolyzed, the metal is deposited on the cathode, and no hydrogen is produced.

For example, the electrolysis of an aqueous copper(II) chloride solution yields Cl_2 gas at the anode and copper metal deposits at the cathode. If the anode is made of copper, it is also oxidized because of the lower voltage requirement relative to water.

Anode reaction: $\quad\quad Cu\ (s)\ \rightarrow\ Cu^{2+}\ (aq)\ +\ 2\ e^-$ $\quad\quad E^o = -0.34$ V

Cathode reaction: $\quad\quad Cu^{2+}\ (aq)\ +\ 2\ e^-\ \rightarrow\ Cu\ (s)$ $\quad\quad E^o = +0.34$ V

Electrolysis of Water

The decomposition of water is a nonspontaneous process that has an amount of energy of about 400 kJ/mol of water. However, the decomposition of water can be effected by electrolysis, where oxygen is formed at the anode and hydrogen at the cathode:

Anode reaction: $\quad\quad 2\ H_2O\ \rightarrow\ O_2 + 4\ H^+\ (aq) + 4\ e^-$ $\quad\quad E^o = -1.23$ V

Cathode reaction: $\quad\quad 4\ H_2O + 4\ e^-\ \rightarrow\ 2\ H_2 + 4\ OH^-\ (aq)$ $\quad\quad E^o = -0.83$ V

Net reaction: $\quad\quad 6\ H_2O\ \rightarrow\ 2\ H_2 + O_2 + 4\ (H^+ + OH^-)$ $\quad\quad E^o = -2.06$ V

$\quad\quad\quad\quad\quad\quad\quad\quad 2\ H_2O\ \rightarrow\ 2\ H_2 + O_2$

This potential assumes an electrolytic cell with $[H^+] = [OH^-] = 1$ M and $P_{H2} = P_{O2}$ = 1 atm. In the electrolysis of pure water, where $[H^+] = [OH^-] = 10^{-7}$ M, the potential for the overall process is –1.23 V. However, applying a voltage of 1.23 V is be sufficient to affect the electrolysis of water. An extra voltage of about 1 V (as overpotential or overvoltage) is needed to force the electrolysis.

Electrolysis of Solution Containing Mixtures of Ions

Consider a solution containing Cu^{2+}, Zn^{2+} and Ag^+ that is electrolyzed using a current with sufficient voltage to reduce all three cations. In such electrolysis, the metal with the smallest potential is the first to be formed. The reduction potentials of these elements are as follows:

$$Ag^+ (aq) + e^- \rightarrow Ag\ (s) \qquad\qquad E^\circ = 0.80\ V$$

$$Cu^{2+} (aq) + 2\ e^- \rightarrow Cu\ (s) \qquad\qquad E^\circ = 0.34\ V$$

$$Zn^{2+} (aq) + 2\ e^- \rightarrow Zn\ (s) \qquad\qquad E^\circ = -0.76\ V$$

Since the reduction of Ag^+ to Ag has the most positive potential, silver is deposited at the cathode before the other metals, which is then followed by Cu and Zn, respectively. If the voltage supply is properly controlled, starting with the lowest voltage possible, it is possible to separate the three metals using electrolysis.

The Stoichiometry of Electrolysis – Total Charge and Theoretical Yield

An electric current that flows through a cell is measured in *ampere* (A), which is the amount of charge in *coulomb* (C) that flows through the circuit per second. That is,

Ampere = Coulomb/second (1 A = 1 C/s)

Coulomb = Ampere × time in seconds (1 C = 1 A·s) = total charge

Joule = Coulomb × Volt (1 J = 1 C.V)

The amount of substances formed at the anode or cathode can be calculated from the magnitude of current (in amperes) and time (in seconds) of electrolysis.

For example, if a current of 1.50 A flows through an aqueous solution of $CuSO_4$ for 25.0 minutes, the amount of charge passing through the solution is:

(1.50 C/s)·(25.0 minutes)·(60 seconds/minutes) = 2,250 C

The number of moles of electrons passing through the solution:

(2,250 C) × (1 mol e⁻) = 0.0233 mol

Since the reduction of Cu^{2+} requires 2 mol e^- per mole of Cu:

$Cu^{2+} + 2\,e^- \rightarrow Cu$, the amount of copper formed at the cathode is:

$$(0.0233 \text{ mol } e^-) \times \frac{(1 \text{ mol Cu})}{(2 \text{ mol } e^-)} \times \frac{(63.55 \text{ g Cu})}{(1 \text{ mol Cu})} = 0.741 \text{ g Cu}$$

If the above process uses a cell with a voltage of 3.0 V, the energy consumed is:

$$3.0 \text{ V} \times 2250 \text{ C} = 6{,}750 \text{ C.V} = 6{,}800 \text{ J} = 6.8 \text{ kJ}$$

Electrolytes

Ions = electrolyte.

Electrolytes conduct electricity by the motion of ions. Without electrolytes, there is no circuit because electricity would not be able to propagate.

Faraday's law relating amount of elements deposited (or gas liberated) at an electrode to current

Current = coulombs of charge per second.

$$I = q / t$$

Faraday's constant = coulombs of charge per mol of electron

= total charge over total moles of electrons.

$$F = q / n.$$

$q = It$ and $q = nF$, thus:

$$It = nF$$

Current × time = moles of e^- × Faraday's constant.

Using this equation, solve for moles of electrons (n). Then, using the half-equation stoichiometry, determine how many moles of element are made for every e^- transferred. For example, 1 mol of Cu is deposited for every 2 moles of electrons for the following half reaction: $Cu^{2+} + 2e^- \rightarrow Cu$.

Faraday's constant = 96,485 C/mol

Electron flow; oxidation and reduction at the electrodes

Electrons originate from the anode because oxidation (loss of electrons) occurs there.

$$M \rightarrow M^+ + e^-.$$

Electrons travel into the cathode, where they join the cations on the surface of the cathode. This is because reduction (gain of electrons) occurs at the cathode.

$$M^+ + e^- \rightarrow M.$$

Mnemonic:

OIL RIG: **O**xidation **I**s **L**osing e^-, **R**eduction **I**s **G**aining e^-.

Oxidation is an increase in charge (more positive) due to the loss of e^-.

Reduction is a decrease in charge (more negative) due to the gain of e^-.

Galvanic (Voltaic) Cell

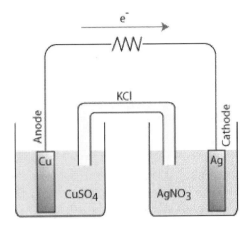

Galvanic (Voltaic) Cell

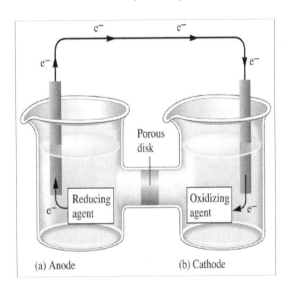

A common application of electrochemistry is the *galvanic cell*, commonly known as a battery. A galvanic cell has the capability of producing a voltage and was invented by Luigi Galvani and Alessandro Volta.

A galvanic cell (voltaic cell) is a device that uses a spontaneous oxidation-reduction reaction to produce electric current.

In Galvanic Cell:

- Oxidation occurs at the anode.

- Reduction occurs at the cathode.

- Salt bridges or porous disks allows ions to flow without extensive mixing of the solutions.

  - *Salt bridge* – contains a strong electrolyte held in a gel–like matrix.

  - *Porous disk* – contains tiny passages for hindered flow of ions.

The following are some examples of spontaneous oxidation-reduction reactions:

1. $Zn\ (s)\ +\ CuSO_4\ (aq)\ \rightarrow\ Cu\ (s)\ +\ ZnSO_4\ (aq)$

   $Zn\ (s)\ +\ Cu^{2+}\ (aq)\ \rightarrow\ Cu\ (s)\ +\ Zn^{2+}\ (aq)$

2. $Cr\ (s)\ +\ 3\ AgNO_3\ (aq)\ \rightarrow\ Cr(NO_3)_3\ (aq)\ +\ 3\ Ag\ (s)$

   $Cr\ (s)\ +\ 3\ Ag^+\ (aq)\ \rightarrow\ Cr^{3+}\ (aq)\ +\ 3\ Ag\ (s)$

3. $MnO_4^-\ (aq) + 5\ Fe^{2+}\ (aq) + 8\ H^+\ (aq) \rightarrow\ Mn^{2+}\ (aq) + 5\ Fe^{3+}\ (aq) + 4H_2O\ (l)$

4. $Zn\ (s)\ +\ 2\ MnO_2\ (s)\ \rightarrow\ ZnO\ (s) + Mn_2O_3\ (s)$

Half-reactions

Redox reactions can be separated into two half-reactions:

Example 1:

Oxidation half-reaction: $\qquad Zn\ (s)\ \rightarrow\ Zn^{2+}\ (aq) + 2\ e^-$

Reduction half-reaction: $\qquad Cu^{2+}\ (aq) + 2\ e^-\ \rightarrow\ Cu\ (s)$

Overall reaction: $\qquad Zn\ (s) + Cu^{2+}\ (aq) \rightarrow\ Cu\ (s) +\ Zn^{2+}\ (aq)$

Example 2:

Oxidation half-reaction: $5 \, Fe^{2+} (aq) \rightarrow 5 \, Fe^{3+} (aq) + 5 \, e^-$

Reduction half-reaction: $MnO_4^- (aq) + 8 \, H^+ (aq) + 5 \, e^- \rightarrow Mn^{2+} (aq) + 4 \, H_2O \, (l)$

Overall reaction: $MnO_4^- (aq) + 5 \, Fe^{2+} (aq) + 8 \, H^+ (aq) \rightarrow Mn^{2+} (aq) + 5 \, Fe^{3+} (aq) + 4 \, H_2O \, (l)$

Oxidation half-reaction describes the species that loses electrons (increases in charge). For example, $Cu \rightarrow Cu^{2+} + 2e^-$

Reduction half-reaction describes the species that gains electrons (decreases in charge). For example, $2 \, Ag^+ + 2 \, e^- \rightarrow 2 \, Ag$

In galvanic cells, redox reactions is split into two half-reactions, each occurring in two separate compartments; *half-cells*. The chemical energy is used to drive electrons through the external circuit connecting the two half-cells, thus producing electric current. For example, consider the following reaction:

$$Zn \, (s) \, + \, CuSO_4 \, (aq) \, \rightarrow \, Cu \, (s) \, + \, ZnSO_4 \, (aq)$$

If zinc metal is placed in $CuSO_4$ solution, an exothermic reaction occurs, producing heat. In a galvanic cell, a zinc metal is placed in $ZnSO_4$ solution in one container, a copper metal in $CuSO_4$ solution in another container, with the two metals are connected by a wire; to complete the circuit, the two solutions are connected by a salt-bridge containing strong electrolytes such as $KCl \, (aq)$ or $K_2SO_4 \, (aq)$ that allow ions to flow between the two half-cells. The reactants—zinc metal and copper ions—are not allowed direct contact.

Due to the potential difference between the two half-cells, electrons are forced to flow from the zinc electrode (the anode) to the copper electrode (the cathode). At the interface between the zinc electrode and $ZnSO_4$ solution, Zn atoms are oxidized to Zn^{2+} ions; at the interface between copper electrode and $CuSO_4$ solution, Cu^{2+} ions combine with incoming electrons and are reduced to Cu atoms.

These oxidation and reduction processes are shown in the following half-reaction equations:

Anode-reaction (oxidation): $Zn\ (s) \rightarrow Zn^{2+}\ (aq)\ + 2\ e^-$

Cathode-reaction (reduction): $Cu^{2+}\ (aq) + 2\ e^- \rightarrow Cu\ (s)$

The two half-cells are represented by notations $Zn|Zn^{2+}$ and $Cu^{2+}|Cu$.

In a galvanic cell, the metal that is more readily oxidized serves as an anode, and the other as a cathode. Determine the tendency of a species to be oxidized from the table of standard reduction potentials, shown below. Zinc is more easily oxidized than copper, so it serves as the anode, while copper forms the cathode. Oxidation half-reaction occurs at anode, and reduction half-reaction at cathode. This galvanic can be represented using the following cell notation:

$$Zn|ZnSO_4\ (aq)\|CuSO_4\ (aq)|Cu$$

(A cell notation is always written with the anode on the left side and cathode on the right.)

At the anode half-cell, Zn^{2+} ions are continuously formed, creating an excess of positive ions. While in the cathode half-cell, Cu^{2+} ions are continuously reduced to Cu, causing a decrease in cation concentration.

To maintain electrically neutral solutions in both half-cells, anions flow into the anode half-cell and cations flows into the cathode half-cell. Thus, electric current is the flow of charged particles – electrons flow from anode to cathode through wire; cations and anions flows in opposite direction through the salt-bridge.

Reduction potentials; cell potential

Reduction potential = potential of the reduction half reaction.

Oxidation potential = potential of the oxidation half reaction = reverse the sign of the reduction potential.

Cell potential = Reduction potential + Oxidation potential.

Standard Reduction Potential

In a galvanic cell, electrons flow from one electrode to the other because there is an electrical potential difference between the two half-cells, simply called the *cell potential*. In the zinc-copper cell, electrons flow from $Zn|Zn^{2+}$ half-cell to $Cu|Cu^{2+}$ half-cell. The $Zn|Z^{2+}$ half-cell has a higher electrical potential than $Cu|Cu^{2+}$.

The magnitude of cell potential depends on the nature of the two half-cells, the concentration of the electrolyte in each half-cell and temperature. The *standard cell potential*, E^{o}_{cell}, is the cell potential measured under standard conditions, (1 atm pressure for gas, 1 M of electrolytes, and at 25 °C). The parameters for a standard cell require the species in solution to have a concentration of 1 M, the partial pressure of gases to be 1 atm and the temperature to be 25 °C (298K).

Using these conditions makes it possible to describe a standard electrode potential (E°) in volts, and calculate the electrical potential of the cell. The superscript, °, denotes standard conditions.

The *standard half-cell potential* or *the reduction potential* of a substance is determined by connecting the half-cell of the substance (under standard conditions) to the *standard hydrogen electrode* (SHE) as reference half-cell. This reference half-cell consists of a Pt-electrode in a solution containing 1 M H^+, into which H_2 gas is purged at a constant pressure of 1 atm. Since the reference half-cell is assigned zero potential, the cell potential measured under these conditions is the standard half-cell potential of the substance.

For example, when a $Zn|Zn^{2+}(aq, 1 M)$ half-cell is connected to the reference half-cell (SHE), the voltage measured at 25 °C is found to be 0.763 V. However electron flows from $Zn|Zn^{2+}$ to SHE; relative to SHE, the reduction potential for $Zn|Zn^{2+}$ half-cell is the negative value of the measured voltage.

$$Zn^{2+}(aq) + 2\ e^- \rightarrow Zn\ (s); \quad E° = -076\ V; \quad \text{(where E° is the reduction potential)}$$

$$2\ H^+(aq) + 2\ e^- \rightarrow H_2\ (s); \quad E° = 0.000\ V$$

$$Cu^{2+}(aq) + 2\ e^- \rightarrow Cu\ (s); \quad E° = 0.34\ V$$

Since values are obtained against the standard hydrogen potential, species with positive reduction potentials are easier to reduce compared to H^+ ions; while those with negative reduction potentials are more difficult to reduce.

Therefore, relative to H^+, Cu^{2+} is easier to reduce, whereas Zn^{2+} is more difficult to reduce. When $Zn|Zn^{2+}$ is connected to $Cu|Cu^{2+}$ half-cells, the spontaneous process is the flow of electrons from $Zn|Zn^{2+}$ to $Cu|Cu^{2+}$ half-cell.

In galvanic cells, species with more positive reduction potential serves as cathode and those with less positive or more negative reduction potential serve as the anode half-cell. The *net cell potential* is the sum of the two half-cell potentials. For the Zn-copper cell,

Anode half-cell reaction: $\quad Zn\ (s) \rightarrow Zn^{2+}\ (aq) + 2\ e^- \qquad E°_{Zn \rightarrow Zn2+} = 0.76$ V

Cathode half-cell reaction: $\quad Cu^{2+}\ (aq) + 2\ e^- \rightarrow\ Cu\ (s) \qquad E°_{Cu2+ \rightarrow Cu} = 0.34$ V

Overall cell reaction: $\quad Zn\ (s) + Cu^{2+}\ (aq) \rightarrow\ Zn^{2+}\ (aq) + Cu\ (s)$

$$E°_{cell} = E°_{Zn \rightarrow Zn2+} + E°_{Cu2+ \rightarrow Cu}$$

$$= 0.76\text{ V} + 0.34\text{ V} = 1.10\text{ V}$$

For a cell consisting of $Cr|Cr^{3+}$ and $Ag|Ag^+$ half-cells, the cell notation and cell potential are:

$$Cr|Cr^{3+}\ (aq, 1\text{ M})\|Ag^+\ (aq, 1\text{ M})|Ag$$

$$\text{(anode)} \qquad \text{(cathode)}$$

Anode half-cell reaction: $\quad Cr\ (s) \rightarrow Cr^{3+}\ (aq) + 3\ e^- \qquad E°_{Cr \rightarrow Cr3+} = 0.73$ V

Cathode half-cell reaction: $\quad Ag^+\ (aq) + e^- \rightarrow Ag\ (s) \qquad E°_{Ag+ \rightarrow Ag} = 0.80$ V

Overall cell reaction: $\quad Cr\ (s) + 3\ Ag^+\ (aq) \rightarrow\ Cr^{3+}\ (aq) + 3\ Ag\ (s)$;

$$E°_{cell} = E°_{Cr \rightarrow Cr3+} + E°_{Ag+ \rightarrow Ag}$$

$$= 0.73\text{ V} + 0.80\text{ V} = 1.53\text{ V}$$

The standard electrode potentials are usually listed as reduction potentials, and are relative to a standard hydrogen electrode (SHE) with a 0 volt potential as a reference point.

The cell potential for all galvanic (voltaic) cells is positive, because the voltaic cell generates potential.

The cell potential for all electrolytic cells is negative, because the electrolytic cell requires potential input.

The *Nernst* equation is used when the cell is not under standard conditions:

$$E_{cell} = E°_{cell} - (RT / nF) \ln Q$$

where E_{cell} = nonstandard cell potential in volts;

$E°_{cell}$ = standard cell potential in volts;

R = constant, 8.314 J/mol·K, T = temperature in Kelvin;

n = moles of electrons transferred;

F = Faraday's constant = 96485 C/mol e⁻   (C represents coulombs)

Q = the reaction quotient expression

Alternative representations of the Nernst Equation may be used if the temperature is standard temperature (298 K) and one has a choice of natural logarithm (ln) or common logarithm, base 10 (log):

$$E_{cell} = E°_{cell} - \frac{0.0257 \, V}{n} \ln Q \quad \text{or} \quad E_{cell} = E°_{cell} - \frac{0.0592 \, V}{n} \log Q$$

Modifying one of the previous cells, as follows:

Zn (s) | Zn^{2+} (*aq*), 3.00M; SO_4^{2-} (3.00M) || Cu^{2+} (*aq*), 0.0015M; SO_4^{2-} (0.0015M) | Cu (s)

It is known that $E°_{cell}$ = +1.10V. Assuming the standard temperature (298K), the Nernst equation expression becomes:

$$E_{cell} = E°_{cell} - \frac{0.0257 \, V}{n} \ln \frac{[Zn^{2+}]}{[Cu^{2+}]} = +1.10 \, V - \frac{0.0257 \, V}{2 \, mol \, e^-} \ln \frac{3.00 \, M}{0.0015 \, M}$$

Evaluating the above expression gives:

$$E_{cell} = +1.10 \, V - 0.098 \, V = 1.00 \, V$$

Cell Potential and Free Energy

The cell potential indicates whether the cell reaction is spontaneous or nonspontaneous. Recall that spontaneity for a process is often associated with its Gibbs free energy change (ΔG).

The mathematical relationship between cell potential and Gibbs free energy change is:

$$\Delta G^\circ = -nF E^\circ \text{ under standard conditions}$$

$$\Delta G = -nF E \text{ under nonstandard conditions}$$

where ΔG = change in Gibbs free energy in Joules, n = moles of electrons transferred

F = Faraday's constant = 98,485 C/mol e⁻, E = cell potential

Using the units of Faraday's constant, coulombs/mol e⁻ and volts for cell potential, the Gibbs free energy units are coulomb-volts. Coulomb-volts are equivalent to Joules.

The cell potential measures the potential difference between the two half-cells. A potential difference of 1 V is equivalent to 1 Joule of work done per coulomb of charge that flows between two points in the circuit. (1 V = 1 J/C or 1 J = 1 C·V)

Maximum work produced = charge × maximum potential

$$W_{max} = -q E_{max} = \Delta G$$

Electrical charge, $q = nF$

$$\Delta G = -nF E_{cell} \text{ or } \Delta G^\circ = -nF E^\circ_{cell}$$

where n = mole of electrons transferred or that flow through circuit,

and Faraday's constant = 96,485 C/mol e⁻.

For example: $Zn\,(s) + Cu^{2+}\,(aq) \rightarrow Zn^{2+}\,(aq) + Cu\,(s)$; $E^\circ_{cell} = 1.10$ V

The standard free energy is $\Delta G^\circ = -2 \text{ mol e}^- \times \dfrac{96,485\,C}{1\,\text{mol e}^-} \times 1.10 \text{ V} = -2.12 \times 10^5 \text{ J}$

2.12×10^2 kJ is the maximum work that can be derived per mole of Zn reacted by Cu^{2+}.

Direction of electron flow

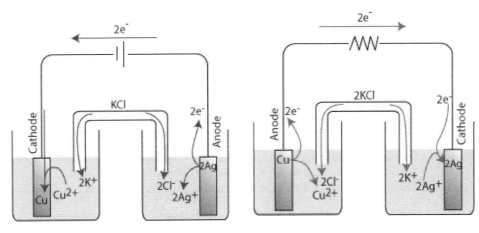

Electrolytic Charge Flow   *Galvanic (Voltaic) Charge Flow*

Electrons always flow from the anode to the cathode. Mnemonic: A to C in alphabetical order. Or, think about AC power - the A comes first and stands for Anode)

Oxidation (at the anode) produces electrons (and cations), and releases electrons toward the cathode. The cathode receives those electrons and uses them for reduction.

Naturally, the species with the highest oxidation potential (lowest reduction potential) is the anode, and the species with the highest reduction potential is the cathode.

In the diagram above, the galvanic (voltaic) cell shows a natural flow because Cu (higher oxidation potential/lower reduction potential) is the anode, and Ag (higher reduction potential) is the cathode.

However, the electrolytic cell shows exactly the opposite. In order to force the Cu to be the cathode and Ag to be the anode, a battery is used to drive the reaction.

Electrons flow in wires and electrodes, while ions flow in the electrolyte solution, thus creating a completed circuit.

Concentration cell

Concentration Cells

A *concentration cell* is an electrochemical cell in which both half-cells are of the same type, but with different electrolyte concentrations. The following cell notations are examples of concentration cells:

$$Cu|Cu^{2+} (aq, 0.0010 \text{ M})||Cu^{2+} (aq, 1.0 \text{ M})|Cu$$

$$Ag|Ag^+ (aq, 0.0010 \text{ M}) ||Ag^+ (aq, 0.10 \text{ M})|Ag$$

In concentration cells, the half-cell with the lower electrolyte concentration serves as an anode half-cell and one with the higher electrolyte concentration is the cathode half-cell. At the anode half-cell, oxidation reaction occurs to increase the electrolyte concentration and at the cathode half-cell, a reduction reaction occurs to decrease its electrolyte concentration. Oxidation-reduction reaction continues until the electrolyte concentrations in both half-cells become equal.

At anode half-cell: $Cu (s) \rightarrow Cu^{2+} (aq) + 2 e^-$ (in 0.0010 M Cu^{2+})

At cathode half-cell: $Cu^{2+} (aq) + 2 e^- \rightarrow Cu (s)$ (in 0.50 M Cu^{2+})

Batteries

Batteries are galvanic cells (or a group of galvanic cells) connected in series, where the total battery potential is equal to the sum of the potentials of the individual cells. There are three types of batteries: – primary batteries, secondary batteries, and fuel cells.

Primary batteries are not re-chargeable, whereas secondary batteries are re-chargeable. Fuel cells will last as long as there is an ample supply of fuel to provide the energy.

<u>Dry Cells</u>: *Primary* batteries include common (acidic) dry batteries, alkaline batteries and mercury batteries. The *acidic dry battery* consists of Zinc casing as container, anode and the reducing agent; graphite rod as (inert) cathode; aqueous NH_4Cl paste as electrolyte and MnO_2 powder as the oxidizing agent.

$$Zn|Zn^{2+}, NH_4^+, NH_3\ (aq)||Mn_2O_3, MnO_2|C\ (s)$$

Anode reaction: $\quad Zn\ (s) \rightarrow Zn^{2+}\ (aq)\ +\ 2\ e^-$

Cathodic reaction: $\quad 2\ MnO_2\ (s) + 2\ NH_4^+\ (aq) + 2\ e^- \rightarrow Mn_2O_3\ (s) + 2\ NH_3\ (aq) + H_2O\ (l)$

Net reaction: $\ Zn\ (s) + 2\ MnO_2\ (s) + 2\ NH_4^+\ (aq) \rightarrow Zn^{2+}\ (aq) + Mn_2O_3\ (s) + 2\ NH_3\ (aq) + H_2O\ (l)$

The reverse reaction is prevented by the formation of $[Zn(NH_3)_4]^{2+}$ ions.

A new dry cell battery has a potential of about 1.5 V regardless of the size, but the amount of energy that a battery can deliver does depend on its size. For example, a D-size battery can deliver more current (greater amperes) than an AAA-size battery. Normal dry batteries use aqueous NH_4Cl paste as electrolyte and are referred to as acidic batteries due to the following ionization: $NH_4^+\ (aq)\ \rightarrow NH_3\ (aq) + H^+\ (aq)$.

Alkaline batteries also use zinc (as the reducing agent) and MnO_2 (as oxidizing agent), but an aqueous paste containing KOH, instead of NH_4Cl, is used as the electrolyte.

The anode and cathode reactions are as follows:

At anode: $\quad Zn\ (s) + 2OH^-\ (aq)\ \rightarrow ZnO\ (s) + H_2O\ (l) + 2\ e^-$

At cathode: $\quad 2\ MnO_2\ (s) + H_2O\ (l) + 2\ e^- \rightarrow Mn_2O_3\ (s) + 2\ OH^-\ (aq)$

Net reaction: $\quad Zn\ (s) + 2\ MnO_2\ (s)\ \rightarrow ZnO\ (s) + Mn_2O_3\ (s)$

Since all reactants involved are solid, alkaline batteries can deliver a fairly constant voltage until the limiting reactant is completely used up. They also last longer because zinc metal corrodes more slowly under basic conditions.

Mercury batteries are used in calculators and watches.

The following reactions occur at the anode and cathode sections of the cell:

Anode reaction: $Zn\ (s) + 2\ OH^-\ (aq) \rightarrow ZnO\ (s) + H_2O + 2\ e^-$

Cathode reaction: $HgO\ (s) + H_2O + 2\ e^- \rightarrow Hg\ (l) + 2\ OH^-\ (aq)$

Net cell reaction: $Zn\ (s) + HgO\ (s) \rightarrow ZnO\ (s) + Hg\ (l)$

Electromotive force, Voltage

Electromotive force (emf), or cell potential (E_{cell}), is the driving force that enables electrons to flow from one electrode to the other, which has the unit volt (V). A volt is one Joule per coulomb, where coulomb is the unit of charge.

Voltage is the driving force for reactions, often called the EMF (electromotive force). The greater the voltage, the greater the driving force.

A voltmeter must have its negative terminal connected to the anode and the positive terminal to the cathode to get the correct polarity (± sign).

Voltage is always positive for a spontaneous reaction.

Lead-storage batteries

Lead-storage batteries are used in automobiles. They contain sulfuric acid as an electrolyte. Each cell contains a number of grids of lead alloy. One set of alternating grids is packed with lead metal and the other with lead(IV) oxide, PbO_2. Each set of grids, which are the electrodes, are connected in a parallel arrangement, which enables the cell to deliver more current; the amount of current delivered depends on the surface area of the electrode.

Each cell in a lead storage battery produces a potential of about 2.01 V. The standard 12-V battery used in most cars contains six cells connected in series.

Spontaneous Reactions that occur in the lead storage battery are:

Anode reaction: $Pb\ (s) + HSO_4^-\ (aq) \rightarrow PbSO_4\ (s) + H^+\ (aq) + 2\ e^-$

Cathode reaction: $PbO_2\ (s) + 3\ H^+\ (aq) + HSO_4^-\ (aq) + 2\ e^- \rightarrow PbSO_4\ (s) + 2\ H_2O\ (m)$

Net reaction:

$Pb\ (s) + PbO_2\ (s) + 2\ H^+\ (aq) + 2\ HSO_4^-\ (aq) \rightarrow 2\ PbSO_4\ (s) + 2\ H_2O\ (l) \rightarrow$ discharging

---

The greatest advantage of lead-storage batteries (i.e., secondary batteries) is that they are re-chargeable. Starting the engine causes the discharge reaction to occur. However, while the car is being driven, the battery obtains energy from the motor through the alternator. The following re-charging reaction occurs:

$$2\ PbSO_4\ (s) + 2\ H_2O\ (l) \rightarrow Pb\ (s) + PbO_2\ (s) + 2\ H^+\ (aq) + 2\ HSO_4^-\ (aq)$$

Lead-storage batteries also have a longer lifetime than other batteries, and they can deliver a relatively large amount of current and electrical energy within a short time. The major disadvantages are: (1) they are very heavy and bulky - non-portable; (2) lead is a toxic metal and its disposal creates environmental problems; (3) the battery must be kept upright, H_2SO_4 is very corrosive.

Nickel-cadmium batteries

Nickel-cadmium batteries are rechargeable batteries used in small appliances such as cordless phones. They contain cadmium as the anode and hydrated nickel oxide as the cathode. The electrolyte is an aqueous KOH paste.

Anode reaction: $Cd\ (s) + 2\ OH^-\ (aq) \rightarrow Cd(OH)_2\ (s) + 2\ e^-$

Cathode reaction: $2\ NiO(OH)\ (s) + 2\ H_2O\ (l) + 2\ e^- \rightarrow 2\ Ni(OH)_2\ (s) + 2\ OH^-\ (aq)$

Net cell reaction: $Cd\ (s) + 2\ NiO(OH)\ (s) + 2\ H_2O\ (l) \rightarrow Cd(OH)_2\ (aq) + 2\ Ni(OH)_2\ (aq)$

Standard Reduction Potentials

Reduction potential is a measure of the tendency of a chemical species to acquire electrons and become reduced (gain of electrons is reduction). Reduction potential is measured in volts (V) or millivolts (mV).

The more positive the E°, the greater the tendency for the species to be reduced (strong oxidizing agent), while the more negative the E°, the greater the tendency for the species to be reduced (weak oxidizing agent).

TABLE OF STANDARD REDUCTION POTENTIALS

Standard Reduction Potentials in Aqueous Solution at 25 ºC	
Acidic Solutions	**Eº (V)**
$F_2 (g) + 2 e^- \rightarrow 2 F^- (aq)$	+2.87
$Co^{3+} (aq) + e^- \rightarrow Co^{2+} (aq)$	+1.82
$Pb^{4+} (aq) + 2 e^- \rightarrow Pb^{2+} (aq)$	+1.8
$H_2O_2 (aq) + 2 H^+ (aq) + 2 e^- \rightarrow 2 H_2O$	+1.77
$NiO_2 (s) + 4 H^+ (aq) + 2 e^- \rightarrow Ni^{2+} (aq) + 2 H_2O$	+1.7
$PbO_2 (s) + SO_4^{2-} (aq) + 4 H^+ (aq) + 2 e^- \rightarrow PbSO_4 (s) + 2 H_2O$	+1.685
$Au^+ (aq) + e^- \rightarrow Au (s)$	+1.68
$2 HClO (aq) + 2 H^+ (aq) + 2 e^- \rightarrow Cl_2 (g) + 2 H_2O$	+1.63
$Ce^{4+} (aq) + e^- \rightarrow Ce^{3+} (aq)$	+1.61
$NaBiO_3 (s) + 6 H^+ (aq) + 2 e^- \rightarrow Bi^{3+} (aq) + Na^+ (aq) + 3 H_2O$	+1.6
$MnO_4^- (aq) + 8 H^+ (aq) + 5 e^- \rightarrow Mn^{2+} (aq) + 4 H_2O$	+1.51
$Au^{3+} (aq) + 3 e^- \rightarrow Au (s)$	+1.5
$ClO_3^- (aq) + 6 H^+ (aq) + 5 e^- \rightarrow 1/2 Cl_2 (g) + 3 H_2O$	+1.47
$BrO_3^- + 6 H^+ (aq) + 6 e^- \rightarrow Br^- (aq) + 3 H_2O$	+1.44
$Cl_2 (g) + 2 e^- \rightarrow 2 Cl^- (aq)$	+1.358
$Cr_2O_7^{2-} + 14 H^+ (aq) + 6 e^- \rightarrow 2 Cr^{3+} (aq) + 7 H_2O$	+1.33
$N_2H_5^+ (aq) + 3 H^+ (aq) + 2 e^- \rightarrow 2 NH_4^+ (aq)$	+1.24
$MnO_2 (s) + 4 H^+ (aq) + 2 e^- \rightarrow Mn^{2+} (aq) + 2 H_2O$	+1.23
$O_2 (g) + 4 H^+ (aq) + 4 e^- \rightarrow 2 H_2O$	+1.229
$Pt^{2+} (aq) + 2 e^- \rightarrow Pt (s)$	+1.2
$IO_3^- (aq) + 6 H^+ (aq) + 5 e^- \rightarrow 1/2 I_2 (aq) + 3 H_2O$	+1.195
$ClO_4^- (aq) + 2 H^+ (aq) + 2 e^- \rightarrow ClO_3^- (aq) + H_2O$	+1.19
$Br_2 (l) + 2 e^- \rightarrow 2 Br^- (aq)$	+1.066
$AuCl_4^- + 3 e^- \rightarrow Au (s) + 4 Cl^- (aq)$	+1
$Pd^{2+} (aq) + 2 e^- \rightarrow Pd (s)$	+0.987
$NO_3^- (aq) + 4 H^+ (aq) + 3 e^- \rightarrow NO (g) + 2 H_2O$	+0.96
$NO_3^- (aq) + 3 H^+ (aq) + 2 e^- \rightarrow HNO_2 (aq) + H_2O$	+0.94
$2 Hg^{2+} (aq) + 2 e^- \rightarrow Hg_2^{2+} (aq)$	+0.92
$Hg^{2+} (aq) + 2 e^- \rightarrow Hg (l)$	+0.855
$Ag^+ (aq) + e^- \rightarrow Ag (s)$	+0.7994
$Hg_2^{2+} (aq) + 2 e^- \rightarrow 2 Hg (l)$	+0.789
$Fe^{3+} (aq) + e^- \rightarrow Fe^{2+} (aq)$	+0.771

Reaction	$E°$
$SbCl_6^- (aq) + 2 e^- \rightarrow SbCl_4^- (aq) + 2 Cl^- (aq)$	+0.75
$[PtCl_4]^{2-} (aq) + 2 e^- \rightarrow Pt (s) + 4 Cl^- (aq)$	+0.73
$O_2 (g) + 2 H^+ (aq) + 2 e^- \rightarrow H_2O_2 (aq)$	+0.682
$[PtCl_6]^{2-} (aq) + 2 e^- \rightarrow [PtCl_4]^{2-} (aq) + 2 Cl^- (aq)$	+0.68
$H_3AsO_4 (aq) + 2 H^+ (aq) + 2 e^- \rightarrow H_3AsO_3 (aq) + H_2O$	+0.58
$I_2 (s) + 2 e^- \rightarrow 2 I^- (aq)$	+0.535
$TeO_2 (s) + 4 H^+ (aq) + 4 e^- \rightarrow Te (s) + 2 H_2O$	+0.529
$Cu^+ (aq) + e^- \rightarrow Cu (s)$	+0.521
$[RhCl_6]^{3-} (aq) + 3 e^- \rightarrow Rh (s) + 6 Cl^- (aq)$	+0.44
$Cu^{2+} (aq) + 2 e^- \rightarrow Cu (s)$	+0.337
$HgCl_2 (s) + 2 e^- \rightarrow 2 Hg (l) + 2 Cl^- (aq)$	+0.27
$AgCl (s) + e^- \rightarrow Ag (s) + Cl^- (aq)$	+0.222
$SO_4^{2-} (aq) + 4 H^+ (aq) + 2 e^- \rightarrow SO_2 (g) + 2 H_2O$	+0.2
$SO_4^{2-} (aq) + 4 H^+ (aq) + 2 e^- \rightarrow H_2SO_3 (g) + H_2O$	+0.17
$Cu^{2+} (aq) + e^- \rightarrow Cu^+ (aq)$	+0.153
$Sn^{4+} (aq) + 2 e^- \rightarrow Sn^{2+} (aq)$	+0.15
$S (s) + 2 H^+ (aq) + 2 e^- \rightarrow H_2S (aq)$	+0.14
$AgBr (s) + e^- \rightarrow Ag (s) + Br^- (aq)$	+0.0713
$2 H^+ (aq) + 2 e^- \rightarrow H_2 (g)$ (reference electrode)	0.0
$N_2O (g) + 6 H^+ (aq) + H_2O + 4 e^- \rightarrow 2 NH_3OH^+ (aq)$	−0.05
$Pb^{2+} (aq) + 2 e^- \rightarrow Pb (s)$	−0.126
$Sn^{2+} (aq) + 2 e^- \rightarrow Sn (s)$	−0.14
$AgI (s) + e^- \rightarrow Ag (s) + I^- (aq)$	−0.15
$Sn^{4+} (aq) + 2 e^- \rightarrow Sn^{2+} (aq)$	+0.15
$S (s) + 2 H^+ (aq) + 2 e^- \rightarrow H_2S (aq)$	+0.14
$AgBr (s) + e^- \rightarrow Ag (s) + Br^- (aq)$	+0.0713
$2 H^+ (aq) + 2 e^- \rightarrow H_2 (g)$ (reference electrode)	0.0
$N_2O (g) + 6 H^+ (aq) + H_2O + 4 e^- \rightarrow 2 NH_3OH^+ (aq)$	−0.05
$Pb^{2+} (aq) + 2 e^- \rightarrow Pb (s)$	−0.126
$Sn^{2+} (aq) + 2 e^- \rightarrow Sn (s)$	−0.14
$AgI (s) + e^- \rightarrow Ag (s) + I^- (aq)$	−0.15
$[SnF_6]^{2-} (aq) + 4 e^- \rightarrow Sn (s) + 6 F^- (aq)$	−0.25
$Ni^{2+} (aq) + 2 e^- \rightarrow Ni (s)$	−0.25
$Co^{2+} (aq) + 2 e^- \rightarrow Co (s)$	−0.28
$Tl^+ (aq) + e^- \rightarrow Tl (s)$	−0.34
$PbSO_4 (s) + 2 e^- \rightarrow Pb (s) + SO_4^{2-} (aq)$	−0.356

$Se\ (s) + 2\ H^+\ (aq) + 2\ e^- \rightarrow H_2Se\ (aq)$	-0.4
$Cd^{2+}\ (aq) + 2\ e^- \rightarrow Cd\ (s)$	-0.403
$Cr^{3+}\ (aq) + e^- \rightarrow Cr^{2+}\ (aq)$	-0.41
$Fe^{2+}\ (aq) + 2\ e^- \rightarrow Fe\ (s)$	-0.44
$2\ CO_2\ (g) + 2\ H^+\ (aq) + 2\ e^- \rightarrow (COOH)_2\ (aq)$	-0.49
$Ga^{3+}\ (aq) + 3\ e^- \rightarrow Ga\ (s)$	-0.53
$HgS\ (s) + 2\ H^+\ (aq) + 2\ e^- \rightarrow Hg\ (l) + H_2S\ (g)$	-0.72
$Cr^{3+}\ (aq) + 3\ e^- \rightarrow Cr\ (s)$	-0.74
$Zn^{2+}\ (aq) + 2\ e^- \rightarrow Zn\ (s)$	-0.763
$2\ H_2O\ (l) + 2\ e^- \rightarrow H_2\ (g) + 2\ OH^-\ (aq)$	-0.8277
$Cr^{2+}\ (aq) + 2\ e^- \rightarrow Cr\ (s)$	-0.91
$Mn^{2+}\ (aq) + 2\ e^- \rightarrow Mn\ (s)$	-1.18
$V^{2+}\ (aq) + 2\ e^- \rightarrow V\ (s)$	-1.18
$Zr^{4+}\ (aq) + 4\ e^- \rightarrow Zr\ (s)$	-1.53
$Al^{3+}\ (aq) + 3\ e^- \rightarrow Al\ (s)$	-1.66
$H_2\ (g) + 2\ e^- \rightarrow 2\ H^-\ (aq)$	-2.25
$Mg^{2+}\ (aq) + 2\ e^- \rightarrow Mg\ (s)$	-2.37
$Na^+\ (aq) + e^- \rightarrow Na\ (s)$	-2.714
$Ca^{2+}\ (aq) + 2\ e^- \rightarrow Ca\ (s)$	-2.87
$Sr^{2+}\ (aq) + 2\ e^- \rightarrow Sr\ (s)$	-2.89
$Ba^{2+}\ (aq) + 2\ e^- \rightarrow Ba\ (s)$	-2.9
$Rb^+\ (aq) + e^- \rightarrow Rb\ (s)$	-2.925
$K^+\ (aq) + e^- \rightarrow K\ (s)$	-2.925
$Li^+\ (aq) + e^- \rightarrow Li\ (s)$	-3.045
Basic Solutions	**E^o (V)**
$ClO^-\ (aq) + H_2O + 2\ e^- \rightarrow Cl^-\ (aq) + 2\ OH^-\ (aq)$	$+0.89$
$OOH^-\ (aq) + H_2O + 2\ e^- \rightarrow 3\ OH^-\ (aq)$	$+0.88$
$2\ NH_2OH\ (aq) + 2\ e^- \rightarrow N_2H_4\ (aq) + 2\ OH^-\ (aq)$	$+0.74$
$ClO_3^-\ (aq) + 3\ H_2O + 6\ e^- \rightarrow Cl^-\ (aq) + 6\ OH^-\ (aq)$	$+0.62$
$MnO_4^-\ (aq) + 2\ H_2O + 3\ e^- \rightarrow MnO_2\ (s) + 4\ OH^-\ (aq)$	$+0.588$
$MnO_4^-\ (aq) + e^- \rightarrow MnO_4^{2-}\ (aq)$	$+0.564$
$NiO_2\ (s) + 2\ H_2O + 2\ e^- \rightarrow Ni(OH)_2\ (s) + 2\ OH^-\ (aq)$	$+0.49$
$Ag_2CrO_4\ (s) + 2\ e^- \rightarrow 2\ Ag\ (s) + CrO_4^{2-}\ (aq)$	$+0.446$
$O_2\ (g) + 2\ H_2O + 4\ e^- \rightarrow 4\ OH^-\ (aq)$	$+0.4$
$ClO_4^-\ (aq) + H_2O + 2\ e^- \rightarrow ClO_3^-\ (aq) + 2\ OH^-\ (aq)$	$+0.36$
$Ag_2O\ (s) + H_2O + 2\ e^- \rightarrow 2\ Ag\ (s) + 2\ OH^-\ (aq)$	$+0.34$

$2 NO_2^- (aq) + 3 H_2O + 4 e^- \rightarrow N_2O (g) + 6 OH^- (aq)$	+0.15
$N_2H_4 (aq) + 2 H_2O + 2 e^- \rightarrow 2 NH_3 (aq) + 2 OH^- (aq)$	+0.1
$[Co(NH_3)_6]^{3+} (aq) + e^- \rightarrow [Co(NH_3)_6]^{2+} (aq)$	+0.1
$HgO (s) + H_2O + 2 e^- \rightarrow Hg (l) + 2 OH^- (aq)$	+0.0984
$O_2 (g) + H_2O + 2 e^- \rightarrow OOH^- (aq) + OH^- (aq)$	+0.076
$NO_3^- (aq) + H_2O + 2 e^- \rightarrow NO_2^- (aq) + 2 OH^- (aq)$	+0.01
$MnO_2 (s) + 2 H_2O + 2 e^- \rightarrow Mn(OH)_2 (s) + 2 OH^- (aq)$	−0.05
$CrO_4^{2-} (aq) + 4 H_2O + 3 e^- \rightarrow Cr(OH)_3 (s) + 5 OH^- (aq)$	−0.12
$Cu(OH)_2 (s) + 2 e^- \rightarrow Cu (s) + 2 OH^- (aq)$	−0.36
$Fe(OH)_3 (s) + e^- \rightarrow Fe(OH)_2 (s) + OH^- (aq)$	−0.56
$2 H_2O + 2 e^- \rightarrow H_2 (g) + 2 OH^- (aq)$	−0.8277
$2 NO_3^- (aq) + 2 H_2O + 2 e^- \rightarrow N_2O_4 (g) + 4 OH^- (aq)$	−0.85
$Fe(OH)_2 (s) + 2 e^- \rightarrow Fe (s) + 2 OH^- (aq)$	−0.877
$SO_4^{2-} (aq) + H_2O + 2 e^- \rightarrow SO_3^{2-} (aq) + 2 OH^- (aq)$	−0.93
$N_2 (g) + 4 H_2O + 4 e^- \rightarrow N_2H_4 (aq) + 4 OH^- (aq)$	−1.15
$[Zn(OH)_4]^{2-} (aq) + 2 e^- \rightarrow Zn (s) + 4 OH^- (aq)$	−1.22
$Zn(OH)_2 (s) + 2 e^- \rightarrow Zn (s) + 2 OH^- (aq)$	−1.245
$[Zn(CN)_4]^{2-} (aq) + 2 e^- \rightarrow Zn (s) + 4 CN^- (aq)$	−1.26
$Cr(OH)_3 (s) + 3 e^- \rightarrow Cr (s) + 3 OH^- (aq)$	−1.3
$SiO_3^{2-} (aq) + 3 H_2O + 4 e^- \rightarrow Si (s) + 6 OH^- (aq)$	−1.7

Practice Questions

1. Nickel-cadmium batteries are used in rechargeable electronic calculators. Given the following reaction for a discharging NiCad battery, what substance is being reduced?

$$Cd\,(s) + NiO_2\,(s) + 2H_2O\,(l) \rightarrow Cd(OH)_2\,(s) + Ni(OH)_2\,(s)$$

A. $Cd(OH)_2$ **B.** H_2O **C.** NiO_2 **D.** Cd

2. How long must a current of 2 amps run for to liberate 3 moles of H_2O when electrolyzed in the following reaction? (Use Faraday's constant = 96,500C/mol and the conversion factor of 1 amp = 1 coulomb/sec)

$$H_2O_2 + 2\,H^+ + 2\,e^- \rightleftarrows 2\,H_2O$$

A. 4.83×10^4 sec **C.** 1.45×10^5 sec

B. 4.83×10^5 sec **D.** 2.41×10^5 sec

3. Which is NOT true for the following redox reaction occurring in an electrolytic cell?

$$\overset{\text{Electricity}}{Cd\,(s) + Zn(NO_3)_2\,(aq) \;\rightarrow\; Zn\,(s) + Cd(NO_3)_2\,(aq)}$$

A. Cd^{2+} is produced at the anode **C.** Oxidation half-reaction: $Cd \rightarrow Cd^{2+} + 2\,e^-$

B. Zn metal is produced at the anode **D.** Reduction half-reaction: $Zn^{2+} + 2\,e^- \rightarrow Zn$

4. Which of the statements is true regarding the following redox reaction occurring in a nonspontaneous electrolytic cell?

$$\overset{\text{Electricity}}{Br_2\,(l) + 2\,NaCl\,(aq) \;\rightarrow\; Cl_2\,(g) + 2\,NaBr\,(aq)}$$

A. Br_2 liquid is produced at the cathode

B. Cl_2 gas is produced at the cathode

C. Reduction half–reaction: $2\,Cl^- \rightarrow Cl_2 + 2\,e^-$

D. Cl_2 gas is produced at the anode

5. Which is true regarding the redox reaction occurring in a spontaneous electrochemical cell?

$$Sn\,(s) + Cu^{2+}\,(aq) \rightarrow Cu\,(s) + Sn^{2+}\,(aq)$$

A. Electrons flow from the Sn electrode to the Cu electrode

B. Anions in the salt bridge flow from the Sn half-cell to the Cu half-cell

C. Sn is oxidized at the cathode

D. Cu^{2+} is reduced at the anode

6. Which of the following is a unit of electrical charge?

A. joule   **B.** volt   **C.** coulomb   **D.** ampere

7. If a galvanic cell has two electrodes, which statement is correct?

A. Oxidation occurs at the negatively charged cathode
B. Oxidation occurs at the positively charged cathode
C. Oxidation occurs at the positively charged anode
D. Oxidation occurs at the negatively charged anode

8. A battery operates by:

A. oxidation   **C.** both oxidation and reduction
B. reduction   **D.** neither oxidation nor reduction

9. What is the term for the electrode in an electrochemical cell where oxidation occurs?

A. oxidation electrode   **C.** anode
B. reduction electrode   **D.** cathode

10. What is the general term for an apparatus that contains two solutions with electrodes in separate compartments that are connected by a wire and salt bridge?

A. electrolytic cell   **C.** battery
B. voltaic cell   **D.** electrochemical cell

11. The electrode with the standard reduction potential of 0 V is assigned as the standard reference electrode and uses the half-reaction:

A. $2\,NH_4^+\,(aq) + 2\,e^- \leftrightarrows H_2\,(g) + 2\,NH_3\,(g)$ **C.** $Cu^{2+}\,(aq) + 2\,e^- \leftrightarrows Cu\,(s)$
B. $2\,H^+\,(aq) + 2\,e^- \leftrightarrows H_2\,(g)$ **D.** $Zn^{2+}\,(aq) + 2\,e^- \leftrightarrows Zn\,(s)$

12. In which type of cell does the following reaction occur when electrons are forced into a system by applying an external voltage?

$$Fe^{2+} + 2e^- \rightarrow Fe\,(s) \qquad E° = -0.44\ V$$

A. concentration cell   **C.** electrochemical cell
B. electrolytic cell   **D.** galvanic cell

13. What is the term for a reaction that represents separate oxidation or reduction processes?

    A. reduction reaction

    B. redox reaction

    C. oxidation reaction

    D. half-reaction

14. What is the term for the providing of electricity to a nonspontaneous redox process to cause a reaction?

    A. hydrolysis

    B. protolysis

    C. electrochemistry

    D. electrolysis

15. How is electrolysis different from the chemical process inside a battery?

    A. They are the same process in reverse

    B. Electrolysis only uses electrons from a cathode

    C. Electrolysis does not use electrons

    D. Chemical changes do not occur in electrolysis

Solutions

1. C is correct.

Determine the oxidation number of each species. The reduced substance has a decrease in the oxidation number.

In NiO_2, the oxidation number of Ni = +4.

In $Ni(OH)_2$, the oxidation number of Ni = +2.

2. C is correct.

3 moles of H_2O need 3 moles of e^-.

Calculate time needed for 3 moles of H_2O:

        (3 moles e^-) × (96,500 coulomb / 1 mole e^-) × (1 sec /2 coulomb)

        time (for 3 moles of H_2O) = 1.45×10^5 sec

3. B is correct.

An electrolytic cell is a nonspontaneous electrochemical cell that requires electrical energy to be supplied (e.g., battery) to initiate the reaction.

The anode is positive and the cathode is the negative electrode.

For both electrolytic and galvanic cells, oxidation occurs at the anode while reduction occurs at the cathode.

Therefore, Zn metal is produced at the cathode because it is a reduction product (from oxidation number of +3 on the left to 0 on the right). Zn will not be produced at the anode.

4. D is correct.

In electrochemical (i.e., galvanic) cells, oxidation always occurs at the anode and reduction occurs at the cathode.

Therefore, Cl_2 gas will be produced at the anode because it is an oxidation product (from oxidation number of −1 on the left to 0 on the right).

5. A is correct.

A spontaneous electrochemical cell is also known as a galvanic cell.

6. C is correct.

The coulomb is a unit of electrical charge.

7. D is correct.

Oxidation (i.e. loss of electrons) occurs at the anode.

8. C is correct.

A battery is an electrochemical (i.e., galvanic) cell, which has both reduction and oxidation reactions happening within them to generate electricity.

9. C is correct.

Oxidation (i.e. loss of electrons) occurs at the anode.

10. D is correct.

The salt bridge should be the most obvious indication that it is an electrochemical cell – electrolytic cells do not have salt bridges.

11. B is correct.

By convention, the reference standard for potential is always hydrogen reduction.

12. B is correct.

Electrolytic cells don't occur spontaneously; the reaction only occurs with the addition of an external electrical energy.

13. D is correct.

A redox reaction, or oxidation-reduction reaction, involves the transfer of electrons between two reacting substances. An oxidation reaction specifically refers to the substance that is losing electrons and a reduction reaction specifically refers to the substance that is gaining reactions.

The oxidation and reduction reactions alone are called half-reactions, because they always occur together to form a whole reaction.

Therefore, half-reaction is the answer because it can represent either a separate oxidation process or a separate reduction process.

14. D is correct.

Electrolysis is a method of using a direct electric current to provide electricity to a nonspontaneous redox process to drive the reaction. The direct electric current must be passed through an ionic substance or solution that contains electrolytes.

15. A is correct.

Electrolysis is the same process in reverse for the chemical process inside a battery.

Electrolysis is often used to separate elements.

Appendix

Periodic Table of the Elements

Atomic Number	Valence Charge
Symbol	
Name	
Atomic Mass	

1 IA 1A	2 IIA 2A	3 IIIB 3B	4 IVB 4B	5 VB 5B	6 VIB 6B	7 VIIB 7B	8 VIII	9 VIII	10	11 IB 1B	12 IIB 2B	13 IIIA 3A	14 IVA 4A	15 VA 5A	16 VIA 6A	17 VIIA 7A	18 VIIIA 8A
1 $^{+1}$ **H** Hydrogen 1.008																	2 ^{0} **He** Helium 4.003
3 $^{+1}$ **Li** Lithium 6.941	4 $^{+2}$ **Be** Beryllium 9.012											5 $^{+3}$ **B** Boron 10.811	6 $^{+4,-4}$ **C** Carbon 12.011	7 $^{+5,+3,-3}$ **N** Nitrogen 14.007	8 $^{-2}$ **O** Oxygen 15.999	9 $^{-1}$ **F** Fluorine 18.998	10 ^{0} **Ne** Neon 20.180
11 $^{+1}$ **Na** Sodium 22.990	12 $^{+2}$ **Mg** Magnesium 24.305											13 $^{+3}$ **Al** Aluminum 26.982	14 $^{+4}$ **Si** Silicon 28.086	15 $^{+5,+3,-3}$ **P** Phosphorus 30.974	16 $^{+6,-2}$ **S** Sulfur 32.065	17 $^{-1}$ **Cl** Chlorine 35.453	18 ^{0} **Ar** Argon 39.948
19 $^{+1}$ **K** Potassium 39.098	20 $^{+2}$ **Ca** Calcium 40.078	21 $^{+3}$ **Sc** Scandium 44.956	22 $^{+4}$ **Ti** Titanium 47.867	23 $^{+5,+4,+3}$ **V** Vanadium 50.942	24 $^{+6,+3,+2}$ **Cr** Chromium 51.996	25 $^{+7,+4,+2}$ **Mn** Manganese 54.938	26 $^{+3,+2}$ **Fe** Iron 55.845	27 $^{+3,+2}$ **Co** Cobalt 58.933	28 $^{+2}$ **Ni** Nickel 58.693	29 $^{+2,+1}$ **Cu** Copper 63.546	30 $^{+2}$ **Zn** Zinc 65.38	31 $^{+3}$ **Ga** Gallium 69.723	32 $^{+4}$ **Ge** Germanium 72.631	33 $^{+3}$ **As** Arsenic 74.922	34 $^{+4,-2}$ **Se** Selenium 78.971	35 $^{+5,-1}$ **Br** Bromine 79.904	36 ^{0} **Kr** Krypton 84.798
37 $^{+1}$ **Rb** Rubidium 84.468	38 $^{+2}$ **Sr** Strontium 87.62	39 $^{+3}$ **Y** Yttrium 88.906	40 $^{+4}$ **Zr** Zirconium 91.224	41 $^{+5}$ **Nb** Niobium 92.906	42 $^{+6,+4}$ **Mo** Molybdenum 95.95	43 $^{+7,+6,+4}$ **Tc** Technetium 98.907	44 $^{+4,+3}$ **Ru** Ruthenium 101.07	45 $^{+3}$ **Rh** Rhodium 102.906	46 $^{+4,+2}$ **Pd** Palladium 106.42	47 $^{+1}$ **Ag** Silver 107.868	48 $^{+2}$ **Cd** Cadmium 112.414	49 $^{+3}$ **In** Indium 114.818	50 $^{+4,+2}$ **Sn** Tin 118.711	51 $^{+5,+3,-3}$ **Sb** Antimony 121.760	52 $^{+4,-2}$ **Te** Tellurium 127.6	53 $^{+5,-1}$ **I** Iodine 126.904	54 ^{0} **Xe** Xenon 131.294
55 $^{+1}$ **Cs** Cesium 132.905	56 $^{+2}$ **Ba** Barium 137.328	57-71	72 $^{+4}$ **Hf** Hafnium 178.49	73 $^{+5}$ **Ta** Tantalum 180.948	74 $^{+6,+4}$ **W** Tungsten 183.84	75 $^{+5,+4,+3}$ **Re** Rhenium 186.207	76 $^{+4}$ **Os** Osmium 190.23	77 $^{+4,+3}$ **Ir** Iridium 192.217	78 $^{+4,+2}$ **Pt** Platinum 195.085	79 $^{+3}$ **Au** Gold 196.967	80 $^{+2,+1}$ **Hg** Mercury 200.592	81 $^{+3,+1}$ **Tl** Thallium 204.383	82 $^{+4,+2}$ **Pb** Lead 207.2	83 $^{+3}$ **Bi** Bismuth 208.980	84 $^{+2}$ **Po** Polonium [208.982]	85 $^{-1}$ **At** Astatine 209.987	86 ^{0} **Rn** Radon 222.018
87 $^{+1}$ **Fr** Francium 223.020	88 $^{+2}$ **Ra** Radium 226.025	89-103	104 unk **Rf** Rutherfordium [261]	105 unk **Db** Dubnium [262]	106 unk **Sg** Seaborgium [266]	107 unk **Bh** Bohrium [264]	108 unk **Hs** Hassium [269]	109 unk **Mt** Meitnerium [268]	110 unk **Ds** Darmstadtium [269]	111 unk **Rg** Roentgenium [272]	112 unk **Cn** Copernicium [277]	113 unk **Uut** Ununtrium unknown	114 unk **Fl** Flerovium [289]	115 unk **Uup** Ununpentium unknown	116 unk **Lv** Livermorium [298]	117 unk **Uus** Ununseptium unknown	118 unk **Uuo** Ununoctium unknown

Lanthanide Series

57 $^{+3}$ **La** Lanthanum 138.905	58 $^{+4}$ **Ce** Cerium 140.116	59 $^{+3}$ **Pr** Praseodymium 140.908	60 $^{+3}$ **Nd** Neodymium 144.243	61 $^{+3}$ **Pm** Promethium 144.913	62 $^{+3}$ **Sm** Samarium 150.36	63 $^{+3}$ **Eu** Europium 151.964	64 $^{+3}$ **Gd** Gadolinium 157.25	65 $^{+3}$ **Tb** Terbium 158.925	66 $^{+3}$ **Dy** Dysprosium 162.500	67 $^{+3}$ **Ho** Holmium 164.930	68 $^{+3}$ **Er** Erbium 167.259	69 $^{+3}$ **Tm** Thulium 168.934	70 $^{+3}$ **Yb** Ytterbium 173.055	71 $^{+3}$ **Lu** Lutetium 174.967

Actinide Series

89 $^{+3}$ **Ac** Actinium 227.028	90 $^{+4}$ **Th** Thorium 232.038	91 $^{+5}$ **Pa** Protactinium 231.036	92 $^{+6}$ **U** Uranium 238.029	93 $^{+5}$ **Np** Neptunium 237.048	94 $^{+7,+4}$ **Pu** Plutonium 244.064	95 $^{+4}$ **Am** Americium 243.061	96 $^{+3}$ **Cm** Curium 247.070	97 $^{+3}$ **Bk** Berkelium 247.070	98 $^{+3}$ **Cf** Californium 251.080	99 $^{+3}$ **Es** Einsteinium [254]	100 $^{+3}$ **Fm** Fermium 257.095	101 $^{+2}$ **Md** Mendelevium 258.1	102 $^{+2}$ **No** Nobelium 259.101	103 $^{+3}$ **Lr** Lawrencium [262]

Common Chemistry Equations

Throughout the test the following symbols have the definitions specified unless otherwise noted.

L, mL	=	liter(s), milliliter(s)	mm Hg	= millimeters of mercury
g	=	gram(s)	J, kJ	= joule(s), kilojoule(s)
nm	=	nanometer(s)	V	= volt(s)
atm	=	atmosphere(s)	mol	= mole(s)

ATOMIC STRUCTURE

$E = h\nu$

$c = \lambda\nu$

E = energy

ν = frequency

λ = wavelength

Planck's constant, $h = 6.626 \times 10^{-34}$ J s

Speed of light, $c = 2.998 \times 10^8$ m s^{-1}

Avogadro's number = 6.022×10^{23} mol^{-1}

Electron charge, $e = -1.602 \times 10^{-19}$ coulomb

EQUILIBRIUM

$K_c = \dfrac{[C]^c[D]^d}{[A]^a[B]^b}$, where $a\,A + b\,B \rightleftarrows c\,C + d\,D$

$K_p = \dfrac{(P_C)^c(P_D)^d}{(P_A)^a(P_B)^b}$

$K_a = \dfrac{[H^+][A^-]}{[HA]}$

$K_b = \dfrac{[OH^-][HB^+]}{[B]}$

$K_w = [H^+][OH^-] = 1.0 \times 10^{-14}$ at 25°C

$\quad = K_a \times K_b$

$pH = -\log[H^+]$, $pOH = -\log[OH^-]$

$14 = pH + pOH$

$pH = pK_a + \log\dfrac{[A^-]}{[HA]}$

$pK_a = -\log K_a$, $pK_b = -\log K_b$

Equilibrium Constants

K_c (molar concentrations)

K_p (gas pressures)

K_a (weak acid)

K_b (weak base)

K_w (water)

KINETICS

$\ln[A]_t - \ln[A]_0 = -kt$

$\dfrac{1}{[A]_t} - \dfrac{1}{[A]_0} = kt$

$t_{1/2} = \dfrac{0.693}{k}$

k = rate constant

t = time

$t_{1/2}$ = half-life

GASES, LIQUIDS, AND SOLUTIONS

$$PV = nRT$$

$$P_A = P_{total} \times X_A, \text{ where } X_A = \frac{\text{moles A}}{\text{total moles}}$$

$$P_{total} = P_A + P_B + P_C + \dots$$

$$n = \frac{m}{M}$$

$$K = °C + 273$$

$$D = \frac{m}{V}$$

$$KE \text{ per molecule} = \frac{1}{2}mv^2$$

Molarity, M = moles of solute per liter of solution

$$A = abc$$

P = pressure
V = volume
T = temperature
n = number of moles
m = mass
M = molar mass
D = density
KE = kinetic energy
v = velocity
A = absorbance
a = molar absorptivity
b = path length
c = concentration

Gas constant, R = 8.314 J mol^{-1} K^{-1}
= 0.08206 L atm mol^{-1} K^{-1}
= 62.36 L torr mol^{-1} K^{-1}
1 atm = 760 mm Hg
= 760 torr
STP = 0.00°C and 1.000 atm

THERMOCHEMISTRY/ ELECTROCHEMISTRY

$$q = mc\Delta T$$

$$\Delta S° = \sum S° \text{ products} - \sum S° \text{ reactants}$$

$$\Delta H° = \sum \Delta H_f° \text{ products} - \sum \Delta H_f° \text{ reactants}$$

$$\Delta G° = \sum \Delta G_f° \text{ products} - \sum \Delta G_f° \text{ reactants}$$

$$\Delta G° = \Delta H° - T\Delta S°$$

$$= -RT \ln K$$

$$= -nFE°$$

$$I = \frac{q}{t}$$

q = heat
m = mass
c = specific heat capacity
T = temperature
$S°$ = standard entropy
$H°$ = standard enthalpy
$G°$ = standard free energy
n = number of moles
$E°$ = standard reduction potential
I = current (amperes)
q = charge (coulombs)
t = time (seconds)

Faraday's constant, F = 96,485 coulombs per mole of electrons

$$1 \text{ volt} = \frac{1 \text{ joule}}{1 \text{ coulomb}}$$

Glossary

A

Absolute entropy (of a substance) – the increase in the entropy (Δs) of a substance as it goes from a perfectly ordered crystalline form at 0 °K (where its entropy is zero) to the temperature in question.

Absolute zero – the zero point on the absolute temperature scale; -273.15 °C or 0 Kelvin; theoretically, the temperature at which molecular motion ceases (i.e., the system does not emit or absorb energy, and all atoms are at rest).

Absorption spectrum – spectrum associated with absorption of electromagnetic radiation by atoms (or other species), resulting from transitions from lower to higher energy states.

Accuracy – how close a value is to the actual or true value; see *Precision*.

Acid – a substance that produces H^+ (*aq*) ions in aqueous solution and gives a pH of less than 7.0; strong acids ionize completely or almost completely in dilute aqueous solution; weak acids ionize only slightly.

Acid dissociation constant – an equilibrium constant for the dissociation of a weak acid.

Acidic salt – a salt containing an ionizable hydrogen atom; does not necessarily produce acidic solutions.

Actinides – the fifteen chemical elements that are between actinium (89) and lawrencium (103).

Activated complex – a structure that forms because of a collision between molecules while new bonds are formed.

Activation energy (E_a) – the amount of energy that must be absorbed by reactants in their ground states to reach the transition state needed for a reaction can occur.

Active metal – a metal with low ionization energy that loses electrons readily to form cations.

Activity (of a component of ideal mixture) – a dimensionless quantity whose magnitude is equal to molar concentration in an ideal solution; equal to partial pressure in an ideal gas mixture; 1 for pure solids or liquids.

Activity series – a listing of metals (and hydrogen) in order of decreasing activity.

Actual yield – the amount of a specified pure product actually obtained from a given reaction; see *Theoretical yield*.

Addition reaction – a reaction in which two atoms or groups of atoms are added to a molecule, one on each side of a double or triple bond.

Adhesive forces – forces of attraction between a liquid and another surface.

Adsorption – the adhesion of a species onto the surfaces of particles.

Aeration – the mixing of air into a liquid or a solid.

Alcohol – hydrocarbon derivative containing a hydroxyl (–OH) group attached to a carbon atom not in an aromatic ring.

Alkali metals – metals of Group IA on the periodic table (Na, K, Rb).

Alkaline battery – a dry cell in which the electrolyte contains KOH.

Alkaline earth metals – group IIA metals on the periodic table; see *Earth metals*.

Allomer – a substance that has a different composition than another but the same crystalline structure.

Allotropes – elements that can have different structures (and therefore different forms), such as carbon (e.g., diamonds, graphite and fullerene).

Allotropic modifications (allotropes) – different forms of the same element in the same physical state.

Alloying – mixing of metal with other substances (usually other metals) to modify its properties.

Alpha (α) particle – a helium nucleus; helium ion with 2+ charge; an assembly of two protons and two neutrons.

Amorphous solid – a non-crystalline solid with no well-defined ordered structure.

Ampere – unit of electrical current; one ampere equals one coulomb per second.

Amphiprotism – ability of a substance to exhibit amphiprotism by accepting donated protons.

Amphoterism – the ability to react with both acids and bases; the ability of a substance to act as either an acid or a base.

Amplitude – the maximum distance that the particles of the medium carrying the wave move away from their rest position.

Anion – a negative ion; an atom or group of atoms that has gained one or more electrons.

Anode – in a cathode ray tube, the positive electrode (electrode at which oxidation occurs); the positive side of a dry cell battery or a cell.

Antibonding orbital – a molecular orbital higher in energy than any of the atomic orbitals from which it is derived; lends instability to a molecule or ion when populated with electrons; denoted with a star (*) superscript or symbol.

Artificial transmutation – an artificially induced nuclear reaction caused by the bombardment of a nucleus with subatomic particles or small nuclei.

Associated ions – short-lived species formed by the collision of dissolved ions of opposite charges.

Atmosphere – a unit of pressure; the pressure that will support a column of mercury 760 mm high at 0 °C.

Atom – a chemical element in its smallest form; made up of neutrons and protons within the nucleus and electrons circling the nucleus.

Atomic mass unit (amu) – one-twelfth of the mass of an atom of the carbon (^{12}C) isotope; used for stating atomic and formula weights; also known as a dalton.

Atomic number (Z) – the number representing an element which corresponds with the number of protons within the nucleus.

Atomic orbital – a region or volume in space in which the probability of finding electrons is highest.

Atomic radius – radius of an atom.

Atomic weight – weighted average of the masses of the constituent isotopes of an element; the relative masses of atoms of different elements.

Aufbau ("building up") principle – describes the order in which electrons fill orbitals in atoms.

Autoionization – an ionization reaction between identical molecules.

Avogadro's law – at the same temperature and the same pressure, equal volumes of all gases will contain the same number of molecules.

Avogadro's number (N) – the number (6.022×10^{23}) of atoms, molecules or particles found in exactly 1 mole of substance.

B

Background radiation – radiation extraneous to an experiment; usually the low-level natural radiation from cosmic rays and trace radioactive substances present in our environment.

Band – a series of very closely spaced, nearly continuous molecular orbitals that belong to the crystal as a whole.

Band of stability – band containing nonradioactive nuclides in a plot of the number of neutrons versus their atomic number.

Band theory of metals – theory that accounts for the bonding and properties of metallic solids.

Barometer – a device used to measure the pressure in the atmosphere.

Base – a substance that produces OH (*aq*) ions in aqueous solution; accepts a proton and has a high pH; strongly soluble bases are soluble in water and are completely dissociated; weak bases ionize only slightly; a common example of a base is sodium hydroxide – NaOH.

Basic anhydride – the oxide of a metal that reacts with water to form a base.

Basic salt – a salt containing an ionizable OH group.

Beta (*β*) particle – an electron emitted from the nucleus when a neutron decays to a proton and an electron.

Binary acid – a binary compound in which H is bonded to one or more of the more electronegative nonmetals.

Binary compound – a compound consisting of two elements; it may be ionic or covalent.

Binding energy (nuclear binding energy) – the energy equivalent ($E = mc^2$) of the mass deficiency of an atom (where E is the energy in Joules, m is the mass in kilograms and c is the speed of light in m/s^2).

Boiling – the phase transition of liquid vaporizing.

Boiling point – the temperature at which the vapor pressure of a liquid is equal to the applied pressure; also the condensation point.

Boiling point elevation – the increase in the boiling point of a solvent caused by the dissolution of a nonvolatile solute.

Bomb calorimeter – a device used to measure the heat transfer between a system and its surroundings at constant volume.

Bond – the attraction and repulsion between atoms and molecules that is a cornerstone of chemistry.

Bond energy – the amount of energy necessary to break one mole of bonds in a substance, dissociating the substance in its gaseous state into atoms of its elements in the gaseous state.

Bond order – half the number of electrons in bonding orbitals minus half the number of electrons in antibonding orbitals.

Bonding orbital – a molecular orbit lower in energy than any of the atomic orbitals from which it is derived; lends stability to a molecule or ion when populated with electrons.

Bonding pair – pair of electrons involved in a covalent bond.

Boron hydrides – binary compounds of boron and hydrogen.

Born-Haber cycle – a series of reactions (and the accompanying enthalpy changes) which, when summed, represents the hypothetical one-step reaction by which elements in their standard states are converted into crystals of ionic compounds (and the accompanying enthalpy changes).

Boyle's law – at constant temperature the volume occupied by a definite mass of a gas is inversely proportional to the applied pressure ($P \propto 1/V$) or $P_1V_1 = P_2V_2$

Breeder reactor – a nuclear reactor that produces more fissionable nuclear fuel than it consumes.

Brønsted-Lowry acid – a chemical species that donates a proton.

Brønsted-Lowry base – a chemical species that accepts a proton.

Buffer solution – resists change in pH; contains either a weak acid and a soluble ionic salt of the acid or a weak base and a soluble ionic salt of the base.

Buret (burette)– a piece of volumetric glassware, usually graduated in 0.1 mL intervals, used to deliver solutions to be used in titrations in a quantitative (drop-like) manner.

C

Calorie – the amount of heat required to raise the temperature of one gram of water from 14.5 °C to 15.5 °C; 1 calorie = 4.184 joules.

Calorimeter – a device used to measure the heat transfer between a system and its surroundings.

Canal ray – stream of positively charged particles (cations) that moves toward the negative electrode in cathode ray tubes; observed to pass through canals in the negative electrode.

Capillary – a tube having a very small inside diameter.

Capillary action – the drawing of a liquid up the inside of a small-bore tube when adhesive forces exceed cohesive forces; the depression of the surface of the liquid when cohesive forces exceed the adhesive forces.

Catalyst – a chemical compound used to change the rate (either to speed it up or slow it down) of a reaction that is regenerated (i.e., not consumed) at the end of the reaction.

Catenation – bonding of atoms of the same element into chains or rings (i.e., the ability of an element to bond with itself).

Cathode – the electrode at which reduction occurs; in a cathode ray tube, the negative electrode.

Cathodic protection – protection of a metal (making a cathode) against corrosion by attaching it to a sacrificial anode of a more easily oxidized metal.

Cathode ray tube – a closed glass tube containing a gas under low pressure, with electrodes near the ends and a luminescent screen at the end near the positive electrode; produces cathode rays when high voltage is applied.

Cation – a positive ion; an atom or group of atoms that has lost one or more electrons.

Cell potential – the potential difference, E_{cell}, between oxidation and reduction half-cells under nonstandard conditions; the force in a galvanic cell that pulls electrons through a reducing agent to an oxidizing agent.

Central atom – an atom in a molecule or polyatomic ion that is bonded to more than one other atom.

Chain reaction – a reaction that, once initiated, sustains itself and expands; a reaction in which reactive species, such as radicals, are produced in more than one step; these reactive species propagate the chain reaction.

Charles' law – at constant pressure the volume occupied by a definite mass of gas is directly proportional to its absolute temperature. $V \propto T$ or $V_1 / T_1 = V_2 / T_2$

Chemical bonds – the attractive forces that hold atoms together in elements or compounds.

Chemical change – a change in which one or more new substances are formed.

Chemical equation – description of a chemical reaction by placing the formulas of the reactants on the left of an arrow and the formulas of the products on the right.

Chemical equilibrium – a state of dynamic balance in which the rates of forward and reverse reactions are equal; there is no net change in concentrations of reactants or products while a system is at equilibrium.

Chemical kinetics – the study of rates and mechanisms of chemical reactions and of the factors on which they depend.

Chemical periodicity – the variations in properties of elements with their position in the periodic table.

Chemical reaction – the change of one or more substances into another or multiple substances.

Cloud chamber – a device for observing the paths of speeding particles as vapor molecules condense on them to form fog-like tracks.

Coefficient of expansion – the ratio of the change in the length or the volume of a body to the original length or volume for a unit change in temperature.

Cohesive forces – all the forces of attraction among particles of a liquid.

Colligative properties – physical properties of solutions that depend upon the number but not the kind of solute particles present.

Collision theory – theory of reaction rates that states that effective collisions between reactant molecules must occur in order for the reaction to occur.

Colloid – a heterogeneous mixture in which solute-like particles do not settle out (e.g., many milks).

Combination reaction – reaction in which two substances (elements or compounds) combine to form one compound.

Combustible – classification of liquid substances that will burn on the basis of flash points; a combustible liquid means any liquid having a flash point at or above 37.8 °C (100 °F) but below 93.3 °C (200 °F), except any mixture having components with flash points of 93.3 °C (200 °F) or higher, the total of which makes up 99% or more of the total volume of the mixture.

Combustion – an exothermic reaction between an oxidant and fuel with heat and often light.

Common ion effect – suppression of ionization of a weak electrolyte by the presence in the same solution of a strong electrolyte containing one of the same ions as the weak electrolyte.

Complex ions – ions resulting from the formation of coordinate covalent bonds between simple ions and other ions or molecules.

Composition stoichiometry – describes the quantitative (mass) relationships among elements in compounds.

Compound – a substance of two or more chemically bonded elements in fixed proportions; can be decomposed into their constituent elements.

Compressed gas – a gas or mixture of gases having (in a container) an absolute pressure exceeding 40 psi at 21.1 °C (70 °F).

Compression – an area in a longitudinal wave where the particles are closer and pushed in.

Concentration – amount of solute per unit volume, mass of solvent or solution.

Condensation – the phase change from gas to liquid.

Condensed phases – the liquid and solid phases; phases in which particles interact strongly.

Condensed states – the solid and liquid states.

Conduction band – a partially filled band or a band of vacant energy levels just higher in energy than a filled band; a band within which, or into which, electrons must be promoted to allow electrical conduction to occur in a solid.

Conductor – material that allows electric flow more freely.

Conjugate acid-base pair – in Brønsted-Lowry terminology, a reactant and a product that differ by a proton (H^+).

Conformations – structures of a compound that differ by the extent of their rotation about a single bond.

Continuous spectrum – spectrum that contains all wave-lengths in a specified region of the electromagnetic spectrum.

Control rods – rods of materials such as cadmium or boron steel that act as neutron absorbers (not merely moderators), used in nuclear reactors to control neutron fluxes and therefore rates of fission.

Conjugated double bonds – double bonds that are separated from each other by one single bond –C=C–C=C–.

Contact process – industrial process by which sulfur trioxide and sulfuric acid are produced from sulfur dioxide.

Coordinate covalent bond – a covalent bond in which both shared electrons are furnished by the same species; a bond between a Lewis acid and a Lewis base.

Coordination compound or complex – a compound containing coordinate covalent bonds.

Coordination number – the number of donor atoms coordinated to a metal; in describing crystals, the number of nearest neighbors of an atom or ion.

Coordination sphere – the metal ion and its coordinating ligands but not any uncoordinated counter-ions.

Corrosion – oxidation of metals in the presence of air and moisture.

Coulomb – the SI unit of electrical charge; unit symbol – c, 1 coulomb = 6.242×10^{18} electrons.

Covalent bond – chemical bond formed by the sharing of one or more electron pairs between two atoms.

Covalent compounds – compounds made of two or more nonmetal atoms that are bonded by sharing valence electrons.

Critical mass – the minimum mass of a particular fissionable nuclide in a given volume required to sustain a nuclear chain reaction.

Critical point – the combination of critical temperature and critical pressure of a substance.

Critical pressure – the pressure required to liquefy a gas (vapor) at its *critical temperature*.

Critical temperature – the temperature above which a gas cannot be liquefied; the temperature above which a substance cannot exhibit distinct gas and liquid phases.

Crystal – a solid that is packed with ions, molecules or atoms in an orderly lattice structure.

Crystal field stabilization energy – a measure of the net energy of stabilization gained by a metal ion's nonbonding d electrons as a result of complex formation.

Crystal field theory – theory of bonding in-transition metal complexes in which ligands and metal ions are treated as point charges; a purely ionic model; ligand point charges represent the crystal (electrical) field perturbing the metal's *d* orbitals containing nonbonding electrons.

Crystal lattice – a pattern of arrangement of particles in a crystal.

Crystal lattice energy – amount of energy that holds a crystal together; the energy change when a mole of solid is formed from its constituent molecules or ions (for ionic compounds) in their gaseous state (always negative).

Crystalline solid – a solid characterized by a regular, ordered arrangement of particles.

Curie (Ci) – the basic unit used to describe the intensity of radioactivity in a sample of material; one curie equals 37 billion disintegrations per second or approximately the amount of radioactivity given off by 1 gram of radium.

Cuvette – glassware used in spectroscopic experiments; usually made of plastic, glass or quartz and should be as clean and clear as possible.

Cyclotron – a device for accelerating charged particles along a spiral path.

D

Daughter nuclide – nuclide that is produced in a nuclear decay.

Debye (*D*)– the unit used to express dipole moments.

Degenerate – in orbitals, describes orbitals of the same energy.

Deionization – the removal of ions; in the case of water, mineral ions such as sodium, iron and calcium.

Deliquescence – substances that absorb water from the atmosphere to form liquid solutions.

Delocalization – in reference to electrons, bonding electrons that are distributed among more than two atoms that are bonded together; occurs in species that exhibit resonance.

Density (*φ*) – mass per unit volume; $\varphi = mV$.

Deposition – settling of particles within a solution or mixture; the direct solidification of a vapor by cooling; see *Sublimation*.

Derivative – a compound that can be imagined to arise from a parent compound by replacement of one atom with another atom or group of atoms; used extensively in organic chemistry to assist in identifying compounds.

Detergent – a soap-like emulsifier that contains a sulfate, SO_3, or a phosphate group instead of a carboxylate group.

Deuterium – an isotope of hydrogen whose atoms are twice as massive as ordinary hydrogen; deuterium atoms contain both a proton and a neutron in the nucleus.

Dextrorotatory – refers to an optically active substance that rotates the plane of plane polarized light clockwise; also known as "dextro" or (+).

Diagonal similarities – refers to chemical similarities in the Periodic Table of Elements of elements of Period 2 to elements of Period 3 one group to the right; especially evident toward the left of the periodic table.

Diamagnetism – weak repulsion by a magnetic field.

Differential Scanning Calorimetry (DSC) – a technique for measuring the temperature, direction and magnitude of thermal transitions in a sample material by heating/cooling and comparing the amount of energy required to maintain its rate of temperature increase or decrease with an inert reference material under similar conditions.

Differential Thermal Analysis (DTA) – a technique for observing the temperature, direction and magnitude of thermally induced transitions in a material by heating/cooling a sample and comparing its temperature with that of an inert reference material under similar conditions.

Differential thermometer – a thermometer used for accurate measurement of very small changes in temperature.

Dilution – process of reducing the concentration of a solute in a solution, usually simply by mixing it with more solvent.

Dimer – molecule formed by combination of two smaller (identical) molecules.

Dipole – electric or magnetic separation of charge; the separation of charge between two covalently bonded atoms.

Dipole-dipole interactions – attractive interactions between polar molecules (i.e., between molecules with permanent dipoles).

Dipole moment – the product of the distance separating opposite charges of equal magnitude of the charge; a measure of the polarity of a bond or molecule; a measured dipole moment refers to the dipole moment of an entire molecule.

Dispersing medium – the solvent-like phase in a colloid.

Dispersed phase – the solute-like species in a colloid.

Displacement reactions – reactions in which one element displaces another from a compound.

Disproportionation reactions – redox reactions in which the oxidizing agent and the reducing agent are the same species.

Dissociation – in an aqueous solution, the process by which a solid ionic compound separates into its ions.

Dissociation constant – equilibrium constant that applies to the dissociation of a complex ion into a simple ion and coordinating species (ligands).

Dissolution or solvation – the spread of ions in a monosaccharide.

Distilland – the material in a distillation apparatus that is to be distilled.

Distillate – the material in a distillation apparatus that is collected in the receiver.

Distillation – the separation of a liquid mixture into its components on the basis of differences in boiling points; the process in which components of a mixture are separated by boiling away the more volatile liquid.

Domain – a cluster of atoms in a ferromagnetic substance, which will all align in the same direction in the presence of an external magnetic field.

Donor atom – a ligand atom whose electrons are shared with a Lewis acid.

d **orbitals** – beginning in the third energy level, a set of five degenerate orbitals per energy level, higher in energy than *s* and *p* orbitals of the same energy level.

Dosimeter – a small, calibrated electroscope worn by laboratory personnel, designed to detect and measure incident ionizing radiation or chemical exposure.

Double bond – covalent bond resulting from the sharing of four electrons (two pairs) between two atoms.

Double salt – solid consisting of two co-crystallized salts.

Doublet – two peaks or bands of about equal intensity appearing close together on a spectrogram.

Downs cell – electrolytic cell for the commercial electrolysis of molten sodium chloride.

DP number – the degree of polymerization; the average number of monomer units per polymer unit.

Dry cells – ordinary batteries (voltaic cells) for flashlights, radios, etc.

Dumas method – a method used to determine the molecular weights of volatile liquids.

Dynamic equilibrium – an equilibrium in which the processes occur continuously with no net change.

E

Earth metal – highly reactive elements in group IIA of the periodic table (includes beryllium, magnesium, calcium, strontium, barium and radium); see *Alkaline earth metal*.

Effective collisions – collision between molecules resulting in a reaction; one in which the molecules collide with proper relative orientations and sufficient energy to react.

Effective molality – the sum of the molalities of all solute particles in a solution.

Effective nuclear charge – the nuclear charge experienced by the outermost electrons of an atom; the actual nuclear charge minus the effects of shielding due to inner-shell electrons (e.g., a set of dx_2-y_2 and dz_2 orbitals); those d orbitals within a set with lobes directed along the x, y and z axes.

Electrical conductivity – the measure of how easily an electric current can flow through a substance.

Electric charge – a measured property (coulombs) that determines electromagnetic interaction.

Electrochemical cell – using a chemical reaction's current; electromotive force is made.

Electrochemistry – study of chemical changes produced by electrical current and the production of electricity by chemical reactions.

Electrodes – surfaces upon which oxidation and reduction half-reactions occur in electrochemical cells.

Electrode potentials – potentials, E, of half-reactions as reductions versus the standard hydrogen electrode.

Electrolysis – process that occurs in electrolytic cells; chemical decomposition that occurs by the passing of an electric current through a solution containing ions.

Electrolyte – a solution that conducts a certain amount of current and can be split categorically as weak and strong electrolytes.

Electrolytic cells – electrochemical cells in which electrical energy causes nonspontaneous redox reactions to occur (i.e., forced to occur by the application of an outside source of electrical energy).

Electrolytic conduction – conduction of electrical current by ions through a solution or pure liquid.

Electromagnetic radiation – energy that is propagated by means of electric and magnetic fields that oscillate in directions perpendicular to the direction of travel of the energy; a type of wave that can go through vacuums as well as material; classified as a "self-propagating wave."

Electromagnetism – fields that have electric charge and electric properties that change the way that particles move and interact.

Electromotive force – a device that gains energy as electric charges are passed through it.

Electromotive series – the relative order of tendencies for elements and their simple ions to act as oxidizing or reducing agents; also known as the "activity series."

Electron – a subatomic particle having a mass of 0.00054858 amu and a charge of –1.

Electron affinity – the amount of energy absorbed in the process in which an electron is added to a neutral isolated gaseous atom to form a gaseous ion with a 1– charge; has a negative value if energy is released.

Electron configuration – the specific distribution of electrons in atomic orbitals of atoms or ions.

Electron-deficient compounds – compounds that contain at least one atom (other than H) that shares fewer than eight electrons.

Electron shells – an orbital around the atom's nucleus that has a fixed number of electrons (usually two or eight).

Electronic transition – the transfer of an electron from one energy level to another.

Electronegativity – a measure of the relative tendency of an atom to attract electrons to itself when chemically combined with another atom.

Electronic geometry – the geometric arrangement of orbitals containing the shared and unshared electron pairs surrounding the central atom of a molecule or polyatomic ion.

Electrophile – positively charged or electron-deficient.

Electrophoresis – a technique for the separation of ions by their rate of migration and direction of migration in an electric field.

Electroplating – plating a metal onto a (cathodic) surface by electrolysis.

Element – a substance that cannot be decomposed into simpler substances by chemical means; defined by its *Atomic number*.

Eluant or eluent – the solvent used in the process of elution, as in liquid chromatography.

Eluate – a solvent (or mobile phase) which passes through a chromatographic column and removes the sample components from the stationary phase.

Emission spectrum – spectrum associated with emission of electromagnetic radiation by atoms (or other species) resulting from electronic transitions from higher to lower energy states.

Empirical formula – gives the simplest whole-number ratio of atoms of each element present in a compound; also known as the simplest formula.

Emulsifying agent – a substance that coats the particles of the dispersed phase and prevents coagulation of colloidal particles; an emulsifier.

Emulsion – colloidal suspension of a liquid in a liquid.

Endergonic (+ΔG) – energy is absorbed by the system: nonspontaneous. Products have more energy than reactants.

Endothermic (+ΔH) – describes processes that absorb heat energy (+ΔH).

Endothermicity – the absorption of heat by a system as the process occurs.

End point – the point at which an indicator changes color and a titration is stopped.

Energy – a system's ability to do work.

Enthalpy (H) – the heat content of a specific amount of substance; E= PV.

Entropy (S) – a thermodynamic state or property that measures the degree of disorder or randomness of a system; the amount of energy not available for work in a closed thermodynamic system.

Enzyme – a protein that acts as a catalyst in biological systems.

Equation of state – an equation that describes the behavior of matter in a given state; the van der Waals equation describes the behavior of the gaseous state.

Equilibrium or chemical equilibrium – a state of dynamic balance in which the rates of forward and reverse reactions are equal; the state of a system when neither forward or reverse reaction is thermodynamically favored.

Equilibrium constant (K) – a quantity that characterizes the position of equilibrium for a reversible reaction; its magnitude is equal to the mass action expression at equilibrium; equilibrium K varies with temperature.

Equivalence point – the point at which chemically equivalent amounts of reactants have reacted.

Equivalent weight – an oxidizing or reducing agent whose mass gains (oxidizing agents) or loses (reducing agents) 6.022×10^{23} electrons in a redox reaction.

Evaporation – vaporization of a liquid below its boiling point.

Evaporation rate – the rate at which a particular substance will vaporize (evaporate) when compared to the rate of a known substance such as ethyl ether; especially useful for health and fire-hazard considerations.

Excited state – any state other than the ground state of an atom or molecule; see *Ground state*.

Exergonic (−ΔG) – a positive flow of energy from the system to surroundings: spontaneous. Products have less energy than reactants.

Exothermic – describes processes that release heat energy.

Exothermicity – the release of heat by a system as a process occurs.

Explosive – a chemical or compound that causes a sudden, almost instantaneous release of pressure, gas, heat and light when subjected to sudden shock, pressure, high temperature or applied potential.

Explosive limits – the range of concentrations over which a flammable vapor mixed with the proper ratios of air will ignite or explode if a source of ignition is provided.

Extensive property – a property that depends upon the amount of material in a sample.

Extrapolate – to estimate the value of a result outside the range of a series of known values; a technique used in standard additions calibration procedure.

F

Faraday constant (*F*) – a unit of electrical charge widely used in electrochemistry and equal to ~ 96,500 coulombs; represents 1 mol of electrons, or the Avogadro number of electrons: 6.022×10^{23} electrons.

Faraday's law of electrolysis – a two-part law that Michael Faraday published about electrolysis: (a) the mass of a substance altered at an electrode during electrolysis is directly proportional to the quantity of electricity transferred at that electrode; (b) the mass of an elemental material altered at an electrode is directly proportional to the element's equivalent weight; one equivalent weight of a substance is produced at each electrode during the passage of 96,487 coulombs of charge through an electrolytic cell.

Fast neutron – a neutron ejected at high kinetic energy in a nuclear reaction.

Ferromagnetism – the ability of a substance to become permanently magnetized by exposure to an external magnetic field.

Flash point – the temperature at which a liquid will yield enough flammable vapor to ignite; there are various recognized industrial testing methods, therefore the method used must be stated.

Fluorescence – absorption of high energy radiation by a substance and subsequent emission of visible light.

First law of thermodynamics – the total amount of energy in the universe is constant (i.e., energy is neither created nor destroyed in ordinary chemical reactions and physical changes); also known as the Law of Conservation of Energy.

Fluids – substances that flow freely; gases and liquids.

Flux – a substance added to react with the charge, or a product of its reduction; in metallurgy, usually added to lower a melting point.

Foam – colloidal suspension of a gas in a liquid.

Formal charge – a method of counting electrons in a covalently bonded molecule or ion; it counts bonding electrons as though they were equally shared between the two atoms.

Formula – combination of symbols that indicates the chemical composition of a substance.

Formula unit – the smallest repeating unit of a substance; the molecule for nonionic substances.

Formula weight – the mass of one formula unit of a substance in atomic mass units.

Fractional distillation – the process in which a fractioning column is used in a distillation apparatus to separate the components of a liquid mixture that have different boiling points.

Fractional precipitation – removal of some ions from a solution by precipitation while leaving other ions with similar properties in the solution.

Free energy change – the indicator of spontaneity of a process at constant temperature (T) and pressure (P); e.g., if ΔG is negative, the process is spontaneous.

Free radical – a highly reactive chemical species carrying no charge and having a single unpaired electron in an orbital.

Freezing – phase transition from liquid to solid.

Freezing point depression – the decrease in the freezing point of a solvent caused by the presence of a solute.

Frequency – the number of repeating corresponding points on a wave that pass a given observation point per unit time; the unit is 1 hertz = 1 cycle per 1 second.

Fuel cells – a voltaic cell that converts the chemical energy of a fuel and an oxidizing agent directly into electrical energy on a continuous basis.

G

Gamma (γ) ray – a highly penetrating type of nuclear radiation similar to x-ray radiation, except that it comes from within the nucleus of an atom and has a higher energy; energy-wise, very similar to cosmic rays except that cosmic rays originate from outer space.

Galvanic cell – battery made up of electrochemical with two different metals connected by a salt bridge.

Galvanizing – placing a thin layer of zinc on a ferrous material to protect the underlying surface from corrosion.

Gangue – sand, rock and other impurities surrounding the mineral of interest in an ore.

Gas – a state of matter in which the particles have no definite shape or volume, though they do fill their container.

Gay-Lussac's law – the expression Gay-Lussac's law is used for each of the two relationships named after the French chemist Joseph Louis Gay-Lussac and which concern the properties of gases; more usually applied to his law of combining volumes.

Geiger counter – a gas filled tube which discharges electrically when ionizing radiation passes through it.

Gel – colloidal suspension of a solid dispersed in a liquid; a semi-rigid solid.

Gibbs (free) energy (ΔG) – the thermodynamic state function of a system that indicates the amount of energy available for the system to do useful work at constant temperature (T) and pressure (P); value that indicates the spontaneity of a reaction.

Graham's law – the rates of effusion of gases are inversely proportional to the square roots of their molecular weights or densities.

Ground state – the lowest energy state or most stable state of an atom, molecule or ion; see *Excited state*.

Group – a vertical column in the periodic table; also known as a family.

H

Haber process – a process for the catalyzed industrial production of ammonia from N_2 and H_2 at high temperature and pressure.

Half-cell – the compartment in which the oxidation or reduction half-reaction occurs in a voltaic cell.

Half-life – the time required for half of a reactant to be converted into product(s); the time required for half of a given sample to undergo radioactive decay.

Half-reaction – either the oxidation part or the reduction part of a redox reaction.

Halogens – group VIIA elements: F, Cl, Br, I; all halogens are non-metals.

Heat – a form of energy that flows between two samples of matter because of their differences in temperature.

Heat capacity – the amount of heat required to raise the temperature of a body (of any mass) one degree Celsius (1 °C).

Heat of condensation – the amount of heat that must be removed from one gram of a vapor at its condensation point to condense the vapor with no change in temperature.

Heat of crystallization – the amount of heat that must be removed from one gram of a liquid at its freezing point to freeze it with no change in temperature.

Heat of fusion – the amount of heat required to melt one gram of a solid at its melting point with no change in temperature; usually expressed in J/g; the molar heat of fusion is the amount of heat required to melt one mole of a solid at its melting point with no change in temperature and is usually expressed in kJ/mol.

Heat of solution – the amount of heat absorbed in the formation of a solution that contains one mole of solute; the value is positive if heat is absorbed (endothermic) and negative if heat is released (exothermic).

Heat of vaporization – the amount of heat required to vaporize one gram of a liquid at its boiling point with no change in temperature; usually expressed in J/g; the molar heat of vaporization is the amount of heat required to vaporize one mole of liquid at its boiling point with no change in temperature and is usually expressed as ion kJ/mol.

Heisenberg uncertainty principle – states that it is impossible to accurately determine both the momentum (p) and the position (x) of an electron simultaneously.

Henry's law – the pressure of the gas above a solution is proportional to the concentration of the gas in the solution.

Hess' law of heat summation – the enthalpy change for a reaction is the same whether it occurs in one step or a series of steps.

Heterogeneous catalyst – a catalyst that exists in a different phase (solid, liquid or gas) from the reactants; a contact catalyst.

Heterogeneous equilibria – equilibria involving species in more than one phase.

Heterogeneous mixture – a mixture that does not have uniform composition and properties throughout.

Heteronuclear – consisting of different elements.

High spin complex – crystal field designation for an outer orbital complex; all t_{2g} and e_g orbitals are singly occupied before any pairing occurs.

Homogeneous catalyst – a catalyst that exists in the same phase (solid, liquid or gas) as the reactants.

Homogeneous equilibria – when all *Reagents* and products are of the same phase (i.e., all gases, all liquids or all solids).

Homogeneous mixture – a mixture which has uniform composition and properties throughout.

Homologous series – a series of compounds in which each member differs from the next by a specific number and kind of atoms.

Homonuclear – consisting of only one element.

Hund's rule – all orbitals of a given sublevel must be occupied by single electrons before pairing begins; see *Aufbau ("building up") principle*.

Hybridization – mixing a set of atomic orbitals to form a new set of atomic orbitals with the same total electron capacity and with properties and energies intermediate between those of the original unhybridized orbitals.

Hydrate – a solid compound that contains a definite percentage of bound water.

Hydrate isomers – isomers of crystalline complexes that differ in whether water is present inside or outside the coordination sphere.

Hydration – reaction of a substance with water.

Hydration energy – the energy change accompanying the hydration of a mole of gas and ions.

Hydride – a binary compound of hydrogen.

Hydrocarbons – compounds that contain only carbon and hydrogen (e.g., methane or octane).

Hydrogen bond – a fairly strong dipole-dipole interaction (but still considerably weaker than the covalent or ionic bonds) between molecules containing hydrogen directly bonded to a small, highly electronegative atom, such as N, O or F.

Hydrogenation – the reaction in which hydrogen adds across a double or triple bond.

Hydrogen-oxygen fuel cell – a fuel cell in which hydrogen is the fuel (reducing agent) and oxygen is the oxidizing agent.

Hydrolysis – the reaction of a substance with water or its ions.

Hydrolysis constant – an equilibrium constant for a hydrolysis reaction.

Hydrometer – a device used to measure the densities of liquids and solutions.

Hydrophilic colloids – colloidal particles that repel water molecules.

I

Ideal gas – a hypothetical gas that obeys exactly all postulates of the kinetic-molecular theory.

Ideal gas law – the product of pressure and the volume of an ideal gas is directly proportional to the number of moles of the gas and the absolute temperature ($PV = nRT$).

Ideal solution – a solution that obeys Raoult's Law exactly.

Indicators – for acid-base titrations, organic compounds that exhibit different colors in solutions of different acidities; used to determine the point at which reaction between two solutes is complete.

Inert pair effect – characteristic of the post-transition minerals; tendency of the electrons in the outermost atomic *s* orbital to remain un-ionized or unshared in compounds of post-transition metals.

Inhibitory catalyst – an inhibitor; a catalyst that decreases the rate of reaction.

Inner orbital complex – valence bond designation for a complex in which the metal ion utilizes *d* orbitals for one shell inside the outermost occupied shell in its hybridization.

Inorganic chemistry – a part of chemistry concerned with inorganic (non carbon-based) compounds.

Insulator – a material that resists the flow of electric current or transfer of heat.

Insoluble compound – a substance that will not dissolve in a solvent, even after mixing.

Integrated rate equation – an equation giving the concentration of a reactant remaining after a specified time; has different mathematical form for different orders of reactants.

Intermolecular forces – forces between individual particles (atoms, molecules, ions) of a substance.

Ion – a molecule that has gained or lost one or more electrons; an atom or a group of atoms that carries an electric charge.

Ion product for water – equilibrium constant for the ionization of water; $K_w = [H_3O^+] \cdot [OH^-] = 1.00 \times 10^{-14}$ at 25 °C.

Ionic bond – electrostatic attraction between oppositely charged ions.

Ionic bonding – chemical bonding resulting from the transfer of one or more electrons from one atom or group of atoms to another.

Ionic compounds – compounds containing predominantly ionic bonding.

Ionic geometry – the arrangement of atoms (not lone pairs of electrons) about the central atom of a polyatomic ion.

Ionization – the breaking up of a compound into separate ions; in aqueous solution, the process by which a molecular compound reacts with water and forms ions.

Ionization constant – equilibrium constant for the ionization of a weak electrolyte.

Ionization energy – the minimum amount of energy required to remove the most loosely held electron of an isolated gaseous atom or ion.

Ionization isomers – isomers that result from the interchange of ions inside and outside the coordination sphere.

Isoelectric – having the same electronic configurations.

Isomers – different substances that have the same molecular formula.

Isomorphous – refers to crystals having the same atomic arrangement.

Isotopes – two or more forms of atoms of the same element with different masses; atoms containing the same number of protons but different numbers of neutrons.

IUPAC – acronym for "International Union of Pure and Applied Chemistry."

J

Joule – a unit of energy in the SI system; one joule is $1 \text{ kg·m}^2/\text{s}^2$, which is also 0.2390 calorie.

K

K capture – absorption of a K shell (n = 1) electron by a proton as it is converted to a neutron.

Kelvin (K) – a unit of measure for temperature based upon an absolute scale.

Kinetics – a sub-field of chemistry specializing in reaction rates.

Kinetic energy (*KE*) – energy that matter processes by virtue of its motion.

Kinetic-molecular theory – a theory that attempts to explain macroscopic observations on gases in microscopic or molecular terms.

L

Lanthanides – elements 57 (lanthanum) through 71 (lutetium); grouped together because of their similar behavior in chemical reactions.

Lanthanide contraction – a decrease in the radii of the elements following the lanthanides compared to what would be expected if there were no f-transition metals.

Lattice – unique arrangement of atoms or molecules in a crystalline liquid or solid.

Law of combining volumes (Gay-Lussac's law) – at constant temperature and pressure, the volumes of reacting gases (and any gaseous products) can be expressed as ratios of small whole numbers.

Law of conservation of energy – energy cannot be created or destroyed, it can only be changed from one form to another.

Law of conservation of matter – there is no detectable change in the quantity of matter during an ordinary chemical reaction.

Law of conservation of matter and energy – the total amount of matter and energy available in the universe is fixed.

Law of definite proportions (law of constant composition) – different samples of a pure compound will always contain the same elements in the same proportions by mass.

Law of partial pressures (Dalton's law) – the total pressure exerted by a mixture of gases is the sum of the partial pressures of the individual gases.

Laws of thermodynamics – physical laws which define quantities of thermodynamic systems, describe how they behave and (by extension) set certain limitations such as perpetual motion.

Lead storage battery – secondary voltaic cell used in most automobiles.

Leclanche cell – a common type of *Dry cell*.

Le Châtelier's principle – states that a system at equilibrium, or striving to attain equilibrium, responds in such a way as to counteract any stress placed upon it; if a stress (change of conditions) is applied to a system at equilibrium, the system will shift in the direction that reduces stress.

Leveling effect – effect by which all acids stronger than the acid that is characteristic of the solvent react with the solvent to produce that acid; a similar statement applies to bases. The strongest acid (base) that can exist in a given solvent is the acid (base) characteristic of the solvent.

Levorotatory – refers to an optically active substance that rotates the plane of plane polarized light counterclockwise; also known as a "levo" or (−).

Lewis acid – any species that can accept a share in an electron pair.

Lewis base – any species that can make available a share in an electron pair.

Lewis dot formula (electron dot formula) – representation of a molecule, ion or formula unit by showing atomic symbols and only outer shell electrons.

Ligand – a Lewis base in a coordination compound.

Light – that portion of the electromagnetic spectrum visible to the naked eye; also known as "visible light."

Limiting reactant – substance that stoichiometrically limits the amount of product(s) that can be formed.

Linear accelerator – a device used for accelerating charged particles along a straight line path.

Line spectrum – an atomic emission or absorption spectrum.

Linkage isomers – isomers in which a particular ligand bonds to a metal ion through different donor atoms.

Liquid – a state of matter which takes the shape of its container.

Liquid aerosol – colloidal suspension of liquid in gas.

London dispersion forces – very weak and very short-range attractive forces between short-lived temporary (induced) dipoles; also known as "dispersion forces."

Lone pair – pair of electrons residing on one atom and not shared by other atoms; unshared pair.

Low spin complex – crystal field designation for an inner orbital complex; contains electrons paired t_{2g} orbitals before e_g orbitals are occupied in octahedral complexes.

M

Magnetic quantum number (mc) – quantum mechanical solution to a wave equation that designates the particular orbital within a given set (s, p, d, f) in which an electron resides.

Manometer – a two-armed barometer.

Mass – a measure of the amount of matter in an object; mass is usually measured in grams or kilograms.

Mass action expression – for a reversible reaction, aA + bB cC + dD; the product of the concentrations of the products (species on the right), each raised to the power that corresponds to its coefficient in the balanced chemical equation, divided by the product of the concentrations of reactants (species on the left), each raised to the power that corresponds to its coefficient in the balanced chemical equation; at equilibrium the mass action expression equals K.

Mass deficiency – the amount of matter that would be converted into energy if an atom were formed from constituent particles.

Mass number (*A*) – the sum of the numbers of protons and neutrons in an atom; always an integer.

Mass spectrometer – an instrument that measures the charge-to-mass ratio of charged particles.

Matter – anything that has mass and occupies space.

Mechanism – the sequence of steps by which reactants are converted into products.

Melting point – the temperature at which liquid and solid coexist in equilibrium.

Meniscus – the shape assumed by the surface of a liquid in a cylindrical container.

Melting – the phase change from a solid to a liquid.

Metal – a chemical element that is a good conductor of both electricity and heat and forms cations and ionic bonds with non-metals; elements below and to the left of the stepwise division (metalloids) in the upper right corner of the periodic table; about 80% of known elements are metals.

Metallic bonding – bonding within metals due to the electrical attraction of positively charged metal ions for mobile electrons that belong to the crystal as a whole.

Metallic conduction – conduction of electrical current through a metal or along a metallic surface.

Metalloid – a substance possessing both the properties of metals and non-metals (B, Al, Si, Ge, As, Sb, Te, Po and At).

Metathesis reactions – reactions in which two compounds react to form two new compounds, with no changes in oxidation number; reactions in which the ions of two compounds exchange partners.

Method of initial rates – method of determining the rate-law expression by carrying out a reaction with different initial concentrations and analyzing the resultant changes in initial rates.

Methylene blue – a heterocyclic aromatic chemical compound with the molecular formula $C_{16}H_{18}N_3SCl$.

Miscibility – the ability of one liquid to mix with (dissolve in) another liquid.

Mixture – a sample of matter composed of two or more substances, each of which retains its identity and properties.

Moderator – a substance, such as hydrogen, deuterium, oxygen or paraffin, capable of slowing fast neutrons upon collision.

Molality (m) – a concentration expressed as number of moles of solute per kilogram of solvent.

Molarity (*M*) – the number of moles of solute per liter of solution.

Molar solubility – the number of moles of a solute that dissolve to produce a liter of saturated solution.

Mole – a measurement of an amount of substance; a single mole contains approximately 6.022×10^{23} units or entities; abbreviated mol.

Molecule – a chemically bonded number of atoms that are electrically neutral.

Molecular equation – equation for a chemical reaction in which all formulas are written as if all substances existed as molecules; only complete formulas are used.

Molecular formula – formula that indicates the actual number of atoms present in a molecule of a molecular substance.

Molecular geometry – the arrangement of atoms (not lone pairs of electrons) around a central atom of a molecule or polyatomic ion.

Molecular orbital (mo) – an orbit resulting from the overlap and mixing of atomic orbitals on different atoms (i.e., a region where an electron can be found in a molecule, as opposed to an atom); an MO belongs to the molecule as a whole.

Molecular orbital theory – a theory of chemical bonding based upon the postulated existence of molecular orbitals.

Molecular weight – the mass of one molecule of a nonionic substance in atomic mass units.

Molecule – the smallest particle of a compound capable of a stable, independent existence.

Mole fraction (X) – the number of moles of a component of a mixture divided by the total number of moles in the mixture.

Monoprotic acid – acid that can form only one hydronium ion per molecule; may be strong or weak.

Mother nuclide – nuclide that undergoes nuclear decay.

N

Native state – refers to the occurrence of an element in an uncombined or free state in nature.

Natural radioactivity – spontaneous decomposition of an atom.

Neat – conditions with a liquid reagent or gas performed with no added solvent or co-solvent.

Nernst equation – corrects standard electrode potentials for nonstandard conditions.

Net ionic equation – equation that results from canceling spectator ions and eliminating brackets from a total ionic equation.

Neutralization – the reaction of an acid with a base to form a salt and water; usually, the reaction of hydrogen ions with hydrogen ions to form water molecules.

Neutrino – a particle that can travel at speeds close to the speed of light; created as a result of radioactive decay.

Neutron – a neutral unit or subatomic particle that has no net charge and a mass of 1.0087 amu.

Nickel-cadmium cell (NiCd battery) – a dry cell in which the anode is Cd, the cathode is NiO2 and the electrolyte is basic.

Nitrogen cycle – the complex series of reactions by which nitrogen is slowly but continually recycled in the atmosphere, lithosphere and hydrosphere.

Noble gases – elements of the periodic Group 0; He, Ne, Ar, Kr, Xe, Rn; also known as "rare gases;" formerly called "inert gases."

Nodal plane – a region in which the probability of finding an electron is zero.

Nonbonding orbital – a molecular orbital derived only from an atomic orbital of one atom; lends neither stability nor instability to a molecule or ion when populated with electrons.

Nonelectrolyte – a substance whose aqueous solutions do not conduct electricity.

Non-metal – an element which is not metallic.

Nonpolar bond – a covalent bond in which electron density is symmetrically distributed.

Nuclear – of or pertaining to the atomic nucleus.

Nuclear binding energy – energy equivalent of the mass deficiency; energy released in the formation of an atom from the subatomic particles.

Nuclear fission – the process in which a heavy nucleus splits into nuclei of intermediate masses and one or more protons are emitted.

Nuclear magnetic resonance spectroscopy – technique that exploits the magnetic properties of certain nuclei; useful for identifying unknown compounds.

Nuclear reaction – involves a change in the composition of a nucleus and can emit or absorb an extraordinarily large amount of energy.

Nuclear reactor – a system in which controlled nuclear fission reactions generate heat energy on a large scale which is subsequently converted into electrical energy.

Nucleons – particles comprising the nucleus; protons and neutrons.

Nucleus – the very small and dense, positively charged center of an atom containing protons and neutrons, as well as other subatomic particles; the net charge is positive.

Nuclides – refers to different atomic forms of all elements; in contrast to isotopes, which refer only to different atomic forms of a single element.

Nuclide symbol – symbol for an atom A/Z E, in which E is the symbol of an element, Z is its atomic number and A is its mass number.

Number density – a measure of concentration of countable objects (e.g., atoms, molecules, etc.) in a space; the number per volume.

O

Octahedral – a term used to describe molecules and polyatomic ions that have one atom in the center and six atoms at the corners of an octahedron.

Octane number – a number that indicates how smoothly a gasoline burns.

Octet rule – many representative elements attain at least a share of eight electrons in their valence shells when they form molecular or ionic compounds; there are some limitations.

Open sextet – refers to species that have only six electrons in the highest energy level of the central element (many Lewis acids).

Orbital – may refer to either an atomic orbital or a molecular orbital.

Organic chemistry – the chemistry of substances that contain carbon-hydrogen bonds.

Organic compound – compounds that contain carbon.

Osmosis – the process by which solvent molecules pass through a semi-permeable membrane from a dilute solution into a more concentrated solution.

Osmotic pressure – the hydrostatic pressure produced on the surface of a semi-permeable membrane by osmosis.

Outer orbital complex – valence bond designation for a complex in which the metal ion utilizes d orbitals in the outermost (occupied) shell in hybridization.

Overlap – the interaction of orbitals on different atoms in the same region of space.

Oxidation – an algebraic increase in the oxidation number; may correspond to a loss of electrons.

Oxidation numbers – arbitrary numbers that can be used as mechanical aids in writing formulas and balancing equations; for single-atom ions they correspond to the charge on the ion; more electronegative atoms are assigned negative oxidation numbers; also known as "oxidation states."

Oxidation-reduction reactions – reactions in which oxidation and reduction occur; also known as "redox reactions."

Oxide – a binary compound of oxygen.

Oxidizing agent – the substance that oxidizes another substance and is reduced.

P

Pairing – a favorable interaction of two electrons with opposite m values in the same orbital.

Pairing energy – energy required to pair two electrons in the same orbital.

Paramagnetism – attraction toward a magnetic field, stronger than diamagnetism but still weak compared to ferromagnetism.

Partial pressure – the pressure exerted by one gas in a mixture of gases.

Particulate matter – fine, divided solid particles suspended in polluted air.

Pauli exclusion principle – no two electrons in the same atom may have identical sets of four quantum numbers.

Percentage ionization – the percentage of the weak electrolyte that will ionize in a solution of given concentration.

Percent by mass – 100% times the actual yield divided by the theoretical yield.

Percent composition – the mass percent of each element in a compound.

Percent purity – the percent of a specified compound or element in an impure sample.

Period – the elements in a horizontal row of the periodic table.

Periodicity – regular periodic variations of properties of elements with their atomic number (and position in the periodic table).

Periodic law – the properties of the elements are periodic functions of their atomic numbers.

Periodic table – an arrangement of elements in order of increasing atomic numbers that also emphasizes periodicity.

Peroxide – a compound containing oxygen in the –1 oxidation state; metal peroxides contain the peroxide ion, O_2^{2-}.

pH – the measure of acidity (or basicity) of a solution; negative logarithm of the concentration (mol/L) of the H_3O^+ [H^+] ion; scale is commonly used over a range 0 to 14, $pH = -\log[H^+]$.

Phase diagram – diagram that shows equilibrium temperature-pressure relationships for different phases of a substance.

Photoelectric effect – emission of an electron from the surface of a metal caused by impinging electromagnetic radiation of a certain minimum energy; the current increases with increasing intensity of radiation.

Photon – a carrier of electromagnetic radiation of all wavelengths, such as gamma rays and radio waves; also known as "quantum of light."

Physical change – in which a substance changes from one physical state to another, but no substances with different composition are formed; physical change may involve a phase change (e.g., melting, freezing etc.) or other physical change such as crushing a crystal or separating one volume of liquid into different containers; never produces a new substance.

Plasma – a physical state of matter which exists at extremely high temperatures in which all molecules are dissociated and most atoms are ionized.

Polar bond – a covalent bond in which there is an unsymmetrical distribution of electron density.

Polarimeter – a device used to measure optical activity.

Polarization – the buildup of a product of oxidation of or a reduction of an electrode, preventing further reaction.

Polydentate – refers to ligands with more than one donor atom.

Polyene – a compound that contains more than one double bond per molecule.

Polymerization – the combination of many small molecules to form large molecules.

Polymer – a large molecule consisting of chains or rings of linked monomer units, usually characterized by high melting and boiling points.

Polymorphous – refers to substances that can crystallize in more than one crystalline arrangement.

Polyprotic acid – an acid that can form two or more hydronium ions per molecule; often at least one step of ionization is weak.

Positron – a nuclear particle with the mass of an electron but opposite charge (positive).

Potential energy – energy stored in a body or in a system due to its position in a force field or due to its configuration.

Precipitate – an insoluble solid formed by mixing in solution the constituent ions of a slightly soluble solution.

Precision – how close the results of multiple experimental trials are; see *Accuracy*.

Primary standard – a substance of a known high degree of purity that undergoes one invariable reaction with the other reactant of interest.

Primary voltaic cells – voltaic cells that cannot be recharged; no further chemical reaction is possible once the reactants are consumed.

Proton – a subatomic particle having a mass of 1.0073 amu and a charge of +1, found in the nuclei of atoms.

Protonation – the addition of a proton (H^+) to an atom, molecule or ion.

Pseudobinaryionic compounds – compounds that contain more than two elements but are named like binary compounds.

Q

Quanta – the minimum amount of energy emitted by a radiation.

Quantum mechanics – the study of how atoms, molecules, subatomic particles, etc. behave and are structured; a mathematical method of treating particles on the basis of quantum theory, which assumes that energy (of small particles) is not infinitely divisible.

Quantum numbers – numbers that describe the energies of electrons in atoms; derived from quantum mechanical treatment.

Quarks – elementary particle and a fundamental constituent of matter; they combine to form hadrons (protons and neutrons).

R

Radiation – high energy particles or rays emitted during the nuclear decay processes.

Radical – an atom or group of atoms that contains one or more unpaired electrons; usually a very reactive species.

Radioactive dating – method of dating ancient objects by determining the ratio of amounts of mother and daughter nuclides present in an object and relating the ratio to the object's age via half-life calculations.

Radioactive tracer – a small amount of radioisotope replacing a nonradioactive isotope of the element in a compound whose path (e.g., in the body) or whose decomposition products are to be monitored by detection of radioactivity; also known as a "radioactive label."

Radioactivity – the spontaneous disintegration of atomic nuclei.

Raoult's law – the vapor pressure of a solvent in an ideal solution decreases as its mole fraction decreases.

Rate-determining step – the slowest step in a mechanism; the step that determines the overall rate of reaction.

Rate-law expression – equation relating the rate of a reaction to the concentrations of the reactants and the specific rate of the constant.

Rate of reaction – the change in the concentration of a reactant or product per unit time.

Reactants – substances consumed in a chemical reaction.

Reaction quotient – the mass action expression under any set of conditions (not necessarily equilibrium); its magnitude relative to K determines the direction in which the reaction must occur to establish equilibrium.

Reaction ratio – the relative amounts of reactants and products involved in a reaction; may be the ratio of moles, millimoles or masses.

Reaction stoichiometry – description of the quantitative relationships among substances as they participate in chemical reactions.

Reactivity series (or activity series) – an empirical, calculated and structurally analytical progression of a series of metals, arranged by their "reactivity" from highest to lowest; used to summarize information about the reactions of metals with acids and water, double displacement reactions and the extraction of metals from their ores.

Reagent – a substance or compound added to a system to cause a chemical reaction or to see if a reaction occurs; the terms reactant and reagent are often used interchangeably, however, a reactant is more specifically a substance consumed in the course of a chemical reaction.

Reducing agent – a substance that reduces another substance and is itself oxidized.

Resonance – the concept in which two or more equivalent dot formulas for the same arrangement of atoms (resonance structures) are necessary to describe the bonding in a molecule or ion.

Reverse osmosis – forcing solvent molecules to flow through a semi-permeable membrane from a concentrated solution into a dilute solution by the application of greater hydrostatic pressure on the concentrated side than the osmotic pressure opposing it.

Reversible reaction – reactions that do not go to completion and occur in both the forward and reverse direction.

S

Saline solution – general term for NaCl in water.

Salts – ionic compounds composed of anions and cations.

Salt bridge – a U-shaped tube containing electrolyte, which connects the two half-cells of a voltaic cell.

Saturated solution – solution in which no more solute will dissolve.

***s*-block elements** – group 1 and 2 elements (alkali and alkaline metals), which includes Hydrogen and Helium.

Schrödinger equation – quantum state equation which represents the behavior of an election around an atom; describes the wave function of a physical system evolving over time.

Second law of thermodynamics – the universe tends toward a state of greater disorder in spontaneous processes.

Secondary standard – a solution that has been titrated against a primary standard; a standard solution.

Secondary voltaic cells – voltaic cells that can be recharged; original reactants can be regenerated by reversing the direction of the current flow.

Semiconductor – a substance that does not conduct electricity at low temperatures but will do so at higher temperatures.

Semi-permeable membrane – a thin partition between two solutions through which certain molecules can pass but others cannot.

Shielding effect – electrons in filled sets of *s, p* orbitals between the nucleus and outer shell electrons shield the outer shell electrons somewhat from the effect of protons in the nucleus; also known as the "screening effect."

Sigma (σ) bonds – bonds resulting from the head-on overlap of atomic orbitals, in which the region of electron sharing is along and (cylindrically) symmetrical to the intermolecular axis connecting the bonded atoms.

Sigma orbital – molecular orbital resulting from head-on overlap of two atomic orbitals.

Single bond – covalent bond resulting from the sharing of two electrons (one pair) between two atoms.

Sol – a suspension of solid particles in liquid; artificial examples include sol-gels.

Solid – one of the states of matter, where the molecules are packed close together and there is a resistance to movement/deformation and volume change.

Solubility product constant (K_{sp}) – equilibrium constant that applies to the dissolution of a slightly soluble compound.

Solubility product principle – the solubility product constant expression for a slightly soluble compound is the product of the concentrations of the constituent ions, each raised to the power that corresponds to the number of ions in one formula unit.

Solute – the dispersed (dissolved) phase of a solution; the part of the solution that is mixed into the solvent (e.g., NaCl in saline water).

Solution – a homogeneous mixture made up of multiple substances; made up of solutes and solvents.

Solvation – the process by which solvent molecules surround and interact with solute ions or molecules.

Solvent – the dispersing medium of a solution (e.g., H_2O in saline water).

Solvolysis – the reaction of a substance with the solvent in which it is dissolved.

***s* orbital** – a spherically symmetrical atomic orbital; one per energy level.

Specific gravity – the ratio of the density (φ) of a substance to the density of water.

Specific heat – the amount of heat required to raise the temperature of one gram of substance one degree Celsius.

Specific rate constant – an experimentally determined (proportionality) constant, which is different for different reactions and which changes only with temperature; k in the rate-law expression: Rate = k [A] × [B].

Spectator ions – ions in a solution that do not participate in a chemical reaction.

Spectral line – any of a number of lines corresponding to definite wavelengths of an atomic emission or absorption spectrum; marks the energy difference between two energy levels.

Spectrochemical series – arrangement of ligands in order of increasing ligand field strength.

Spectroscopy – study of radiation and matter, such as X-ray absorption and emission spectroscopy.

Spectrum – display of component wavelengths (colors) of electromagnetic radiation.

Speed of light – the speed at which radiation travels through a vacuum (c = 299,792,458 m/sec).

Square planar – a term used to describe molecules and polyatomic ions that have one atom in the center and four atoms at the corners of a square.

Square planar complex – complex in which the metal is in the center of a square plane, with ligand donor atoms at each of the four corners.

Standard conditions for temperature and pressure (STP) – a standardization used in order to compare experimental results (25 °C and 100.000 kPa).

Standard electrodes – half-cells in which the oxidized and reduced forms of a species are present at unit activity (1.0 M solutions of dissolved ions, 1.0 atm partial pressure of gases, pure solids and liquids).

Standard electrode potential – by convention, potential (E^o) of a half-reaction as a reduction relative to the standard hydrogen electrode when all species are present at unit activity.

Standard entropy (*s*) – the absolute entropy of a substance in its standard state at 298 K.

Standard molar enthalpy of formation (H^o_f) – the amount of heat absorbed in the formation of one mole of a substance in a specified state from its elements in their standard states.

Standard molar volume – the volume occupied by one mole of an ideal gas under standard conditions; 22.4 L.

Standard reaction – a reaction in which the numbers of moles of reactants shown in the balanced equation, all in their standard states, are completely converted to the numbers of moles of products shown in the balanced equation, also all at their standard state.

State of matter – matter having a homogeneous, macroscopic phase (e.g., as a gas, plasma, liquid or solid, in increasing concentration).

Stoichiometry – description of the quantitative relationships among elements and compounds as they undergo chemical changes.

Strong electrolyte – a substance that conducts electricity well in a dilute aqueous solution.

Strong field ligand – ligand that exerts a strong crystal or ligand electrical field and generally forms low spin complexes with metal ions when possible.

Structural isomers – compounds that contain the same number of the same kinds of atoms in different geometric arrangements.

Subatomic particles – particles that comprise an atom (e.g., protons, neutrons and electrons).

Sublimation – the direct vaporization of a solid by heating without passing through the liquid state; a phase transition from solid to limewater fuel or gas.

Substance – any kind of matter, all specimens of which have the same chemical composition and physical properties.

Substitution reaction – a reaction in which an atom or a group of atoms is replaced by another atom or group of atoms.

Supercooled liquids – liquids that, when cooled, apparently solidify but actually continue to flow very slowly under the influence of gravity.

Supercritical fluid – a substance at a temperature above its critical temperature.

Supersaturated solution – a solution that contains a higher than saturation concentration of solute; slight disturbance or seeding causes crystallization of excess solute.

Suspension – a heterogeneous mixture in which solute-like particles settle out of the solvent-like phase some time after their introduction.

T

Talc – a mineral representing the one on the Mohs Scale and composed of hydrated magnesium silicate with the chemical formula $H_2Mg_3(SiO_3)_4$ or $Mg_3Si_4O_{10}(OH)_2$.

Temperature – a measure of the kinetic energy of particles.

Ternary acid – a ternary compound containing H, O and another element, often a nonmetal.

Ternary compound – a compound consisting of three elements; may be ionic or covalent.

Tetrahedral – a term used to describe molecules and polyatomic ions that have one atom in the center and four atoms at the corners of a tetrahedron; ideal bond angle equals $109.5°$.

Theoretical yield – maximum amount of a specified product that could be obtained from specified amounts of reactants, assuming complete consumption of the limiting reactant according to only one reaction and complete recovery of product; see *Actual yield*.

Theory – an established model describing the nature of a phenomenon.

Thermal conductivity – a property of a material to conduct heat (often noted as k).

Thermal cracking – decomposition by heating a substance in the presence of a catalyst and in the absence of air.

Thermochemistry – the study of absorption/release of heat within a chemical reaction.

Thermodynamics – the study of the effects of changing temperature, volume or pressure (or work, heat, and energy) on a macroscopic scale.

Thermodynamic stability – when a system is in its lowest energy state with its environment (equilibrium).

Thermometer – device that measures the average energy of a system.

Thermonuclear energy – energy from nuclear fusion reactions.

Third law of thermodynamics – the entropy of a hypothetical pure, perfect crystalline substance at absolute zero temperature is zero.

Titration – a procedure in which one solution is added to another solution until the chemical reaction between the two solutes is complete; the concentration of one solution is known and that of the other is unknown.

Torr – a unit to measure pressure; 1 Torr is equivalent to 133.322 Pa or 1.3158×10^{-3} atm.

Total ionic equation – equation for a chemical reaction written to show the predominant form of all species in aqueous solution or in contact with water.

Transition elements (metals) – B Group elements except IIB in the periodic table; sometimes called simply transition elements, elements that have incomplete d sub-shells; may also be referred to as "the *d*-block elements."

Transition state theory – theory of reaction rates that states that reactants pass through high-energy transition states before forming products.

Transuranic element – an element with an atomic number greater than 92; none of the transuranic elements are stable.

Triple bond – the sharing of three pairs of electrons within a covalent bond (e.g., N_2 as $N\equiv N$).

Triple point – the place where the temperature and pressure of three phases are the same; water has a special phase diagram.

Tyndall effect – the effect of light scattering by colloidal particles (a mixture where one substance is dispersed evenly throughout another) or by suspended particles.

U

Uncertainty – the characteristic that any measurement that involves the estimation of any amount cannot be exactly reproducible.

Uncertainty principle – knowing the location of a particle makes the momentum uncertain, while knowing the momentum of a particle makes the location uncertain.

Unit cell – the smallest repeating unit of a lattice.

Unit factor – statements used in converting between units.

Universal or ideal gas constant – proportionality constant in the ideal gas law (0.08206 L·atm/(K·mol)).

UN number – a four-digit code used to note hazardous and flammable substances.

Unsaturated hydrocarbons – hydrocarbons that contain double or triple carbon-carbon bonds.

V

Valence bond theory – assumes that covalent bonds are formed when atomic orbitals on different atoms overlap and the electrons are shared.

Valence electrons – outermost electrons of atoms; usually those electrons involved in bonding.

Valence shell electron pair repulsion theory – assumes that electron pairs are arranged around the central element of a molecule or polyatomic ion so that there is maximum separation (and minimum repulsion) among regions of high electron density.

Van der Waals' equation – an equation of a state that extends the ideal gas law to real gases by inclusion of two empirically determined parameters, which are different for different gases.

Van der Waals force – one of the forces (attraction/repulsion) between molecules.

Van't Hoff factor – the ratio of moles of particles in solution to moles of solute dissolved.

Vapor – when a substance is below the critical temperature while in the gas phase.

Vaporization – the phase change from liquid to gas.

Vapor pressure – the particle pressure of a vapor at the surface of its parent liquid.

Viscosity – the resistance of a liquid to flow (e.g., oil has a higher viscosity than water).

Volt – one joule of work per coulomb; the unit of electrical potential transferred.

Voltage – the potential difference between two electrodes; measure of chemical potential for a redox reaction.

Voltaic cells – electrochemical cells in which spontaneous chemical reactions produce electricity; also known as "galvanic cells."

Voltmeter – an instrument that measures the cell potential.

Volumetric analysis – measuring the volume of a solution (of known concentration) in order to determine the concentration of the substance being measured within said solution; see *Titration*.

W

Water equivalent – the amount of water that would absorb the same amount of heat as the calorimeter per degree of temperature increase.

Weak electrolyte – a substance that conducts electricity poorly in a dilute aqueous solution.

Weak field ligand – a ligand that exerts a weak crystal or ligand field and generally forms high spin complexes with metals.

X

X-ray – electromagnetic radiation between gamma and ultraviolet (UV) rays.

X-ray diffraction – a method for establishing structures of crystalline solids using single wavelength X-rays and studying the diffraction pattern.

X-ray photoelectron spectroscopy – a spectroscopic technique used to measure the composition of a material.

Y

Yield – the amount of product produced during a chemical reaction.

Z

Zone melting – a way to remove impurities from an element by melting it and slowly traveling it down an ingot (cast).

Zone refining – a method of purifying a bar of metal by passing it through an induction heater; this causes impurities to move along a melted portion.

Zwitterion (formerly known as a dipolar ion) – a neutral molecule with both a positive and a negative electrical charge; multiple positive and negative charges can be present; distinct from dipoles at different locations within that molecule; also known as "inner salts."

To access online AP tests at a special pricing visit:
http://ap.sterling-prep.com/bookowner.htm